175903

D1766138

## DATE OF RETURN

|  |  |  |
|---|---|---|
|  |  |  |
|  |  |  |
|  |  |  |
|  |  |  |
|  |  |  |
|  |  |  |
|  |  |  |
|  |  |  |
|  |  |  |
|  |  |  |
|  |  |  |
|  |  |  |

Entrepreneurship and Innovations in Functional Regions

# Entrepreneurship and Innovations in Functional Regions

*Edited by*

## Charlie Karlsson

*Professor of the Economics of Technological Change and Director of CISEG (Centre for Innovation Systems, Entrepreneurship and Growth), Jönköping International Business School, Jönköping University and Guest Professor of Economics, University West, Trollhättan, Sweden*

## Roger R. Stough

*Vice President for Research and Economic Development, NOVA Endowed Chair and Professor of Public Policy, George Mason University, USA*

## Börje Johansson

*Professor of Economics, Jönköping International Business School, Jönköping University and Director of CESIS (Centre of Excellence for Science and Innovation Studies), Royal Institute of Technology, Stockholm, Sweden*

**Edward Elgar**
Cheltenham, UK • Northampton, MA, USA

Published by
Edward Elgar Publishing Limited
The Lypiatts
15 Lansdown Road
Cheltenham
Glos GL50 2JA
UK

Edward Elgar Publishing, Inc.
William Pratt House
9 Dewey Court
Northampton
Massachusetts 01060
USA


A catalogue record for this book
is available from the British Library

Library of Congress Control Number: 2009933362


ISBN 978 1 84720 074 7

Printed and bound by MPG Books Group, UK

# Contents

# Contributors

**Vito Albino**, Department of Innovation in Mechanics and Management (DIMEG), Politecnico di Bari, Italy.

**Francisco Alvarez**, Universidad Nacional de Mar del Plata, Argentina.

**Martin Andersson**, Jönköping International Business School and Centre of Excellence for Science and Innovation Studies (CESIS), Royal Institute of Technology, Stockholm, Sweden.

**Gary A.S. Cook**, University of Liverpool Management School, UK.

**Lei Ding**, Center for Community Capitalism, Frank Hawkins Kenan Institute of Private Enterprise, University of North Carolina, Chapel Hill, NC, USA.

**Olof Ejermo**, Centre for Innovation, Research and Competence in the Learning Economy (CIRCLE), Lund University, Sweden.

**Ilaria Giannoccaro**, Department of Innovation in Mechanics and Management (DIMEG), Politecnico di Bari, Italy.

**Jack A. Goldstone**, School of Public Policy, George Mason University, Fairfax, VA, USA.

**Urban Gråsjö**, University West, Trollhättan, Sweden.

**Kingsley E. Haynes**, School of Public Policy, George Mason University, Fairfax, VA, USA.

**Börje Johansson**, Jönköping International Business School and Centre of Excellence for Science and Innovation Studies (CESIS), Royal Institute of Technology, Stockholm, Sweden.

**Astrid Kander**, Centre for Innovation, Research and Competence in the Learning Economy (CIRCLE), Lund University, Sweden.

**Charlie Karlsson**, Jönköping International Business School, Centre for Innovation Systems, Entrepreneurship and Growth (CISEG) and University West, Sweden.

**Hans Lööf**, Centre of Excellence for Science and Innovation Studies (CESIS), Department of Transport and Economics, Royal Institute of Technology, Stockholm, Sweden.

**Rosina Moreno**, AQR Research Group-IREA, Department of Econometrics, Statistics and Spanish Economy, University of Barcelona, Spain.

**Kristina Nyström**, The Ratio Institute, Stockholm, Sweden.

**Raquel Ortega-Argilés**, European Commission, Joint Research Centre, Institute for Prospective Technological Studies (IPTS), Spain.

**Naresh R. Pandit**, Norwich Business School, University of East Anglia, UK.

**Waldemar Pfoertsch**, Pforzheim University of Applied Sciences, Pforzheim, Germany.

**Keith Pond**, Business School, Loughborough University, UK.

**Tõnu Roolaht**, University of Tartu, Faculty of Economics and Business Administration, Department of International Business, Tartu, Estonia.

**Amy Ryder-Olsson**, Centre for Banking and Finance (CEFIN), Royal Institute of Technology, Stockholm, Sweden.

**Roger R. Stough**, School of Public Policy, George Mason University, Fairfax, VA, USA.

**Reha Tözün**, Geography Institute, University of Stuttgart, Stuttgart, Germany.

# Preface

The contributions forming the different chapters in this book were first presented and discussed at the *Eighth Uddevalla Symposium* on Innovations and Entrepreneurship in Functional Regions, 15–17 September 2005. The aim with this international conference was to explore and analyze further the role of innovations and entrepreneurship in functional regions. It was organized by the University West, Uddevalla campus, Sweden in cooperation with the Jönköping International Business School, Sweden, the School of Public Policy at George Mason University, USA, CESIS (Centre of Excellence for Science and Innovation Studies, Stockholm, Sweden), FSF (Swedish Foundation for Small Business Research, Sweden), McGill University, Faculty of Management, Montreal, Canada and The Nordic Section of the Regional Science Association (NS-RSA).

It was held at and hosted by the University West, Uddevalla, Sweden and it was totally incorporated with the Eighth McGill International Entrepreneurship Conference 2005. The first annual international Uddevalla Symposium, took place in 1998, and aimed to bring together the leading-edge views of academic scholars and insightful practitioners from the fields of entrepreneurship, economics, geography, public policy and regional science in order to examine the cause(s), pattern(s) and consequences of these developments.

The organizers of the Eighth Uddevalla Symposium would like to thank The Foundation of Gustaf B. Thordén, the Swedbank of Uddevalla, The Savings Bank Foundation Väst, Swedish Research Council, The Region Västra Götaland, Sweden and The Municipality of Uddevalla, Sweden for financial support.

The authors and the editors thank Iréne Johansson, University West, Sweden, Jiamin Wang, George Mason University, USA, Emilia Catalina Istrate, George Mason University, USA and Debasree Das Gupta, George Mason University, USA for editorial assistance.

Charlie Karlsson and Börje Johansson
Jönköping
Roger R. Stough
Fairfax, VA

# 1. Introduction: Innovation and Entrepreneurship in Functional Regions

## Charlie Karlsson, Roger R. Stough and Börje Johansson

## INNOVATION, ENTREPRENEURSHIP AND REGIONAL DEVELOPMENT

In recent decades, the world has witnessed the emergence of a global knowledge economy, in which functional (urban) regions increasingly play a role as independent, dynamic marketplaces, which are integrated with other functional regions by means of flows of information, knowledge, and commodities. Each functional region has its own specific base of scientific, technological, and entrepreneurial knowledge in the form of knowledge assets of firms and other organisations located in the region and the human and social capital associated with the region's population. A functional region is also characterised by its education system, its ongoing knowledge-production activities in universities, research laboratories, and firms, as well as its import and export of knowledge, where all these knowledge aspects may be classified as components of its regional innovation system (Andersson and Karlsson, 2006).

The functional (urban) region is a geographical area for knowledge creation, appropriation, diffusion, and absorption, as well as for transformation of knowledge to innovations via entrepreneurial initiatives (Jaffe et al., 1993; Glaeser, 1999). A functional region can encompass these activities, because it is an arena for exploiting communication externalities (Fujita, and Thisse, 2002), which requires that the spatial extent of the region must be limited so that economic actors in the region can and do exercise frequent face-to-face interaction. The functional region is also a labour market region, in which knowledge spreads as individuals change their job affiliation and place of employment (Zucker et al., 1998a and b).

# INNOVATION, ENTREPRENEURSHIP AND LOCALISED KNOWLEDGE

It is often argued that processes of innovation and entrepreneurship are prerequisites for sustainable growth of regions and that knowledge and knowledge creation are prerequisites for innovation and entrepreneurship. However, the conditions for innovation and entrepreneurship vary substantially between functional regions since knowledge and knowledge-creating activities tend to be localised and to cluster in certain regions and not others. Knowledge in the form of firm assets, such as patents, technology employed and research and development (R&D) capacity is concentrated in space to the extent that knowledge-rich firms decide to co-locate in the same region. Knowledge in the form of human capital becomes localised as a result of clustering processes, where concentrations of persons embodying knowledge and creativity attract other knowledge-intensive persons to migrate to such regions and to stay there.

Localised knowledge has a long-term influence on the future development of functional regions, and the knowledge resources of regions normally change slowly. This implies that a functional region with limited knowledge resources can accumulate substantially more knowledge only over an extended period, whereas a knowledge-rich region will tend to be knowledge rich far into the future. Thus, knowledge location patterns are quite invariant over long periods. Large urban functional regions, for example, often have a history that can be measured in centuries. There are two basic factors behind this temporal–spatial phenomenon. The first comprises the infrastructure and the amenities that operate as attractors for both firms and households, and which constitute slowly changing location attributes (Johansson and Karlsson, 1992). The second factor refers to a fundamental externality in the New Economic Geography theory. This externality can be formulated in the following way (Krugman, 1991a; Karlsson and Johansson, 2006):

- Knowledge-intensive labour is attracted to functional regions where knowledge-dependent firms are located.
- Firms with knowledge-dependent activities are attracted to functional regions where knowledge-intensive labour is located.

In some regions more than in others the externality effects of knowledge and related infrastructure can generate cumulative growth through innovation and entrepreneurship (Acs and Audretsch, 1988; Acs, 2000). At the same time, the growth process is making the co-location of knowledge-rich labour and knowledge-demanding firms and industries resilient to change. The pertinent firms remain in the functional region because of its favourable accessibility to knowledge resources and their use, and the labour force has a corresponding advantage of remaining in a functional region with favourable accessibility to knowledge-handling and knowledge-using job opportunities.

## KNOWLEDGE, INNOVATION AND ENTREPRENEURSHIP

Given the critical role of knowledge and knowledge generation for innovation and entrepreneurship, it is necessary to identify the main types of knowledge used by a firm. The following four components comprise a firm's primary types of knowledge:

- knowledge about firm routines;
- knowledge about product varieties;
- knowledge about markets and customers' willingness to pay for different product characteristics; and
- knowledge about how to perform R&D.

Firm routines include techniques and approaches that are applied in production, administration, logistics, distribution, and transaction activities. In this way, the routines (traditionally called 'production technique') are a manifestation of the firm's know-how, where the latter also includes the firm's capability to combine product attributes of its variety of outputs. For an innovative firm, routines also comprise its procedures to improve – gradually or stepwise – its routines, to develop its product varieties, and to find new markets, that is, its entrepreneurial procedures.

The above considerations are illustrated in Figure 1.1, which emphasises that the know-how about how to develop routines is a combination of the firm's experiences, the inflow of knowledge from outside the firm, and the firm's know-why. In the case of a pure start-up, it is instead the entrepreneur's experience, knowledge network and know-why that is in focus. The most important observation in Figure 1.1 is that the interaction between firms and entrepreneurs in a functional region can be a major generator of the region's compound knowledge. Given the structure outlined in the figure, how do economic models describe the influence of knowledge? In orthodox theory, we identify two approaches:

- Knowledge affects (augments or amplifies) the production function of a firm, which implies that it improves the productivity of its inputs (Chambers, 1988).
- Knowledge affects the value ladder of product varieties produced by the firm (Grossman and Helpman, 1991).

In microeconomic models, knowledge is often represented by a factor that influences a firm's production function. The latter describes how a firm transforms (i) current inputs, (ii) labour, and (iii) physical, human, and organisational capital to outputs. In its most naked form, the production function describes how labour and capital can be used to obtain output. In this case, knowledge is a factor that shifts the productivity of labour and capital upwards. Here, innovation is a very abstract phenomenon and entrepreneurship is unknown.

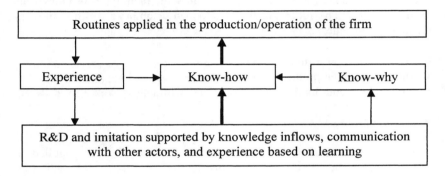

*Source:* Karlsson and Johansson (2007).

*Figure 1.1  Knowledge development of a firm*

The microeconomic production function isolates the study of knowledge to a question of the existing routines of established firms. However, it excludes important temporal phenomena by not considering the routines that are available to a firm when improving its production process or to an entrepreneur when considering starting a new firm. When such issues are at the forefront, researchers take a step into evolutionary economics. Attempts to study product and market development and new firm formation takes the analyses even further into the territory of industrial dynamics and evolutionary processes (Nelson and Winter, 1982; Dosi et al., 1988).

How is it possible to take the step from the model outlined in Figure 1.1 to a model description of how knowledge affects the economy of a functional region? Obviously, such a step requires heroic efforts. Following a mainstream approach leads to a regional production-function model of the following kind:

$$Y = F(K, L, N)A \tag{1.1a}$$

$$A = \int_{t} \dot{A} dt \qquad (1.1b)$$

$$\dot{A} = G(\hat{K}, \hat{L}, \hat{N})A \qquad (1.1c)$$

where $K$, $L$ and $N$ represent capital, labour and human capital employed in the production of an aggregate output, while $\hat{K}$, $\hat{L}$ and $\hat{N}$ represent capital, labour and human capital employed in the production of knowledge (know-how) as signified by $A$, where $\dot{A} = dA/dt$ signifies the change of $A$ per time unit. The three equations also need to be supplemented by a specification of the temporal motion of $K$, $L$ and $N$ as wells as of $\hat{K}$, $\hat{L}$ and $\hat{N}$. When equation (1.1c) is excluded and (1.1b) is exogenously given, we have an aggregate regional production model of the Solow type (Solow, 1994). Otherwise, the equation system represents a regional endogenous-growth model (Romer, 1994). In either case, the model outlined tries to capture knowledge interaction and creation of all actors in a functional region into equations (1.1b) and (1.1c). In particular, it disregards all knowledge flows to and from the functional region. Moreover, if one specifies the equation system for individual sectors of a regional economy, one has to consider knowledge flows between sectors (Romer, 1986).

## KNOWLEDGE SOURCES, KNOWLEDGE FLOWS AND KNOWLEDGE CREATION

Innovation and entrepreneurship processes generate new products, new markets, and new routines of innovating firms as well as new firms (Nelson and Winter, 1982). The knowledge employed and applied in innovative and entrepreneurial activities has several sources in each individual case. For firms and entrepreneurs in a functional region, we can identify the following three principal sources of knowledge:

- Knowledge that originates from knowledge created in the functional region, based on R&D efforts in firms, research laboratories and universities – partly carried out as interactive processes in regional innovation systems.
- Knowledge flows between economic actors inside a functional region, due to unintended local diffusion, knowledge interaction including interaction between suppliers and customers, and movement of employees when individuals change employer, and when firms employ individuals who leave education or research organisations.
- Knowledge flows from outside the functional region based on immigration of labour and various forms of interregional interaction, imports and

exports, foreign direct investment (FDI) and flows inside each company group's internal networks (in particular inside multinational companies).

The literature offers a steady progression of methods and frameworks to examine the role of both intra- and inter-regional knowledge flows for innovation and entrepreneurship. These approaches examine the importance of knowledge flows for a firm's patenting, R&D efforts, innovation output in the form of novel products or more valuable export products (Gråsjö, 2006) as well as for new firm formation (Karlsson and Nyström, 2006). In these studies, the knowledge-production function has been used as a major workhorse, relating basically the knowledge inputs of firms to their innovative output in most cases measured in terms of patent applications (Varga, 1997; Zucker et al., 1998b). These studies have shown for the US that innovative firms normally are dependent on knowledge generated by local university R&D (Feldman and Audretsch, 1999). The intra-regional knowledge transfer from and exchange with universities may rely on a whole spectrum of mechanisms, such as (i) a flow of newly trained graduates from universities to industry, (ii) technological spillovers of newly created knowledge from universities to industry, (iii) industrial purchases of intellectual property from universities, (iv) university researchers working as R&D consultants or serving on company boards, (v) university researchers leaving universities to work for industry, and (vi) university researchers starting new firms. In addition, universities may create incubators, enterprise centres, and science parks to improve interaction with industry and to facilitate knowledge exchange between industry and university.

Some scholars have used the knowledge production function to discriminate between localised knowledge flows and knowledge exchange in long-distance networks (Varga, 2002; Andersson and Ejermo, 2005). At the same time, many empirical analyses emphasise that the relevant sources are local, based on R&D that takes place in the region hosting the innovative firm that makes use of the R&D results.

Recent studies have also compared a firm's accessibility to R&D activities in universities and other firms, where accessibility here refers to the possibility of getting in touch with R&D activities, as well as the costs of the associated contacts. A clear outcome is that the accessibility to other firms' R&D activities has a much stronger impact on the knowledge production than the accessibility to R&D resources in universities (Andersson and Ejermo, 2005; Gråsjö, 2006). In this case, the accessibility measures imply that local knowledge flows are persistently important, whereas long-distance flows have a very small impact – except in one case. Firms that belong to a company group, can utilise the internal networks of their company group to overcome long distances. These company groups are invariably multinational enterprises. Obviously, a multinational enterprise can locate subsidiaries in the proximity of places with specialised excellence, from which novelties can be developed and transferred through the internal networks of such enterprises (Dunning and Narula, 1995).

Evidently, the R&D efforts by an individual firm are a main factor in its knowledge production. However, the R&D resources and R&D efforts of a firm have a second motivation. Firms with a large and active R&D staff also have a large absorptive capacity with regard to external knowledge flows. Pfaffermayr and Bellak (2002) argue that this gives them an advantage in both knowledge absorption and knowledge creation. Recalling that we have concluded that knowledge flows are largely local in nature, it seems natural to conjecture that regions may improve their absorptive capacity as a consequence of hosting firms with such capacities.

Variations in institutional frameworks between functional regions generate potentially strong variations between regions as regards the opportunities for innovation and entrepreneurship. Effective institutions bring down transaction costs and thus costs associated with introducing innovations and establishing new firms. They also play an important role in improving incentives, efficiency, and rates of innovation and entrepreneurship and more generally in the definition and protection of property rights. Variations in institutional frameworks between functional regions create variations in opportunities for knowledge flows and appropriating rents from innovations and entrepreneurship.

## INNOVATION, ENTREPRENEURSHIP AND CREATIVITY

It has been observed that the last decades of the twentieth century were characterised by a transformation from the traditional industrial society characterised by knowledge-handling activities to a C-society characterised by knowledge development and knowledge handling (Noyelle and Stanback, 1984; Andersson 1985a and b; Hall and Preston, 1988; Castells, 1989; Hall, 1990). Development of new knowledge and the handling and presentation of knowledge and information employ a steadily increasing share of the labour force and have strong spillover effects in innovative and entrepreneurial activities in manufacturing as well as service production. At the same time, the composition of infrastructure is changing. Traditional means of transportation are complemented and partly replaced by the communication networks created by modern information and telecommunication technologies. Among the traditional means of transportation, road and air traffic have gradually achieved a more dominating role. Overall, access to material and non-material networks are becoming more critical for regional competitiveness.

The major driving force behind the observed transformation has been creative activities in a broad sense, involving not only the creation of new knowledge but also the creation of new goods and services, new firms, new artistic expressions and so on. With the emergence of the 'C-society', the resource base in developed economies is no longer natural resources, energy, and so on, but human capital and assets evolving through creative endeavours. However, a strong resource base in terms of human capital and non-material assets is not enough for knowledge generation, innovation and entrepreneurship to flourish. Rich import networks and a diversified flow of import products is also critical, since novelties from the world economy are important inputs in all creative processes.

During the transformation process in recent decades, many traditional industrial regions have lost their previous comparative advantages and have been forced to try to restructure to regain prosperity. Winners in the process have been regions that have been able to preserve and upgrade an existing creative milieu or to create a new one. Andersson (1985a) summarises the characteristics of creative milieus. To be creative, a regional economic milieu must be large scale but still culturally versatile, rich with profound original knowledge and competence, and characterised by good communication internally and externally for generating potentially synergetic situations (Andersson, 1985c). It must also contain a specific set of relationships of production based on a social organisation that by and large shares a work culture and instrumental goals aimed at generating new knowledge, new processes and new products (Castells, 1989). Since innovation according to Joseph Schumpeter is the result of novelty by combination, a region to be a creative milieu must also contain a large enough supply of creative individuals and teams of creative individuals to generate such combinations. This aspect has been emphasised by Florida (2002, 2005a and b) who recognises the critical role of talented individuals. This implies that the potential of different functional regions to generate innovations will be influenced by the location preferences of the individuals belonging to the 'creative class'.

Creative regions can also be characterised as learning regions (see Morgan, 1997) reflecting the increasing recognition of the role of knowledge and learning as a catalyst for economic development (Knight, 1995; Cooke and Morgan, 1998). The fundamental idea here is that the competitiveness of a region is directly influenced by its ability to rapidly generate, access, understand and transform relevant knowledge into learning (Keane and Allison, 1999). The overall concept of a learning economy recognises knowledge as the most fundamental resource in the 'C-society' and learning therefore as the most fundamental process (Lundvall and Johnson, 1994). Of particular importance is the degree of 'collective learning', which connotes a broad notion of the capacity of a particular regional creative milieu to generate or facilitate innovative and entrepreneurial behaviour by the economic agents who are members of that milieu (Camagni, 1991).

Learning regions function as collectors and repositories of knowledge and ideas, and provide the underlying environment or knowledge infrastructure that facilitates the flow and exchange of knowledge and ideas (Andersson, 1985a; Florida, 1995; Jin and Stough, 1998). The knowledge infrastructure is critical for the transformation of knowledge into learning. It consists of two major parts: (i) the physical transport, communication and interaction infrastructure, which connects nodes internally as well as with other nodes and which provides arenas for human interaction, and (ii) the knowledge networks with universities, research institutes, knowledge-intensive firms, and other centres of learning but also knowledge-generating and knowledge-handling individuals as their major nodes. The importance of the tangible infrastructure cannot be overstated in this context, since it provides accessibility to knowledge locally, intra-regionally and inter-regionally (Karlsson and Manduchi, 2001).

The comparative advantages of learning regions are based upon their capacity to generate new ideas, knowledge creation, organisational learning and continuous improvements. Their transportation and communication infrastructure including electronic connections is globally oriented as well as providing high intra-regional accessibility to maximise knowledge flows and knowledge exchange. The human infrastructure in learning regions is based on knowledge workers, continuous improvements of human resources and continuous education and training. Their industrial governance system is based upon network organisations with mutually dependent relationships and a flexible regulatory framework. They seem to be characterised by institutional thickness (Indergaard, 1997) with a high level of interaction based on relationships of trust and reciprocity (Keeble and Lawson, 1998), and with a mutual awareness of a common purpose (Keane and Allison, 1999). At the same time, the institutional setting should not be 'too thick' since this would bring rigidities, hindering new combinations.

A substantial part of the production in learning regions is knowledge based, with a recurrent creation of new knowledge as the main source of value and with a synthesis combining innovation, entrepreneurship, and production. Networks between firms in multi-firm companies and supplier–customer networks are critical sources that provide ideas for innovation. In particular, it is the existing and often larger firms that engage in the production of knowledge as an input for their innovation processes. Thus, these firms may outsource innovation activities to external firms including subsidiaries, while orchestrating such interaction distributes innovation efforts. The possibility of turning internal and accessible external knowledge into innovations depends on the capacity of existing firms in a region to appropriate existing learning opportunities through both own R&D and internal learning, and also by the systematic absorption of the specific knowledge externalities available in the regional creative milieu (Antonelli, 1998). However, knowledge often spills over for possible exploitation by economic agents other than those who created it. Learning regions offer economic agents better conditions than other regions to discover, evaluate, and exploit opportunities emerging as a result of knowledge spillovers through entrepreneurial actions.

Maillat and Kebir (2001) take the discussion of learning regions one step further by highlighting the processes that turn a region into a learning region. They claim that one must give the learning concept a dynamic substance. For them, learning is a process of acquisition and transformation of knowledge, which allows for permanent adaptation in the face of the uncertainty of the environment. They characterise the learning region as a dynamic and evolving region. It is dynamic because each economic actor, be it an individual, a firm, a public organisation or a network, is in continuous interaction (directly or indirectly) with its environment. It is evolving because each actor in the region participates in sequences of ongoing experiments. The learning region is also characterised by three types of ongoing processes: (i) a process of territorial implementation of innovation, (ii) a process of territorialisation of actors, and (iii) complex learning processes. These processes occur not only within the different regions, that is, actors interacting with each other within a region, but also through relationships that each region fosters with other regions, that is, through cross-border interaction of actors.

## INNOVATION, ENTREPRENEURSHIP AND SIZE OF FUNCTIONAL REGIONS

There are very substantial variations in the opportunities for innovations and entrepreneurship in functional regions of various sizes due to the variation in their demand and supply conditions. Regional variations in demand conditions, in terms of regional market potential and regional demand for new goods and services, generate spatial variations in opportunities for innovation and entrepreneurship. There is also a strong variation between functional regions to the extent that they offer opportunities for individual economic agents to discover, create and exploit innovations and new firms due to variations in the knowledge base, information supply, industrial structure, company structure, infrastructure supply, institutions, business climate and so on. Conditions that can generate potentially synergetic situations and support for learning are mostly available in large functional regions, that is, metropolitan regions.

The best opportunities for innovations and entrepreneurial initiatives are offered by functional regions with a large home market and high access to markets in other regions, that is, large functional urban regions. Economic agents engaging in innovation and entrepreneurship in large functional regions may take advantage of the close proximity to concentrations of (potential) customers, that is, purchasing power, which of course could be and often are other firms. Under certain conditions, new firms may take market shares from incumbents if they locate near them (Hotelling, 1929). Admittedly, this gain may be short-lived if further new firms enter, or if incumbents in the region react to this unwanted competition. On the other hand, innovators and entrepreneurs may suffer less from the proximity of similar firms when competition in the product market is imperfect, such that firms supply differentiated products (Fujita and Thisse, 2002).

A third reason why large functional regions bring advantages to innovators and entrepreneurs may be more long term. In a large region, they will generally be better exposed to customers. Searching is costly for the customer who, *ceteris paribus*, will prefer to minimise search costs by purchasing in areas of concentrated supply. This is particularly relevant in markets with discerning potential customers with specific requirements, who wish to search before purchasing. This applies to consumers but probably even more to other innovative firms that have specific requirements as regards input goods and services. Transaction costs, and in particular search costs for customers, suppliers, services and knowledge are lower in larger functional regions (Quigley, 1998).

A fourth advantage offered by large functional regions is the positive information externalities in such regions, through which economic agents receive signals about the strength of regional demand by observing established suppliers' successful trade. There are generally large potentials for production knowledge to spill over in large functional regions, not least because large regions are generally dense regions. Such observations also inform about varieties of existing goods and services, and can of course trigger the development of new varieties. The fundamental role of large functional regions in the creative process depends in particular upon their role as communication centres due to their more developed physical infrastructure. They are centres of international communication in culture, business, politics and science. Actually, large functional urban regions are each a nucleus of numerous networks ranging from the local to the global (Nijkamp, 2003) and offer network thickness, which tends to encourage innovation and entrepreneurship, since involvement in such networks makes it easier to externalise some of the risks involved (Shapero, 1984). They also offer good opportunities to develop closely knit intra-regional communication networks within as well as between sectors of society, by offering various interaction arenas. Economies of information flows (Acs et al., 1992) on both the demand and the supply side are greater in large functional regions than in small ones.

One important reason why creative activities are concentrated in large functional regions is that these regions offer physical proximity, which facilitates the integration of multi-disciplinary knowledge that is tacit and therefore 'person embodied' rather than 'information embodied' as well as allowing the rapid decision-making needed to cope with uncertainty (see Patel and Pavitt, 1991). Due to urbanisation economies, these regions also offer diversity, that is, economies of scope, in information, skills, knowledge, competence, producer services and other inputs, which is crucial in creative, innovative and entrepreneurial processes. This diversity advantage is fundamental since these processes are critically dependent upon knowledge, which is complex and perhaps tacit in nature (Jaffe et al., 1993). This advantage includes access to a large pool of well-educated and specialised labour (Marshall, 1920), particularly specialised workers in accounting, law, finance, advertising and various technical fields. This reduces the costs for innovation and for starting up and expanding new businesses (Krugman, 1993). Furthermore, densely populated agglomerations are conducive to a greater provision of non-traded inputs, since their service infrastructure is more developed. Such inputs are provided both in greater variety and at lower costs in large functional regions (Krugman, 1991b and c).

Generally speaking, the larger and richer the functional region, the larger the number of potential innovators and entrepreneurs, since economic agents in such regions are better educated, have more varied work experience, and so on. We may even assume that large and rich functional regions offer increasing returns in the acquisition of innovative and entrepreneurial skills due to more effective and numerous interactions in denser areas (Glaeser, 1999; Desmet, 2000).

The implications of the above discussion are far-reaching. Since larger functional regions afford larger opportunities and higher capacity for innovation and entrepreneurship and a higher probability of successful innovation and entrepreneurship, these regions will experience a long-term build-up of innovative and entrepreneurial knowledge. This will stimulate future innovation and entrepreneurship. Furthermore, innovators and entrepreneurs are change agents who also shape regional economic environments and institutions. They develop resources and relationships that further their own interests as well as the interests of potential innovators and entrepreneurs, through the creation of a positive local environment for innovation and entrepreneurship (Feldman, 2001). Good conditions for innovation and entrepreneurship in large functional regions stimulate potential innovators and entrepreneurs, often well-educated people, in smaller regions to move to larger regions. When more potential innovators and entrepreneurs gather in large functional regions, conditions for innovation and entrepreneurship improve due to increased supply and increased availability of relevant knowledge. This will further induce innovation and entrepreneurship as well as further in-migration of potential innovators and entrepreneurs from smaller regions. In this sense the spatial behaviour of potential innovators and entrepreneurs generates a dynamic cumulative spatial concentration process.

However, the effects of innovation and entrepreneurship go much further, since they involve the introduction of new products and new processes in the market. Accordingly, they provide a major challenge to incumbent firms and encourage them to improve product quality and services, or to reduce prices or go out of business. This implies that innovation and entrepreneurship play a fundamental role in the renewal of the economies of functional regions by strengthening competition and initiating competitive processes that often lead to the creative destruction of existing modes of production.

## STRUCTURE AND CONTRIBUTIONS OF THIS BOOK

In Chapter 2, Jack A. Goldstone discusses economic growth as an inherently organic process. His view is that economic growth emerges from a set of complex interactions among different sets of individuals in dynamic exchange, circulating ideas, designs, products and marketing plans. These interactions are nurtured by an engineering culture, which fosters innovation. The result is that there is no single aggregate additive to add to a national or regional economy to encourage growth – not capital, or R&D, or 'knowledge'. Rather, the engine of growth tends to be regional centres of innovation, clustered around small firms launching products or processes that will eventually lead to mature markets in which they are the dominant producer. Goldstone discusses the measures to develop such regional centres but is careful also to point to the limits of these measures. There is no guarantee that measures will always produce the wanted breakthrough in the functional regions where the investments are made.

The discussion of economic growth is continued in Chapter 3, where Olof Ejermo and Astrid Kander discuss the so-called 'Swedish paradox', that is, the very widespread belief in Sweden that the high R&D expenditures do not produce sufficient economic results at the societal level. This empirical paradox is part of a more general debate concerning the relations between R&D and economic growth. The authors show that the theoretical underpinnings of the paradox are rather weak. There is a long chain of different gears between R&D, high-tech and growth, which should lead to expectations of high variation among countries. Previous evidence suggests that Sweden appears to have problems in two of these gears, the entrepreneurial climate, and innovation to high-tech production. The authors support this conclusion by new empirical results. First, they show that the high persistence in concentration of R&D to a few multinational companies remains, which in itself is an indication of weak entrepreneurship. Second, Sweden is still behind the OECD in high-tech and medium-high-tech exports, given its R&D intensity, although it is catching up. Moreover, employment figures in the high-tech sectors point to a more favourable development.

In Chapter 4, Börje Johansson, Amy Ryder-Olsson and Hans Lööf elucidate how firm location and corporate structure influence innovation efforts and innovation results. Innovation efforts comprise innovativeness, R&D intensity, and participation in innovation systems. Innovation results include innovation sales and productivity. Their study is based on 1,907 firm-level observations, and the firms are distinguished with regard to (i) location, where the analysis compares an integrated functional region – the Stockholm region – with four other regional areas in Sweden, and corporate structure, where the major classification is between multinational enterprises (MNEs) and other categories of firms. When investigating the influence of location and corporate structure, the econometric analysis controls for a range of other firm attributes of Schumpeterian type. The findings can be arranged in two groups. First, firms with a location in the Stockholm region have a significantly higher probability of being innovative, and innovative firms in the Stockholm region have higher innovation sales and productivity per employee, reflecting superior returns to R&D investments. Second, MNEs have a significantly higher probability of being innovative, and innovative MNEs have a significantly higher R&D intensity, and they are more likely to participate in regional innovation systems.

In Chapter 5, Kristina Nyström investigates the commonly debated issue about the relationship between R&D and firm age. Are product and process R&D made by incumbent firms, and does R&D therefore constitute a barrier to entry, or is conducting product and process R&D a way for new firms to compete successfully? She further investigates the relationship between firm size and R&D investments. Do investments in product and process R&D constitute a way for small firms to compete or is R&D a large-firm phenomenon? Data from 1997 and 1999 on product and process R&D, firm size and age in the Swedish manufacturing industry are used in the empirical analysis. A multinomial logit model is used to estimate the probability of performing product and process R&D as a function of firm size and age. The results show that there are complementarities between product and process R&D, and very few firms conduct only process R&D. The probability of product R&D and combined product and process R&D is higher for large firms, and firms that are older than 80 years. Size and age effects are more pronounced for firms that carry out both product and process R&D.

The main purpose of Chapter 6 by Urban Gråsjö is to establish to what extent accessibility to R&D and university-educated labour can explain regional export performance. This is done by estimating knowledge-production functions, with total export value and number of high-value exports in Swedish municipalities from 1997 to 1999 as outputs. In order to account for geographical proximity, the explanatory variables are expressed as accessibility to R&D and university-educated labour. The total accessibility is divided into three geographical levels: local (within the municipality), intra-regional and inter-regional accessibility to R&D and university-educated labour. R&D conducted at universities and in companies is measured in man-years and university-educated labour is measured by the number of people with at least three years of university education. The estimations are conducted with quantile regressions since the distributions of the dependent variable are highly skewed with a few very influential outliers. The results in the chapter indicate that accessibility to university-educated labour has the greatest positive effects. The value of exported products is mainly affected by local accessibility to university-educated labour (and company R&D). The intra- and inter-regional accessibilities play a more important role when the number of high-value export products in Swedish municipalities is the output.

Preference for variety on behalf of consumers suggests that variety in supply is a pertinent characteristic of individual firms. In Chapter 7, Martin Andersson studies the relationship between export variety and exports on a cross-section of exporting firms, which adds to a recent literature devoted to how different characteristics of firms affect their export behaviour. Extensive and intensive margins are computed by firm as well as by firm and export market such that the respective contribution of each margin to the estimated relationship is revealed. Firms with larger export variety export more, of which 54 per cent can be ascribed to a larger set of export markets (the extensive margin).

The purpose of Chapter 8 by Raquel Ortega-Argilés and Rosina Moreno is to analyse the differences in the survival rate of firms according to different competitive strategies. The authors consider these strategies to be related to both specific and technological competitive differentiation. Among the latter strategies, is that which is based on advertising and the introduction of new products into the market. As for the technological differentiation, the authors analyse those based on R&D expenses or the development of new production processes. They study the effect of these firm-specific competitive strategies in a set of Spanish manufacturing firms during the 1990s. First, they include the comparison between the Kaplan-Meier and Cox models for the different samples, that is, those firms that develop the described strategies and those that do not. Second, several non-parametric tests for equality of survival functions are computed to check the diversity of the survival rates across different competitive characteristics of firms.

In Chapter 9, Gary A.S. Cook, Naresh R. Pandit and Keith Pond employ the resource-based view to access the use of bankruptcy law to promote entrepreneurship. The UK Company Voluntary Arrangement (CVA) is an early example of a regime designed to sustain entrepreneurship by aiding the rescue of financially distressed but viable firms. Analysis of empirical evidence from the UK provides support for the central proposition that a firm that has resource strength but is pushed into bankruptcy by temporary factors, will be more likely to succeed in a rescue. The authors conclude that the resource-based view is useful for analysing the performance of bankrupt small and medium-sized enterprises and that the design of bankruptcy law can promote entrepreneurship.

In Chapter 10, Vito Albino, Francisco Alvarez and Ilaria Giannoccaro examine the concept of knowledge externalities by focusing on the role of interactive learning processes and by adopting a single-firm perspective. As a comparison, the literature has mainly analysed the role of knowledge spillovers by adopting the system perspective. To pursue their aim, an agent-based model of geographical clustering is developed, based on knowledge externalities produced by learning by imitation and learning by interaction. A simulation analysis is then carried out to observe the emergence of cluster patterns and to study influence of agent heterogeneity and the existence of knowledge centres on the geographical clustering process. Their results show that knowledge externalities based on learning motivate firms to cluster geographically.

Chapter 11 by Waldemar Pfoertsch and Reha Tözün presents research into the East Württemberg optics industry, whose characteristics display an intriguing and mixed picture. The strengths and weaknesses of the industry are discussed from the learning regions' perspective, and the solutions devised by firms that are willing to overcome the regional deficiencies are exemplified. The aim is to draw attention to learning firms' capability to pursue solutions to their problems. Additionally, the benefits of non-profit or public initiatives for regional economies are emphasised and questions for further research into the East-Württemberg situation are suggested.

In Chapter 12, Gary A.S. Cook and Naresh R. Pandit provide insights from two major studies of the broadcasting industry. The first was a two-year comparative case study of three important city-regions in the broadcasting industry in the UK, based on the cities of London, Bristol and Glasgow. This drew on semi-structured interviews with industry practitioners and policy makers. The second was an in-depth questionnaire survey of broadcasting and related media activities in London. Both studies clearly indicate that the sources of advantage gained by firms in these strong media clusters are typical of those found in leading manufacturing clusters. Above all, personal relationships are easier to build and maintain in a compact space, and help both knowledge flows, and also the close cooperation of many specialised suppliers, underpinned by trust, to deliver complex products and services to demanding customers. However, the importance of particular cluster benefits, such as informal knowledge flows and personal interaction, vary significantly by precise location and line of activity.

The closing of the gap in competitive capacity between developing and developed economies is explored in Chapter 13 by Lei Ding and Kingsley E. Haynes with reference to China's telecommunications industry. Since the entry of Chinese domestic mobile handset manufactures in 1998, domestic suppliers have successfully surpassed the market share of joint ventures while direct imports have been largely phased out. By examining China's telecommunications in general and its mobile handset manufacturing sector in particular, the authors found several factors including market conditions, competition and government support that contributed to the competitiveness of China's domestic manufacturers.

In Chapter 14, Roger R. Stough examines the role of entrepreneurship or enterprise development in regional economic development in general and more specifically its expression through a case study of the US National Capital Region. The chapter first presents a general assessment of enterprise development patterns nationally and globally and then examines trends and the institutional infrastructure in a specific region. Models of the policy environment are then developed, and the interpretative analysis above used to deductively offer policies aimed at optimising enterprise development processes.

The aim of Chapter 15 by Tõnu Roolaht is to model the formation of university-led entrepreneurial business support networks for business start-ups, where the focal role is played by technology transfer and incubation initiatives of the leader institution. This model is then used as the basis for an exploratory case study about the entrepreneurial initiatives in the entrepreneurship support network around the University of Tartu in Estonia. A dynamic support network that constantly looks for new ways to update its service portfolio, procedures and contacts can offer potentially more efficient help to start-ups than formalised and rigid promotion measures. Therefore, in order to understand the changing needs of entrepreneurial start-up companies, the support institutions also benefit from adopting an entrepreneurial attitude. In order to lift the barriers to entrepreneurship faced by small start-ups, all sides should work closely together in order to find customised solutions that serve the joint purpose of facilitating development.

## REFERENCES

Acs, Z.J. (ed.) (2000), *Regional Innovation, Knowledge and Global Change*, London: Frances Pinter.
Acs, Z.J. and D.B. Audretsch (1988), 'Innovation in Large and Small Firms: An Empirical Analysis', *American Economic Review*, **78**, 678–90.
Acs, Z.J., D.B. Audretsch and M.P. Feldman (1992), 'Real Effects of Academic Research: Comment', *American Economic Review*, **82**, 363–67.
Andersson, Å.E. (1985a), *Kreativitet – Storstadens framtid*, Stockholm: Prisma.
Andersson, Å.E. (1985b), 'Creativity and Economic Dynamic Modelling', in Batten, D., J. Casti and B. Johansson (1985) (eds.), *Economic Evolution and Structural Adjustment*, Berlin: Springer, 27–45.
Andersson, Å.E. (1985c), 'Creativity and Regional Development', *Papers of the Regional Science Association*, **56**, 5–20.
Andersson, M. and O. Ejermo (2005), 'How does Accessibility to Knowledge Sources Affect the Innovativeness of Corporations? – Evidence from Sweden', *Annals of Regional Science*, **39**, 741–65.
Andersson, M. and C. Karlsson, (2006), 'Regional Innovation Systems in Small and Medium-Sized Regions', in B. Johansson, C. Karlsson and R.R. Stough (eds), *The Emerging Digital Economy. Entrepreneurship, Clusters and Policy*, Berlin: Springer, 55–81.
Antonelli, C. (1998), 'Localised Technological Change, New Information Technology, and the Knowledge-Based Economy: The European Evidence', *Journal of Evolutionary Economics*, **8**, 177–98.
Camagni, R. (1991), 'Local "Milieu", Uncertainty and Innovation Networks: Towards a New Dynamic Theory of Economic Space', in R. Camagni (1991) (ed.), *Innovation Networks: Spatial Perspectives*, London: Belhaven, 121–42.
Castells, M. (1989), *The Informational City*, Oxford: Blackwell.
Chambers, R.G. (1988), *Applied Production Analysis: A Dual Approach*, Cambridge: Cambridge University Press.
Cooke, P. and K. Morgan (1998), *The Associational Economy*, Oxford: Oxford University Press.
Desmet, K. (2000), 'A Perfect Foresight Model of Regional Development and Skill Specialisation', *Regional Science and Urban Economics*, **30**, 221–42.
Dosi, G., C. Freeman, R. Nelson, G. Silverberg and L. Soete (eds) (1988), *Technical Change and Economic Theory*, London: Pinter Publishers.
Dunning, H.H. and R. Narula (1995), 'The R&D Activities of Foreign Firms in the United States', *International Studies of Management and Organization*, **25**, 39–73.
Feldman, M.P. (2001), 'The Entrepreneurial Event Revisited: Firm Formation in a Regional Context', *Industrial and Corporate Change*, **10**, 861–91.
Feldman, M.P. and D.B. Audretsch (1999), 'Innovation in Cities: Science-Based Diversity, Specialisation and Localized Competition', *European Economic Review*, **43**, 409–29.

Florida, R. (1995), 'Toward the Learning Region', *Futures* **27**, 527–36.

Florida, R. (2002), *The Rise of the Creative Class*, New York: Basic Books.

Florida, R. (2005a), *The Flight of the Creative Class. The New Global Competition for Talent*, New York: Harper Business.

Florida, R. (2005b), *Cities and the Creative Class*, New York: Routledge.

Fujita, M. and J.F. Thisse (2002), *Economics of Agglomeration – Cities, Industrial Location and Regional Growth*, Cambridge: Cambridge University Press.

Glaeser, E. (1999), 'Learning in Cities', *Journal of Urban Economics*, **100**, 254–77.

Gråsjö, U. (2006), '*Spatial Spillovers of Knowledge Production: An Accessibility Approach*, JIBS Dissertation Series No. 034, Jönköping International Business School.

Grossman, G.M. and E. Helpman (1991), 'Quality Ladders and Product Cycles', *Quarterly Journal of Economics*, **106**, 557–86.

Hall, P. (1990), 'High-Technology Industry and the European Scene', in *SOU 1990:33, Urban Challenges*, Stockholm: Statens offentliga utredningar, 117–33.

Hall, P. and P. Preston (1988), *The Carrier Wave: New Information Technology and the Geography of Innovation*, London: Unwin Hyman, 1846–2003.

Hotelling, H. (1929), 'The Stability of Competition', *Economic Journal*, **39**, 41–57.

Indergaard, M. (1997), 'Community-based Restructuring? Institution Building in the Industrial Midwest', *Urban Affairs Review*, **32**, 662–82.

Jaffe, A.B., M. Trajtenberg and R. Henderson (1993), 'Geographical Localisation of Knowledge Spillovers as Evidenced by Patent Citations', *Quarterly Journal of Economics*, **108**, 577–98.

Jin, D. and R.R. Stough (1998), 'Learning and Learning Capability in the Fordist and Post-Fordist Age: An Integrative Framework', *Environmental and Planning*, **30**, 1255–78.

Johansson, B. and C. Karlsson (1992), 'Transportation Infrastructure of the Mälar Region', *Regional Studies* **28**, 169–85.

Karlsson, C. and B. Johansson (2006), 'Dynamics and Entrepreneurship in a Knowledge-Based Economy', in C. Karlsson, B. Johansson and R.R. Stough (eds), *Entrepreneurship and Dynamics in the Knowledge Economy*, New York: Routledge, 12–46.

Karlsson, C. and B. Johansson (2007), 'Regional Development and Knowledge', CESIS Working Paper No. 76, CESIS/Jönköping International Business School, Jönköping.

Karlsson, C. and A. Manduchi (2001), 'Knowledge Spillovers in a Spatial Context: A Critical Review and Assessment', in M.M. Fischer and J. Fröhlich (eds), *Knowledge, Complexity and Innovation Systems*, Berlin: Springer, 101–23.

Karlsson, C. and K. Nyström (2006), 'Knowledge Accessibility and New Firm Formation', CESIS Working Paper No. 70, CESIS/Jönköping International Business School, Jönköping.

Keane, J. and J. Allison (1999), 'The Interaction of the Learning Region and local and Regional Economic Development: Analysing the Role of Higher Education', *Regional Studies*, **33**, 896–902.

Keeble, D. and C. Lawson (eds) (1998), *Collective Learning Processes and Knowledge Development in the Evolution of Regional Clusters of High Technology SMEs in Europe*, ESRC Centre for Business Research, University of Cambridge.

Knight, R.V. (1995), 'Knowledge Based Development: Policy and Planning Implications for Cities', *Urban Studies*, **32**, 225–60.

Krugman, P. (1991a), *Geography and Trade*, Leuven: Leuven University Press.

Krugman, P. (1991b), 'Increasing Returns and Economic Geography', *Journal of Political Economy*, **99**, 483–99.

Krugman, P. (1991 c), 'History and Industry Location: The Case of the Manufacturing Belt', *American Economic Review*, **81**, 80–83.

Krugman, P. (1993), 'First Nature, Second Nature and Metropolitan Location', *Journal of Regional Science*, **33**, 129–44.

Lundvall, B.-Å. and B. Johnson (1994), 'The Learning Economy', *Journal of Industrial Studies*, **1**, 23–42.

Maillat, D. and L. Kebir (2001), 'The Learning Region and Territorial Production Systems', in B. Johansson, C. Karlsson and R.R. Stough (eds), *Theories of Endogenous Regional Growth: Lessons for Regional Policies*, Berlin: Springer, 255–77.

Marshall, A. (1920), *Principles of Economics*, 8th ed., London: Macmillan.

Morgan, K. (1997), 'The Learning Region: Institutions, Innovation and Regional Renewal', *Regional Studies*, **31**, 491–503.

Nelson, R.R. and S.G. Winter (1982), *An Evolutionary Theory of Economic Change*, Cambridge, MA: Harvard University Press.

Nijkamp, P. (2003), 'Entrepreneurship in a Modern Network Economy', *Regional Studies*, **37**, 395–405.

Noyelle, T.J. and T.M. Stanbeck (1984), *The Economic Transformation of American Cities*, Totowa, NJ: Rowman & Allanheld.

Patel, P. and K. Pavitt (1991), 'Large Firms in the Production of the World's Technology: An Important Case of "Non-Globalisation"', *Journal of International Business Studies*, **22**, 1–21.

Pfaffermayr, M. and C. Bellak (2002), 'Why Foreign-Owned Firms are Different: A Conceptual Framework and Empirical Evidence from Austria', in R. Jungnickel (2002) (ed.), *Foreign-Owned Firms, Are They Different?*, London: Palgrave Macmillan, 13–57.

Quigley, J.M. (1998), 'Urban Diversity and Economic Growth', *Journal of Economic Perspectives*, **12**, 127–38.

Romer, P. (1986), 'Increasing Returns to Scale and Long-Run Growth', *Journal of Political Economy*, **94**, 1002–37.

Romer, P. (1994), 'The Origins of Endogenous Growth', *Journal of Economic Perspectives*, **8**, 3–32.

Shapero, A. (1984) 'The Entrepreneurial Event', in C.A. Kent (ed.), *The Environment for Entrepreneurship*, Lexington, MA: Lexington Books, 21–40.

Solow, R.M. (1994), 'Perspectives of Growth Theory', *Journal of Economic Perspectives*, **8**, 45–54.

Varga, A. (1997), *University Research and Regional Innovation: A Spatial Econometric Analysis of Academic Technology Transfers*, Boston, MA: Kluwer Academic Publishers.

Varga, A. (2002), 'Knowledge Transfers from Universities and the Regional Economy: A Review of the Literature', in A. Varga, and L. Szerb (eds), *Innovation, Entrepreneurship, Regions and Economic Development: International Experiences and Hungarian Challenges*, Pécs: University of Pécs Press, 147–71.

Zucker, L.G., M.R. Darby and J. Armstrong (1998a), 'Geographically Localised Knowledge: Spillovers or Markets?', *Economic Inquiry*, **36**, 65–86.

Zucker L.G., M R. Darby and M.B. Brewer (1998b), 'Intellectual Human Capital and the Birth of U.S. Biotechnology Enterprises', *American Economic Review*, **88**, 290–306.

# 2. Engineering Culture, Innovation, and Modern Wealth Creation

## Jack A. Goldstone

## SOURCES OF ECONOMIC GROWTH

Neoclassical economics and Marxism/socialism have opposite formulas for growth. The neoclassical paradigm is one of free-market efficiency; the socialist paradigm is one of government direction and intervention in the market for the common good.

In fact both paradigms offer something of value. The market remains an unparalleled method of coordinating the activity of diverse firms to achieve maximum efficiency. Government intervention, however, as institutional economists have pointed out, is often necessary to provide public goods, to counter monopolistic or oligopolistic behavior, and to provide the framework of law and contract enforcement and open communication that makes the smooth and rapid operation of markets possible.

However, both the neoclassical and socialist paradigms share a major limitation in their view of growth – they see growth as simply a result of the accumulation of capital. More capital, and more investment to create yet more capital, is the root of economic growth.

Yet empirical research shows that this is simply wrong, as a statement of fact. The collapse of the Soviet economy in the 1980s was in fact a crisis of unproductive over-investment. The economy was so badly structured and so badly manned and directed that while ever more capital was spent on investment (perhaps 40 percent of GDP in the last years of the 1980s) the product was unwanted surplus and shoddy goods that piled up in warehouses and on railroad sidings, or simply went to replace prior goods that were breaking down at a rate that required rapid replacement (Allen, 2003).

Nor is a surplus of capital a problem only in socialist economies. Capitalist economies in the US and East Asia have in recent years been embarrassed by surpluses of capital that served only to inflate bubbles in property (the US Saving and Loan debacle of the late 1980s) or currencies (the East Asian financial crisis of the late 1990s), which when burst led to major depressions rather than growth.

What, then, is the true source of growth? The Solow–Swan growth model (Solow, 1956, 1970) was the first to point out that since capital accumulation ran into diminishing returns, continuous growth could only come from technological change. As to how technical change arises and spreads through the economy, new endogenous growth models (Romer, 1986) point to research and development (R&D) and technological spillovers as the key.

Yet while technological change is critical to sustained growth, such models are often interpreted in a misleading fashion. First, empirically, it is not true that simply increasing investment in R & D increases the rate of economic growth, any more than increases in capital investment in general. The largest firms, which invest the largest amount of dollars in R&D, are generally not the main motors of growth in an economy.

What the research of my colleague Zoltan Acs (2002), among others, has shown, is that a crucial, often the leading, source of growth in modern economies is not the growth of large, existing firms. Such firms generally operate in mature and saturated markets, where the goods or services being produced have been available for a long time and most consumers of those goods are already consuming it at near maximum-desired levels. In such markets, most of the growth of firms comes from taking market share from competitors, and much research and innovation goes into marketing efforts for that purpose, or incremental product changes designed to increase market share. At this point, most of the gains in productivity from economies of scale and learning-by-doing have already been achieved and gone into the production of these goods. Thus there is little room left for routine increases in productivity. Rather, for such companies, their rate of growth is limited by the increase in overall levels of population and income in the markets that they serve. This, of course, explains why large companies serving mature domestic markets in Europe and the US have been willing to recklessly throw huge amounts of capital into the prospect of expansion into new and emerging markets, such as China, in the desperate hope of finding an avenue for rapid expansion without radically changing the products or the production processes that they have already mastered.

Breakthroughs that lead to dramatic changes in productivity, however, involve either the creation of wholly new products or services – such as airplanes, video recorders, portable personal music systems, or automated teller machines (ATMs) – or changes in production processes that make existing products either dramatically cheaper or dramatically superior in performance and/or quality or design. Unlike incremental changes in productivity, which allow a firm to command a small price premium and thus gain increased market share, major changes in products or processes change the nature of the market itself. Major improvements in quality or features for the same price will change the market from a mature 'replacement' market in which consumers seek to buy only when their current product is worn-out, or to maintain their current level of services, to a 'new' market in which most consumers want to acquire the product with higher quality or new features now. The second way to create a 'new' market is to create a wholly new product that is widely desired, and thus escape the constraints of mature markets. The creator of a new product faces the prospect of extremely rapid growth as the product penetrates markets where the product is unknown or previously unavailable; and because desire is high and supply is limited compared to that vast demand, prices can be kept high, resulting in the wonderful combination of high profit margins and rapid growth. Note that this is the opposite of conditions in mature and technologically stable markets, where the rule is small margins and incremental growth.

These types of productivity gain are only rarely made by large companies who have invested heavily in a given production process and in marketing certain goods. For such companies, who have reached a dominant or major position in their product markets, the risks of gambling on volume production of a new product, or a radical change in their established production processes, are usually outweighed by the more certain but incremental gains that they believe they can tweak from their existing production processes and marketing arrangements, in which, after all, they have enormous experience and have achieved a high level of excellence. Thus the major gains in productivity generally come from small companies, or middling companies entering new markets, where survival and growth are completely dependent on finding a breakthrough product or process that will propel rapid growth (Baumol, 2002a).

It is therefore the case that critical elements of the growth in modern economies come not from large and established or dominant companies, but from small companies that become large and dominant companies (Acs, 2002). It is not the companies with a hundred thousand or more employees that are the motors of growth (companies this size often look to cut employment and costs when seeking efficiencies in mature markets), but companies with one hundred or one thousand employees that grow in the course of a decade or two to employ over one hundred thousand employees. In short, in the last several decades it has been Microsoft, Dell, Intel, Cisco, Nokia, Honda, Toyota, Airbus, Wal-Mart and similar companies that have generated the most employment growth and economic growth, not General Motors, Xerox, or AT&T.

It should also be noted that the emergence and expansion of such small and middling companies not only provides substantial growth for that company itself, but also has remarkable regional and national propulsive effects. Such rapidly-expanding firms need and attract associated suppliers, advertisers, marketers, shippers and transport, banking and insurance and media to create and move and market their products and help manage their business. Secondary business may also be invigorated that can benefit from the use of the new product or new processes to create new sources of added value (thus, for example, new processes that create cheaper or higher-quality specialized steel can benefit existing or new industries that create steel-based products).

Moreover, the people who work for and profit from these rapidly expanding firms and associated suppliers/shippers/marketers create a large source of new demand for construction, consumer products, and services. The results are dynamic regional economies that develop around the centers of innovation.

While this type of expansion is often associated today with high-tech companies, the same story has held true of earlier industrial expansions, most notably that of Japan from the 1950s, in which new production methods for steel and motor cars, and new products in consumer electronics, drove expansion, as we shall note in more detail below.

In short, the key to modern economic growth is not merely greater accumulation of capital, or investment *per se*, or even investment in R&D. Rather, the key to modern economic growth is successful innovation to raise productivity through the creation of new products or new production processes. In a sense, this is an old story, advocated by Joseph Schumpeter, and validated by much modern empirical work (e.g., Florida, 2002; High, 2004). And yet it is a lesson that seems to have been lost in the obsession of the economics profession with growth models, neoclassical or endogenous, which elide over the really radical characteristics of discontinuous innovations in long-term economic transformation. A region seeking to create or increase economic growth should therefore not aim mainly to attract investment, which may or may not be fruitful. Rather, a region seeking growth should seek to attract innovation, as the presence of firms who are successful innovators will naturally draw large-scale investment, and translate that investment into multiple avenues of rapid growth.

This is not to deny, of course, that some incremental and continuous innovations in products or production processes, including those financed by large-company R&D, can have a substantial cumulative impact on economic growth. They do (Nelson and Winter, 1982; Nelson, 1993; Rosenberg, 1994). Examples include the motor vehicle industry, aerospace, construction, microchips, consumer electronics, and metallurgy, where continuous innovation has produced products of increasingly higher value. However, the most fruitful pathways of incremental and continuous innovation are those that lead to the creation of new products using incrementally improved technology, or conversely, developing radically innovative ways of manufacturing goods or supplying services even if the products or services are only incrementally changed. For example, the motor car has undergone amazing and continuous incremental development since its inception. Although the basic product has remained the same for a hundred years – an enclosed passenger compartment mounted on a four-wheeled platform driven by an internal-combustion engine with gear shafts mechanically transmitting power to the wheels – improvements in the components and materials have transformed the comfort and performance of the vehicle. Nonetheless, it was the creation of the motor car to replace other modes of transport that launched the industry and created huge companies from small ones. Since the 1950s, not a single new automobile company within the existing mature markets of that time (Europe and the US) has arisen with a radically new product or technology of production. Yet while the basic technology of motor cars has changed only incrementally over time, the rise of a smaller company to become a dominant firm – Toyota – came from a major innovation in production processes, i.e., Toyota's 'lean production' methods (Womack et al., 1990).

Similarly, the development of semi-conductors could be treated as one of incremental improvement, allowing ever more transistors and components to be placed on a single microcircuit, or chip. Yet what mattered for economic growth was not the simple incremental improvements in chip capacity, but such major product breakthroughs as the cellular phone, digital camera, and personal computer, all building on the humble transistor. It was these novel products that laid the foundation for vast new markets and rapidly growing firms. In some cases, innovations that seem to be incremental but which in fact created new products for existing firms have created rapid growth for firms that had apparently reached limits to their growth with their older products, such as the development of the SUV as a new form of motor-car did for Chrysler, or the iPod personal music player did for Apple.

All of which is to say that it may be difficult to draw a clear line between radical innovations that produce new products or processes, and innovations that are incremental in some respects but still capable of launching new industries or hugely invigorating and expanding existing firms. Yet either way, the key source of modern growth remains successful innovation, not merely greater efficiency or expanded investment in the production of existing and well-established products.

There is, of course, another pathway to growth, which is advocated by the classical model of 'comparative advantage'. If a country possesses a product in which it has unique resources for production (either a raw material, such as minerals or a locally produced agricultural product, or a labor force that has a higher skill level/cost ratio for such production than any other country), it is likely that it can produce that product for relatively lower costs, compared to other items it may produce and consume, than other countries. By concentrating on production of this good that it produces most efficiently and exporting it, and importing other items that it consumes, it can greatly increase the efficiency of its overall economy and thus achieve economic growth. There are, however, a number of problems with this model. First, it assumes that countries can freely export their relatively efficient products and freely import other consumables. Obviously, while free trade has grown, this is still something of a utopian ideal rather than a real-world reality. From sugar and banana producers in the developing world to producers of nuclear technology, import/export markets are in fact highly constricted by a variety of economic and political considerations.

Moreover, utilizing the complementarity of relative advantage works best when the prices and production of imports and exports are such that they involve comparable value-added and encourage similar levels of productivity. It may be more efficient for Nepal to produce carpets and handicrafts and import capital-intensive goods such as aircraft and electric power plants. Nonetheless, the amount of foreign exchange that Nepal must acquire to achieve this pattern in practice is either unobtainable by producing products for which global prices are low and markets are limited, or requires such a vast deployment of workers into unskilled and low value-added work as to limit Nepal's own movement into higher productivity avenues. It is one thing for the US to concentrate on production of larger long-haul aircraft while Canada and Brazil concentrate on the production of smaller short-haul aircraft. But for developing countries with little industry, unskilled workforces, and low value-added industries to rely on exploiting relative advantage does not direct them into pathways that promise to rapidly raise the productivity of their workforce and modernize their economy as a whole.

In the short term, exploiting natural relative advantages, as with mineral or agricultural production for export, or low-cost labor, can certainly generate profits. This justifies the prescription for growth that suggests focusing on improving the ability of a country to produce those goods in which it has a comparative advantage by investing in additional production, and in improving infrastructure to bring those products to market. If those profits are invested in industrial facilities, and upgrading human capital and infrastructure, a long-term growth trajectory can be achieved. However, all too often the benefits of relative advantages are treated as 'rents' earned simply from possession of a desired commodity, and those rents are concentrated in and spent by a narrow circle of elites who control those rents. The result is the 'resource curse', in which countries that have exploitable comparative advantages find their economies plundered and exploited by selfish elites, while the majority of their population fails to benefit (Karl, 1997).

Even countries that make good use of their comparative advantage face limited prospects. China has transformed its economy from one of widespread extreme poverty to one of substantial middle-income regions and far less poverty by allowing peasants to produce for the market and encouraging production of labor-intensive goods. Allowing peasants to produce for the market led to major gains in efficiency and output and created a substantial internal market for inexpensive consumer goods. Encouraging and attracting investment in production of labor-intensive goods (exploiting China's comparative advantage in skill/labor cost ratios) both served the growing internal market and created a vast export sector that took market share from less-efficient producers worldwide. In some cases, the gains from doing so were so great as to create new markets by turning formerly costly luxury goods (e.g., cashmere sweaters) into affordable items of mass consumption. Nonetheless, in the near future, China will face the limits of growth based on comparative advantage (as did Argentina and Australia with their reliance on raw material production, or Mexico with its reliance on high labor skill/cost ratios, all of which made great economic strides for a period on this basis). Eventually, there will be no further market share to gain from higher-cost producers; rather, as Chinese wages grow, China will be in danger of losing market share to countries with now higher skill/labor cost ratios (e.g., Bangladesh, Vietnam), or find itself unable to take market share in more capital-intensive goods from countries with comparable ratios and advantages in location and market access (Eastern Europe).

In order for China to sustain investment and growth, it must start to produce innovations that will allow it to become not merely a global leader in low-cost labor-intensive production, but a global leader in the production of higher value-added items so that its own consumers and export markets will continue to seek Chinese-made goods and services with higher profit margins, which will continue to provide higher incomes for Chinese producers. Chinese leaders are aware of this, but so far Chinese firms have shown no signs of being able to move in the direction of being competitive innovators rather than merely cost-competitive manufacturers (Kash, 2003).

## FOSTERING INNOVATION: THE ENGINEERING CULTURE

In preindustrial and prescientific eras, societies relied on artisanal improvements for technological advance. Once a certain machine was developed, such as the horse collar, or the pallet pump, or the windmill, it was often operated in the same way for centuries, with only tiny and mostly insignificant improvements. Given that prescientific societies had no precise way to measure the efficiency with which a given machine converted energy into work, this is hardly surprising.

It is the ability to draw on the accumulated systematic knowledge of modern science, the instrumentation and machinery of modern engineering, and the advanced marketing and finance capabilities of modern capitalist economies with regimes favorable to entrepreneurship, that keep innovations coming at a historically rapid clip. Modern economic growth changed the world by changing the length of the cycle of innovation /diffusion/commodification from centuries to decades, and by multiplying the number of distinct fields in which these cycles occur (Baumol, 2002b; Mokyr, 2004). For example, aviation, pharmaceuticals and computers are three areas of rapid advance which themselves did not exist prior to modern scientific innovation. By greatly enlarging the number of fields in which advances take place, and enormously accelerating the rate of advance, modern scientific engineering has increased the pace of technological innovation by several orders of magnitude.

How was the pattern of innovation established, in general and in specific areas and regions? As Richard Florida (2002) has shown, it starts with creative people. The leading centers of economic growth, from eighteenth-century Glasgow, London and Birmingham to contemporary San Jose and Mumbai, are places that attract a wealth of creative talent. Yet it is not just any such talent, in any combination, that is sufficient to ignite growth. Rather, to take the steps of pioneering new knowledge, identifying the opportunities for such knowledge to be turned to practical use in desirable and marketable products, and to implement the production and marketing of such products – from fine art and entertainment to exceptional goods and services – requires a certain arrangement, or network, of people and skills. In particular, it takes the marrying of creators, designers, engineers and entrepreneurs in networks that encourage their fruitful collaboration.

The creation of a successful innovation has at least three discrete stages. First is the creation of a new design, or idea, for a product or service. This is more likely to happen where more people who are interested in pursuing a novelty – that is, creative people – congregate and interact. To some degree, of course, ideas can be exchanged and developed over the internet, just as they were by letters and periodicals in an earlier age. But to a significant degree, creativity is sparked by the direct interaction of creative people pushing each other to do something new and worthwhile.

Second is the translation of the new design or idea into a workable prototype – something that is practical and can actually be produced, often called the stage of 'invention'. This is the domain of the engineer or technically skilled craftsman, sometimes the same person as the creator, sometimes not. However, a creative center needs a significant number of people who have the training and skills to take raw materials and ideas or designs and turn them into reality.

Third is the utilization of the idea or design in a product that can be profitably produced and marketed to users or consumers. This is the domain of both the engineer and the entrepreneur. The engineer needs to create a production process so that the product or service can be produced at a reasonable cost in needed volumes; the entrepreneur needs to identify the market or consumers who will pay for the new idea or product or service, and determine how much they will pay for how many, and so set the boundaries for the engineers to deliver products whose production will be profitable. The entrepreneur also needs to bring the financing, marketing, and distribution know-how to make the marketing of the product a success.[1]

Without the combination of all three stages – and most crucially, the networks to bring them fruitfully together – economic growth does not occur. No doubt, many great ideas remain impractical because of design and production issues that go unresolved. Easier to identify are the innovations that were created by engineers, but which were not brought to the attention of those entrepreneurs who were fated to create successful products out of those inventions – videotape for recording invented at Ampex, or the transistor invented at Stanford University, or the mouse and graphics computer interface invented at Xerox. Perhaps most striking is the action of the 'venture capitalist' – the entrepreneur who moves continually among the scientific and engineering and ideas men of a creative region, on the lookout for those with a commercially promising idea, and then seeking to bring together the designers, engineers, and entrepreneurs who will create a company to bring products to market.[2]

We have noted that recent theories of economic growth (Romer, 1986; Jones, 1994; Mokyr, 2002) have emphasized that accelerating economic growth depends on the expansion of knowledge, and more formally on investment in R&D of new products and production processes. This in turn has given rise to a huge theoretical and empirical literature on how investment in R&D drives long-term economic growth, and how human capital and physical capital embody and promote technological change (Nelson and Winter, 1982; Rosenberg, 1982, 1994; Nelson, 1993).

A vast literature has also arisen on the 'institutions' – laws and organizational attributes – necessary for growth to occur in modern societies (North, 1990; De Soto, 2000), and on the 'co-evolution' of markets and institutions in the dynamics of innovation (Nelson, 1994; Malerba, 2006). Yet while private property and rule of law may be necessary to undergird economic growth, they are far from being a sufficient explanation of why growth occurs, or where, or when. These conditions allow for the efficient exploitation of existing resources and technologies, but they in no way assure or promote innovation. As we have seen, innovation is the product of specialized and localized networks of individuals and firms that take advantage of these background conditions (Kash, 1989, pp. 44ff.); such networks do not spontaneously arise everywhere the background conditions are present.

The basic framework of English laws and institutions held in backwards and impoverished southeastern England, not just in industrializing Manchester; the basic laws of the United States hold throughout the country, not just in Silicon Valley and Hollywood. Centers of innovation are far more narrowly defined and tightly clustered than the general domain in which certain institutions hold sway.

Moreover, while the specific institutional conditions of eighteenth- and nineteenth-century England – bourgeois-led parliamentary rule, the Common Law, and a mix of Scots, Irish, and English, Protestants and Catholics – allowed for growth in Britain, it is not at all clear that these are general requisites. Japan has been hostile to ethnic and religious minorities, South Korea and Taiwan were run by military dictatorships for decades, Singapore has a notoriously strong executive, and China is run by an authoritarian party that does not provide secure private property; yet these are precisely the countries that have been the most spectacular growers of the post-World War II period. Their governments promoted innovation and entrepreneurship for global markets, but hardly on the British/US institutional model.

Furthermore, as we have argued repeatedly above, a focus on the aggregate, or national average conditions, often is misleading – the real action often takes place through specific local social formations that may in fact be atypical of national conditions. This is precisely what we find in the basis for creating modern wealth. In Japan, world-beating steel, auto, and consumer electronics industries grew up alongside an enormously costly, inefficient, and heavily subsidized agricultural sector, while the domestic retail and distribution sector was notoriously overmanned and stuffed with politically-protected local monopolies (Posen, 2002). How was this possible?

Many economists have focused on the growth of 'knowledge' as the key to the origins of modern growth (Baumol, 2002b; Mokyr, 2002; Malerba, 2006), and we have come to refer to modern economies as 'knowledge' economies. A key problem with this literature, however, as pointed out by Keely and Quah, is that despite shifting attention in their models from capital accumulation and investment to the growth of knowledge and technology, economists have nonetheless used the same basic model, treating 'knowledge' like capital: as a single undifferentiated entity whose accumulation leads to growth. Although economists grant that knowledge, or its embodiment in human capital, can produce increasing returns – unlike physical capital, which depreciates and has diminishing returns – their models still feature a 'uni-dimensionality of technology where it is only the aggregate patented stock of knowledge … that matters' (Keely and Quah, 2000, p. 93).

In fact, knowledge shows precisely the same kind of behavior as capital that we described above. That is, simply piling up more and more knowledge can be as inefficient as simply piling up more and more tractors; and indeed one can go broke in doing so. Knowledge is not all of a piece – some kinds of new knowledge render old kinds of knowledge obsolete or useless, while some kinds of old knowledge act as 'sunk capital' and block the adoption of new knowledge or its application and learning by doing.

To take an early example from the North Sea region, Holland achieved technological leadership in the seventeenth century in part by its exploitation of knowledge regarding water management and wind power. But this knowledge base was not fruitful for further development, and the technology based on it was rendered obsolete by the late eighteenth century. More importantly, Holland never developed the network of engineers and artisans working with steam power that England built up in the eighteenth and nineteenth centuries. As a result, even though Holland had ideal institutional conditions for entrepreneurship, including low interest rates, limited government, and easy access to markets, it did not develop steam-powered industry. Oddly, what Holland did develop in the eighteenth century, drawing on its established skilled networks in typesetting and printing, was the leading publishing industry in Europe (and to this day, Dutch publishers are global leaders in academic publishing), publicizing the scientific and technical developments arrived at in England and diffusing them throughout the continent. But this did not lead to innovation in the critical areas of metallurgy and engine-power for manufacturing and transport that transformed Britain.[3]

This highly specific character of knowledge is not just a feature of old, preindustrial or early industrializing economies. In the last decade, the American telecommunications industry generated new knowledge that made possible the internet, and fiber-optic transmission of data. This particular combination seemed like a sure engine of growth – the internet would generate increasing transmission of data, and fiber-optic networks would grow to handle the load. The result was huge investment in all kinds of internet-supporting activities, such as server farms and equipment production, and huge investment in building fiber-optic networks. But this story in fact had a sad outcome. While internet access spread, there was no innovation that provided a lucrative use of the internet for producers – no services that people wanted to pay for. In fact, people remain quite satisfied using the internet for e-mail, purchasing travel services, auctioneering, and information searches – beyond that they have been largely unwilling to pay for additional services that would require greater bandwidth. Innovators are still looking for the 'killer application' that will turn internet use *per se* into a major stream of revenue. In the meantime, most of the equipment providers, server farms, and other internet-support firms have gone bust, drowned in wasted capital investments.

Moreover, another new kind of innovation was developing – knowledge of how to multiplex light-wave signals so as to increase the volume of data that could be carried on a given capacity of fiber-optic network by a hundred-fold. This particular bit of knowledge made most of the huge investment in fiber-optic networks redundant. Even though internet use did increase a hundred-fold, this increase could now be carried without much strain through a small portion of the greatly expanded fiber-optic networks. Thus fiber-optic and communications companies went bankrupt as well, having wasted billions investing in now-redundant fiber-optic capacity.

Of course, some day an innovation will come along that will spur huge increases in demand for internet traffic; at that point, the existing fiber-optic networks may become valuable, and a new cycle of innovation and growth will have begun. But for the moment, as of this writing, the innovation cycle of internet/fibre optic communication has created its boom of growth and run out. Piling up knowledge and investment in the latest technology did not produce unending sustained growth; it produced a boom and then a bust – just like piling up too much of anything that cannot be profitably marketed.

These cautionary tales suggest that while knowledge growth is essential to modern economic growth, it is not sufficient to think in terms of simply accumulating more and more knowledge. While some economists do argue that what matters is 'useful' knowledge (Mokyr, 2002), it is in fact impossible to know what knowledge is useful and what is not until long after it appears.

And of course even the same bit of knowledge may be useful in some contexts, with properly complementary knowledge and capabilities, but useless in others. What matters for sustaining the growth of useful knowledge is innovation – and for that matter, not just innovation, but innovation coupled to entrepreneurial needs through networks that produce new products and new production processes that can be competitively marketed (most innovation in abstract philosophy or even in historical interpretation, for example, has less economic impact than innovation in computer games).

Knowledge, however crucial, is thus of little use without the skills of the right kinds of people to apply it and work with it to develop marketable products. Economic theory has tried to capture the role of people in producing innovation by developing the concept and measurement of 'human capital', that is, the added capabilities and knowledge acquired by people through a combination of formal education and practical experience (Mankiw et al., 1992). The problem, again, is that like other forms of capital or knowledge, 'human capital' is treated as all of a piece, and subjected to the false logic of accumulation. Thus Lensink and Kuper (2000) stress the importance of 'the accumulation of human capital for economic growth'. In its simplest formulation, it might be measured simply as aggregate years of schooling in a population, or years of schooling plus years of work experience.

Yet in fact there is little evidence that added years of schooling as such will spur economic growth. As Pritchett (2001) has shown, huge increases in schooling in developing countries in recent decades have had little effect on growth. As we all know, not all experience or schooling is equally useful. One should note the ironic but very real study of Murphy et al. (1991), which showed that countries with more engineers have higher growth rates than countries with more lawyers, or the work of Rogers (2003), which showed that sending modest numbers of students abroad for an engineering education may have more impact than schooling large numbers at home.

That is an almost jocular example of a more general principle – that certain kinds of education are more likely to produce entrepreneurs and engineering advances than others. It is no accident that rapidly growing computer software firms developed around the Indian Institute of Science in Bangalore, or that computer hardware firms developed around the Massachusetts Institute of Technology, or that circuit and computer design firms developed around Stanford University. Even the Soviet Union, in its rapid growth days, had the sense to develop technical training institutes in greater numbers than liberal arts universities. Japan, South Korea, and Taiwan followed a similar course. While other developing countries designed their educational systems around the British university model – which had developed mainly to train professional civil servants, lawyers, clergy, professors, and the like – the East Asian economic tigers 'quietly dismantled [that model and instead] education was harmonized with ... national manpower requirements for rapid economic development'. Technical education was emphasized, and 'education was [aimed at] entrepreneurial development' (Mehmet, 1999, p. 138).

Aside from the positive benefit of training engineers, there are often truly negative effects of training too many liberal arts or law graduates. Without economic innovations to create a complex and rapidly growing economy, there is no demand for such graduates; in this case, investment in the liberal arts and law education is wasted. Even worse, in economies not generating innovation and rapid growth, skilled and educated people will likely turn their attention to exploiting whatever opportunities are available, such as the gains available from controlling streams of natural resources or foreign assistance. To the extent that education is turned to this kind of rent-seeking behavior, rather than productive innovation, it does more harm than good to economic growth (Baumol 1993; Barthélemy et al., 2000). As Easterly sagely warns: 'Creating people with high skills in countries where the only profitable activity is lobbying the government for favors is not a formula for success' (2001, p. 73).

In addition, once rent-seeking, corruption or stultifying government planning has damaged the prospects for economic growth, even production of talented engineers will not produce desired outcomes. Without access to networks of entrepreneurs, and opportunities to create firms and market products, the skills that engineers have will not pay off; thus in such countries engineers will do the logical thing and leave. It is precisely because of the value of access to such networks, which are critical to translating skills into marketable innovations, that a trained engineer – with a given amount of human capital – can earn $55,000 per year in the United States, but only $2,300 per year in India (ibid., p. 81). The return on human capital is thus extremely dependent on context.[4]

Finally, not all years of formal education or job experience are of equal worth. In too many schools in developing nations, schooling takes place in underfunded schools with large classes, few or no texts, and poorly trained teachers (Mehmet, 1999, p. 137; Easterly, 2001, p. 83). Such education may be better than none, and providing basic literacy skills is often conducive to self-respect, independence, and small-scale enterprise.[5]   But one cannot expect the same skills for developing future innovations to come from such education as from the education that takes place in better-supported institutions.

For all of these reasons, the results of empirical studies of returns to investment in human capital are ambiguous (Wolf, 2003). While in general, it appears that having more knowledgeable and more skilled people in a society would be a plus for economic growth, it is also true that there are so many differences in the quality and kinds of knowledge acquired, that the general principle so often found at the heart of simple economic models – 'more is better, so accumulation of human capital leads to growth' – again fails to capture the complexity of social and economic reality.

The critical quality among engineers and entrepreneurs, who together are immersed in fruitful networks of interaction, is the spread of what I call the 'engineering culture'. This is not simply a matter of being conversant with technical terms or comfortable with quantitative thinking, although these are parts of it. Much more important is the relentless commitment to optimization as a goal. Looking for the 'elegant' solution or the 'optimal' approach is the hallmark of the creative engineer; looking for the 'killer application' or the 'monster' product is the hallmark of the aggressive entrepreneur. Both share in the belief that a product or process can always be improved, and that doing so is the path to improving the world. The pursuit of riches is something that follows in consequence of having the 'best' or 'optimal' solution to a particular problem. But it is solving the problem in an elegant fashion that is a crucial part of the goal.

Entrepreneurs, after all, have been making money for centuries by seizing opportunities to buy low and sell high. While those skills and actions do contribute to efficient use of existing resources and technologies, they generally do not lead to major innovations in products or production. The modern scientific engineer is a much more recent product of the development of modern empirical and experimental science, with its rapid advances in the production of useful knowledge in many fields. The scientifically-trained engineer sees it as his/her task to bring to bear the latest fruits of science to improve the efficiency and utility of the products that underpin material life. However, engineers excel in invention, not necessarily in production and marketing, and thus often need the assistance of entrepreneurs to maximize their influence on the economy at large. But together, scientific engineering and entrepreneurship can operate to continually change products and production, and in many cases to create radical changes that lead to dramatic episodes of economic growth. It is precisely such processes that are at the core of many of the most dramatic regional success stories in the global economy.

## EVIDENCE ON MODERN WEALTH CREATION

The latest research on the empirical patterns of industrial productivity shows that since the 1960s, the global economy appears to be bifurcating into two distinct groups of economies – those with relatively high productivity, and those with relatively low productivity (Quah, 1996; Kumar and Russell, 2002). The high-productivity economies are reaping the benefits of science-based engineering married to capable entrepreneurship. They are producing innovative products, new sources of energy, new materials, novel designs, and new and improved processes for manufacturing, transportation, and other technology. They are thus producing what I call distinctively 'modern' wealth. The low-productivity economies are instead focusing on the production of widely available commodities for competitive markets, as has been the standard practice of producers and merchants in traditional societies for thousands of years, and that is what I call the production of 'traditional' wealth.

Whether producing cacao, coffee, computer chips, oil or diamonds, phone-answering services or assembly of simple components, the production of widely available commodities – even if using skilled labor – may increase incomes and lead to modest prosperity. In some cases, and in the short-term, rapid increases in the output of certain raw materials, such as oil and natural gas, gold and diamonds, or of basic assembly or service enterprises, may even lead to pockets of considerable wealth. But such production of traditional wealth eventually runs into diminishing returns, as additional producers come on-stream and increase supplies. Thus the production of sugar was the basis of fabulous fortunes in the eighteenth-century Caribbean; today with global markets glutted with sugar production (as with coffee, or other items), it barely supports producers at modest incomes. If one country finds it profitable to produce coffee (or memory chips, or cotton, or any other product that can be easily produced with off-the-shelf technology, semi-skilled labor, and is fairly uniform regardless of who produces it), then other countries will find it profitable, and eventually will enter the market, and increase supplies until such production is barely profitable. This is precisely what the general-equilibrium theory of economics tells us. The final result may be good for consumers around the world, but it is not very good for lagging economies trying to catch up by increasing their output of such commodities. It is therefore not in production of cotton, or oil, or coffee that the creation of modern wealth can be found. Rather, it is in the design of new clothing lines with global appeal, the creation of new petrochemicals and plastics, and the purveying of innovative beverages and environments for their consumption (thus the daily wage of a coffee-picker in many places in the world is a bit less than the cost of a grande mocha latte in San Francisco or New York). Creative engineering and entrepreneurship producing new products and even new markets is what creates modern wealth.[6]

The difference between the creation of 'traditional' versus 'modern' wealth has little to do with ambitions for profit. Rather, it is the difference between seeking profit by exploiting existing markets versus creating new ones. In what I label 'the sector of traditional wealth creation', producers create products with few or no unique characteristics; such commodities are readily produced by additional producers. Producers in this sector inevitably tend toward competitive equilibrium with minimal profits, and can be forced out by lower-cost producers. By contrast, in the sector of modern wealth creation, producers create products by engineering in unique characteristics or production advantages, allowing them exceptionally high margins and high and growing demand. Such sectors may mature with the diffusion of designs or production technologies and become producers of traditional sector commodities, for example, production of generic drugs or computer chips. But modern sectors continually renew themselves, in these cases, through development of custom circuit designs and new pharmaceuticals. The emergence and maintenance of modern wealth-creating sectors depended on the emergence of scientific engineering to help entrepreneurs systematize the development of new products and production processes at an accelerating rate. Schumpeter (1934) of course saw the same difference, and focused on technological change as its driver. Yet he placed all his emphasis on the spirit of the entrepreneur who puts together 'new combinations'; he allows little place for the progress of science and in particular of scientific engineering as a factor that dramatically changes the rate at which new combinations can be realized.

We see this pattern in the shift of centers of production innovation around the world from the onset of the Industrial Revolution. Great Britain became the initial leader of industrialization through its innovation in textile machinery, steel production and fabrication, and above all in the utilization of steam power. Having a substantial lead in the networks of expertise in the development and application of these technologies, England remained the center of advances in steam technology for over a century and a half. But England did not remain alone as a center of modern wealth creation – what happened?

While much has been written on the defects of Victorian Britain in seeking an explanation for why Britain lost its economic leadership, the problem was not specific to Britain, but rather part of the general pattern of modern wealth creation – namely the way that modern wealth is created not merely through accumulation of capital or education or other resources, but through specific networks of innovation. Such networks inevitably acquire specialized skills through 'learning by doing' (David, 1975) that gives them preeminence in a particular field. But such leadership does not necessarily transfer to other fields, where innovation may provide new and yet greater gains.

Britain did not lose its economic leadership because other countries developed superior steam engines. Other countries did catch up in steam technology, importing engineers, engines, railways, and learning to emulate and manufacture their own. But this did not create superior networks in the development of these technologies to those that had developed in Britain. Instead, other countries developed their own specialized networks of innovation in other fields, by training their own cadres of engineers, mechanics, and supporting their own entrepreneurial enterprises, thus building up their own discrete fields of technological leadership. As Hobday has put it, latecomer learning and innovation was often a 'hard slog, rather than a leapfrog' (1995, p. 1188).

Thus nineteenth-century Germany, through its pioneering development of the research-focused university system, trained a generation of innovators in modern chemical and mechanical engineering, who had more systematic knowledge of chemical engineering than chemists in Britain (Mokyr, 1990, p. 263). The result was German dominance in chemistry and related fields (e.g., dyeing, chemical synthesis) (Murmann, 2003).

> The German states ... pioneered a new form of technical education, based on France's Ecole Polytechnique but more oriented toward industry, and they were particularly well able to provide the scientific talent upon which financial success depended. German chemists [working with coal tars to develop synthetic aniline dyes] soon developed whole new 'families' of colors and also learned to synthesize such popular natural dyestuffs as indigo and madder. Consequently, German scientific discoveries drove natural dyestuffs from the commercial market and Germany came to dominate the dyestuffs industry, the profits from which then allowed them to branch out into pharmaceuticals and explosives. ... By 1914 Germany produced about 75% of the world's supply of dyes and dyestuffs. (Smithsonian Institution, 1998)

Building on the coal revolution, Germany produced coal-based dyes that transformed the textile industry. But an even bigger breakthrough from chemistry was the production of synthetic fertilizers. If the steam engine was the pivotal innovation of the initial phase of the Industrial Revolution, because it allowed the inorganic carbon in coal to be converted to energy useful for propulsion and locomotion, then the pivotal innovation of chemical phase of the Industrial Revolution was the Haber–Bosch process for creating chemical fertilizers from inorganic petrochemicals (Smil, 2001). The steam engine removed one of the critical constraints on preindustrial societies – the need for all motive energy to come from organic or natural sources (muscle, wind, water power) – by allowing people to convert plentiful inorganic substances to sources of useful motion. Similarly, the Haber–Bosch process removed another one of the critical constraints on preindustrial societies: the need for all food production to rely on organic fertilizers (recycling wastes or planting legumes) to undergird crop production. Instead, it allowed people to convert plentiful inorganic substances to food (albeit indirectly; by using the inorganic fertilizer to sustain and boost food supplies without the need for the usual organic inputs). The ammonia synthesis at the heart of modern chemical fertilizers was invented in Germany by Fritz Haber in 1908. Again demonstrating the critical importance of combining scientific engineering with entrepreneurial networks, the commercial application was developed slightly later by Carl Bosch (and is hence known as the Haber–Bosch process), and was implemented by BASF just before World War I. German engineers also pioneered the development of the diesel engine, which was eventually to displace the steam engine in most applications. Again German advances were diffused and copied, and the next advance to economic leadership occurred in the United States, with the creative exploitation of mass production for the large-scale assembly of cars and other large machines overcoming yet another constraint on prior production.

Yet in addition, and equally important if generally far less noted, alongside the mass production sector in the US there grew up a highly innovative, small-scale sector of design and machinery firms that constantly supplied useful new products and processes to the mass producers. It was in many ways these small-scale, highly innovative firms that maintained the appeal of products from mass producers, whose products were thus continually differentiated, enhanced and which retained unique advantages.

In his wonderful book *Endless Novelty*, Scranton points out that the standard tale of modern industrialization in America from 1865 to 1925 focuses on the rise of the large corporation and mass production; yet in fact such corporations were extremely atypical, never employing more than a tiny fraction of all manufacturing employment and a similar portion of the value added (Scranton, 1997, p. 7). Few things were more emblematic of the advance of technology in this era than railway locomotives – yet locomotives were never mass produced. The director of Baldwin Locomotive Works in Philadelphia described his work as follows:

> Sharp fluctuation of demand; impossibility of manufacturing in advance of orders; impracticability of mass production; necessity for employing [skilled] specialists; high cost of each completed item and varying conditions under which it is sold and used call for unusual adjustability, flexibility, ingenuity, and resourcefulness (Cited in Scranton, 1997, p. 12)

It was thus in the specialty sector, as much or more than in mass production, that advanced engineering skills married with entrepreneurial agility led American economic growth. 'Specialty sectors not only crafted the hardware that made mass production feasible and the styled goods that helped define American consumer society, but also initiated the technological and organizational transformations distinct from, but comparably significant to, the creation of routinized assembly' (Scranton, 1997, p. 3).

If we look at one of the leading sectors of the world economy today – computer software and hardware – we again find it concentrated in regional centers, such as Ireland, Bangalore, and Silicon Valley, where the specific mix of engineering talent and entrepreneurial skill, along with access to markets and non-intrusive but supportive government institutions, have come together. Not routinized mass production, but highly skilled and specialized production for ever-changing and specific markets, is often at the center of these enterprises.

Thus innovation leading to rapid growth is not something that simply occurs in an ongoing fashion in economies, cumulating like capital or wealth. Rather, innovations tend to be clustered in specific fields and embodied in particular networks of human relations, skills, and techniques.[7] Such centers of innovation tend to be localized, even within nations, and have a certain period in which they enjoy 'leading-edge' advantages, before their advances become diffused, the technology becomes routinized, and the products become widely produced commodities. The diffusion phase, of course, creates considerable growth and advance in living standards. But the diffusion phase itself is not an engine for future growth; its success depends on the prior center of innovation.

This process of innovation in particular centers and networks, diffusion of advances, and the slowing of the engine of growth, is not a characteristic unique to industrial times. Rather, this pattern is the general pattern of economic growth throughout history. Just as Renaissance Italy pioneered in techniques of finance and ceramics, silk, and textile design and production, only to be eclipsed by Holland's production based on peat and windmill-driven power and improvements in shipping, warehousing, and credit, and as Holland was then surpassed by British innovations in water-powered textile machinery and then steam-engine-driven production, so too the US steel industry and Soviet heavy machinery production 'ran out of steam' as engines of growth, to be succeeded by centers of advance in computing, software, and circuit design.

What is distinctive about modern wealth creation is the pace of change, the rapidity with which innovations are found and applied to production, creating a rapid succession of advances in different areas of the production frontier (Kash, 1989). It might be thought that Japanese, South Korean, and Taiwanese companies became leaders in the various fields of automobiles, semiconductors, liquid crystal displays, and the like through heavy investment in R&D. But that is not what actually happened. Rather, companies like Sony, Toyota, Matsushita, and Samsung developed large R&D programs after becoming leaders in their field, in order to sustain future growth, not as the precondition for their early advances.

Instead, the Asian economies started their trajectory to growth by developing new products around existing technologies – such as the transistor radio – that they could supply cheaply to world markets (ibid., pp. 192–4). These economies also did a lot of subcontracting and assembly work for foreign corporations. But it was not cheap labor *per se* that made them attractive for such work. It was the availability of low-cost, high-quality engineering. Investments in technical education had provided a skilled, but relatively low-cost, pool of talent that could reproduce foreign technologies. At first, this was used to produce products specified by foreign companies to their designs. But Asian supplier firms then began to investigate and reverse-engineer the products they were producing, finding ways to improve them or their production processes (Hobday, 1995).

Japanese companies then gained world-class status not by 'catching up' to existing technologies, or simply by taking existing production processes and plugging in cheaper labor. Quite the contrary. They made their mark by adopting more advanced technologies than those current in western countries, especially redesigning processes for production. For example, in the case of steel, the dominant steel manufacturer in the 1950s was the United States, which used the open-hearth furnace to smelt iron ore (itself a major advance over the Bessemer furnace earlier developed and used by Britain). But the Japanese did not simply adopt this technology; they enthusiastically adopted the newer basic oxygen furnace, invented in Austria in 1952. This newer technology was not adopted by the United States, which had a huge investment in existing open-hearth furnaces and was already the world leader, with little competition. But Japan not only adopted the new smelting technology; they found that doing so also revolutionized downstream elements in the process of making steel, allowing them to develop continuous casting instead of going through the intermediate stage of creating ingots (as in the open-hearth furnace) for later casting (Easterly, 2001, p. 183). The result was a considerable leap in productivity that was due to innovation in production processes, not cheap labor.

Similarly, in auto manufacturing, the Japanese pioneered a variety of innovations designed to make production more efficient, including just-in-time inventory techniques and tougher quality control (Womack et al., 1990). These techniques were not the result of R&D, nor borrowed from existing leading manufacturers. Rather, they were the result of adopting new ideas (especially those regarding quality control and employee relations advanced by the American W.E. Deming) that were long known but which current leading producers did not bother to adopt. However, once adopted, the emphasis on quality and just-in-time inventory led to complementary innovations in the design of cars themselves (such as using fewer connections and simpler and fewer parts), making them easier and cheaper to assemble but also stronger and more reliable. Again, the result was to catapult Japanese productivity ahead of that of then-current leading producers.

In both cases, the innovations in production could not have been adopted without the prior existence of a large cadre of workers with solid technical skills. This was even more true of the semiconductor and software industries that arose in the 1990s. However, the key again was a broad complementarity of skills. Japanese and other Asian economies benefited not only from cadres of trained engineers, but also from substantial training of the workforce in 'low-tech' technical specialties. That is, without 'human resources trained across a wide range of basic craft, technician, engineering and industrial skills [including] capabilities in fields such as plastics, moldings, machinery, assembly', plating, and metal work, these countries could not have emerged as export leaders (Hobday, 1995, p. 1188).

Different East Asian countries also developed varied but explicit mechanisms for bringing together engineering capability with entrepreneurs and financing. Japan encouraged close relationships, involving extensive stock cross-holdings, among banks and production firms. In South Korea, the government set up incentives, subsidies, and targets for local firms to help them compete in world markets. In Taiwan, investment in electronics was encouraged from overseas Chinese entrepreneurs, while in areas with large capital requirements, such as semiconductors, steel, and petrochemicals, state ownership underwrote investment. In Singapore, partnerships with multi-national corporations were welcomed (Hobday, 1995; Orru et al., 1996). But in every case, the basis of growth was the combination of a workforce with broad technical skills, encouragement for advanced engineering, and support for entrepreneurship. Much the same has been true for new or newly dominant clusters of production in Europe in financial services in London (Thrift et al., 1994), cell phones in Finland (Ojala et al., 2006), and electronics in Ireland (O'Riain, 2004); and in outsourced software and information services in India (Bhagwati and Calomiris, 2007).

## CONCLUSION: GROWING ECONOMIC GROWTH

It is no accident that one of the most common concepts for encouraging economic growth today is that of the 'growth incubator', for as I have laid it out in this chapter, economic growth is inherently an organic process. Growth grows out of a set of complex interactions among different sets of individuals in dynamic exchange, circulating ideas, designs, products, and marketing plans.

There is thus no single aggregate additive to add to a national economy to encourage growth – not capital, or research, or 'knowledge'. Rather, the engines of growth tend to be regional centers of innovation, clustered around small firms launching new products or processes that will eventually lead to mature markets in which they are the dominant producers.

To encourage the formation of such regional centers, certain requisites can be identified. First, there must be conditions that attract or develop creative people. These might be new educational institutions in areas of already dense but underskilled populations, such as Ireland or northern India. Or they might be pleasant living and working environments that attract skilled talent from other areas. Second, the creative mix of people must include a substantial number of engineers, imbued with the engineering culture and the skills to translate ideas into inventions and marketable products. Third, the engineers need to be complemented by a cadre of technical workers who can execute the designs and man production facilities (although this is becoming less and less important, as manufacturing can be outsourced provided the regional creative center has good communications and transportation so that the designers and engineers can be in constant touch with their manufacturing operations). Fourth, the creative mix must include a substantial number of entrepreneurs who are able to easily set up firms and develop new products, or services, or production processes, for the market. This means that the legal conditions must make the movement of capital and the formation of new firms relatively easy and secure, with solid intellectual as well as capital and physical property rights clearly specified and enforced. Finally, the mix must operate in a social environment where different groups can easily meet to exchange ideas, discuss plans, and spark new thoughts. Thus a rigid separation of different occupational groups or sterile isolated residential communities is highly dysfunctional for this project; rather a concentrated or sprawling array of mixed-use properties and entertainment venues, with ample opportunities for socialization and movement of people as well as ideas across different circles, will maximize the chances for a fruitful meeting of the minds.

This is not to say that these ingredients will always produce a breakthrough. Moreover, established clusters often retain advantages in the pools of talent and experience they have accumulated in producing specific products (e.g., Hollywood for entertainment, Silicon Valley for technical hardware, even Detroit for motor vehicles) that are hard to overcome. Nonetheless, it is only through venturing into the creative process that firms and regions can hope to attain a position on the leading edge of the global economy, and the rapid economic growth that comes with it.

## NOTES

1.  Von Hippel (2005) has suggested a fourth stage – the sophisticated consumer hungry for innovation. Yet part of good entrepreneurship is identifying the market for a product, even if consumers are unaware of their need. No doubt a vigorous and innovation-seeking group of consumers makes an entrepreneurs' task somewhat easier, but new products that offer real advantages – from the 'Green revolution' seed/fertilizer combinations in south Asia to DDT-impregnated mosquito nets in Africa – can be successfully marketed even where no prior consumer markets were present.
2.  Perhaps the first modern venture capitalist was Matthew Boulton, who immersed himself in the 'Lunar Society' of creative scientists, engineers, and inventors in Birmingham, England, in the eighteenth century. Spotting the potential of the 'fire engine' patented by fellow Society member James Watt, Boulton sponsored Watt's further research into making a practical engine, arranged for financing and production of the engine, and marketed and sold the key components through a new firm that he created with Watt for that purpose (Uglow, 2002).

3.    Mokyr (2002, pp. 28–9) argues that diffusion of scientific knowledge through publication was a major factor in creating economic growth in eighteenth century Europe. I fear this is an anachronistic view. While scientific publishing did aid diffusion and growth of innovation in the late nineteenth and twentieth centuries, in the eighteenth century the 'scarce' factor in technology was not so much the 'book learning' awareness of scientific ideas, as the practical skills of engineers and technicians embodied in the British labor force, which far exceeded that of other nations through the eighteenth century. These practical skills, based in experience with processes of machine fabrication, design, and operations, were much harder to transfer across societies than were books and journals. Thus the irony that the leading publisher of scientific books and journals in Europe – Holland – remained technologically backwards in many fields until the nineteenth century.

4.    The Indian software industry around Bangalore is an exception. How did this arise? The reason was, in fact, an accidental benefit of central planning. Because the Indian government's planning commissions did not foresee an Indian software industry, there was no effort to create regulations to cover one. The industry thus could grow up without much of the stifling regulatory apparatus that controlled most Indian enterprises. It was also, of course, fortunate that the capital requirements for a software industry are low (a personal computer and software per engineer), and the raw-material inputs are negligible, otherwise the industry would have been unable to secure the required inputs from the planned economy, as they would have already been allocated elsewhere.

5.    There is in fact evidence that on a global scale, increases in basic literacy are associated with improvements in the rate of economic growth (Pereira, 2003).

6.    The diffusion of economic market activities into 'traditional' and 'modern' realms goes back at least to Max Weber (1958 [1904–05], pp. 64ff.). Weber argued that under 'traditionalistic capitalism' production and marketing operated according to rational and market-based rules, but the goods, their production, and their sale were governed by 'traditional' norms, so that nothing changed. By contrast, in 'modern capitalism' businessmen – inspired by ascetic Protestantism in Weber's view – aimed to renovate production, markets, and products, to squeeze out more profits (Swedberg, 2003, p. 230).

7.    Lamoreaux and Sokoloff (1999) have pointed out that in America, patent awards tended to be granted in tight geographical clusters, among firms that comprised a network of shared talent, skills, and worked in similar products. High (2004) has demonstrated that a large portion of the value-added in American manufacturing is concentrated in a few specific regions and industries, which have high rates of innovation.

# REFERENCES

Acs, Z. (2002), *Innovation and the Growth of Cities*, Cheltenham, UK and Northhampton, MA, USA: Edward Elgar.

Allen, R.C. (2003), *Farm to Factory: A Reinterpretation of the Soviet Industrial Revolution*, Princeton, NJ: Princeton University Press.

Barthélemy, J.C., C. Pissarides and A. Varoudakis (2000), 'Human Capital and Growth: The Cost of Rent Seeking Activities', in Oosterbaan et al. (eds), pp. 209-29.

Baumol, William J. (1993), *Entrepreneurship, Management, and the Structure of Payoffs*, Cambridge, MA: MIT Press.

Baumol, William J. (2002a), 'Entrepreneurship, Innovation and Growth: The David-Goliath Symbiosis', *Journal of Entrepreneurial Finance and Business Ventures*,7, 1–10.

Baumol, William J. (2002b), *The Free Market Innovation Machine: Analyzing the Growth Miracle of Capitalism*, Princeton, NJ: Princeton University Press.

Bhagwati, J. and C.W. Calomiris (2007), *Sustaining India's Growth Miracle*, New York: Columbia University Press.

David, P.A. (1975), *Technical Choice, Innovation and Economic Growth*, Cambridge: Cambridge University Press.

De Soto, H. (2000), *The Mystery of Capital*, New York: Basic Books.

Easterly, W. (2001), *The Elusive Quest for Growth: Economists' Adventures and Misadventures in the Tropics*, Cambridge, MA: MIT Press.

Florida, R. (2002), *The Rise of the Creative Class*, New York: Basic Books.

High, J.C. (2004), 'The Roles of Entrepreneurship in Economic Growth', in H. de Groot, P. Nijkamp and R.R. Stough (eds), *Entrepreneurship and Regional Economic Development*, Cheltenham, UK and Northampton, MA, USA: Edward Elgar.

Hobday, M. (1995), 'East Asian Latecomer Firms: Learning the Technology of Electronics', *World Development*, **23** 1171–93.

Jones, E.L. (1994), 'Patterns of Growth in History', in John A. James and Mark Thomas (eds), *Capitalism in Context: Essays On Economic Development and Cultural Change in Honor of R.M. Hartwell*, Chicago, IL: University of Chicago Press.

Karl, Terry (1997), *The Paradox of Plenty*, Berkeley, CA: University of California Press.

Kash, D. (1989), *Perpetual Innovation: the New World of Competition*, New York: Basic Books.

Kash, D. (2003), Personal Communication.

Keely, L.C. and D. Quah (2000), 'Technology in Growth', in Oosterbaan et al. (eds), pp. 75-102.

Kumar, Subodh and Robert Russell (2002), 'Technological Change, Technological Catch-Up, and Capital Deepening: Relative Contributions to Growth and Convergence', *American Economic Review*, **92**, 527–48.

Lamoreaux, N.R. and K.L. Sokoloff. (1999), 'The Geography of the Market for Technology in the Late-Nineteenth- and Early-Twentieth Century United States', in Gary D. Libecap (ed.), *Advances in the Study of Entrepreneurship, Innovation, and Economic Growth*, Amsterdam: Elsevier, **11**, pp. 67–121.

Lensink, B.W. and G.H. Kuper (2000), 'Recent Advances in Economic Growth: A Policy Perspective', in Oosterbaan et al. (eds) pp. 235-65. pp.

Malerba, Franco (2006), 'Innovation and the Evolution of Industries', *Journal of Evolutionary Economics*, **16**, 3–23.

Mankiw, G., D. Romer and D. Weil (1992), 'A Contribution to the Empirics of Economic Growth', *Quarterly Journal of Economics*, **107**, 407–37.

Mehmet, O. (1999), *Westernizing the Third World: The Eurocentricity of Economic Development Theories*, 2nd edn, London: Routledge.

Mokyr, J. (1990), *The Lever of Riches: Technological Creativity and Economic Progress*, Oxford and New York: Oxford University Press.

Mokyr, J. (2002), *The Gifts of Athena: Historical Origins of the Knowledge Economy*, Princeton, NJ: Princeton University Press.

Mokyr, J. (2004), 'The New Economic History and the Industrial Revolution', in J. Mokyr (ed.), *The British Industrial Revolution: An Economic Perspective*, 2nd edn, Boulder, CO: Westview.

Murmann, Johann P. (2003), *Knowledge and Competitive Advantage*, Cambridge: Cambridge University Press.

Murphy, K.M., A. Schleifer and R.W. Vishnay (1991), 'The Allocation of Talent: Implications for Growth', *Quarterly Journal of Economics*, **106**, 503–30.

Nelson. R.R. (ed.) (1993), *National Innovation Systems: A Comparative Analysis*, Oxford and New York: Oxford University Press.

Nelson, R.R. (1994), 'The Co-evolution of Technology, Industrial Structure and Supporting Institutions', *Industrial and Corporate Change*, **3**, 47–63.

Nelson, R.R. and S.G. Winter (1982), *An Evolutionary Theory of Economic Change*, Cambridge, MA: Harvard, Belknap Press.

North, D. (1990), *Institutions, Institutional Change and Economic Performance*, Cambridge: Cambridge University Press.

O'Riain, Sean (2004), *The Politics of High-Tech Growth*, Cambridge: Cambridge University Press.

Ojala, Jari, Jari Eloranta and Jukka Jalava (eds), (2006), *The Road to Prosperity: An Economic History of Finland*, Helsinki: Suomalaisen Kirjallisuuden Seura.

Oosterbaan, M.S., T. de Ruyter van Stevenink and N. Van der Windt (eds), (2000), *The Determinants of Economic Growth*, Boston, MA: Kluwer.

Orru, Marco, Nicole W. Biggart and Gary G. Hamilton (1996), *The Economic Organization of East Asian Capitalism*, Beverly Hills, CA: Sage.

Pereira, Alvaro S. 2003 'When did Modern Economic Growth Really Start? The Empirics of Economic Growth from Malthus to Solow', *Journal of Economic Literature* **39**, 11–33.

Posen, Adam (2002), 'Japan', in Benn Steil, David G. Victor and Richard R. Nelson (eds), *Technological Innovation and Economic Performance*, Princeton, NJ: Princeton University Press, pp. 74–111.

Pritchett, L. "Where Has All the Education Gone?" *World Bank Economic Review*, December 2001.

Quah, D.T. (1996), 'Twin Peaks: Growth and Convergence in Models of Distributional Dynamics', *Economic Journal*, **106**, 1045–55.

Rogers, Mark (2003), 'Directly Unproductive Schooling: How Country Characteristics Affect the Impact of Schooling on Growth', Economics Series Working Papers 166, University of Oxford, Department of Economics.

Romer, Paul (1986), 'Increasing Returns and Long-Run Growth', *Journal of Political Economy*, **44**, 110–37.

Rosenberg, N. (1982), *Inside the Black Box: Technology and Economics*, Cambridge and New York: Cambridge University Press.

Rosenberg, N. (1994), *Exploring the Black Box: Technology, Economics, and History*, Cambridge: Cambridge University Press.

Schumpeter, J.A. (1934), *The Theory of Economic Development*, Cambridge, MA: Harvard University Press.

Scranton, P. (1997), *Endless Novelty: Specialty Production and American Industrialization*, Princeton, NJ: Princeton University Press, pp. 1865–1925.

Smil, Vaclav (2001), *Enriching the Earth: Fritz Haber, Carl Bosch, and the Transformation of World Food Production*, Cambridge, MA: MIT Press.

Smithsonian Institution (1998). 'True Colors', Website of the Lemelson Center for the Study of Invention and Innovation, National Museum of American History, Smithsonian Institution, Washington DC.

Solow, Robert M. (1956), 'A Contribution to the Theory of Economic Growth', *Quarterly Journal of Economics*, **70**, 65–94.

Solow, Robert M. (1970), *Growth Theory: An Exposition*, Oxford: Clarendon Press.

Swedberg, Richard (2003), 'The Economic Sociology of Capitalism: Weber and Schumpeter', *Journal of Classical Sociology*, **2** 227–55.

Thrift, Nigel, Stuart Corbridge and Ron Martin (eds) 1994,  *Money, Power, and Space*, Oxford: Blackwell.
Uglow, Jenny (2002), *The Lunar Men*, New York:  Farrar, Straus & Giroux.
von Hippel, E.  (2005), *Democratizing Innovation*,  Cambridge, MA: MIT Press.
Weber, M.  (1958), *The Protestant Ethic and the Spirit of Capitalism*, New York: Scribners.
Wolf, A. (2003), *Does Education Matter?*, Hamondsworth, UK: Penguin Books.
Womack, J.P., D.T. Jones,and D.R. Roos (1990), *The Machine That Changed the World: The Story of Lean Production*, New York: Harper Perennial.

# 3. The Swedish Paradox Revisited

## Olof Ejermo and Astrid Kander

## INTRODUCTION

The idea of a Swedish paradox has appeared in three different versions, sharing the common stance that Swedish research and development (R&D) expenditures do not produce sufficient economic results. Common for all these paradox ideas is that they think there are some problems on the societal level, while firms carry out R&D according to their expected private returns to these investments.

The first formulation of the Swedish paradox is that there was surprisingly low production of high-tech products in Sweden in relation to its high R&D expenditures (Edquist and McKelvey, 1998).[1] The second formulation states that high-tech exports are low, given the high R&D investments (Braunerhjelm, 1998). The third formulation is more general and states that Sweden is inefficient in transforming its high R&D expenditures into productivity and growth (Andersson et al., 2002) or more generally that economic performance is poor (Klofsten, 2002). One fact that has been used to demonstrate the existence of a Swedish paradox in this version is that Swedish growth has been relatively sluggish since the early 1970s. Sweden's GDP per capita dropped from fourth to fifteenth place among OECD countries between 1970 and 2003 (Marklund et al., 2004). Also, Sweden invests more R&D in relation to GDP than any other country.

We aim here to examine the Swedish paradox, and start with a discussion about the relationships between R&D and growth. We argue that in a strict meaning there is no paradox, since there are more reasons to expect high variation among countries, than there are to expect a simple and strong relationship, where R&D efforts automatically are transformed into growth. We focus the discussion on four links on the long journey between R&D and growth: A: R&D to inventions; B: inventions to innovations; C: innovations to high-tech production; and D: high-tech production to growth.

In 'The Swedish paradox: three formulations', the different previous formulations of the Swedish paradox are discussed at some length. 'Swedish

R&D and growth: the facts' gives up-to-date evidence of R&D and growth. 'Turning inventions into innovations: the entrepreneurial function (link B)' explores the link between inventions and innovations, by looking at the empirical facts of Swedish entrepreneurship, including academic entrepreneurship. 'A high-tech paradox? (Link C)' discusses another link: that between innovations and high-tech production. The final section summarizes our results, gives some policy implications and makes suggestions for further research.

## A PROPORTIONAL RELATION BETWEEN R&D AND GROWTH?

Growth theory provides a natural starting-point for discussing the relationship between R&D and growth. Endogenous growth models ultimately compromise a growing stock of knowledge contributing to growth, where the best-known models (Romer, 1986, 1990, 1994; Grossman and Helpman, 1991a, b, 1994; and Aghion and Howitt, 1992) all imply a proportional relationship between R&D and GDP growth in the steady state. Solow (1994, p. 52) however, finds this assumption of proportionality too strong and stresses:

> [I]f innovation generates a proportionate increase in A (TFP [total factor productivity]) then we have a theory of easy endogenous growth. Spend  more resources on R&D, there will be more innovations and the growth rate of A will be higher.  But suppose an innovation generates only an absolute  increase in A: then greater allocation of resources to R&D buys only a one time jump in productivity, but not a faster rate of productivity growth. I do not know which is the better assumption, and these are only two of many possibilities.

The first possibility Solow mentions of course justifies the expectation of a strong linear relationship between levels of R&D and the growth rate of GDP/cap. It would mean that growth rates will increase, as long as levels of R&D grow. We then have a truly endogenous theory of growth, where productivity is explained within the system. The second possibility is more pessimistic: R&D investments work basically like other kinds of capital investments, with decreasing marginal returns. Then *levels of R&D* are only able to influence *levels of GDP*, not the *trend* (its growth rate).  If this is true, it will only be possible to sustain a certain growth rate by increasing the investment ratio, which means that the prospects for high sustained growth rates are gloomy in the long run.  In addition it means that the endogenous growth theory has failed to explain TFP.

The true relation between R&D and growth may be somewhere between these two extremes. This insecurity in theory means that there is no reason to expect a strong linear relation between levels of innovation and productivity growth, but perhaps a weak one.

Jones (1995 a, b) questions this proportional implication by pointing out that the number of scientists engaged in R&D in advanced countries has grown dramatically over the last 40 years, while growth rates have either exhibited a constant mean or even declined on average. This empirical critique of the idea of a simple proportional relationship between R&D and growth led Aghion and Howitt in one of their model variants (1998, 404 ff.) to modify their original (1992) model so that rising R&D in a steady state does not cause an increased growth rate. In this model, due to increasing complexity of technology and since R&D at a higher level gives rise to relatively smaller spillover effects, a constant innovation rate requires a rise in R&D over time. The term 'spillovers' is often implicitly referred to as positive side-effects on actors beyond those intended by the producer of a good and suffices for the discussion in this chapter.[2]

Easterly and Levine (2001) contest the claim by Jones (1995 a, b) that growth rates have not been increasing. They also claim that no growth model to date can adequately fit the growth experience of all countries and periods. Thus, there is no automatic reason to expect a very high return from R&D investments on growth.

Going beyond the somewhat mechanistic view of formal growth theory, we propose an analytical scheme (See Figure 3.1), to illuminate why there is no proportional relationship between R&D and growth. We argue that variations in R&D to growth ratios among countries should be large. One reason not to expect a simple, linear and common relation between R&D and productivity for all countries is that firms and sectors vary in this relation, so the composition of firms and sectors in each country, the structure, will influence the aggregate effects.

The distinction between 'return' and 'variation' is important. The return aspect can be addressed by the concepts 'low- versus high-linked relationships' that form intermediate steps in the chain ranging from R&D to GDP. The variation in R&D to GDP is addressed by the concepts 'weak or strong linear relationships'. Generally every reason put forward for low-linked relations also has the potential to affect variations among countries, since the link can be different.

In the following we discuss some of the links that lead to different R&D-growth relationships for different countries – and hence is a way of systematizing why Sweden may have lower-linked relationships than many other countries. Our arguments are summarized in Figure 3.1, with arrows labeled A, B, C and D for the different links. Even though the linear model of innovation has been condemned by innovation scholars (e.g., Kline and Rosenberg, 1986), for reasons of dynamic feedback loops, we think it would be a mistake not to have an idea of the *main direction* of relationships. This means in terms of our Figure 3.1 that we believe that R&D mainly contributes in the direction of *invention*; inventive activity normally contributes to *innovation* which affects high-tech production, which in turn makes up part of GDP. Some of the relationships between the boxes in Figure 3.1, marked by dashed lines, are only briefly touched upon in the present chapter. The reason why we do not put much emphasis on these links is that they may not constitute the core of the 'link-relationships', but also because research may be lacking in these areas. By innovation we refer in this chapter to useful applications 'new to the world'. Commercialization is not necessary, since many innovations are introduced only in the internal processes of the firm.

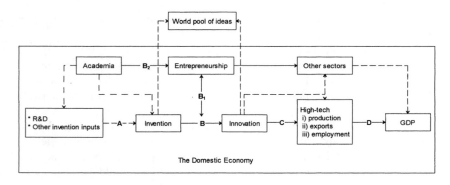

*Figure 3.1   The interrelations between R&D and growth*

1. *Link A: R&D to Inventions* The first link is from R&D to invention. Not only has the innovation literature questioned the automatic link going from inventive inputs to invention; it also stresses that other inputs of less formal, yet inventive, character, may also lead to an inventive outcome[3] and are crucial to the innovation process. Moreover, the empirical construct of R&D statistics is somewhat problematic. R&D here denotes resources specifically set aside for the purpose of inventing. This means that staff also engaged in production do not count. This tends to bias data towards showing larger firms to conduct more R&D by virtue of their larger resource endowments. This means that R&D data should ideally be complemented by other invention data, and economies with a high proportion of large firms may report relatively higher R&D figures.

2. *Link B: Inventions to Innovations* A second reason not to expect too strong linear relations between R&D and growth is that it is not sufficient for R&D efforts to translate into inventions. In order for them to become actual innovations, there is a need for *entrepreneurial activities* (link $B_1$), broadly defined as entrepreneurial acts which take place within existing firms and activities that lead to new business formation. The entrepreneurial link has lately been amended to endogenous models of economic growth (Acs et al., 2004). In addition, academic life may be more or less beneficial for link B. *Academia* (link $B_2$) can have a direct positive effect on entrepreneurship, which is the case when there are spin-offs (new enterprises created by people employed in academia). A well-functioning higher education system in addition has more important effects on R&D and growth than this direct one. It provides the skill and knowledge basis for inventions in general and may affect the efficiency in transforming R&D into inventions.

3. *Link C: Innovations to High-Tech Production* There is a link between innovations and domestic production. This link depends on the exchange with the global economy, because knowledge is partly a public good and therefore diffuses internationally. Generally the growth rates of countries are more similar than the R&D investment ratios among countries. This partly common process of worldwide economic growth implies less reason to expect linear relations between own R&D and high-tech production for small, open countries, and more reason to expect this for larger integrated economies like the US. Countries more talented in absorbing knowledge from this common pool by imitation than others may perform better in high-tech production than their own R&D investments would allow. In addition, not only are there spillovers due to imitation, but it may also be the case that inventions or innovations generated in one country will not result in any related production there at all. They may instead directly lead to production in other countries. Thus the link for individual countries between innovations and high-tech production is affected by the exchange-flow of innovations with the 'world pool' of ideas.

Whether a country is capable of reaping the fruits of its own R&D or not has been measured by production indicators such as high-tech production, high-tech exports and employment in high-tech industries (Braunerhjelm, 1998; Edquist and McKelvey, 1998). The construct 'high-tech' is built on R&D intensity, so focusing on its production is a natural consequence of studying the effects of business R&D.

4.  *Link D: High-Tech Production to GDP* High-tech indicators only
    partly reflect total production in a country, which also consist of low-
    and medium-tech industries, service production and so on. Moreover,
    even though high-tech industries are the most R&D-intensive ones,
    R&D is conducted elsewhere, also in the low- and medium-tech
    industries. One rationale for focusing on high-tech industries rests in
    their spillover-generating capability, for example they influence
    growth in other sectors. However, market structures (e.g.,
    monopolistic or competitive) and other factors may limit spillover
    characteristics or generate spillovers outside the high-tech industry.

To sum up, the many links between R&D and GDP growth make it quite
natural that countries may differ, and we should perhaps not be so surprised
to find that Sweden (or any other country) may differ from the average with
respect to the R&D–GDP relationship. In the remainder of the chapter we
shall focus on the empirical evidence for there being any spectacular results,
or a paradox, for Sweden and to what degree such results may be due to
malfunctioning links.

## THE SWEDISH PARADOX: THREE FORMULATIONS

Edquist and McKelvey (1996) had a rather precise definition of a Swedish
paradox. It referred to the finding that the production of R&D-intensive
products in Sweden was relatively lower than in other countries, despite a
high R&D intensity. The OECD uses R&D intensity to divide industries into
low-, medium- and high-tech. A reason why high-tech, and hence R&D-
intensive, production may be considered particularly beneficial, rests in its
potential for generating externalities or spillovers. This may, for instance,
contribute to the emergence of firms in the formation of geographical clusters
based on so-called 'Marshallian localization externalities' (Marshall, 1920).
These encompass the emergence of 'subsidiary trades' around an industry,
labor pooling and increased flows of knowledge about inventions and
machinery ('knowledge spillovers').

Edquist and McKelvey (1998) prefer to examine production rather than
export data, since they argue that it is 'production and development of
technologies which lead to significant long term positive externalities such as
cumulative development of knowledge. Export data only imperfectly reflects
this'. Edquist (2002) maintains that a notion of paradoxical R&D investments
should at least partially be related to the (in)ability to generate commercially
viable innovations. In a preliminary investigation, Bitard et al. (2005)

maintain that a paradox still exists when Sweden is compared to other small countries.

A second and slightly different version of the Swedish paradox is proposed by Braunerhjelm (1998) who argues that due to the theory of comparative advantage, a country that invests heavily in R&D should also be exporting high-tech products. In contrast to production, exports may reflect innovative advantage that extends beyond the borders of the own nation. Braunerhjelm finds that this is not the case for Sweden, since the Swedish technology balance of payments had a higher surplus (in relative terms) than any other OECD country, suggesting that Swedish technology may be commercialized elsewhere.[4] Braunerhjelm also reports a high concentration, about 75–80 percent in 1994, of Swedish R&D to multinationals. Four multinationals together accounted for slightly more than 70 percent of this, or roughly half of all Swedish business R&D. It also seems from Braunerhjelm's material that the concentration of R&D in the four most R&D-intensive multinationals has increased over 1965–94. This is potentially important since a high concentration of R&D may imply a slow diffusion of new results that can be applied to other sectors and firms, since application of R&D generally requires own investments in R&D to generate absorptive capacity (Cohen and Levinthal, 1989, 1990). Studies confirm that there may indeed be limited spillovers due to R&D where Swedish firms are involved, whether internationally (Braconier et al., 2005) or domestically (Ejermo, 2004).

A third formulation of the paradox is more general and concerns the link between R&D and growth. Andersson et al. (2002) state that the Swedish paradox comes from large investments that lead to doubtful results in terms of output, although they do not give a precise definition. Klofsten (2002) states that a basic problem of the Swedish innovation system is its inability to generate output related to inputs (research money vs. commercial results). He claims that Swedish firms bring few new products to the market, and that there are few growing enterprises. The above stories are all related to the industry structure, and internationalization of Swedish firms. Highly related to this is the possibility that these firms outsource or relocate their production chains so that while still being competitive in the product development phases (R&D) which is kept within domestic borders, production activities are increasingly undertaken abroad. Since it seems probable that the latter may be more labor intensive, this means a net emigration of job opportunities.

## SWEDISH R&D AND GROWTH: THE FACTS

Sweden is a small open economy; a large share of its industrial production is exported, which means that it is highly influenced by international markets and conditions. The industrial structure has become dominated by big multinationals, many of which originated in one major innovation that was successfully sold abroad (Ejermo, 2004). Subsequent expansion was based on the ability of these firms to innovate incrementally and sometimes radically. Thus these big firms conducted a lot of R&D domestically, while also generating substantial employment in Sweden, as well as in other countries. In addition, some large companies enjoyed (indirect) support, or were directly owned by the national government.[5] The governmental influence in these firms, however, has declined from the 1980s and onwards.

First, we should update and possibly reconfirm the 'established notion' that: (i) business R&D expenditures are high, and (ii) recent growth has been sluggish.

The first point can easily be confirmed. Official statistics on R&D expenditures, that is, the sum of current costs and R&D investments, should be related to some size measure, customarily GDP. Table 3.1 shows gross R&D expenditures (GERD), which covers both public and business R&D, and Table 3.2 gives business R&D expenditures (BERD) separately. Both measures are given as a share of GDP, and the countries are ranked. These figures reveal that Sweden had the highest GERD and BERD as a share of GDP in 2001 and also the highest BERD/GDP ratio in 2003. Moreover, Sweden has climbed compared with the 1991 ranking. Sweden ranked second in GERD/GDP and third in BERD/GDP in 1991. Furthermore, the relative gap increased over this decade. Sweden invested 1.9 percent in 1991, compared to the OECD average of 1.5 percent. In 2001, its BERD/GDP ratio was 3.3 percent, compared to a near unchanged mean for OECD of 1.6 per cent. Among other business R&D-intensive countries we find Finland, Japan, Korea and the United States.

However, some researchers distrust the reliability or at least comparability, of R&D figures, and claim that the high Swedish figures originate from specific Swedish features. One reason could be its high dependence on a few large firms. For academia, Jacobsson (2002) and Jacobsson and Rickne (2004) argue that to compare R&D expenditures of the higher education sector in different countries is misleading. Many countries allocate a lot of R&D resources to specific research institutes, while this type of research is allocated to the higher education sector in Sweden.

It has been customary in the Swedish debate to choose 1970 as a starting-point for GDP/capita comparisons. Material from Groningen Growth and Development Centre and the Conference Board (GGDC) which covers a

*Table 3.1*    *Gross domestic expenditure on R&D (GERD) as a percentage of*
               *GDP*

| Country | 1991 | 2000 | 2001 | 2002 | 2003 | Rank 1991 | Rank 2001 |
|---|---|---|---|---|---|---|---|
| Australia | | 1.56 | | 1.62 | | | |
| Austria | 1.44 | 1.91 | 2.04 | 2.12 | 2.2 | 16 | 12 |
| Belgium | 1.62 | 2.04 | 2.17 | 2.23 | 2.31 | 14 | 10 |
| Canada | 1.6 | 1.93 | 2.08 | 1.96 | 1.94 | 15 | 11 |
| Czech Republic | 1.9 | 1.23 | 1.22 | 1.22 | 1.26 | 10 | 16 |
| Denmark | 1.64 | | 2.41 | 2.53 | | 12 | 8 |
| Finland | 2.04 | 3.4 | 3.41 | 3.44 | 3.49 | 8 | 2 |
| France | 2.37 | 2.18 | 2.23 | 2.26 | 2.19 | 5 | 9 |
| Germany | 2.52 | 2.49 | 2.51 | 2.53 | 2.55 | 4 | 7 |
| Greece | 0.36 | | 0.65 | | | 26 | 24 |
| Hungary | 1.06 | 0.8 | 0.95 | 1.02 | 0.95 | 19 | 20 |
| Iceland | 1.17 | 2.75 | 3.06 | 3.09 | 3.04 | 18 | 4 |
| Ireland | 0.93 | 1.14 | 1.11 | 1.12 | | 21 | 18 |
| Italy | 1.23 | 1.07 | 1.11 | 1.16 | | 17 | 18 |
| Japan | 2.94 | 2.99 | 3.07 | 3.12 | 3.15 | 1 | 3 |
| Korea | 1.82 | 2.39 | 2.59 | 2.53 | 2.64 | 11 | 6 |
| Luxembourg | | 1.71 | | | | | |
| Mexico | | 0.37 | 0.39 | | | | 27 |
| Netherlands | 1.97 | 1.9 | 1.88 | 1.8 | | 9 | 13 |
| New Zealand | 0.98 | | 1.14 | | 1.16 | 20 | 17 |
| Norway | 1.64 | | 1.6 | 1.67 | 1.75 | 12 | 15 |
| Poland | 0.76 | 0.66 | 0.64 | 0.58 | 0.56 | 23 | 25 |
| Portugal | 0.57 | 0.8 | 0.85 | 0.94 | | 24 | 22 |
| Slovak Republic | 2.13 | 0.65 | 0.64 | 0.58 | 0.58 | 6 | 25 |
| Spain | 0.84 | 0.94 | 0.95 | 1.03 | 1.1 | 22 | 20 |
| **Sweden** | **2.72** | | **4.27** | | | **2** | **1** |
| Switzerland | | 2.57 | | | | | |
| Turkey | 0.53 | 0.64 | 0.72 | 0.66 | | 25 | 23 |
| United Kingdom | 2.07 | 1.86 | 1.87 | 1.9 | 1.89 | 7 | 14 |
| United States | 2.71 | 2.72 | 2.73 | 2.66 | 2.6 | 3 | 5 |
| EU-25 | | 1.8 | 1.83 | 1.85 | 1.85 | | |
| **Total OECD** | **2.21** | 2.23 | **2.27** | 2.25 | 2.24 | | |

*Source:* OECD (2005).

*Table 3.2    Business enterprise expenditure on R&D (BERD) as a
            percentage of GDP*

| Country | 1991 | 2001 | 2002 | 2003 | Rank 1991 | Rank 2001 | Rank 2003 |
|---|---|---|---|---|---|---|---|
| Australia | 0.58 | 0.81 | 0.79 | | 17 | 15 | |
| Austria | | | 1.42 | | | | |
| Belgium | 1.08 | 1.60 | 1.63 | 1.71 | 10 | 9 | 7 |
| Canada | 0.79 | 1.27 | 1.09 | 1.03 | 14 | 12 | 11 |
| Czech Republic | 1.32 | 0.74 | 0.75 | 0.77 | 8 | 19 | 15 |
| Denmark | 0.96 | 1.65 | 1.75 | | 12 | 8 | |
| Finland | 1.16 | 2.42 | 2.41 | 2.46 | 9 | 2 | 2 |
| France | 1.46 | 1.41 | 1.43 | 1.36 | 6 | 11 | 9 |
| Germany | 1.75 | 1.75 | 1.75 | 1.78 | 4 | 7 | 6 |
| Greece | 0.09 | 0.21 | 0.20 | 0.20 | 24 | 28 | 21 |
| Hungary | 0.44 | 0.38 | 0.36 | 0.35 | 19 | 24 | 19 |
| Iceland | 0.26 | 1.80 | 1.77 | 1.67 | 20 | 6 | 8 |
| Ireland | 0.59 | 0.78 | 0.77 | 0.80 | 16 | 18 | 14 |
| Italy | 0.68 | 0.55 | 0.56 | 0.55 | 15 | 20 | 17 |
| Japan | 2.08 | 2.26 | 2.32 | 2.36 | 1 | 3 | 3 |
| Korea | | 1.97 | 1.90 | 2.01 | | 5 | 4 |
| Luxembourg | | | | | | | |
| Mexico | 0.09 | 0.12 | | | 24 | 29 | |
| Netherlands | 0.98 | 1.10 | 1.02 | 0.99 | 11 | 15 | 13 |
| New Zealand | 0.26 | 0.42 | | 0.47 | 20 | 23 | 18 |
| Norway | 0.89 | 0.96 | 0.96 | 1.00 | 13 | 16 | 12 |
| Poland | | 0.23 | 0.12 | 0.15 | | 27 | 22 |
| Portugal | 0.13 | 0.27 | 0.30 | | 22 | 25 | |
| Slovak Republic | 1.59 | 0.43 | 0.37 | 0.32 | 5 | 22 | 20 |
| Spain | 0.47 | 0.50 | 0.56 | 0.60 | 18 | 21 | 16 |
| **Sweden** | **1.87** | **3.31** | | **2.95** | **3** | **1** | **1** |
| Turkey | 0.11 | 0.24 | 0.19 | | 23 | 26 | |
| United Kingdom | 1.39 | 1.24 | 1.26 | 1.24 | 7 | 13 | 10 |
| United States | 1.97 | 1.99 | 1.87 | 1.79 | 2 | 4 | 5 |
| EU-25 | | 1.17 | 1.17 | 1.17 | | | |
| **Total OECD** | **1.52** | **1.57** | 1.53 | **1.51** | | | |

*Source:* OECD (2005).

longer period spanning 1950–2004 (see Figure 3.2) reveals that Swedish
growth has in fact been relatively high over the last 10-year period. Figure 3.2

shows real GDP per capita in 1950–2004. As seen from the figure, Sweden was actually ahead of OECD (excluding Sweden) for the whole period up to 1970. However, by 1980 most of this difference had gone, and by 1990 the OECD had overtaken Sweden. Following in the wake of a Swedish crisis in the early 1990s, Sweden lagged substantially behind, but beginning in 1994 its growth has on average been higher than that of other OECD countries, so that by 2004 the gap was again miniscule. All in all, this seems to indicate close convergence of the GDP time series in the long run between Sweden and the rest of the OECD. Sweden is (presently) not underperforming compared to other OECD countries. A different issue is of course if it is underperforming in relation to its R&D.

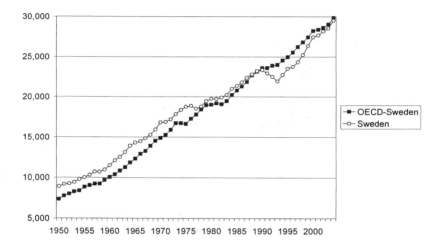

*Note:* * The EKS method adjusts for the effect that lower prices generally induce higher demand, and hence the comparison basket of goods differs between countries.

*Source*: Groningen Growth and Development Centre and the Conference Board, Total Economy Database, August 2005, http://www.ggdc.net. Data include West Germany before 1988 and Germany from 1989 onwards.

*Figure 3.2   GDP per capita 1950–2004, in constant 2002 year's prices, using OECD's EKS* PPP method;  the OECD group is defined based on pre-1994 OECD membership*

These results show that the second 'established fact' which we have examined no longer prevails, since the more recent growth experience has not been sluggish. In recent years, overall economic performance in Sweden has clearly been better than the OECD average.

## TURNING INVENTIONS INTO INNOVATIONS: THE ENTREPRENEURIAL FUNCTION (LINK B)

Entrepreneurs play a key role in introducing competitive pressure, which leads to the transformation of economies. Much of this pressure seems to be absent in the Swedish economy (Henrekson and Jakobsson, 2001). However, some authors have stressed that industrial transformation and innovation sometimes take place in industries characterized by 'swarms of innovation' and sometimes in industries dominated by big corporations (Schumpeter, 1934, 1950; Breschi et al., 2000). But there may be lock-in risks for an economy which for a long time has been path dependent on the cumulative inventive capabilities of big corporations. Even though these firms may be highly successful, they may prevent restructuring and renewal that is essential for growth. There may be two ways in which these firms hinder such renewal: (i) the institutional framework becomes adapted to the dominant business model and (ii) crowding out of nascent businesses. As an indicator of entrepreneurial activities in existing firms, we examine initially to what degree Sweden is characterized by dynamic pressure or, alternatively, has a high concentration of R&D to big firms. We then examine the evidence regarding business formation and the entrepreneurial link between academia and new firms.

### Concentration of R&D

As discussed above, high concentration of R&D in business has long been a distinguishing feature of the Swedish National Innovation System. We now examine whether this pattern prevails using the latest available data. Given data on R&D on the firm level, concentration of R&D may be examined from two perspectives, both of which can be used to examine R&D expenditures and R&D man-years. The first perspective is to construct R&D concentration measures (Table 3.3). There are two measures used in the table. First, the Hirschmann–Herfindahl index (HHI)[6] which is a standard measure for concentration. Second, we report on C5 and C20, which show the 5 and 20 most man-year-intensive, and R&D-expenditure-intensive firms, respectively. Statistics Sweden has improved their sampling so that now more firms are covered by the micro-data that they provide. This in itself would contribute to more dispersion, other things equal. C5 and C20 have the benefit that they are less dependent on samples over time. Table 3.3 demonstrates that it is obvious that the Swedish structure is marked by a continued high concentration of R&D. Concentration as measured by HHI has gone up over time. The share of man-years among the top 5 has been ever increasing; only among the top 20 is the trend less clear, and if anything there is a slight downward trend. We conclude that concentration of R&D remains a distinctive feature of Swedish business R&D. This means that the findings of concentration in Braunerhjelm (1998) remain unchallenged.

*Table 3.3 Concentration of R&D in Swedish companies*

|  | HHI Man-years | HHI R&D exp | C5 man-years | C5 R&D exp | C20 man-years | C20 R&D exp |
|---|---|---|---|---|---|---|
| 1991 | 0.026 | 0.034 | 27.8% | 34.0% | 60.1% | 65.9% |
| 1993 | 0.026 | 0.031 | 29.4% | 31.8% | 58.2% | 64.9% |
| 1995 | 0.024 | 0.031 | 27.9% | 33.2% | 56.1% | 62.5% |
| 1997 | 0.026 | 0.032 | 30.0% | 32.7% | 56.9% | 62.3% |
| 1999 | 0.028 | 0.040 | 30.1% | 36.8% | 57.0% | 65.4% |
| Trend | + | + | + | + | − | ~ 0 |

*Source:* Own calculations.

The measures reported there do not consider changes in the composition of firms, such as if one company stops doing R&D, while another starts. The second perspective examines the stability of firms. Although R&D is concentrated in a small number of firms, firms may change over time. The stability of R&D performers is illustrated in Table 3.4.

*Table 3.4 Share of firms that are the same from one survey to the next in R&D concentration measures*

|  | C5 man-years | C5 R&D exp. | C20 man-years | C20 R&D exp. |
|---|---|---|---|---|
| 1991 to 1993 | 80% | 70% | 100% | 70% |
| 1993 to 1995 | 80% | 85% | 60% | 80% |
| 1995 to 1997 | 100% | 80% | 80% | 85% |
| 1997 to 1999 | 60% | 90% | 80% | 90% |
| 1991 to 1999 | 60% | 55% | 40% | 65% |

*Source:* Own calculations.

Concentration may be a problem since R&D not only contributes to inventions but is also often related to capabilities to access new knowledge (absorptive capacity). The big concentration of Swedish R&D may thus be a problem for a wide diffusion of knowledge and productivity gains. However, a lot of innovative activity is going on that is not adequately captured by R&D. That is, new firms most likely add a new kind of R&D that in a sense could be more 'radical'. Clearly, the innovation process also entails an element of bringing new knowledge to the market through its embodiment in new firms. We can actually trace the percentage of firms that are the same from one survey to the next in the C5 and C20 measures discussed above. Table 3.4 shows this and it is clear there is considerable stability in terms of which firms belong to the top R&D performers. Roughly half of the firms are the same throughout the 1991–99 period, whether we use C5 or C20 as our stability indicator.

## Employment Effects in R&D-intensive Companies

A widely felt concern in Swedish society to date is that multinationals, which used to be successful in creating and maintaining jobs in Sweden, nowadays generate most of their employment abroad.

This seems to be true, but is still somewhat misleading. Recent evidence from ITPS (2004) shows that many employment changes are related to internationalization in ownership structure, as was the case when ASEA merged with Swiss Brown Boveri to form ABB in 1987. Hence, registered data cannot always be used to assess whether employment is transferred abroad. But the evidence shows that more people are employed in other countries by companies that have Swedish origin, and by the same token more personnel than ever in Sweden are now employed by a company which is foreign owned. Hence, cross-border ownership has become increasingly important over the 1996–2001 period. Since 1998, Swedish multinational groups have more people employed in other countries than domestically.

## Business Formation (Link B₁)

One indication of business renewal is given by the frequency of start-ups. Despite having low barriers to trade, investment and entrepreneurship, according to the Global Entrepreneurship Monitor (2005), Sweden consistently scores among the countries with the lowest entrepreneurial activities out of 40 countries (Andersson and Ejermo, 2005b). In the US the share of entrepreneurs in the population is 11.3 percent, while in Sweden only 3.7 percent take on this role. This rate is lower than, for instance, in Denmark (5.3 percent) and Norway (7 percent) (Global Entrepreneurship Monitor,

2005). The Confederation of Swedish Enterprise reports that only one of the 50 largest Swedish companies were started after 1970, Tele2 in 1993 (Wallen and Fölster, 2005). However, some of the 50 largest companies were established from spin-offs or mergers from existing firms or foreign firms establishing in Sweden (Johanson and Karlson, 2006). This can be contrasted with the situation in the US where the largest companies are frequently exchanged, and those with highest stock value are commonly quite young. This pessimistic view of Swedish entrepreneurship does not accord with evaluations of its general competitiveness. Sweden ranks very high (3rd in 2004 and 2003) on the World Economic Forum's list of competitiveness. This ranking is based on sub-indices comprising technology, public institutions and the macroeconomic environment. Entrepreneurship and business renewal do not play more than indirect roles, but are especially important indicators for domestic employment generation.[7]

### Academia and Entrepreneurship (Link B₂)

Lindholm Dahlstrand (1997a) examines the origins of 60 small Swedish technology-based firms. Of these, 30 represent entrepreneurial spin-offs. Two-thirds of these 30 spin-offs have originated in private firms and only one-sixth in universities. The spin-offs grew faster than the 30 non-spin-offs, but there was a difference in the level of inventiveness. In Lindholm Dahlstrand (1997b), employment growth and technological development in terms of patenting of university spin-offs from Chalmers University of Technology in Gothenburg are compared with the development of other new technology-based firms. A result is that corporate spin-offs have higher employment growth, while university spin-offs are more engaged in patenting activities.

Delmar et al. (2005) investigate the total Swedish population of academics with at least three years' university education in natural sciences, technology and medicine. They find that such persons run their own businesses slightly more frequently than Swedes in general, but this result is entirely attributed to those specializing in medicine; otherwise the number of businesses per capita is the same. Moreover, data show that this business involvement mainly comprises consultancy as a side activity to their ordinary employment. Delmar et al. conclude that academic entrepreneurship is unlikely to be a major factor behind economic development in the future. Similarly, Wiklund (2005) reports on the poor ambitions with regard to starting a new business among final-year engineers' future career plans. These new engineers think that starting a business ranks as less likely, in decreasing order, than being employed, continued studies, or unemployment. The conclusion is that the incentives to start a business are too poor, which is related to the reliance of the welfare system on the status of being an employee. Incentives to be an entrepreneur should be more balanced relative to those of being employed.

Goldfarb and Henrekson (2003) point to large differences between how the American and the Swedish university systems are run.[8] The American system is based on a 'bottom-up' perspective; the universities have a considerably larger degree of freedom in deciding their own 'rules of the game', that is how teaching should respond to market signals, how universities should best make use of the commercialization abilities of innovations and so on. In contrast to Sweden, universities in the US have owned the right to patented inventions ever since the implementation of the so-called Bayh Dole Act of 1983. It is stressed that the Swedish organizational setup may not be conducive to innovations, since universities have nothing to gain from allowing their researchers to engage in commercialization activities. Instead, it is argued that if the incentives between university and the inventor are aligned, they may work better towards the goal of commercialization. However this argument in favor of transferring the ownership right somewhat fuzzy, since Swedish inventors do in fact have the right to transfer ownership a priori to the engagement in inventive activities. For example, inventors may negotiate a deal that part of the invention falls to the university, and part to the researcher, prior to their engagement in a research project. The only difference to the US system is then where the ownership rests by default.

Sellenthin (2004) argues that there may be a selection mechanism at hand, so that excellent inventions are commercialized outside and mediocre ones within the university. Goldfarb and Henrekson (2003) also consider the risk that university resources may be too scanty for efficient caretaking of inventions. To assess the importance of academic entrepreneurship it is important to know how many inventions are produced by academia and how valuable these are. Knowledge about this is almost entirely lacking in Sweden.[9]

## A HIGH-TECH PARADOX? (LINK C)

A lot of attention in the discussion of the Swedish paradox has been given to link C, linking innovations to production, employment and production in high-tech sectors. Braunerhjelm (1998) and Edquist and McKelvey (1998) concluded that in the early 1990s Sweden was not efficient in transforming its research in hightech into high-tech production or high-tech exports. We widen the analysis from a pure high-tech focus to a view where we also take in lower technology levels. This analysis is carried out by comparing R&D intensities on industries classified by the OECD's recent division into four different technology levels: (i) low-tech, (ii) medium-low-tech, (iii) medium-high- tech (MHT), and (iv) high-tech (HT). We relate these R&D intensities to exports and employment performance on the different technology levels and compare this to the performance of OECD countries (Table 3.5).

*Table 3.5*   *R&D intensity and export performance in low-, medium-, to medium-high- and high-tech industries*

|  | High-tech | | Medium-high-tech | | Medium-low-tech | | Low-tech | |
|---|---|---|---|---|---|---|---|---|
|  | 1995 | 2000 | 1995 | 2000 | 1995 | 2000 | 1995 | 2000 |
| A. Sweden: R&D intensity | 41.0 | 48.9 | 12.5 | 12.8 | 2.6 | 2.5 | 1.7 | 1.4 |
| B. G7: R&D intensity | 23.0 | 22.3 | 8.6 | 9.7 | 2.2 | 2.2 | | 1.1 |
| C = A/B | 1.8 | 2.2 | 1.5 | 1.3 | 1.2 | 1.1 | | 1.3 |
| D. Sweden export index, OECD = 100 | 100.0 | 106.5 | 84.6 | 84.6 | 112.0 | 111.5 | 120.8 | 114.9 |
| E = D/C | 56.1 | 48.6 | 58.2 | 64.1 | 94.8 | 98.1 | | 90.3 |

*Source:* Own calculations.

We have previously shown that Sweden has the world's highest business R&D intensity. By looking at the R&D intensity, here defined as R&D as a share of value added in HT and MHT industries for available countries from the OECD's STAN databases, we find that Sweden ranks as the country with the highest R&D intensity in high-tech industries in 1990, 1995 and 2000 out of 13–18 countries. The gap is large to Canada (the second highest), which had an R&D intensity of roughly half that of Sweden. In MHT, Sweden ranked as 1–3 in 1990, 1995 and 2000 out of 12–17 countries, and the gap is as large as in HT. In medium-low-tech and low-tech, Sweden does not have quite the same leading role in R&D intensities. The data show that Sweden ranked as the country with the 4th to 6th highest R&D intensity in medium-low-tech industries and the 1st to 4th in low-tech.[10] Sweden's R&D intensity compared to other countries is relatively higher in HT industries than in industries with a lower-tech level.

Turning to the performance measures of these sectors we compare the export performance of the four technology levels *relative* to R&D intensity.[11] The following expression is evaluated:

$$E_i = D_i / C_i,$$

where $D_i$ is exports in Sweden in technology level $i$ relative to OECD countries, and $C_i$ is Sweden's R&D intensity relative to that of the G7 countries.[12] It is clear that Sweden underperforms in HT and MHT exports compared to R&D intensities. Only 50 per cent of the average value of other developed countries is reached. In medium-low- and low-tech, on the other hand, it is almost average level. Relative employment performance is given in Table 3.6, together with a comparison of the results from the previous studies by Braunerhjelm (1998) and Edquist and McKelvey (1998). In order to make our results comparable with these studies, the measures are not adjusted for R&D intensities as they were in Table 3.5.

Table 3.6 shows that while Swedish employment in HT has increased more than in other countries, the share of Swedish HT exports has not risen to the same degree. In fact Swedish HT exports are fluctuating around the OECD average. There is a significant drop in 2003 which can be attributed to the poor performance of one single actor in high-tech: Ericsson, which was hit by the crises in the telecommunications sector in the early 2000s. Annual growth in telecommunications exports (current prices), according to data from Statistics Sweden (2005), are shown in Figure 3.3. Of the 50 largest Swedish export performers, Ericsson alone was responsible for 27 percent in 1999 (Sönne, 2000); exports which for the most part fall under the heading of the telecommunications sector. The late 1990s and the year 2000 saw two-digit increases in export growth of this sector, which was replaced by a negative development in 2001–03. In 2004 and 2005, Ericsson managed to turn this problematic situation around, and growth is again very impressive. This means that Swedish high-tech development is very dependent on one single company. This is an unfortunate situation for Sweden as a nation, since it implies high vulnerability, and it also reveals that the choice of reference year is crucial for outcome of comparisons.

How does Sweden compare to other OECD countries in medium-high-tech industries? In terms of employment, it had the second-largest share of jobs in the MHT sectors throughout the period, second only to Germany. In MHT exports, Sweden ranks as an average country consistently over time.

In conclusion, Sweden seems to be doing well in employment in both HT and MHT, whereas exports from these sectors are around the same as for other OECD countries. The discrepancy between employment and export figures for HT and MHT is largely due to path dependence, where Swedish

*Table 3.6    Summary of 'high-tech' performance and corresponding results from Braunerhjelm (1998) and Edquist and McKelvey (1998)*

| Paper | Method | Production index | Employment ranking | Employment index | Exports ranking | Exports index |
|---|---|---|---|---|---|---|
| Ejermo & Kander<br>Employment:<br>21 countries<br>Exports:<br>30 countries | Ranking for available countries/average comparison.<br>4 technology categories | | HT:<br>7th in 1990<br>3rd in 2000<br>MHT:<br>2nd in 1990<br>2nd in 2000 | | HT:<br>8th in 1990<br>12th in 2003<br>MHT:<br>12th in 1990<br>14th in 2003 | HT:<br>82.3 in 1990<br>88.6 in 2003<br>MHT:<br>88.4 in 1990<br>91.8 in 2003 |
| Braunerhjelm<br>Employment:<br>12 countries<br>Exports:<br>12 or 14 countries | Average comparison.<br>3 technology categories | | | HT:<br>75 in 1970<br>79 in 1993<br>MT:<br>96.3 in 1970<br>117.2 in 1993 | | HT:<br>74 in 1970<br>85 in 1993<br>MT:<br>84 in 1970<br>88 in 1993 |
| Edquist & McKelvey<br>Production and employment:<br>14 countries | Average comparison.<br>3 technology categories | HT:<br>72 in 1970<br>72 in 1980<br>71 in 1990 | | HT:<br>75 in 1970<br>80 in 1980<br>79 in 1990 | | |

*Notes:* Index 100 = OECD average. MT refers to medium-tech. OECD employment data for different technology levels are expressed as employment shares of the manufacturing sector, not as shares of total employment in the economy. However, data of employment shares are not provided for the OECD as a whole, and the necessary information for computing such an average is not provided. Hence, an index where Sweden is compared to the OECD could not be calculated.

a.  Index data for Braunerhjelm's employment figures have been calculated from his information given in his Table 3.

b.  The data have been taken from visual inspection of Figure 1 in their paper, and may as such differ somewhat from the actual numbers the figure is based on.

production is heavily natural-resource based. These industries are capital rather than labor intensive. In addition, the favorable employment figures have more important direct effects on jobs and welfare than exports as such

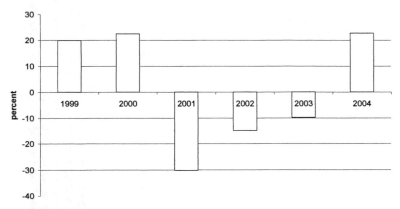

*Source*: Statistics Sweden (2005).

*Figure 3.3     Export development in the Swedish telecommunications sector (1999–2004) annual percentage growth, current prices*

The very large depreciation of the Swedish currency that occurred in 1992 stimulated export-led growth. In real terms, exports have grown 7 percent per year in 1995–2004 (Statistics Sweden, 2005). Natural-resource-intensive exports (e.g., iron, steel and forest-based industries) grew only by 3 percent per year in this period and HT and MHT exports increased even faster than the average 7 percent.

It seems that Sweden's specialization is moving only slowly in a more high-tech direction. This is still more spectacular in view of the increasing R&D-specialization of the economy.  We would like to suggest a possible explanation to the R&D-intensive mode of production chosen by Swedish industry: low costs for engineers and academic staff in general. These relatively low costs contributed to high R&D intensity in all sectors, but particularly in high-tech industries. This would explain why Sweden has an R&D intensity relatively higher than the G7 countries in high-tech industries. Such an argument on relative costs would also imply a comparative advantage in the sense that R&D is conducted in Sweden, while the high-tech products are produced elsewhere, where R&D is more expensive.

# CONCLUDING DISCUSSION

In this final section we shall sum up our main arguments and results and in addition make some suggestions for further studies in the field. The Swedish paradox has been formulated in three versions, with the common feature of stressing high R&D efforts in relation to meagre results:

1. Edquist and McKelvey's (1998) original formulation of the paradox was that the manufacturing of R&D-intensive products in Sweden was surprisingly low given its large R&D expenditures.
2. Braunerhjelm (1998) found that the technology balance of payments was a higher surplus in relative terms than for any other country. In addition, Swedish high-tech exports were found to be lacking and this was hence formulated as a Swedish export paradox.
3. Andersson et al. (2002) talk of output in a more abstract sense, referring to growth and productivity at the national level. Klofsten (2002) claims that Sweden brings few new goods to the market and that there are few new enterprises.

Is there anything paradoxical in high R&D and more modest high-tech production, exports and growth? We argue that in a strict sense there is no reason to talk of a Swedish paradox, once we look at the theoretical underpinnings of such an idea. There is no sound reason to expect a strong proportional relationship between the level of R&D in a country and its growth performance. This is because of several links on the journey from R&D to growth. The larger the possible variation in these links, the larger possible variation could result in the R&D to GDP ratios of different countries, and thus the weaker the proportional relationship. The four reasons we proposed for this lack of a simple proportional relationship are:

A. R&D does not necessarily result in a proportional amount of inventions;
B. inventions do not always become innovations, due to a lack of entrepreneurial functions or a lack of demand.
C. innovations do not always result in domestic high-tech production, because of an exchange with the world pool of innovations; and
D. there are other sources for growth than the direct contribution from the growth of high-tech sectors, or spillover effects from high-tech to other sectors.

That the relationship between R&D and growth is not a simple proportional one may seem obvious, but apparently is not so for many policy makers or even academic researchers, something which is presently expressed in the Lisbon strategy of increasing the R&D/GDP ratio of EU member states to 3 percent to increase their growth rates and possibly make the European economy surpass that of the US. This strategy determines current R&D investments of billions of euros. We therefore think that there are reasons for a wider audience to consider the actual relations. Sweden is already at a level above 3 per cent. It currently invests more than 4 percent of its GDP in R&D. If this does not produce expected results in terms of growth, why would there be such results on the EU level?

Although there is no reason to talk of a paradox in a strict meaning, we still think it is worthwhile to look into the somewhat surprising results for Sweden that drew our predecessors' attention to these issues in the first place. We use links A–D to organize our discussion on possible explanations for the Swedish paradox, examine some recent evidence on indicators used by our predecessors and add some new indicators.

Our empirical examination focuses strongly on links B and C. This is symptomatic of how the discussions have been carried out so far and shows that links A and D have been pretty much neglected. We recommend that future research devotes more attention to these two links, as they are also important for explaining returns and variations in the R&D to growth relation.

There seems to be a problem with the transformation of inventions into innovations (link B). One problem that seems to prevail in the Swedish innovation system is the reluctance of people to take on an entrepreneurial role (link $B_1$). There is a uniform picture given by different investigations that Swedes are not keen on becoming entrepreneurs (e.g., Delmar et al., 2005; Wiklund 2005). This suggests, that the incentive structure may need to be changed.

One weakness of the Swedish innovation system that prevails according to our examination here is the high concentration of R&D in a few large enterprises. We showed that this pattern has not weakened during the last few years. It seems possible that this industrial structure is detrimental for spillover effects within Sweden (Ejermo, 2004), and prevents innovative behavior and start-ups of small businesses (Henrekson and Jakobsson, 2001; Goldfarb and Henrekson, 2003). In particular, the possible hindrance to innovative behavior needs further empirical support.

Some researchers, for example, Henrekson and Rosenberg (2001), Andersson and Henrekson (2003) and Goldfarb and Henrekson (2003) claim that an important component of the Swedish paradox is rooted in a sub-paradox: high expenditures of university R&D and poor output from this. In terms of output from academic research, Sweden ranks second both in terms of publications in all sciences and in natural sciences, medicine and engineering (Jacobsson and Rickne, 2004). A more important issue than sheer academic output is the wider influence from academia on entrepreneurship (link $B_2$). The few studies available on this issue do not show that Swedes with academic degrees are more likely to start up new enterprises than the average population, especially not ones that generate employment. This is another field of study that deserves more attention.

There seems to be some leakage of innovative ideas (link C). Sweden does not seem to reap all the benefits from her innovations in terms of high-tech production. Our results show that exports and employment in high-tech are much better than previous authors have claimed. Exports have improved relatively since 1990. Braunerhjelm (1998) did not acknowledge in his data that there was in fact a positive trend for high-tech exports between 1970 and 1993. We show that this trend has continued. The export shares for HT are sensitive to the year picked for comparison, since Sweden fluctuates around the OECD average between 1990 and 2003. Employment in high-tech and medium-high tech has improved. The HT employment ranking was 7th in 1990 and 3rd in 2003. In medium-high-tech, Sweden maintained the second largest share of employment throughout the 1990-2003 period.

There is more reason to focus on the more optimistic figures of employment in HT and MHT than to look at export shares for HT and MHT. Relatively low export shares for HT and MHT depend on Swedish comparative advantage in natural-resource-intensive exports. This advantage has its root in the fact that Sweden is richly endowed with iron and forests and has over time built up specialist competence in the refinement of these goods. The forest and iron industries are capital intensive, thus not providing many job opportunities. The HT and MHT industries provide many job opportunities, because highly qualified people such as engineers and researchers can be hired at low cost. The Swedish wage structure is very compressed in an international perspective. This is the result of many years of policy directed towards decreasing wage differences, where strong unions have played an important role.[13] It could be argued that employment is more directly connected to welfare than to exports.

We find it likely that Sweden, a small open economy with lots of international trade and good skills in English, has an unusually large exchange with other countries in terms of innovative ideas. Sweden's absorptive capacity (imitative skill) is high according to the Community Innovation Surveys (as shown by Bitard et al., 2005) and this is likely to result in many spillovers to other countries. As long as there is a balance in the in- and outflows of knowledge, this should hardly be thought of as a problem, but as a strength. The net balance of this international exchange however, is not easy to measure, but there is no a priori reason to assume that it is negative for Sweden. From a Swedish policy perspective, the exchange of ideas is a neglected dimension and something that should be studied more.

With respect to link D (high-tech to growth) we have demonstrated that Swedish R&D is particularly pronounced in high-tech and medium-high-tech, but also above average in low-tech and medium-low-tech industries. Sweden has managed to achieve high exports in low-tech and medium-low-tech industries and hence the return in Sweden from R&D efforts in these sectors has been good. This is a perspective that has not previously been addressed in the R&D and growth debate and in doing so we would also like to stress that a more coherent growth theory that takes all the dynamic interactions between domestic sectors and the global economy into account is needed. R&D is not the sole driving force for growth in any sector. To investigate R&D and production in high-tech industries and talk of a paradox is too simplistic a perspective.

## ACKNOWLEDGEMENTS

This chapter has benefited from the many useful suggestions made at a seminar held in Lund in October 2005, and an earlier version presented at the Uddevalla symposium in September 2005. In particular we thank our commentators in Lund, Merle Jacob and Annika Rickne, and two anonymous referees.

## NOTES

1. According to Edquist (2002), this 'paradox' was already noted in 1991 although not labeled as a Swedish one. The notion of a Swedish paradox originally appeared in a working paper in 1996 (Edquist and McKelvey, 1996), which was later published as Edquist and McKelvey (1998).
2. Griliches (1992) distinguishes between rent and knowledge spillovers and Scitovsky (1954) discusses technological spillovers. For discussions on 'local knowledge spillovers', see Ejermo (2005a) and Andersson and Ejermo (2005a).
3. These include lead time, learning curve advantages, marketing and customer service, as stressed by Levin et al. (1987).
4. The technology balance of payments consists of sales of licenses and acquisition of R&D. With this definition, Swedish technology exports were roughly US$350 million in 1997 – imports were only US$45 million.
5. Former state-owned Televerket is now partially private owned under the name Telia-Sonera. This company formed a powerful and semi-public partnership together with Ericsson. Another important partnership was in the defense industry, between SAAB, Bofors and others with Technology for Sweden's Security – a government agency (FMV, Försvarets Materielverk).
6. The HHI measure is $HHI = \sum s_i^2$, where $S_i$ is the share of man-years/R&D expenditures in firm $i$. Total dispersion would imply that an infinite number of firms have an equal share, a figure that approaches zero, and hence the measure becomes zero. On the other end of the scale, just one firm has all the activity and the measure becomes 1.
7. Recently, whether Sweden should be considered entrepreneurial or not has been debated in the Swedish media by representatives from two Swedish authorities: the Swedish Institute for Growth Policy Studies (ITPS) and the Swedish Agency for Economic and Regional Growth (Nutek).

8. They claim that their findings have a bearing on the larger group of the continental European university system as well.
9. We know of only two researchers who are dealing with this. Ingrid Schild at Umeå University is investigating patenting among inventors active at Linköping University and Devrim Göktepe at Lund University has a similar project regarding inventors at Lund University. However, we do not know the value of the inventions created, and these are only two out of several universities.
10. Data available on request.
11. For employment, the available data forced us to choose between employment as a share of all employed or as a share of all employed in manufacturing. The former measure would capture changes in the distribution between services and manufacturing and relative changes in employment shares between high-tech and medium-high-tech. The latter measure only captures relative changes within manufacturing employment. For Sweden both measures revealed very similar patterns, so we chose the practical approach of using shares of manufacturing employment since data were available for more countries.
12. Unfortunately R&D intensities and exports data were not available for all years for either the G7 or the OECD group, but the data indicate that this approximation does not alter the results.
13. Together with Denmark, Sweden has the lowest Gini coefficient among the OECD countries (Andersson and Ejermo, 2005b).

# REFERENCES

Abramovitz, M. (1956), 'Resource and Output trends in the United States since 1870', *American Economic Review, Papers and Proceedings*, May, 5–23.
Acs, Z.J., D.B. Audretsch, P. Braunerhjelm, and B. Carlsson (2004), 'The Missing Link – the Knowledge Filter and Entrepreneurship in Endogenous Growth', CEPR Discussion Paper 4783, London: Center for Economic policy Research.
Aghion, P. and P. Howitt (1992), 'A model of growth through creative destruction', *Econometrica*, **60** (2), 323–51.
Aghion, P. and P. Howitt (1998), *Endogenous Growth Theory*, Cambridge, MA: MIT Press.
Andersson, M. and O. Ejermo (2005a), 'How Does Accessibility to Knowledge Sources Affect the Innovativeness of Corporations? – Evidence from Sweden', *Annals of Regional Science* **39**, 741–65.
Andersson, T. and O. Ejermo (2005b), 'Country Report: Efforts and Performance of R&D in Sweden', Malmö: IKED
Andersson, T., O. Asplund and M. Henrekson (2002), *Betydelsen av Innovationssystem, Utmaningar för Samhället och för Politiken [The Importance of Innovation Systems, Challenges for Society and Politics]*, Stockholm: VINNOVA.
Andersson, T. and M. Henrekson (2003), 'A Critique of Staffan Jacobsson's paper "Universities and industrial transformation"', *Science and Public Policy*, **30** (6), 455–61.
Bitard, P., C. Edquist, L. Hommen and A. Rickne (2005), 'The Swedish System, Report within the Project "National Innovation Systems in Ten Small Countries"', Unpublished, Lund: Division of Innovation.
Braconier, H., P.-J. Norbäck, and D.M. Urban, (2005), 'Multinational Enterprises and Wage Costs: Vertical FDI Revisited', *Journal of International Economics*, 67:2, pp. 446-470.

Braunerhjelm, P. (1998), 'Varför leder inte ökade FoU-satsningar till mer högteknologisk export?' (Why does not increased R&D-efforts result in more export of high-tech?), *Ekonomiska samfundets tidskrift*, **2**, 113–23.

Breschi, S., F. Malerba and L. Orsenigo (2000), 'Technological Regimes and Schumpeterian Patterns of Innovation', *Economic Journal*, **110**, 388–410.

Cohen, W.M., and D.A. Levinthal (1989), 'Innovation and Learning: The Two Faces of R&D', *Economic Journal*, **99**, 569–96.

Cohen, W.M. and D.A. Levinthal (1990), 'Absorptive Capacity: A New Perspective on Learning and Innovation', *Administrative Science Quarterly*, **35**, 128–52.

Comin, D. (2004), 'R&D: A Small Contribution to Productivity Growth', *Journal of Economic Growth*, **9**, 391–421.

Delmar, F., K. Wennberg, K. Sjöberg and J. Wiklund (2005), 'Self-employment among the Swedish Science and Technology Labor Force: The Evolution of the Firms between 1990 and 2000', Research Report A2005:001, Swedish Institute for Growth Policy Studies (ITPS): Östersund.

Easterly, W. and R. Levine (2001), 'It's Not Factor Accumulation: Stylized Facts and Growth Models', *World Bank Economic Review*, **15** (2), 177–219.

Eaton, J. and S. Kortum (1999), 'International technology and diffusion: theory and measurement', *International Economic Review*, **40** (3), 537–70.

Edquist, C. (ed.) (1997), *Systems of Innovation: Technologies, Institutions and Organizations*, London: Pinter.

Edquist, C. (2002), 'Innovationspolitik för Sverige – mål, skäl, problem och åtgärder' (Innovation politics for Sweden – goal, reasons, problems and measures), VINNOVA Forum Innovationspolitik i Fokus VFI 2002, 2.

Edquist, C. and M. McKelvey (1996), 'High R&D Intensity, Without High Tech Products: A Swedish Paradox?', Working Paper 161, Department of Technology and Social Change, Linköping University, Linköping.

Edquist; C. and M. McKelvey (1998), 'The Swedish paradox: High R&D intensity without high-tech products', in K. Nielsen and B. Johnson (eds), *Institutions and Economic Change: New Perspectives on Markets, Firms and Technology*, Cheltenham UK and Northhampton, MA: Edward Elgar Publishing Ltd.

Ejermo, O. (2004), 'Perspectives on Regional and Industrial Dynamics of Innovation', PhD thesis, Jönköping: Jönköping International Business School.

Ejermo, O. (2005), 'Technological Diversity and Jacobs' Externality Hypothesis Revisited', *Growth and Change*, **36** (2), 167–95.

European Commission (2005), *European Trend Chart on Innovation – Annual Innovation Policy Trends and Appraisal Report Sweden 2004 – 2005*, preliminary version.

Global Entrepreneurship Monitor (2005), *GEM 2004 global report*, accessed online: http://www.gemconsortium.org/download/1120560514625/GEM_2004_Exec_Repo rt.pdf, on 2005-07-05.

Goldfarb, B. and M. Henrekson (2003), 'Bottom-up Versus Top-down Policies towards the Commercialization of University Intellectual Property', *Research Policy*, **32**, 639–58.

Granberg, A. and S. Jacobsson (2005), 'Myths or Reality: a Scrutiny of Dominant Beliefs in the Swedish Science Policy Debate', 1st draft, unpublished.

Griliches, Z. (1992), 'The Search for R&D Spillovers', *Scandinavian Journal of Economics*, **94**, S29–S47.

Grossman, G.M. and E. Helpman (1991a), 'Trade, Knowledge Spillovers and Growth', *European Economic Review*, **35** (3), 517–26.

Grossman, G.M. and E. Helpman (1991b), *Innovation and Growth in the World Economy*, Cambridge, MA: MIT Press.

Grossman, G.M. and E. Helpman (1994), 'Endogenous Innovation in the Theory of Growth', *Journal of Economic Perspectives*, **8** (1), 23–44.

Henrekson, M. and U. Jakobsson (2001), 'Where Schumpeter Was Nearly Right: the Swedish Model and Capitalism, Socialism and Democracy', *Journal of Evolutionary Economics*, **11**, 331–58.

Henrekson, M. and N. Rosenberg (2001), 'Designing Efficient Institutions for Science-Based Entrepreneurship: Lesson from the US and Sweden', *Journal of Technology Transfer*, **26** (3), 207–31.

INNO and Technopolis (2004), *Benchmarking Technology R&D*, Brighton and Stockholm: VINNOVA.

ITPS (2004), *Näringslivets Internationalisering – Effekter På Sysselsättning, Produktivitet och FoU*, Stockholm: Elanders Gotab.

Jacobsson, S. (2002), 'Universities and Industrial Transformation: an Interpretative and Selective Literature Study with Special Emphasis on Sweden', *Science and Public Policy*, **29** (5), 345–65.

Jacobsson, S. and A. Rickne (2004), 'How Large is the Swedish "Academic" Sector really? A Critical Analysis of the Use of Science and Technology Indicators', *Research Policy*, **33**, 1355–72.

Johanson, D. and N. Karlson (2006), *Svensk utvecklingkraft*, (Swedish development power) Stockholm: Ratio.

Jones, C.I. (1995a), 'Time series tests of endogenous growth models', *Quarterly Journal of Economics*, **110** (2), 495–525.

Jones, C.I. (1995b), 'R&D-Based Models of Economic Growth', *Journal of Political Economy*, **103**, 759–84.

Jones, C.I. (2002), 'Sources of U.S. Economic Growth in a World of Ideas', *American Economic Review*, **92**, 220–39.

Kendrick, J.W. (1961), *Productivity Trends in the United States*, Princeton, NJ: Princeton University Press.

Kline, S. and N. Rosenberg (1986), An overview of the process of innovation, in: G. Landau and N. Rosenberg, Editors, *The Positive Sum Strategy:Harnessing Technology for Economic Growth*, National Academy Press, Washington.

Klofsten, M. (2002), 'Bidrag som svar på förfrågan från Näringsdepartementet om underlag för utarbetande av en svensk innovationspolitik' (Contribution as response to the Ministry of Enterprise, energy and communciation about the elaboration of a Swedish innovation policy), Mimeo.

Levin, R.C., A.K. Klevorick, R.R. Nelson and S.G. Winter (1987), 'Appropriating the Returns from Industrial Research and Development', *Brookings Papers on Economic Activity*, (3), 783–820.

Lindholm Dahlstrand, Å. (1997a), 'Growth and Inventiveness in Technology-based Spin-off Firms', *Research Policy*, **26** (3), 331–4.

Lindholm Dahlstrand, Å. (1997b), 'Entrepreneurial Spin-off Enterprises in Göteborg, Sweden', *European Planning Studies*, **5** (5), 659–73.

Lundvall, B.-Å. (1992), *National Systems of Innovation: Towards a Theory of Innovation and Interactive Learning*, London: Pinter.

Marklund, G., R. Nilsson, P. Sandgren, J. Granat Thorslund and J. Ullström (2004), *The Swedish National Innovation System*, Stockholm: VINNOVA.

Marshall, A. (1920), *Principles of Economics*, London: Macmillan.

76	*Entrepreneurship and Innovations in Functional Regions*

NSF (2002), *Science and Engineering Indicators–2002*, National Science Foundation, Arlington, VA: Division of Science Resources Statistics.

OECD (2005), *Main Science and Technology Indicators*, Paris: OECD.

Romer, P.M. (1986), 'Increasing Returns and Long-Run Growth', *Journal of Political Economy*, **94**, 1002–37.

Romer, P.M. (1990), 'Endogenous Technological Change', *Journal of Political Economy*, **98**, 71–102.

Romer, P.M. (1994), 'The Origins of Endogenous Growth', *Journal of Economic Perspectives*, **8**, 3–32.

Schön, L. (1991), 'Development Blocks and Transformation Pressure in a Macro Economic Perspective: a Model of Long-Cyclical Change', *Skandinaviska Enskilda Banken Quarterly Review*, no. 3–4, 11-23.

Schön, L. (1998), 'Industrial Crises in a Model of Long Cycles; Sweden in an International Perspective', in T. Myllyntaus (ed.), *Economic Crises and Restructuring in History*, Berlin: Scripta Meracaturae, pp. 63-75.

Schön, L. (2000), 'En modern svensk ekonomisk historia', Tillväxt och omvandling under två sekel, Stockholm: SNS.

Schumpeter, J. (1934), *The Theory of Economic Development*, Cambridge, MA: Harvard University Press.

Schumpeter, J. (1950), *Capitalism, Socialism, and Democracy*, New York: Harper & Row.

Scitovsky, T. (1954), 'Two Concepts of External Economies', *Journal of Political Economy*, **62**, 143–51.

Sellenthin, M. (2004), 'Who should own university research? An Exploratory Study of the Impact of Patent Rights Regimes in Sweden and Germany on the Incentives to Patent Research Results', Report A2004:013, Östersund: Institute for Growth Policy Studies (ITPS).

Solow, R.M. (1994), 'Perspectives on growth theory', *Journal of Economic Perspectives*, **8** (1), 45–54.

Sönne, A. (2000), 'Skanska klättrar på exporttoppen', Dagens Industri 2000-06-28, http://di.se/Nyheter/?page=%2fAvdelningar%2fArtikel.aspx%3fO%3dIndex%26Ar ticleId%3d2000%5c06%5c28%5c1202, accessed 13 September, 2005.

SOU (2005), *Nyttiggörande av högskoleuppfinningar*, Stockholm: Ministry of Education, Research and Culture, SOU 2005, 95.

Statistics Sweden (2005), http://www.ssd.scb.se/databaser/makro/start.asp, accessed 1st October, 2005.

Swedish Research Council (2003), *En Stark Grundforskning i Sverige, Vetenskapsrådets forskningsstrategi 2005 –2008*, Stockholm.

Wallen, F. and S. Fölster (2005), *Utflyttningens konsekvenser*, Stockholm: The Confederation of Swedish Enterprise (Svenskt Näringsliv).

Wiklund, J. (2005), 'Nästan alla högutbildade ratar jobb som företagare', Dagens Nyheter 2005-06-01, http://www.dn.se/DNet/jsp/polopoly.jsp?d=572anda=422548, accessed 5th November, 2005.

# 4. Firm Location, Corporate Structure and Innovation

## Börje Johansson, Amy Ryder-Olsson and Hans Lööf

### INTRODUCTION

This chapter examines how firm location and corporate structure relate to innovation and productivity. The propensity of firms to agglomerate is associated with the benefits that large urban regions can afford, both proximity advantages and special qualities of regions in fostering innovation and economic growth. As suggested by Acs (1994), Glaeser (1999), Harhoff (1999) and others, large urban regions can be expected to have higher rates of innovation and adopt innovations more rapidly.

Regional features can capture proximity externalities in the innovation process. What, then, is the role of corporate structure? A multinational firm is a multi-unit network in which knowledge can also flow with small friction over long distances. When located in a metropolitan region, such a firm can combine proximity advantages with network advantages.

This chapter adds to the literature on innovation by combining two questions. First, how does a firm's location affect its innovation behavior? Second, how does the innovation behavior differ between multinational enterprises (MNEs) and other firms, while observing that an MNE is a multi-location organization? We examine the role of domestic and foreign MNEs, in view of the fact that research and developmet (R&D) has become increasingly internationalized in recent decades (Zander, 1994; Cantwell, 1998; and Kuemmerle, 1999). In particular, foreign-owned firms have increased their share of Swedish manufacturing production from 21 percent in 1985 to 34 percent in 2001. In addition, foreign-owned firms increased their share of R&D investments in Sweden to 40 percent in 2001. In the same year, Swedish firms carried out almost half of their R&D activities abroad (Lööf, 2005). Our empirical analysis shows that MNEs differ clearly from other enterprise categories by making more frequent and larger innovation efforts. However, there are no signs of any greater returns to R&D investments among multinational firms.

There is widely held agreement in the modern literature that an R&D facility's capacity to exploit and augment its technological competency is a function not just of its own resources, but also of the efficiency with which it can utilize complementary resources (formal and informal linkages) and complex interdependencies among small local geographical units. Our analysis looks closely at ownership, because it may affect local embeddedness in innovation systems in the light of globalization trends in R&D.

The chapter uses the Community Innovation Survey (CIS) data for regional analysis. In European countries and also in some others (Canada, Brazil, South Korea, Australia, New Zealand, Japan and China) there is a growing group of studies that employ information from the internationally harmonized CIS, which contains observations of firm attributes such as R&D, patents, innovation collaboration, physical capital, human capital, firm size and sales (for an overview, see Kleinknecht and Mohnen, 2002). The CIS data, containing 1,907 firm-level observations for the 1998–2000 period, has been merged with register data derived from annual accounts and includes both manufacturing and service firms.

The Swedish capital region (Stockholm) is compared with four other Swedish regions. The Stockholm region is a functional urban region proper in that it forms an integrated labor market region and hence an arena for face-to-face contacts. Each of the other regional areas in this study contains several functional regions, which are all smaller than the Stockholm region. Moreover, the concentration of MNEs and universities is higher, and the share of innovative firms larger, in the Stockholm region than in other Swedish functional regions. The average firm in Stockholm has both a higher R&D intensity and a higher human capital intensity compared to firms in other regions. Among innovative firms, the Stockholm region's share of newly established firms and of firms launching non-imitation innovations is larger compared to other regions.

In sum, the Stockholm region has a denser and richer economic environment than other parts of Sweden. Urban economic theory tells us that this should result in higher floor-space costs in Stockholm, and we would expect innovative firms in the Stockholm region to have higher sales value per employee than similar firms elsewhere in the country. The chapter tests these hypotheses using empirical evidence. Our empirical analyses reveal that firms in the Stockholm region – with varying corporate structures – are more innovative than firms in other regions. Moreover, the returns to R&D investments are higher for firms in the Stockholm region. Controlling for R&D intensity, firm size, physical capital, human capital, corporate structure and sector classification, innovation sales per employee as well as labor productivity are larger in the large metropolitan region. This finding is not well documented in the literature.

This chapter is structured as follows. In 'Background and previous research' we elaborate on the key questions posed in this study and relate them to recent literature. 'Data and descriptive statistics' introduces the data used and presents descriptive statistics that illuminate our research topic. 'Methodology' discusses the econometric approach, which includes a probit model and a two-stage selection model. 'Results from the econometric analysis' presents the empirical analysis, and 'Summary discussion' concludes.

## BACKGROUND AND PREVIOUS RESEARCH

### Innovation Activities and Knowledge Flows

Knowledge is an input to an innovation process, which – if successful – generates new products and new production routines used by the innovating firm. Knowledge for innovation takes several forms: (i) scientific knowledge in the form of basic principles, (ii) technological knowledge in the form of 'technical solutions', and (iii) entrepreneurial knowledge about product attributes, customer preferences and market conditions, business concepts and so on. (Karlsson and Johansson, 2004). With these distinctions it becomes clear why knowledge networks may have many different participants representing different types of knowledge (Batten et al., 1989).

The first type of knowledge interaction is that which is internal to the firm and the group to which it may belong. This may be the result of formal knowledge transfer processes or 'water cooler conversations'. Several studies have noted the importance of both firm organization and key individuals. An effective organization can facilitate the transfer of codified information among knowledge workers and also provide (or thwart) opportunities for sharing ideas and collaborating on new projects. Because knowledge has a strong tacit component, it is embedded in the firm's 'knowledge workers'. These workers are mobile primarily inside the same functional region, so their role in diffusing knowledge includes both interacting with others in one firm and also imparting some of the knowledge gained during that tenure to future employers. This observation implies that a functional region can be a special milieu for knowledge diffusion.

A single firm will often simultaneously participate in a range of discrete or interlinked networks of suppliers, customers, or neighboring firms (Karlsson and Johansson, 2004). This study uses the distinctions offered by Cox et al.,

(2003) between a firm's horizontal and vertical innovation systems. Firms are embedded in horizontal innovation network relationships with similar firms (competing, consulting and collaborating) and in vertical innovation network relationships with suppliers and customers.

This study considers a third type of innovation system, 'scientific innovation networks', comprising channels for knowledge flows of (i) newly trained graduates from universities to industry, (ii) technological spillovers of newly created knowledge from universities to industry, (iii) industrial purchases of newly created university knowledge or intellectual property, (iv) university researchers as consultants to industry or serving on company boards, (v) university researchers leaving universities to work for industry, and (vi) university researchers creating new firms, that is, academic entrepreneurship.[1]

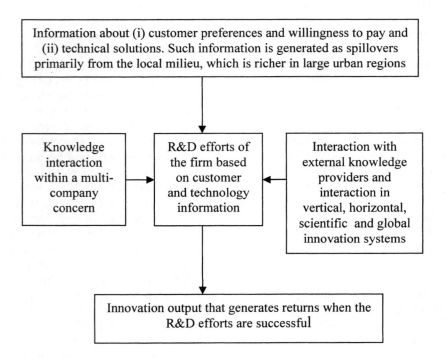

*Figure 4.1  Knowledge and information flows in a firm's innovation process*

Figure 4.1 illustrates how a firm can gain innovation advantages by means of knowledge flows in innovation networks, inside an MNE, and in the urbanization context of a large urbanized region. Urbanization advantages obtain when information about both customers and technical solutions spreads more easily when actors are in proximity to each other. The second knowledge source is a firm's interaction in different local innovation systems, where the privatization of the created knowledge is crucial. That is less problematic with regard to knowledge that is generated inside the organization of a multi-company group. In addition, empirical observations indicate that knowledge interaction within a multi-company concern may be much less dependent on the proximity principle (Andersson and Ejermo, 2004). The suggestion is that multinational firms tend to internalize the knowledge interaction process, which may partly explain the very existence of multinationals.

**Regions and Innovation**

Over several decades, scholars have argued that the proximity afforded by locating in large urban regions creates an advantage for firms by facilitating information and knowledge flows, following arguments presented early in Artle (1959) and Vernon (1962), and later in Feldman and Audretsch (1999) and Glaeser (1999). The nature of this phenomenon may be classified as a proximity-based communication externality (Fujita and Thisse, 2002). The exchange of ideas as embodied in technology spillovers has also been used by Cockburn and Henderson (1996) to account for the clustering of economic activity across space.

Within a functional region, delimited by housing and labor market perimeters, firms have better accessibility to customers, input suppliers, the scientific community, and competing firms all important sources for intellectual capital and innovation-relevant knowledge and information. As noted earlier, labor mobility inside a functional region is also an important source for both knowledge transfer and internal firm activities leading to growth and maintenance of intellectual capital. Some studies have estimated that proximity of within less than one hour's travel time from the firm location is sufficient to enjoy or produce the positive externalities associated with agglomeration (e.g., Johansson et al., 2002).

Functional regions in the Swedish context are known as 'LA regions', and they consist of local government areas (municipalities). Inside a region, the average travel time between zones in a municipality is about 10 minutes, between municipalities the average travel time is about 30 minutes, and from the central (largest) municipality all other municipalities in the region can be reached within less than 50 minutes. Because of this, LA regions form local labor market regions, and they provide an arena for frequent person-to-person interaction. The Stockholm region is one such functional LA region.

A large LA region offers special advantages to innovative firms in terms of knowledge flows and spillovers, since they offer both clusters in specific industries as well as a diverse range of industries. They combine the advantages of industrial clustering to knowledge transfer and spillover associated with Alfred Marshall, Kenneth Arrow and Paul Romer with the advantages of firm diversity for fostering and incubating innovative ideas as described by Jacobs (1969). Such contact opportunities are especially important when knowledge must be specified as a commodity for which property rights are clearly defined. The CIS, employed in this study, identifies sources of information for innovation as well as collaboration with national scientific, vertical and horizontal innovation systems. In this study we assume that these contacts primarily take place inside each LA region.

The Stockholm region has many of the preconditions identified in the literature as essential to the creation of regional innovation systems supporting innovative firms. Compared to other Swedish regions, the Stockholm region has a higher share of R&D workers in the local labor supply, as well as a higher share of persons with university education (higher than average knowledge intensity). Nearly one in three multinational companies with facilities in Sweden are located in the Stockholm region; about one in two are in the Mälar Valley (which includes Stockholm). Since multinationals account for approximately 60 percent of industrial output and overall export, and almost 90 percent of Sweden's industrial R&D spending in 1990 (Fors and Svensson, 2002), the Stockholm region has by far Sweden's most significant concentration of R&D spending.

The Stockholm region has better conditions than other Swedish regions for both short- and long-distance interaction with R&D institutions and knowledge providers in general. As a large region with good connections, both among regional clusters and agglomerations and with other regions (both Swedish and international), Stockholm offers the agglomeration and network advantages described earlier as important to knowledge creation, transfer and spillover.

## Corporate Structure and Ownership

In the empirical analyses we focus on the location of a firm and its corporate structure and ownership. The corporate structure dimension is captured by means of a classification of firms into the following four groups: (i) non-affiliates, (ii) uninationals (domestic multi-firm groups), (iii) domestic multinationals, and (iv) foreign multinationals. All other firm attributes are employed as control variables.

A firm's corporate structure can contribute both to the generation and transmission of knowledge and therefore to its stock of intellectual capital.

Although these processes are complex and not completely understood, it is generally accepted that multinational firms may have advantages over uni-national and unaffiliated firms in both the creation and transmission of knowledge for innovation (Pfaffermayr and Bellak, 2002). Multinational firms, with many affiliated locations in several countries, have both the 'reach' to access new information and the closed system necessary to protect temporary monopolies on intellectual capital.

Followers of Joseph Schumpeter argue that firms' incentive to innovate is their ability to enjoy at least temporary monopoly profits from their innovations. Multinational corporations thus seem to provide the best of both 'worlds', both access to a large stock of external knowledge (due to the number of locations, including international locations) and the ability to share and develop proprietary information within the corporation. For a detailed discussion, see Dunning (1993), Cantwell and Janne (1999), Kuemmerle (1999) and Criscuolo et al. (2002).

This could indicate that formal incorporation of strategic partners within a multinational corporation is an attempt to appropriate their innovation output. Multinationals may also be more skilful in their interactions with R&D organizations, increasing their likelihood of benefiting from embeddedness in regional innovation systems. Moreover, multinationals tend to have a larger average size than other firms and can thereby attract knowledge providers and specialized input suppliers. They have access to a richer base of customer and technological information and use the structure of the firm as a network for knowledge flows between the different units of the company.

Recent studies have confirmed the advantages of multi-location firms for innovative activities. Anderstig and Karlsson (1989) have shown that both advanced process innovations and all product innovations are positively correlated with the size of customer networks. A recent study by Ebersberger and Lööf (2005), using data from Swedish firms, indicates that multinational firms have a significantly larger probability of patenting and introducing radical innovations than uninational firms. Ebersberger et al., (2007) also note an important distinction between Swedish-owned multinational firms (domestic multinationals) and foreign-owned multinational firms. Domestic multinationals tended to be more embedded in their home country's innovation systems and had a higher value of R&D investments.

# DATA AND DESCRIPTIVE STATISTICS

## The CIS III DataSet

This study uses data from the CIS III for Sweden. The survey was conducted in 2001 and covers the 1998–2000 period for both the manufacturing sector and business services. The CIS has become a popular data source for statistical studies regarding innovation, since it allows for broad comparisons across firms and countries. However, its usefulness in assessing the importance of R&D and other innovation engagement in a regional perspective is somewhat limited. As noted above, firms are, for instance, not asked to report on the proximity of their domestic collaboration on innovation with external partners. The reporting units are firms whose geographical locations are known, but R&D and production activities in plants located in other places may also be included in the data obtained from the reporting unit. Having made this observation, motivated by resent research we chose to assume that a firm's R&D activities as well as its collaboration in innovation processes mostly are enclosed in the same location area as that of the reporting firm. Several authors exploit patent citation data in order to trace possible links between geographical proximity and innovation (Jaffe et al., 1993; Almeida, 1996; Eaton and Kortum, 1999; Bottazzi and Peri, 2003; Verspagen and Schoenmakers, 2004). This research typically shows that proximity in the creation of economically useful knowledge is important, and some authors also suggest that inventors increasingly use close by knowledge more than long-distant knowledge (Sonn and Stolper, 2003).

## Variables Describing Innovation Inputs and Outputs

Table 4.1 introduces the selection variable 'innovative firms' and the eight dependent variables posited as potential determinants for each specific variable. We define a firm as innovative if it satisfies one or more of the following criteria during the most recent three-year period: it has introduced a new product, it has carried out a process innovation, or it has ongoing innovation activities. In addition, this type of estimation has the role of a selection equation embedded in all other regressions.

The study considers two aspects of innovation: input and output. Innovation inputs or innovation efforts are recognized by the following four categories: (i) R&D intensity which measures the firms' expenditures on R&D per employee; (ii) embeddedness in the domestic science base is a composite dummy variable indicating firms' collaboration with universities, and private and public R&D laboratories; (iii) embeddedness in the domestic vertical innovation system is a composite variable indicating collaboration on innovation with customers and suppliers; and (iv) global sources of knowledge for innovation is a variable that reflects a firm's global knowledge interaction with suppliers, customers, competitors, consultancies, commercial R&D laboratories, universities and public R&D laboratories. In the regression analyses we disregard interaction in horizontal innovation systems since a sensitivity analysis shows that this variable is non-significant and that it does not affect other coefficient estimates.

*Table 4.1 Description of variables*

| Dependent variables | Definition |
| --- | --- |
| Innovative firm | Innovative firms are firms reporting a product and/or process innovation and/or reporting ongoing innovation activities |
| Innovation input | The firm's expenditures on R&D and other innovation activities per employee, log |
| Embeddedness in the regional science base | Composite dummy variable indicating whether firms collaborate on innovation with universities and private and public R&D laboratories |
| Embeddedness in the regional vertical innovation system | Composite dummy variable indicating whether firms collaborate on innovation with customers or suppliers |
| Global collaboration on innovation | Composite dummy variable indicating whether firms collaborate globally on innovation with suppliers, customers, competitors, consultancies, commercial R&D laboratories, universities and public R&D laboratories |
| Non-imitation innovations | Dummy variable, indicates whether the firm has introduced a product to the market that is new or significantly improved |
| Innovation sales | The firm's sales income from new products per employee, log |
| Gross labor productivity | Sales per employee, log |
| Net labor productivity | Value added per employee, log |

*Table 4.2 Explanatory variables*

| Explanatory variables | Definition |
| --- | --- |
| *Regional localization* | |
| Stockholm | |
| East Central Sweden | Uppsala, Sörmland, Örebro, Östergötland |
| South Sweden | Blekinge, Skåne |
| West Sweden | Västra Götaland, Halland |
| Other Sweden | Småland, Öland, Gotland, Värmland, Dalarna, Gävleborg, Västernorrland, Jämtland, Västerbotten, Norrbotten |
| *Firm structure* | |
| Non-affiliated enterprises | Domestically owned firms without affiliates |
| Uninational enterprises | Domestically owned firms belonging to a group with only Swedish affiliates |
| Domestically owned MNEs | Domestically owned firms belonging to a group with foreign affiliates |
| Foreign-owned MNEs | Foreign-owned firms belonging to a multinational group |
| *Firm characteristics* | |
| Size | Number of employees |
| Gross productivity | Turnover per employee |
| Profit margin | Profit as a share of turnover |
| Human capital | Share of the employment with a university degree |
| Physical capital | Tangible assets |
| Innovation input | See Table 4.1 |
| Persistent R&D | Dummy for continuous R&D engagement |
| Process innovation | Dummy variable indicating whether the firm has introduced onto the market a new or significantly improved process |
| Newly established | The enterprise has been established during the last three years |
| Recent history of merging and acquisition | The enterprise has been involved in M&A during the last three years |

| Explanatory variables | Definition |
|---|---|
| *Collaboration on innovation* | |
| Embeddedness in the regional science base | See Table 4.1 |
| Embeddedness in the regional vertical innovation system | See Table 4.1 |
| Global collaboration on innovation | See Table 4.1 |
| *Market* | |
| Significant market area local | The firms' most significant market |
| Significant market area national | The firms' most significant market |
| Significant market area global | The firms' most significant market |
| *Sector* | |
| High-technology manufacturing sectors | Nace 353, Nace 2423, Nace, 30, Nace 32, Nace 33 |
| Medium-high-technology manufacturing sectors | Nace 24 excl Nace 2423, Nace 29, Nace 31, Nace 34, Nace 352, Nace 359 |
| Medium-low-technology manufacturing sectors | Nace 23, Nace 25, Nace 26, Nace 37, Nace 28, Nace 351, Nace 354 |
| Low-technology manufacturing sectors | Nace 15, Nace 16, Nace 17, Nace 18, Nace 19, Nace 20, Nace 21, Nace 36, Nace 37 |
| Knowledge-intensive services | Nace 64, Nace 65, Nace 66, Nace 67, Nace 71, Nace 72–74 |
| Other services | Other services than knowledge intensive services |

To examine innovation output, the study uses four different measures of firm output performance. The first is non-imitation innovations, a dummy variable that indicates whether a firm has introduced a product to the market that is either partly or completely new. The second measure is innovation sales, that is, sales income from new products. The variable innovation sales is expressed in intensity terms (per employee). The third output measure is total sales per employee, or gross labor productivity. Finally, we report on value added per employee.

Table 4.2 describes the definitions of the explanatory variables. It should be noted that some of the dependent variables presented in Table 4.1 are also used as explanatory variables in other steps of the empirical model. In the study, the Stockholm region is compared with the rest of Sweden which consists of four areas: East Central Sweden, South Sweden, West Sweden and Other Sweden (mainly north Sweden).

Based on findings by Doms and Jensen (1999), Bellman and Jungnickel (2002), Pfaffermayr and Bellak (2002), Criscuolo and Martin (2004), Ebersberger and Lööf (2005) and others, we also control for differences in corporate structure when exploring the relationship between innovative activities and location. In order to do this we divide our sample into four separate categories of ownership: non-affiliate enterprises (firms not belonging to a group), uninational enterprises (firms belonging to a group with only domestic affiliates), domestic multinationals and foreign-owned multinationals.

The main firm characteristics in the study are firm size, gross labor productivity, profit margin, human capital (university educated/total employment), physical capital, knowledge capital (current and recurrent R&D), process innovation and the firms' recent history (establishment, merger and acquisition: M&A). In order to control for industry-specific factors, six sector dummies are included in the analysis, as well as information about the firm's most significant market.

**Summary Descriptive Statistics**

Tables 4.3–4.6 present descriptive and comparative statistics for all firms and innovative firms, respectively. The sample contains 1,907 firms from manufacturing and service enterprises with 10 or more employees, of which 815 (43 percent) are non-affiliated enterprises, 691 (36 percent) uninational enterprises and 401 (21 percent) multinationals, as described in Table 4.3. The Swedish capital Stockholm (REG 1) has a smaller share of non-affiliated enterprises compared to other regions, and a larger share of multinationals. Nearly 50 percent of all MNEs in Sweden are located in Stockholm or its close neighbor-region East Central Sweden (REG 2).

The Stockholm region has a larger share of innovative firms (57 percent) compared to the other four regions (48–53 percent). A decomposition of the average figures in Table 4.4 shows that the relatively higher share of innovative firms in Stockholm is due to the region's lower share of non-affiliated and uninational enterprises. Somewhat surprisingly, the share of innovative firms among multinationals is considerably smaller in Stockholm than in the four other regions. On the other hand, the share of multinationals is higher in the Stockholm region than elsewhere.

*Table 4.3  Number of observations*

|  | REG 1 | REG 2 | REG 3 | REG 4 | REG 5 | SWE |
|---|---|---|---|---|---|---|
| Non-affiliate | 160 | 103 | 125 | 181 | 246 | 815 |
| Uninational | 144 | 105 | 93 | 135 | 214 | 691 |
| Multinational | 117 | 67 | 58 | 78 | 81 | 401 |
| Average | 421 | 275 | 276 | 394 | 541 | 1,907 |

*Table 4.4  Share of innovative firms\**

|  | REG 1 | REG 2 | REG 3 | REG 4 | REG 5 | SWE |
|---|---|---|---|---|---|---|
| Non-affiliate | 0.47 | 0.44 | 0.42 | 0.39 | 0.37 | 0.41 |
| Uninational | 0.65 | 0.50 | 0.44 | 0.47 | 0.47 | 0.50 |
| Multinational | 0.63 | 0.75 | 0.77 | 0.72 | 0.78 | 0.72 |
| Average | 0.57 | 0.53 | 0.50 | 0.48 | 0.47 | 0.51 |

*Notes:\** Innovative firms are firms reporting a product and/or process innovation and/or reporting ongoing innovation activities.

*Table 4.5  Number of employees, (mean)*

|  | REG 1 | REG 2 | REG 3 | REG 4 | REG 5 | SWE |
|---|---|---|---|---|---|---|
| Non-affiliate | 325 | 102 | 46 | 50 | 50 | 110 |
| Uninational | 587 | 198 | 157 | 254 | 151 | 270 |
| Multinational | 648 | 381 | 324 | 567 | 417 | 494 |
| Average | 504 | 207 | 142 | 222 | 145 | 249 |

Table 4.5 shows the distribution of firm size by region and corporate structure/ownership. Stockholm firms have on average twice the number of employees compared to firms in other parts of Sweden. MNEs tend to be larger than other types of firms, but in Stockholm multinational and multi-location uninational firms are not significantly different in size.

Table 4.6 outlines the characteristics of firms regarding key economic variables. Panel A reports the statistics for all firms and Panel B only for the subgroup of innovative firms. First, we see in Panel A that sales per employee are not larger in Stockholm than the average for Sweden. Second, in all five regions we find that multinational firms have higher average sales than other firms. Third, the Stockholm region has a lower profit margin than the average for the rest of Sweden.

The bottom part of Panel A shows that the typical firm in Stockholm is distinguished from the typical firm in other parts of Sweden in several respects; the number of employees is larger, the share of newly established firms is larger, the human capital intensity is about twice as high as in Sweden as a whole, while the capital intensity and global market orientation is considerably lower. In addition, the occurrence of M&A is somewhat more common in Stockholm than in Sweden as a whole.

*Table 4.6 Firm characteristics (mean and standard deviation)*

*Panel A: All firms*

|  | REG 1 | REG 2 | REG 3 | REG 4 | REG 5 | SWE |
|---|---|---|---|---|---|---|
| Sales [a] |  |  |  |  |  |  |
| Non-affiliate | 4.73 | 4.72 | 4.81 | 4.77 | 4.68 | 4.74 |
|  | (1.00) | (0.61) | (0.74) | (0.69) | (0.71) | (077) |
| Uninational | 5.05 | 5.03 | 5.06 | 4.96 | 5.01 | 5.02 |
|  | (1.23) | (0.85) | (0.77) | (0.74) | (0.77) | (0.89) |
| Multinational | 5.33 | 5.18 | 5.32 | 5.38 | 5.27 | 5.30 |
|  | (1.01) | (0.64) | (0.59) | (0.67) | (0.67) | (0.77) |
| Profit margin | 0.05 | 0.06 | 0.07 | 0.05 | 0.06 | 0.06 |
|  | (0.32) | (0.19) | (0.20) | (0.06) | (0.26) | (0.26) |
| Firm size, log | 4.22 | 4.09 | 3.84 | 3.88 | 3.83 | 3.97 |
|  | (1.69) | (1.46) | (1.30) | (1.40) | (1.29) | (1.44) |
| Newly established [b] | 0.10 | 0.05 | 0.06 | 0.06 | 0.04 | 0.07 |
|  | (0.30) | (0.22) | (0.23) | (0.24) | (0.20) | (0.25) |
| M&A [b] | 0.11 | 0.07 | 0.10 | 0.08 | 0.10 | 0.10 |
|  | (0.31) | (0.26) | (0.31) | (0.29) | (0.30) | (0.30) |
| Human capital, share [c] | 0.19 | 0.08 | 0.09 | 0.10 | 0.06 | 0.11 |
|  | (0.21) | (0.13) | (0.13) | (0.16) | (0.10) | (0.16) |
| Physical capital [a] | 2.06 | 2.74 | 2.78 | 2.71 | 3.06 | 2.68 |
|  | (1.68) | (1.67) | (1.61) | (1.64) | (1.47) | (1.64) |
| Global market [b] | 0.25 | 0.31 | 0.32 | 0.33 | 0.26 | 0.29 |
|  | (0.43) | (0.46) | (0.46) | (0.47) | (0.44) | (0.45) |

*Panel B: Innovative firms*

| | REG1 | REG2 | REG3 | REG4 | REG5 | SWE |
|---|---|---|---|---|---|---|
| Firm size, log | 4.45 | 4.51 | 4.20 | 4.33 | 4.19 | 4.33 |
| | (1.74) | (1.50) | (1.37) | (1.55) | (1.42) | (1.55) |
| Physical capital [a] | 1.84 | 2.80 | 2.88 | 2.63 | 3.08 | 2.59 |
| | (1.66) | (1.54) | (1.53) | (1.52) | (1.55) | (1.64) |
| Global market [b] | 0.31 | 0.44 | 0.44 | 0.40 | 0.39 | 0.38 |
| | (0.46) | (0.49) | (0.50) | (0.49) | (0.49) | (0.49) |
| Newly established [b] | 0.09 | 0.05 | 0.07 | 0.09 | 0.03 | 0.06 |
| | (0.28) | (0.21) | (0.26) | (0.28) | (0.17) | (0.25) |
| M&A [b] | 0.14 | 0.10 | 0.12 | 0.12 | 0.14 | 0.13 |
| | (0.35) | (0.30) | (0.32) | (0.33) | (0.35) | (0.33) |
| Human capital, share [c] | 0.20 | 0.10 | 0.11 | 0.12 | 0.07 | 0.12 |
| | (0.21) | (0.14) | (0.15) | (0.17) | (0.12) | (0.17) |
| R&D personnel [c] | 0.09 | 0.07 | 0.07 | 0.07 | 0.04 | 0.07 |
| | (0.18) | (0.14) | (0.20) | (0.16) | (0.09) | (0.15) |
| Process innovation [b] | 0.55 | 0.51 | 0.51 | 0.48 | 0.49 | 0.51 |
| | (0.50) | (0.50) | (0.50) | (0.50) | (0.50) | (0.50) |
| Persistent R&D [b] | 0.48 | 0.53 | 0.50 | 0.47 | 0.48 | 0.49 |
| | (0.50) | (0.50) | (0.50) | (0.50) | (0.50) | (0.50) |
| Innovation input [a] | 1.36 | 1.25 | 1.03 | 1.06 | 1.00 | 1.14 |
| | (1.86) | (1.65) | (1.85) | (1.70) | (1.60) | (1.73) |
| Scientific IS collaboration [b] | 0.19 | 0.29 | 0.19 | 0.25 | 0.23 | 0.23 |
| | (0.39) | (0.45) | (0.39) | (0.43) | (0.42) | (0.42) |
| Vertical IS collaboration [b] | 0.27 | 0.37 | 0.25 | 0.29 | 0.31 | 0.30 |
| | (0.44) | (0.48) | (0.44) | (0.45) | (0.46) | (0.45) |
| Global collaboration on innovation. [b] | 0.25 | 0.30 | 0.22 | 0.23 | 0.20 | 0.24 |
| | (0.43) | (0.46) | (0.42) | (0.42) | (0.40) | (0.43) |
| Patent application [b] | 0.23 | 0.38 | 0.36 | 0.33 | 0.31 | 0.31 |
| | (0.42) | (0.48) | (0.48) | (0.47) | (0.46) | (0.46) |

|                          | REG1   | REG2   | REG3   | REG4   | REG5   | SWE    |
|--------------------------|--------|--------|--------|--------|--------|--------|
| Non-imitation            | 0.39   | 0.36   | 0.31   | 0.39   | 0.35   | 0.37   |
| innovations [b]          | (0.48) | (0.48) | (0.46) | (0.48) | (0.48) | (0.48) |
| Innovation sales [a]     | 2.37   | 1.84   | 2.03   | 2.14   | 1.94   | 2.08   |
|                          | (2.09) | (1.78) | (1.84) | (1.75) | (1.80) | (1.88) |
| Total sales [a]          | 5.12   | 5.01   | 5.08   | 5.02   | 5.07   | 5.07   |
|                          | (1.03) | (0.73) | (0.66) | (0.71) | (0.75) | (0.81) |
| Value added [a]          | 3.96   | 3.93   | 3.98   | 3.95   | 4.01   | 3.97   |
|                          | (0.92) | (0.88) | (0.50) | (0.53) | (0.62) | (0.72) |

*Notes:*
a. In 1000 euros, per employee, log.
b. Share of firms.
c. Share of employees.

Panel B reveals that the average innovative firm in Stockholm is clearly more R&D intensive than the average firm in other Swedish regions. But on average, innovative firms in Stockholm participate less with the Swedish scientific and vertical innovation systems (IS). This is a phenomenon that will be further examined in the econometric analyses, and it partly contradicts the suggestions in the literature that we have reviewed in previous sections. However, there are other aspects of innovation efforts, for which the Stockholm region differs positively from the rest of Sweden, such as (i) a higher human-capital share, (ii) a larger share of R&D personnel, and (iii) a higher R&D intensity.

Innovation output, measured as new product sales per employee, is larger for the typical Stockholm firm. Non-imitation innovations are somewhat more common in Stockholm than in the rest of Sweden. It is notable that the average innovative firm in Stockholm applies for patents less frequently than other firms. The explanation is that Stockholm is a considerably more service-intensive region than other parts of Sweden. In particular, Stockholm has a far higher share of knowledge-intensive services, and such service firms do not apply for patents on a regular basis. In view of this and in order to reduce space, application for a patent as an indicator of R&D productivity is not included in the econometric analysis. Instead, we employ two other innovation output variables and observe that among innovative firms the sales income per employee as well as the value added per employee (labor productivity) is bigger in the Stockholm region compared to other areas.

In this study, the better innovation-output performance by firms in the Stockholm region cannot be attributed to conscious participation by the firms in the regional innovation system. There are a number of reasons for this, one being the prevalence of multinational firms that can utilize a broad base of intra-corporate knowledge In addition, Panel B shows that the difference between Stockholm and the mean for Sweden is small with regard to global sources of knowledge for innovation.

The overall picture of the regional comparison indicates that some local characteristics that attract multinationals to Stockholm, such as the presence of a high-quality labor force, high concentration of R&D, large local markets, good infrastructure, and good administration, also enhance innovation output and productivity of other firms in this region. Thus, a priori we would expect that the econometric analyses suggest that the typical innovative Stockholm firm is more successful with regard to innovation output than the corresponding firm in other parts of Sweden.

## METHODOLOGY

A simple econometric approach is used to determine the relationships among factors affecting firms' innovation activities. Our first task is to examine a firm's probability of being innovative. In this case we apply a probit estimation model. Our second task is to estimate factors that influence a firm's innovation efforts and innovation results, given that the firm is recognized as innovative. For this second purpose we apply a generalized Tobit model (the Heckman two-step estimator), comprising the selection equation in (4.1) and the performance equation in (4.2), using observations on both innovative and other firms. This approach provides consistent and asymptotically efficient estimates for all parameters in the model.

The described two-step estimation procedure is designed to solve the econometric problem of selection bias. Our approach takes into account that not all firms are engaged in innovative activities. Suppose that we examine only the sample of innovative firms in some part of the model, then the firms would not be randomly drawn from the larger population, and selection bias might arise. The two-step model used in the analyses accounts for this possible problem by formulating the following choice structure. In the first step, firms decide whether to engage in innovation activities or not (selection equation). Given that a firm has decided to spend resources on innovation projects, the different performance variables – describing innovation efforts and innovation results – are estimated. More specifically, we are using the following model:

$$y0_i = \begin{cases} 1 & \text{if } y^*0_i = X0_i\,\beta_0 + \varepsilon_{0i} > 0 \\ 0 & \text{if } y^*0_i = X0_i\,\beta_0 + \varepsilon_{0i} \leq 0 \end{cases} \qquad (4.1)$$

$$y1_i = y*1_i = X1_i\beta_1 + \varepsilon1_i \quad \text{if} \quad y*0_i = 1 \tag{4.2}$$

where $y_{1i}^*$ is a latent innovation decision variable measuring the propensity to innovate, $y_{0i}$ is the corresponding observed binary variable being 1 for innovative firms and zero for others. $y_{1i}$ signifies the different dependent variables. $X_{0i}$ and $X_{1i}$ are vectors of various variables explaining innovation decision and innovation performance. The $\beta$-vectors contain the unknown parameters for each equation. $\varepsilon_{0i}$ and $\varepsilon_{1i}$ are independent and identically distributed drawings from a normal distribution with zero mean. In addition, we also estimate the correlation, $\rho$, of the two residuals in equations (4.1) and (4.2). For each estimated selection equation a chi-square test is conducted to decide whether $\rho$ is significantly different from zero. The selection equation is not necessary when there is no correlation.

## RESULTS OF THE ECONOMETRIC ANALYSIS

### The Propensity to be an Innovative Firm

In accordance with the Oslo manual, which contains the guidelines used by the CIS (OECD, 2005), an innovative firm in this chapter is associated with new products, new processes and ongoing innovation efforts. New products, in this context, are new both to the firm and to the market. Our regression results from the probit equation (see Table 4.7) indicate that the propensity to be innovative is positively associated with being located in Stockholm. We also find that multinational firms have a greater likelihood of planning or launching new product and process innovations than other firms. The profitability, expressed as the profit margin, is not a significant determinant of a firm's decision to engage in innovation activities.

In accordance with the Schumpeterian literature (see, for instance, Cohen and Klepper, 1996, Crepon et al., 1998 and Lööf and Heshmati, 2006), Table 4.7 shows that an 'innovative firm', is an increasing function of firm size,[2] capital intensity (physical capital per employee) and human capital (share of the workforce with three years' university education). The incidence of history of a firm in terms of merger or acquisition in a firm's recent history is positively associated with innovativeness. One explanation is that large firms may be 'buying innovation' by acquiring smaller, innovative firms. In addition, when we control for region and corporate structure, the coefficient estimate for newly established firms is negative, but not significant.

*Table 4.7   Probit parameter estimates of determinants of 'innovative firms'* [a]

|  | Coeff. | Std.err. |
|---|---|---|
| *Regions* | | |
| Stockholm | 0.209[**] | 0.094 |
| East Central | 0.073 | 0.098 |
| South | 0.057 | 0.099 |
| West | 0.107 | 0.088 |
| Other Sweden | Ref | |
| *Corporate Structure* | | |
| Non-affiliate | Ref | |
| Uninational | 0.128[*] | 0.069 |
| Multinational | 0.435[***] | 0.089 |
| *Firm Characteristics* | | |
| Profit margin | 0.010 | 0.119 |
| Firm size | 0.166[***] | 0.022 |
| Physical capital per employee, log | 0.064[***] | 0.020 |
| Human capital | 0.931[***] | 0.249 |
| Newly established | 0.036 | 0.120 |
| M&A | 0.356[***] | 0.100 |
| Local market | Ref | |
| National market | 0.464[***] | 0.073 |
| Global market | 0.785[***] | |
| *Sector classification* | | |
| High-technology manufacturing | 0.537[***] | 0.150 |
| High-medium-technology manufacturing | 0.180[*] | 0.096 |
| Low-medium-technology manufacturing | 0.067 | 0.097 |
| Low-technology manufacturing | Ref | |
| Knowledge-intensive service | 0.075 | 0.122 |
| Other services | 0.385[***] | 0.092 |

*Note:*
a. designates firms reporting a product and/or a process innovation and/or reporting ongoing
   innovation activities.
b. Significant at the 1% (***), 5% (**) and (*) 10% level of significance.

Innovativeness is related to the firm's market profile and perspective, which is a classic result (e.g., Fischer and Johansson, 1994). A firm that recognizes the global market as its most important market has a significantly greater likelihood of being engaged in innovative activities compared to a firm selling on a local market. Finally and not surprisingly, high-technology manufacturing firms have a significantly greater propensity to be innovative than other firms.

**Innovation Investment and National Innovation Collaboration**

Tables 4.8 and 4.9 report results for innovative firms, from the second step of the selection equation, or the outcome equation. By using the selection model, we have relaxed the assumption that the factors determining participation in innovation activities and the outcome of innovation effort are identical and of the same sign. In order to reduce space, the coefficient estimates for the selection variables (the first step of the selection equation) are not depicted but they are all in accordance with the results reported in Table 4.7.

Table 4.8, Panel A, Column 1, presents determinants of R&D and other innovation input per employee. All other things being equal, none of the point estimates for regions is significantly different from zero, implying that *per se* the location of the firm does not influence the size of R&D investments for the group of innovative firms.

However, controlling for location, the average domestic MNE invests considerably more in R&D compared to other domestic firms and foreign-owned enterprises. Persistent R&D expenditures are positively and closely associated with the size of innovation investments. This may be interpreted as a learning-by-doing effect in innovation processes and indicates the importance of accumulated R&D investments. The results depicted in Column 1 also confirm previous studies regarding the sign of the firm size variable; innovation investment per employee is a decreasing function of firm size. Finally, process innovations are positively associated with the size of R&D investments.

Columns (2)–(3) in Table 4.8 show a starkly consistent pattern regarding collaboration on innovation with universities and vertical partners: Swedish-owned multinational firms have a significantly greater propensity to collaborate with domestic innovation systems than all other categories of

*Table 4.8*    Innovation investment and collaboration on innovation

| Equation | (1) | | (2) | | (3) | | (4) | |
|---|---|---|---|---|---|---|---|---|
| | R&D and other innovation input per employee, log | | Collaboration on innovation within scientific IS | | Collaboration on innovation within vertical IS | | Global collaboration on innovation | |
| | Coeff | Std.err | Coeff | Std.err | Coeff | Std.err | Coeff | Std.err |
| *Regions* | | | | | | | | |
| Stockholm | 0.126 | 0.142 | −0.474 *** | 0.154 | −0.335 ** | 0.142 | 0.000 | 0.137 |
| East Central | 0.208 | 0.153 | 0.079 | 0.149 | 0.127 | 0.144 | 0.174 | 0.140 |
| South | −0.022 | 0.155 | −0.309 * | 0.168 | −0.298 * | 0.156 | −0.108 | 0.152 |
| West | 0.033 | 0.141 | −0.046 | 0.144 | −0.168 | 0.139 | −0.036 | 0.137 |
| Other Sweden | Ref | | Ref | | Ref | | Ref | |
| *Corporate Structure* | | | | | | | | |
| Uninational | Ref | | Ref | | Ref | | Ref | |
| Multinational D | 0.842 *** | 0.235 | 0.983 *** | 0.221 | 1.338 *** | 0.230 | 1.198 *** | 0.225 |
| Multinational F | 0.175 | 0.128 | 0.170 | 0.130 | 0.254 ** | 0.123 | 0.421 *** | 0.125 |
| Non-affiliate | −0.014 | 0.115 | 0.265 ** | 0.125 | 0.253 ** | 0.117 | 0.326 *** | 0.117 |
| *Knowledge* | | | | | | | | |
| R&D investment | − | − | 0.136 *** | 0.038 | 0.104 *** | 0.094 | 0.170 *** | 0.036 |
| Persistent R&D | 1.220 *** | 0.109 | 0.710 *** | 0.139 | 0.732 *** | 0.103 | 0.624 *** | 0.127 |
| *Characteristics* | | | | | | | | |
| Firm size | 0.412 *** | 0.039 | 0.204 *** | 0.055 | 0.115 *** | 0.032 | 0.149 *** | 0.034 |
| Newly established | −0.097 | 0.215 | −0.252 | 0.224 | 0.060 | 0.193 | 0.173 | 0.195 |
| M&A | −0.274 * | 0.163 | −0.325 ** | 0.153 | 0.024 | 0.145 | −0.104 | 0.143 |
| Process innovation | 0.222 ** | 0.095 | 0.201 * | 0.098 | 0.230 ** | 0.094 | 0.057 | 0.090 |
| Selection equation | Included | | Included | | Included | | Included | |

*Notes:*

a. Outcome equation. Number of observations: 1,907 of which 972 uncensored observations.

b. The following selection variables are included in equations (4.1)–(4.4): Firm size, Sales, Newly established, M&A, Physical capital, Human capital, Market orientation and six sector dummies.

c. Significant at the 1% (***), 5% (**) and (*) 10% level of significance. Six sector dummies are included: High-technology manufacturing (HI-M), high-medium-technology manufacturing (HM-M), low-medium-technology manufacturing (LM-M), low-technology manufacturing (LO-M), knowledge-intensive services (KI-S) and other services (O-S).

*Table 4.9 Innovation investment and collaboration on innovation*

| Equation | (5) Non-imitation innovations | | (6) New product sales/ employee | | (7) Total sales/ employee | | (8) Value added/ employee | |
|---|---|---|---|---|---|---|---|---|
| | Coeff | Std err | Coeff | Std err | Coeff | Std err | Coeff | Std err |
| *Regions* | | | | | | | | |
| Stockholm | 0.146 | 0.131 | 0.390 *** | 0.163 | 0.296 *** | 0.080 | 0.135** | 0.054 |
| East Central | 0.023 | 0.139 | −0.242 | 0.173 | 0.027 | 0.086 | −0.004 | 0.057 |
| South | −0.123 | 0.144 | 0.009 | 0.173 | 0.040 | 0.087 | −0.041 | 0.058 |
| West | 0.128 | 0.129 | 0.160 | 0.159 | 0.020 | 0.080 | −0.020 | 0.053 |
| Other Sweden | Ref | | Ref | | Ref | | Ref | |
| *Corporate Structure* | | | | | | | | |
| Uninational | Ref | | Ref | | Ref | | Ref | |
| Multinational D | 0.609 *** | 0.210 | 0.688 ** | 0.290 | −0.053 | 0.136 | −0.031 | 0.093 |
| Multinational F | 0.210 * | 0.118 | 0.520 *** | 0.150 | 0.101 | 0.072 | −0.015 | 0.049 |
| Non Affiliate | 0.389 *** | 0.106 | 0.232 * | 0.130 | −0.137 ** | 0.064 | −0.084 ** | 0.043 |
| *Knowledge* | | | | | | | | |
| R&D invest | 0.031 | 0.030 | 0.131 *** | 0.036 | 0.069 *** | 0.014 | 0.031 ** | 0.012 |
| Persistent R&D | 0.440 *** | 0.110 | 0.273* | 0.139 | −0.065 | 0.065 | 0.018 | 0.044 |
| Science IS | 0.333 ** | 0.133 | 0.009 | 0.172 | 0.115 * | 0.069 | 0.059 | 0.058 |
| Vertical IS | 0.136 | 0.123 | 0.167 | 0.157 | −0.089 | 0.065 | −0.108 | 0.054 |
| Global collaboration | 0.048 | 0.132 | 0.217 | 0.169 | 0.112* | 0.067 | 0.076 | 0.057 |
| *Characteristics* | | | | | | | | |
| Firm size | −0.103 ** | 0.041 | −0.406 *** | 0.055 | −0.043 * | 0.023 | −0.109 *** | 0.017 |
| Physical capital | −0.029 | 0.032 | −0.119 *** | 0.046 | 0.129 *** | 0.016 | 0.161 *** | 0.016 |
| Newly established | 0.181 | 0.174 | −0.272 | 0.271 | −0.309 *** | 0.116 | −0.280 *** | 0.095 |
| M&A | −0.020 | 0.138 | 0.063 | 0.209 | 0.033 | 0.089 | −0.279 *** | 0.072 |
| Process innovation | 0.216 ** | 0.087 | −0.051 | 0.102 | 0.028 | 0.053 | 0.055 | 0.035 |
| Selection equation | Included | | Included | | Included | | Included | |

*Notes:*
a.  Outcome equation. Number of observations: 1,907 of which 972 uncensored observations.
b.  The following selection variables are included in equations (5)–(6): Firm size, Sales, Newly established, M&A, Physical capital, Human capital, Market orientation and six sector dummies. In equations (7) and (8) all these variables are included except sales.
c.  Significant at the <1% (***), <5%(**) and (*) <10% level of significance. Six sector dummies are included: High-technology manufacturing (HI-M), high-medium-technology manufacturing (HM-M), low-medium-technology manufacturing (LM-M), low-technology manufacturing (LO-M), knowledge-intensive services (KI-S) and other services (O-S). (a) Reference is local market.

firms in Sweden. There is also a significant and positive correlation between collaboration propensity and non-affiliate firms. Moreover, foreign-owned firms and are more embedded in the vertical innovation system compared to the reference group (uninational firms).

At the same time, there is also a regional factor, such that firms – in general – that are located in Stockholm have a lower propensity to utilize domestic innovation systems, compared to (nearly) identical firms in other Swedish regions. As expressed before, this is surprising given the wealth of literature on the importance of innovation systems in vibrant metropolitan regions. Either these metropolitan firms are utilizing internal resources (at home and abroad) or they are enjoying the benefits of the metropolitan milieu in a typically Marshallian fashion; where pure spillover effects generate agglomeration externalities that 'are, as if it were, in the air' (Marshall, 1920). Collaboration on innovation is an increasing function of both current and persistent R&D investments as well as firm size.

Column 4 reports that no regional differences can be found with regard to the utilization of global sources of information for innovation. Looking at the corporate structure variables, we see that multinational firms and non-affiliate firms are significantly more globally oriented in their innovation process compared to uninational firms. In this context we observe that the domestic MNEs, which are more embedded in the regional and national innovation systems than other firms, share knowledge with international partners to a larger extent than all other categories of firms. Global collaboration on innovation is a positive function of R&D intensity, persistent R&D investments and firm size.

**Innovation Output and Productivity**

As described in Table 4.9, Column 5, none of the regional variables is significant when non-imitation innovations (products new to the market) are considered. In a sense this indicates that possible influences from the regional milieu are already taken into account by other determinants in the model. However, there is a corporate structure effect, reflected by a highly significant and positive point estimate for domestic multinationals and non-affiliate firms. There is also a path-dependence effect, such that enterprises reporting that they are engaged in R&D on a regular basis have a larger propensity to launch non-imitation innovations than other firms. The estimated relationship between non-imitation innovation and collaboration with the scientific innovation system is positive and significant. Evidence is also given that non-imitation innovation is a decreasing function of firm size. Process innovation is positively associated with non-imitation innovations.

Column 6 describes the relationship between the log value of new product sales per employee and its determinants. Interestingly, there is a strong relationship between company location and this form of innovation productivity. The estimate for Stockholm is highly significant and quite sizable, 0.4. This means that, all other things being equal (such as firm size, industry classification, corporate owner structure and R&D investment), a firm's research productivity is superior if it is located in Stockholm rather than in other regions. In other words, the return to R&D investment in terms of new product sales is evidently greatest for firms in the Stockholm region.

In accordance with the innovation literature, the point estimate for R&D and other innovation investments is closely associated with innovation output, and the order of magnitude, 0.13, is within the range of results reported from most other studies. There is also a corporate structure effect, such that the income from innovations is larger for multinational firms than for other firms. Somewhat unexpectedly, the three embeddedness variables are not significantly associated with innovation sales per employee, everything else being equal.

Columns 7 and 8 report productivity estimates and distinguish between total sales per employee (gross productivity) and value added per employee (labor productivity proper). Both measures describe a significant regional effect: the average innovative firm in Stockholm has larger or higher sales and value added per employee compared to a corresponding firm in other Swedish regions. Hence, the advantage of being located within Sweden's most significant concentration of R&D spending, universities, human capital and MNEs with their global networks is reflected in a superior economic performance, controlling for factors such as firm size, human capital, physical capital, R&D intensity, market orientation and sector classification. Note also that we control for R&D intensity.

No significant difference in gross or net productivity can be established between foreign multinationals, domestic multinationals and uninational firms. However, non-affiliated firms have significantly lower productivity than other firms. R&D investment and the firm's capital stock are closely associated with the sales and value-added performance. The point estimates for new establishments (both sales and value added) and M&As (only value added) are both negative and highly significant. Finally, according to existing literature we should expect the variable firm size to be insignificant (e.g., Klette and Kortum, 2004). However, our parameter estimate is negative and significant. One possible explanation for our conflicting result is the inclusion of region and corporate structure in the analysis. The regression also indicates a negative relationship between productivity and M&A, and for this result we can suggest no clear explanation. The literature on this topic is mixed, showing both positive and negative effects.

# SUMMARY DISCUSSION

This study analyzes how corporate ownership and structure and location influence innovation activities among firms in Swedish regions. It attempts to illuminate some of the many complex relationships within and between firms and their interface with innovation systems (other firms, universities, public actors, etc.). Essentially the Stockholm region is being compared with the rest of Sweden. Thus the study examines how the functional metropolitan region Stockholm differs from the rest of Sweden. This comparison seems relevant in that none of the other four macro regions contains any city region comparable with the Stockholm region.

The dataset contains extensive information on the characteristics of firms with 10 or more employees. The survey-based dataset has been merged with register data derived from annual accounts. With this background, we ask the following question: how does (i) corporate structure and (ii) location affect innovation efforts and innovation results? Among innovation efforts we focus on innovativeness, R&D intensity and interaction in innovation systems. The innovation results that are highlighted comprise innovation sales, total sales per employee and value added per employee.

A major observation is that the Stockholm region satisfies widely accepted criteria regarding what characterizes a functional urban region (Cheshire and Gordon, 1995). In particular, a functional region is integrated in such a way that frequent face-to-face contacts are possible, which facilitates knowledge flows that can stimulate innovation activities and knowledge interaction. The other four 'regional areas' are not functional in the above sense. These macro regions East, North, South and West have the following features: (i) South includes the functional urban region Malmo, which is a small metropolitan region, (ii) West includes the functional urban region Gothenburg (Göteborg), which is about half the size of the Stockholm region, and none of the other macro regions contain any large functional urban region.

In terms of innovativeness, we can observe that Stockholm is different from each of the four macro regions. At the same time we can observe that there is no significant difference between East, North, South and West. Thus, the fact that West is dominated by the functional metropolitan region Gothenburg does not make West different from East and North. The same conclusion applies when comparing South with East and North.

An issue for further research is to investigate what the result would be if Stockholm was compared to another but somewhat smaller functional region such as Gothenburg. The most recent wave of CIS (CIS 4 which was conducted in Sweden in 2005) also allows us to detect metropolitan effects outside Stockholm. The Stockholm region is the only true metropolitan region in Sweden. Gothenburg, in region West, is about half the size of the Stockholm region.

If we could separate Gothenburg from the rest of region West, there might be a Gothenburg effect, and that would be compatible with the conclusions of the chapter. Assume instead that we cannot find any strong Gothenburg effect. Then this would tell us that the metropolitan effect is present only for a larger metropolitan region, in which the innovation milieu is rich enough to bring about the higher probability of finding an innovative firm. Hence in either case this chapter has demonstrated an innovativeness effect in large metropolitan regions. There might be a metropolitan effect in Gothenburg and Malmo  or such an effect may not be present because of their smaller size. In either case our conclusions about the Stockholm metropolitan region will remain valid.

The analysis starts with a probit model to examine innovativeness. The regression results show that the likelihood of being an innovative firm is higher when the firm is located in the Stockholm region, and when controlling for Schumpeterian variables such as corporate structure, human capital, firm size, and high-technology classification. From the same regression we can also conclude that multinational firms have a larger probability of being innovative, when we control for location and the other Schumpeterian variables. Thus, the results are in concordance with previous findings, while adding the influence from location and corporate structure.

Given these results, we then examined the subgroup of innovative firms across the five regional areas using the Heckman selection model (Heckman, 1979), which allowed us to use the same type of variables in the selection equation and in the performance equations, relaxing the strict association between a variable's influence on a firm's innovativeness and R&D intensity, for example. We found that a firm's location in the Stockholm region has no positive effect on (i) its R&D intensity or (ii) its participation in innovation systems. This means that the location is associated with innovation efforts by increasing the probability of being engaged in innovation activities, but it does not increase the intensity of these efforts. How can this be interpreted? One may conjecture that Stockholm offers greater opportunities to internalize R&D efforts, because of the region's greater knowledge intensity, and its greater functional integration because of proximity effects are more concentrated there. It may also be that the innovation milieu in Stockholm allows for informal knowledge spillovers that are not captured in the CIS survey.

The result with regard to location influences is contrasted with the effects from corporate structure. Multinational firms are not only more likely to be innovative, but they also have a significantly higher R&D intensity and they are more likely to participate in local innovation systems. Thus, corporate structure affects innovation efforts in all the dimensions we have examined.

With the above observations, are there any other positive consequences for R&D-intense firms of being located in the Stockholm region? Does the location affect the innovation results? The answer to both these questions is yes. We have three equations with a positive and significant regional dummy for the Stockholm region only. In the first of these the dependent variable is new product sales, in the second, it is total sales per employee, and in the third it is value added per employee. In contradistinction to these findings, we can conclude that corporate structure does not reveal any effect on innovation results.

Hence, the returns to innovation efforts are positively influenced by the Stockholm location. Combining this with our previous findings about formal R&D collaboration, this suggests the presence of pure (knowledge) spillovers in the Stockholm region. In addition, there is a positive Stockholm impact on sales per employee and value added per employee. The first impact allows Stockholm firms to afford higher floor-space cost, which in itself reflect positive agglomeration effects. The second impact allows Stockholm firms to pay higher labor costs, and these are partly related to the high knowledge intensity of employees in Stockholm firms.

Thus, the Stockholm region provides a milieu that stimulates innovativeness in a more pronounced way than in the rest of Sweden, as well as in each of the regions: South, West, East and North. South and West each include a smaller metropolitan region. There might be a metropolitan effect in Malmo and Gothenburg or such an effect may not be present because of their smaller size. In either case our conclusions about the Stockholm metropolitan region will remain valid.

## NOTES

1.  Slaughter and Leslie (1997) provide a comprehensive overview of this phenomenon.
2.  Recent research in organization theory suggests that the higher innovativeness of large firms isoften associated with conservative selection of certain approaches to decision making and risky options. See, for instance, Snull (1999) and Woodman (1999).

## REFERENCES

Acs, Z.J. (ed.) (1994), *Regional Innovation, Knowledge and Global Change*, London: Frances Pinter.

Almeida, P. (1996), 'Knowledge sourcing by foreign multinationals: Patent citation analysis on the semiconductor industry', *Strategic Management Journal*, **17**, 155–65.

Andersson, M. and O. Ejermo (2004), 'How does Accessibility to Knowledge Sources Affect the Innovativeness of Corporations? Evidence from Sweden', CESIS Electronic Working Paper Series, No 3.

Anderstig, C. and C. Karlsson (1989), 'Spatial Diffusion of Information Technology in Sweden', in A.E. Andersson, D.F. Batten and C. Karlsson (eds), *Knowledge and Industrial Organization*, Berlin: Springer-Verlag, 157–76.

Artle, R. (1959), 'The Structure of the Stockholm Economy – Toward a Framework for Projecting Metropolitan Community Development', Business Research Institute of the Stockholm School of Economics.

Batten, D.F., K. Kobayashi and Å.E. Andersson (1989), 'Knowledge, Nodes and Networks: An Analytical Perspective', in A.E. Andersson, D.F. Batten and C. Karlsson (1989) (eds), *Knowledge and Industrial Organization*, Berlin: Springer-Verlag, 31–46.

Bellman, L. and R. Jungnickel (2002), '(Why) do Foreign-owned Firms in Germany Achieve Above-Productivity?', in R. Jungnickel (ed.), *Foreign-owned Firms – are They Different?*, London: Palgrave Macmillan.

Bottazzi, L. and G. Peri (2003), 'Innovation and spillovers in regions: Evidence from European patent data', *European Economic Review*, **47**, 687–710.

Cantwell, J. (1998), 'The Globalisation of Technology: what Remains of the Product-Cycle Model?', in A. Chandler, P. Hagström, and Ö. Sölvell (eds), *The Dynamic Firm*, New York: Oxford University Press, 263–88.

Cantwell, J. and O. Janne (1999), 'Technological globalisation and innovative centres: the role of corporate technological leadership and location hierarchy', *Research Policy*, **28**, 119–144.

Cheshire, P.C. and I.R. Gordon (1995), 'Territorial competition and the predictability of collective (in)action', *International Journal of Urban and Regional Research*, **20**, 383–99.

Cockburn, I. and R. Henderson (1996), 'Scale, Scope and Spillovers: The Determinants of Research Productivity on Drug Discovery', *Rand Journal of Economics*, Spring, **27** (1), 32-59.

Cohen, M. and S. Klepper (1996), 'A reprise of size and R&D', *Economic Journal*, **106**, 925–51.

Cox, H., S. Mowatt and M. Prevezar (2003), 'New Product Development and Product Supply within a Network Setting: The Chilled Ready-Meal Industry in the UK', *Industry and Innovation*, **10**, 197–217.

Crepon, B., E. Duguet and J. Mairesse (1998), 'Research, Innovation and Productivity: An Econometric Analysis at the Firm Level', *Economics of Innovation and New Technology*, **7**, 115–58.

Criscuolo, C. and R. Martin (2004), 'Multinationals and US productivity leadership: Evidence from Great Britain', STI working paper 2004/5.

Criscuolo, P., R. Narula and B. Verspagen (2002), 'The relative importance of home and host innovation systems in the internationalisation of MNE R&D: a patent citation analysis', Ecis working paper series 02.12.

Doms, M.E. and J. Brandford Jensen (1998), 'Comparing Wages, Skills, and Productivity between Domestically and Foreign-Owned Manufacturing Establishments in the United States', in R.E. Baldwin, E. Lipsey and J.D. Richardson (eds), *Geography and Ownership as Bases for Economic Accounting, Studies in Income and Wealth*, **59**, Chicago: University of Chicago Press, 235–58.

Dunning, J.H. (1993), 'Multinational Enterprises and the Global Economy', Wokingham: Addison-Wesley.

Eaton, J. and S. Kortum (1999), 'International technology diffusion: Theory and Measurement', *International Economic Review*, **40** (3), 537–70.

Ebersberger, B., B. Johansson and H. Lööf (2007), 'Does Ownership Matter? The Impact of Foreign Takeovers on Innovation and Productivity Performance', in A. Heshmati, Y.B. Sohn and Y.R. Kim (eds), *Commercialization and Transfer of Technology: Major Country Case Studies*, 157–77, Hauppauge, NY: Nova Science.

Ebersberger, B. and H. Lööf (2005) 'Multinational Enterprises, Spillover, Innovation and Productivity', *International Journal of Management Research*, December.

Feldman, M.P. and D.B. Audretsch (1999), 'Innovation in Cities: Science-Based Diversity, Specialisation and Localised Competition', *European Economic Review*, **43**, 409–29.

Fischer, M.M. and B. Johansson (1994), 'Networks for Process Innovation by Firms: Conjectures from Observations in Three Countries', in B. Johansson, C. Karlsson and L. Westin (eds), *Patterns of a Network Economy*, Berlin: Springer-Verlag, 261–74.

Fors, G. and R. Svensson (2002), 'R&D and Foreign Sales in Swedish Multinationals: a Simultaneous Relationship', *Research Policy*, **31**, 95–107.

Fujita, M. and J.F. Thisse (2002), *Economics of Agglomeration: Cities, Industrial Location and Regional Growth*, Cambridge: Cambridge University Press.

Glaeser, E. (1999), 'Learning in Cities', *Journal of Urban Economics*, **46**, 254–77.

Harhoff, D. (1999), 'Firm Formation and Regional Spillovers', *The Economics of Innovation and New Technology*, **8**, 27–55.

Heckman, J.J. (1979), 'Sample Selection Bias as a Specification Error', *Econometrica*, **47**, 153–62.

Jacobs, J. (1969), 'The Economy of Cities', New York: Vintage.

Jaffe, A., M. Trajtenberg and R. Hendersson (1993), 'Geographical localization of knowledge spillovers as evidence by patent citations', *Quarterly Journal of Economics*, **108**, 577–99.

Johansson, B., J. Klaesson and M. Olsson (2002), 'Time Distances and Labor Market Integration', *Papers on Regional Science*, **81**, 305–27.

Karlsson, C. and B. Johansson (2004), 'Towards a Dynamic Theory for the Spatial Knowledge Economy', CESIS Electronic Working Paper Series, No. 20.

Kleinknecht, A. and P. Mohnen (2002), *Innovation and Firm Performance – Econometric Explorations of Survey Data*, Basingstoke: Palgrave.

Klette, T.J. and S. Kortum (2004), 'Innovating Firms and Aggregate Innovation', *Journal of Political Economy*, **112** (5), 986–1018.

Kuemmerle, W. (1999), 'Foreign direct investment in industrial research in the pharmaceutical and electronic industries – results from a survey of multinational firms', *Research Policy*, **28** (2–3), 179–93.

Lööf, H. (2005), 'Den växande utlandskontrollen av ekonomierna i Norden. Effekter på FoU, innovation and produktivitet', ITPS A2005:005, Stockholm.

Lööf, H. and A. Heshmati (2006), 'On the Relationship Between Innovation and Performance: A Sensitivity Analysis', *Economics of Innovation and New Technology*, **15** (4–5), 317–45.

Marshall, A. (1920), *Principles of Economics*, 8th edition, London: Macmillan.

OECD (2005), *Oslo Manual: Guidelines for Collecting and Interpreting Innovation Data*, 3rd Edition, Paris: OECD.

Pfaffermayr, M. and C. Bellak (2002), 'Why Foreign-owned firms are Different: A Conceptual Framework and Empirical Evidence for Austria', in R. Jungnickel (ed.), *Foreign-owned Firms – are They Different?*, London: Palgrave MacMillan.

Slaughter, S. and L.L. Slaughter (1997), *Academic Capitalism: Politics, Policies, and the Entrepreneurial University*, Baltimore, MD: The John Hopkins University Press.

Snull, D.N. (1999), 'Why good companies go bad', *Harvard Business Review*, 77 (4), 42–52.

Sonn, J.W. and M. Stolper (2003), 'The Increasing Importance of Geographical Proximity in Technological Innovation, An Analysis of U.S. Patent Citations, 1975–1997', Paper presented at the conference: 'What do we know about Innovation?', in Honour of Keith Pavitt, Sussex, 13–15 November, 2003.

Vernon, R. (1962), *Metropolis 1985*, Cambridge, MA.: Harvard University Press.

Verspagen, B., and W. Schoenmakers (2004), 'The spatial dimension of patenting by multinational firms in Europe', *Journal of Economic Geography* , 4, 23–42.

Woodman, L.A. (1999), 'The phenomenon of lock-in in business in light of complexity theory', unpublished doctoral dissertation, The Union Institute.

Zander, I. (1994), 'The Tortoise Evolution of the Multinational Corporation-Foreign Technological Activity in Swedish Multinational Firms 1890–1990', PhD-dissertation, Institute of International Business, Stockholm.

# 5. Firm Size, Firm Maturity and Product and Process R&D in Swedish Manufacturing Firms

**Kristina Nyström**

## INTRODUCTION

Innovations and new firm formation are both regarded as important factors for economic growth since they are strongly associated with the structural adjustment process and the introduction of new production techniques and new products. Therefore many researchers have been interested in how new firm formation and innovations are interrelated. This question has been debated from a theoretical perspective. The outcome of this discussion is two major seemingly contradictory models or approaches. One is a barrier to entry approach, as suggested by early theoretical contributors such as Bain (1956) and Yip (1982). According to this approach, innovations constitute a barrier to entry and imply that most innovations are made in incumbent firms. Empirical evidence and alternative theoretical models as suggested by, for example, Acs and Audretsch (1989) and Geroski (1999), conclude that innovation can be an important way for new firms to compete with already incumbent firms.

There are of course several ways for a firm to try to create innovations. One is to invest in research and development (R&D) activities,[1] which the firm expects to result in innovations. This chapter will focus on Swedish manufacturing firms' efforts to create innovations by investing in R&D.

The two theoretical explanations, mentioned above, regarding the interrelationship between new firm formation and innovation give a somewhat confusing picture that indeed corresponds to the mixed empirical evidence that is currently available. In their review article of empirical studies on entry and exit studies, Siegfried and Evans (1994, p. 142) even state: Overall, the empirical evidence about the role of research and development intensity is either encouraging or impeding entry is confusing, perhaps even chaotic. This chapter will explicitly study the relationship between firm age and the probability of investing in R&D activities.

The question of R&D in large and small firms is related to the question of firm maturity and R&D. In the literature, both advantages and disadvantages for large firms in performing R&D activities have been discussed. Large firms might have advantages in raising capital to finance their R&D investments, whereas small firms might have more incentives to try to innovate in order to gain a competitive advantage. All these issues will be discussed more thoroughly in the next section. However, a particularly interesting issue is to look at process and product innovation efforts separately. Product innovation can be defined as 'the generation, introduction and diffusion of a new product (with the production process being unchanged' (Stoneman, 1995, p. 3) and process innovation is defined as 'the generation, introduction and diffusion of a new production process (with the products remaining unchanged)' (ibid. p. 3). Distinguishing between product and process R&D, we shall also analyze the relation between it and firm size and age. The empirical part of this chapter will analyze the probability of doing process R&D in Swedish manufacturing firms. Which firms conduct product and process R&D? Large or small firms? Old and mature firms or recent entrants? Do the firms choose to perform either process R&D or product R&D or do they choose to combine them?

The chapter is organized as follows: first, it presents the theoretical arguments regarding the relationship between firm size and age on the one hand and product and process R&D on the other. Earlier empirical findings regarding this issue are also presented. The sources of data and the multinomial logit model that will be used in the empirical analysis are then described, and empirical results are presented. Finally, conclusions and suggestions for future research are presented.

## R&D AND FIRM DEMOGRAPHY

The issue of which firms are more innovative than others has been discussed in a number of articles during recent years. Much of the literature does not explicitly distinguish between process and product innovation but rather discusses innovation more generally. The incentives, advantages and disadvantages connected to the firm characteristics when it comes to performing process and product R&D are in many cases similar. Therefore our discussion will also initially take a more general approach but eventually be more explicitly focused on process and product R&D.

## R&D and Firm Size

The discussion about the role of innovation usually takes its starting-point in the writings of Joseph Schumpeter (1934, 1942). In Schumpeter (1934), industry dynamics are described as a process of 'creative destruction' where most new firms are created by 'new men'. In Schumpeter (1942), this process is instead described as 'creative accumulation' and in this description of how innovations are created, large established firms play an important role because they are able to accumulate knowledge (e.g., R&D and product and process knowledge) and financial resources. Cohen and Levin (1989) and Mansfield (1963) among others summarize a number of arguments regarding advantages for small and large firms in the innovation process. Explanations why large firms should perform a larger share of innovations include the following:

- Capital market imperfections: It is easier for large firms to finance risky R&D projects. One reason for this large-firm advantage is that many large firms have well-established contacts with banks and other instiutions that can provide financing. It is also plausible that large firms have larger and more stable internal funds available for financing these projects and they are therefore less dependent on external capital. Large firms can in this way afford large and expensive R&D projects (Hoshi et al., 1991). An additional explanation why large firms allocate more resources to inventions and R&D is, according to Arrow (1962), that R&D investments are very risky projects. A large firm can, in such situations, act as its own insurance company by investing in several small-scale R&D and invention activities and therefore reduce the risk.
- Innovation and industry competition: An additional issue regarding the incentives to innovate is that such incentives are larger in more competitive industries than in monopolistic environments. This issue has been debated by, among others, Arrow (1962) and Demsetz (1969). Arrow concluded that there are fewer incentives to innovate in monopolistic conditions than in a competitive environment. Demsetz stated that the theoretical analysis in the paper by Arrow suffered from some fallacies and instead concluded that the incentives to innovate are the reverse. If Demsetz's conclusions are correct, one would expect fewer incentives to innovate for firms that operate in competitive industries compared to firms in a monopolistic environment. Hence, if one assumes that monopolistic industries consist of fewer and larger firms, one would expect large firms to be more innovative. With regard to this it is appropriate to mention that most empirical studies in this field report a positive relationship between market concentration and R&D (Cohen, 1995). Empirical evidence

presented by Pavitt et al. (1987) and Acs and Audretsch (1987), for example, suggests that large firms are more innovative in concentrated industries with high entry barriers and small firms are innovative in less-concentrated industries that are less mature. When discussing the relationship between R&D and industry concentration one must mention that there is also the issue of causality. Sutton (1998) thinks that the discussion of how technological competition shapes the size distribution of firms might have been emphasized too much. He does not find any significant differences regarding size inequality in industries where R&D has an important role compared with a group of control industries where R&D does not play any important role. Since it is possible that industry concentration also influences innovative behavior, one could expect that there is a mutual relationship between these variables.

- Economies of scale: The returns from R&D are larger if output is large, since in the large firm the fixed cost of innovation can be spread over a larger output. This is especially true for process innovations (Cohen, 1995; Cohen and Klepper, 1996). An implication of this advantage for large firms would be that R&D increases more than proportionally with firm size.
- Economies of scope: Because of complementarities between R&D and other activities in the firm that might be more developed in large firms, R&D tends to be more productive in large firms. Cohen (1995) mentions that there might be complementarities between non-manufacturing activities such as marketing and the production of innovation. For the present discussion of process and product R&D, the presence of economies of scope means that there might be advantages in performing product and process R&D simultaneously. This raises the question about how product and process R&D are related to each other. If there are complementarities between product and process R&D, a firm that chooses to conduct such R&D can expect the marginal profitability of the complementing innovation activity to increase (Milgrom and Roberts, 1990).
- Access to knowledge networks and research cooperation: Through their larger number of employees, large firms can be expected to have access to a larger number of knowledge sources. It is therefore probable that new information about product and process R&D in the industry can more easily be accessed by large firms. Larger firms can also be expected to be involved in research cooperation activities more frequently than smaller firms (Karlsson, 1988).
- Management advantages: A large firm is more able to respond to new technology in terms of better access to managerial skills (Mansfield, 1971). Even if the managerial skills necessary to implement a new product

or process innovations are not available in the firm, the large firm is better to obtain these skills through the acquisition of specialized services.

According to the discussion above, the advantages of being a large firm seem to be quite convincing, but the literature also provides some explanations for why large firms have some disadvantages in producing innovation, that is, there are advantages for small firms. The following arguments have been put forward:

- Loss of managerial control: As firms grow large, they tend to lose managerial control of the activities in the firm and therefore they might lose efficiency in R&D activities (Cohen and Levin, 1989).
- Weaker R&D incentives for researchers: The incentives for researchers and entrepreneurs to be innovative diminish since individual benefits from their R&D efforts usually decrease with firm size. Researchers employed in most large companies have fewer opportunities for patenting or benefiting in other ways from their achievements (ibid, 1989).
- Cooperation opportunities: One possibility for small firms to overcome their size disadvantages regarding R&D is to establish cooperation with other firms that have similar interests and complementary assets. Cooperation can result in various types of contracts between the firms, such as a joint venture.

Incentives to invest in R&D in large and small firms have been empirically investigated in several studies. Before the empirical findings regarding R&D and firm size are presented, it is important to note that there are some difficulties in measuring R&D in small firms. Many small firms do not have a formal R&D function, that is, a unit that explicitly works with product and process development, but considerable R&D can still be performed outside a formal R&D function. This means that there might be some problems with capturing all R&D expenditures, especially in small firms (ibid, 1989).

The empirical evidence on the relationship between firm size and R&D has to some extent shifted over the years. From the mid-1960s to the mid-1980s, most studies found that R&D intensity (R&D as a ratio of sales) was increasing with firm size. Many studies also found that R&D increased more than proportionately with firm size (Cohen, 1995). Studies performed after the mid-1980s show a somewhat different pattern. A U-shaped form for the relationship between R&D intensity and size was found, indicating that initially R&D intensity decreases but then again starts to increase with size (Cohen and Levin, 1989). In his review article on the empirical evidence of studies of innovative activity, Cohen (1995) on the other hand concludes that there is a monotonic relationship between R&D and firm size.

Acs and Audretsch (1990) try to overcome the empirical difficulties of measuring R&D in small firms, mentioned above, and find that small firms make substantial contributions to technological change if one takes informal R&D activities into consideration. Audretsch et al. (2002) state that small firms use external sources as a source of knowledge input. More specifically, Audretsch and Feldman (1996) show that spillovers from universities are more important to small firms than to large firms. Johansson et al. (2005) discuss the importance of the corporate structure for innovative behavior and conclude that multinationals have a much higher R&D intensity than other firms.

Fritsch and Meschede (2001) investigate the relationship between product R&D, process R&D and firm size. They find that R&D expenditure rises less than proportionately to size for both product and process R&D expenditures, but the size effect is somewhat more apparent regarding process R&D. Mansfield (1981), Link (1982), Scherer (1991) and Cohen and Klepper (1996) argue that firm size influences the composition of R&D. Mansfield (1981) found that product and process development increases less than proportionately with firm size. The choice between product and process innovation varies substantially between industries. If we summarize the empirical evidence presented, we can expect a positive relationship between R&D and firm size but it is possible that this relationship has a non-linear pattern.

A particularly interesting issue is the possible existence of complementarities between product and process innovations. Miravete and Pernias (2006) study the Spanish ceramic tiles industry and find that there are significant complementarities between process and product innovation. The data in their study are based on interviews with firm managers stating whether the firm are involved in process and product innovations. In their sample, 50 percent of the firms do not innovate at all and 30 percent either product innovation or process innovation, whereas 20 percent conduct both. They also find that firms that conduct both process and product innovation are smaller than the firms that choose not to innovate, and that older firms invest more in cost-reducing innovations. Process innovations are more profitable for multi-product firms. Comparing the returns of process and product innovations they find that there are high returns on product innovations for multi-product firms, but also smaller firms obtain larger returns on product innovations (ibid.).

## R&D and Firm Age

The discussion about the relationship between firm size and investments in R&D can be connected more explicitly with theories of new firm formation. Investment in R&D can, according to different theoretical views, have a dual role for the entry of firms since it can both stimulate and discourage entry. Below, the advantages and disadvantages of being an old versus being a new or young firm when deciding to conduct R&D activities, will be discussed:

- R&D investments as a barrier to entry: The traditional entry-barrier literature represented by, among others, Bain (1956), Orr (1974) and Yip (1982), suggests that innovations, along with, for example, high capital intensity, advertising and scale economies, will work as barriers to entry and exit, since all these factors imply large costs associated with entering the market. If new and young firms need to make costly investments in R&D in order to compete, it will become more risky and less attractive to enter an industry and hence R&D investments will work as a barrier to entry.
- Innovation as a competitive advantage: Another type of literature is represented by, among others, Griliches (1979), Acs and Audretsch (1989) and Geroski (1999). These contributions suggest instead that innovation can be a competitive advantage for entering firms. Acs and Audretsch (1989) suggest that small potential firm entrants can compensate for their size disadvantage by having higher innovation intensity. Geroski (1999) states that entrants can be 'forced' to conduct product differentiation since they cannot compete with price in an already heavily competitive market situation. These arguments suggest that innovation and hence investments in R&D may be a competitive advantage.
- Capital market imperfections: In the previous section it was claimed that larger firms can have better access to capital due to their well-established contacts with banks or other external sources of financing. A similar argument can also be used when discussing innovation and firm age. To a certain extent older firms might also be able to accumulate internal capital that could be used for R&D projects that feature large risks.
- Learning-by-doing economies: It is reasonable to expect that the productivity of R&D projects increases as the skills and experiences of people involved in the R&D projects increase with time. This would constitute an advantage for older firms compared with new and young firms. It is, however, possible that some of the human capital in old firms may have become obsolete.
- The business stealing effect: Tirole (1988) and Aghion and Howitt (1992) discuss the incentives for incumbent firms to innovate. The business

stealing effect refers to the fact that as a new innovation is created, old innovations will become obsolete. This means that existing rents from previous innovations will be destroyed when the new innovations are created. This can be seen as a disincentive for old firms to innovate since they probably have a larger amount of rents from previous R&D projects, whereas new or young firms have fewer accumulated rents that will be destroyed if they continue to invest in R&D and new innovations.

- The stage of the product life cycle: The decision to make product or process innovations, or perhaps both, can be expected to depend on the stage of the product life cycle of the market in which a potential entrant or incumbent firm is competing. Agarwal and Gort (1996) describe a stylized pattern of how the number of incumbent firms and entry and exit vary over the product life cycle. According to this stylized pattern, many firms enter during the initial stages of the product life cycle. In the initial stages, firms compete mainly by offering differentiated products, and hence product innovations are important. In the later stages, it becomes more important to reduce production costs, since firms compete with lower prices. Hence, in order for firms to survive, process innovations become more important (Karlsson, 1988). In the model of entry exit and innovation over the product life cycle presented by Klepper (1996), it is shown that the relative effort put into process R&D, compared to product R&D, increases with time. Hence, according to these stylized patterns, we can expect that young firms in an early stage of the product life cycle would be more likely to invest in product R&D, whereas older firms in the later stages of the product life cycle would put more effort into process R&D.

The general empirical evidence on the relationship between entry and R&D investments is, as mentioned earlier, somewhat mixed. Researchers such as Gort and Klepper (1982), find a positive causal relationship between innovations and entry. Empirical studies by, among others, Geroski (1995), show that small firms and entering firms make a substantial contribution to the generation and diffusion of innovations. Furthermore, the relationship between R&D, entry and exit is especially closely associated with the relationship between innovation and firm size, since many of the entering firms are very small. More explicitly focusing on R&D investments, Orr (1974) finds, for example, that entry in Canadian manufacturing was deterred by high R&D rates. A similar conclusion was made by Baldwin and Gorecki (1987), who found plant creation to be negatively correlated with R&D.

Distinguishing between process and product innovations, empirical work by Huergo and Jaumandreu (2004) shows that the relationship between firm age and product and process innovations can be characterized as non-linear.

In their empirical analysis, where the innovation indicator is based on response to questionnaires, they show that the probability of both product and process innovation is higher in the early years of the life of a firm, but that it decreases with age and then starts to increase again when the firm has reached the age of about 20 years. They also show that the pattern differs substantially between industries.

## Summing Up and Formulation of Hypotheses

Before turning to the empirical part of this chapter it is appropriate to summarize the previous discussion and formulate some explicit hypotheses that will be tested. Table 5.1 summarizes the arguments regarding innovations and R&D related to firm size and age that were discussed in the previous section.

*Table 5.1   R&D and firm size and age*

| | Advantages |
|---|---|
| Small firms | *Innovation as a competitive advantage |
| | *Higher R&D incentives for researchers |
| | *Cooperation opportunities can compensate for the scale disadvantages |
| | *Large firms may lose managerial control of R&D projects |
| Large firms | *Capital market imperfections |
| | *Innovation and industry competition |
| | *Economies of scale |
| | *Economies of scope |
| | *Access to knowledge networks and research cooperation |
| | *Management advantages |
| New/young firms | *Innovation as a competitive advantage |
| | *The business stealing effect |
| | *The stage of the product life cycle (higher probability of product innovations) |
| Old firms | *R&D as a barrier to entry |
| | *Learning-by-doing economies |
| | *Capital market imperfections (easier to find capital for R&D projects) |
| | *The stage of the product life cycle (higher probability of process innovations) |

The theoretical discussion above and the lessons from previous empirical studies can be summarized by formulating three main hypotheses that will be tested in the empirical part of the chapter. A first hypothesis concerns the relationship between process and product R&D and the economies of scope between these two activities:

Hypothesis 1: Process and product R&D are complementary.

As mentioned earlier, the relationship between R&D and firm size has been extensively investigated. This chapter will contribute to the discussion by investigating this relationship for the Swedish manufacturing industry and explicitly distinguish between process and product R&D.

Hypothesis 2: The probability of the firm conducting process and product R&D increases with firm size, possibly in a non-linear pattern.

The third hypothesis concerns the relationship between firm maturity and the probability of doing process and product R&D:

Hypothesis 3: Old and mature firms are expected to have a higher probability of conducting process and product R&D, but the relationship between firm age and R&D can be expected to exhibit a non-linear pattern.

## DATA, METHOD AND DESCRIPTON OF VARIABLES

In order to empirically investigate the propositions stated in the previous section, data from two different sources will be used. The datasets 'Research and development in the business enterprise sector' and 'Financial accounts for enterprises' are both collected by Statistics Sweden and are described below. The empirical part in this chapter focuses on the manufacturing industry. This focus is motivated by the fact that most R&D is conducted in the manufacturing industries and that the recorded observations are more reliable for these industries than for others.

### Financial Accounts for Enterprises (FA)

The dataset 'Financial accounts for enterprises', denoted FA, makes it possible to identify entering and exiting firms since it includes individual firm-level data coded in order to make it possible to identify entry and exit. However, the dataset does not allow us to distinguish between firms that are 'de novo entrants' or if they are 'spin-offs' from larger firms. In the dataset whether information regarding the financial situation of enterprises outside the financial sector is available. This means that financial information from joint-stock companies, cooperatives, partnerships, limited partnerships, associations and some foundations is included. The FA dataset includes financial information from the profit and loss account and the balance sheet but also information about the industrial classification according to the SIC[2] code at the 5-digit level, the number of employees and sales value. For firms with more than 50 employees the data are based on a survey conducted by Statistics Sweden, and for firms with fewer than 50 employees, the data are based on other administrative sources.

## Research and Development in the Business Enterprise Sector (BERD)

The dataset 'Research and development in the business enterprise sector', denoted BERD, is based on a biennial survey covering enterprises in the non-financial sectors with more than 50 employees. Data for 1997 and 1999 are used in the empirical study. Firms that in the FA database declare that they had R&D expenditures or firms that previously reported R&D expenditures in the BERD database are included in the survey, as are firms that satisfy the above description and report R&D expenditures exceeding 5 million SEK and also all firms with more than 200 employees. For firms with 50–199 employees and R&D expenditures of less than 5 million SEK, a sample of firms is surveyed. Thereby, the total number of observations for 1999 adds up to 1,096 firms. The survey includes questions about, among other things, the number of persons in the R&D staff and their education, R&D expenditure, and the distribution of R&D expenditure by type of activity.

The questionnaire includes questions about the purpose of the R&D activities. Because of this it is possible to characterize activities in terms of product or process R&D. Product R&D is defined as development of new products (not existing on the market), development of products that are new to the firm (but already existing on the market) and improvement of already existing products. Process development is defined as development of new processes and improvement of already existing processes.

The data from the two databases described above have been supplemented by information from a third database[3] providing data about firm age. An interesting characteristic about the age structure of the firms is that many of the largest firms are old firms. Henreksson (2003) shows that 31 of the 50 largest firms in Sweden were established before 1913. Figure 5A.1 presents the relationship between size and age for the sample of the 573 firms included in the chapter. The figure shows that the age and size structure is not as pronounced as in the study by Henreksson. For the purpose of this chapter we shall investigate whether the very oldest firms have a higher probability of conducting R&D. Therefore a dummy variable for firms that are older than 80 years is included in the empirical analysis. This means that the dummy variable is used for 64 firms, which corresponds to roughly 10 percent of the firms.

Since the number of firms included in the survey increases each year, the data from the latest year available, 1999, were used as a starting-point, in order to match as many firms as possible from the two databases. For the year 1999 it was possible to match 573 manufacturing firms in the FA and BERD databases.[4] Some 362 of these firms were also present in the 1997 survey. In the empirical analysis in the next section the results for 1999 are emphasized, since the statistical material can be considered better for that year. The purpose of including the material from 1997 is to strengthen the implications and conclusions presented. In addition to the size and age variables, industry specificities such as capital intensity and the profitability of the industry can be expected to influence the probability of innovation. In the theoretical section it was also emphasized that innovative behavior can be expected to differ substantially between industries. Hence, dummy variables for each 2-digit SIC-level industry are also included in order to account for additional industry-specific effects. The detailed construction of variables used in the regression analysis is described in Table 5.2. The correlation matrix for the variables is presented in Table 5A.1 and the reported correlations do not indicate any serious multicollinearity problems.

*Table 5.2  Description of explanatory variables*

| Variable name | Description | Expected sign |
| --- | --- | --- |
| Size | Number of employees | Positive |
| Size2 | Squared number of employees | Open question |
| Capital intensity | Fixed assets divided by sales value | Positive |
| Profitability | Profit margin defined as the firm's result before financial revenues and expenses divided by production value | Positive |
| Age80 | Dummy variable 1 if the firm is older than 80 years, 0 otherwise. | Positive |
| Industry dummy | Industry dummy variables for each 2-digit SIC industry. Manufacturing of fabricated metal products is the base category (SIC code 28) | Positive or negative |

## Multinomial Logit Model of R&D Decisions

Each individual firm has four different choices with regard to R&D: to conduct no R&D at all (outcome 1, denoted NO R&D) to conduct only process R&D (outcome 2, denoted PROC. R&D), to conduct only product R&D (outcome 3, denoted PROD. R&D) or to combine product and process R&D (outcome 4, denoted COMB. R&D). Note that this choice set fulfils the criterion to be exhaustive, that is, that all possible alternatives are included in the choice set (Train, 2003). An appropriate model when the dependent variable consists of a choice set with several outcomes, is the multinomial logit model. In the model, $Y_i$ denotes the choice of type of R&D for firm $i$. The different R&D choices are denoted $j$. In this case $j = 1, 2, 3$ and $4$. $x_i$ denotes a set of explanatory variables, which describe the characteristics of firm $i$ (in our case the explanatory variables defined in Table 5.3). A multinomial logit model for four choices can be formulated (see, for example, Train 1993, 2003 and Green 2003) as:

$$\text{Prob } (Y_i = j) = \frac{e^{\beta'_j x_i}}{\sum\limits_{k=1}^{4} e^{\beta'_k x_i}} \tag{5.1}$$

With this formulation the probability of choosing the four different alternatives is determined in the model, $\beta_j$ is the set of coefficients associated with each choice $j$ and in this case four vectors of coefficients $\beta_1$, $\beta_2$, $\beta_3$ and $\beta_4$ corresponding to the different choices are estimated. The model formulated in equation (5.1) is unidentified. This can be resolved by setting the coefficients in one of the $\beta$ vectors equal to zero. In this case $\beta_1$ (corresponding to the choice NO R&D) was chosen as the zero vector, which means that the remaining coefficients should be interpreted as the change relative to $\beta_1$. The probabilities for each of the four choices are then:

$$\text{Prob}(Y_i = 1) = \frac{1}{1 + \sum\limits_{k=2}^{4} e^{\beta'_k x_i}}$$

$$\text{Prob.}(Y_i = 2,3,4) = \frac{e^{\prime\beta\, x_i}}{1 + \sum\limits_{k=2}^{4} e^{\prime\beta\, x_i}} \tag{5.2}$$

The multinomial logit is estimated by a maximum likelihood procedure. The $\beta$ coefficients resulting from this estimation are difficult to interpret and cannot be interpreted in the way we are accustomed to analyzing coefficients. In order to analyze the results, marginal effects have to be calculated, which can then be interpreted as usual. White's robust variance estimator was used in the estimation in order to control for heteroskedasticity.[5]

In order to evaluate a multinomial logit model further, a goodness-of-fit measure (called pseudo $R^2$) is also calculated. This goodness-of-fit measure is a log likelihood measure and is defined as $1 - (L_n L / L_n L_0)$ where $L_0$ is the loglikelihood for a model including only a constant, and $L$ is the log likelihood of the full model. This log-likelihood measure is bounded between zero and one and can be interpreted in a similar way as the $R^2$ measure.

## EMPIRICAL FINDINGS

Before we consider the results from the estimation of the multinomial logit model, we should examine the statistics used in the empirical analysis at a more aggregated level. Tables 5.3 and 5.4 present some descriptive statistics for 1999 and 1997, respectively. These tables show clearly that there seem to be substantial complementarities in combining both process and product R&D. During both years, less than 1 per cent of the firms choose to carry out only process R&D. It is, however, more common to confine efforts to only product R&D, but most of those firms that make any process R&D efforts at all, combine process and product R&D. The latter firms are also on average larger and older than the other firms. An exception is the set of firms that only conduct process R&D in 1999. These firms are on average larger than the other firms. The very few firms that concentrate on process R&D only are on average more capital intensive than the other firms.

Tables 5.5 and 5.6 present the results from the estimation of the multinomial logit model for 1999 and 1997, respectively. As mentioned above, a vector of coefficients, $\beta_j$, for each choice is estimated. Note that the results regarding the different choices should be interpreted in comparison with the choice NO R&D. Since the number of observations for the choice PROC. R&D is so small (only three firms for each year), the estimation for this choice does not provide any results that can be meaningfully interpreted.[6] The analysis therefore concentrates on the choices PROD. R&D and COMB. R&D.

In hypothesis 2 it was suggested that the probability of conducting process and product R&D increases with firm size and that there is a possibility that the relationship has a non-linear pattern. The empirical analysis shows that the size and the squared size variables are significant both in 1997 and in

1999 for both alternatives, PROD. R&D and COMB. R&D. The size variable has a positive sign, whereas the squared size variable has a negative sign, which implies that there is a non-linear relationship between the probability to innovate and firm size. Hence, the probability of conducting R&D increases with size but at a decreasing rate.

*Table 5.3  Descriptive statistics, 1999*

|  | Number of firms | Percent share | Average size | Average age | Average capital intensity | Average profitability |
|---|---|---|---|---|---|---|
| NO R&D | 325 | 56.72 | 198.49 | 41.12 | 0.21 | 0.05 |
| PROC. R&D | 3 | 0.52 | 2039.33 | 44.33 | 0.37 | 0.10 |
| PROD. R&D | 74 | 12.91 | 537.03 | 44.36 | 0.21 | 0.07 |
| COMB. R&D | 171 | 29.84 | 1064.90 | 50.04 | 0.25 | 0.07 |
| Total | 573 | 100.00 | 511.71 | 44.32 | 0.22 | 0.06 |

*Table 5.4  Descriptive statistics, 1997*

|  | Number of firms | Percent share | Average size | Average age | Average capital intensity | Average profitability |
|---|---|---|---|---|---|---|
| NO R&D | 163 | 45.03 | 262.08 | 45.10 | 0.21 | 0.10 |
| PROC. R&D | 3 | 0.83 | 652.33 | 47.00 | 0.37 | 0.09 |
| PROD. R&D | 64 | 17.68 | 576.44 | 47.05 | 0.17 | 0.09 |
| COMB. R&D | 132 | 36.46 | 1382.02 | 56.17 | 0.24 | 0.06 |
| Total | 362 | 100.00 | 730.40 | 49.60 | 0.21 | 0.08 |

The theoretical section of this chapter concludes that the empirical evidence on the relationship between innovations and firm maturity is rather unclear. Therefore hypothesis 3 has been given a general formulation regarding the possibly non-linear pattern. The result from the estimation adds to the previous literature in one respect by making use of the distinction between product and process R&D. The regression shows that the age variable is significant only regarding the choice COMB. R&D. In the regressions for both 1999 and 1997, the firms that are older than 80 years have a higher probability of conducting combined process and product R&D.

*Table 5.5  Results of the multinomial logit model, 1999*

| Variable | Coeff. | Robust std err. | $z$ | $p$ | Marginal effect |
|---|---|---|---|---|---|
| PROD. R&D | | | | | |
| Constant | −3.528 | 0.855 | −4.13* | 0.000 | |
| Size | 0.005 | 0.001 | 6.03* | 0.000 | $1.32*10^{-4}$ |
| Size2 | $-2.07*10^{-7}$ | $3.56*10^{-8}$ | −5.82* | 0.000 | $-5.82*10^{-9}$ |
| Cap | 0.406 | 1.234 | 0.33 | 0.742 | 0.014 |
| Age80 | 0.832 | 0.554 | 1.50 | 0.133 | 0.014 |
| Profit | 2.165 | 1.611 | 1.34 | 0.179 | 0.063 |
| COMB. R&D | | | | | |
| Constant | −3.424 | 0.613 | −5.58* | 0.000 | |
| Size | 0.005 | 0.001 | 6.79* | 0.000 | 0.001 |
| Size2 | $-2.25*10^{-7}$ | $3.49*10^{-8}$ | −6.45* | 0.000 | $-4.28*10^{-8}$ |
| Cap | 0.208 | 0.830 | 0.25 | 0.802 | 0.037 |
| Age80 | 1.281 | 0.433 | 2.96* | 0.003 | 0.278 |
| Profit | 2.199 | 1.231 | 1.79** | 0.074 | 0.416 |

Number of observations: 530
Loglikelihood function: −373.092
Pseudo $R^2$ = 0.287

*Note:* *denotes significance at the 5 percent level. ** denotes significance at the 10 percent level

We can compare the size of the marginal effects for the choice PROD. R&D and COMB. R&D. Such a comparison shows that the marginal effects for COMB. R&D are generally higher for both years. Thus, the size and age effects are more pronounced for firms that choose to combine process and product R&D. This result may be interpreted in the framework of a product life cycle perspective by observing that as firms grow old and large they do not stop doing product innovation. Rather they continue with product R&D, combining this with process R&D. When the firm starts to combine product with process R&D, the relative efforts into process R&D, as predicted in the model by Klepper (1996), will increase.

Finally, a few words about the capital and profitability variables which do not have any significant coefficients at the 5 percent level for any of the choices. The profitability variable is, however, significant at the 10 percent level for the choice of COMB. R&D. These results could have been expected in the light of the descriptive statistics in Table 5.4, which showed very small differences in average capital intensity and profitability between the four different types of firms.

*Table 5.6  Results of the multinomial logit model, 1997*

| Variable | Coeff. | Robust std err | z | p | Marginal effect |
|---|---|---|---|---|---|
| PROD. R&D | | | | | |
| Constant | −2.673 | 0.883 | −3.02 | | |
| | | | | 0.002 | |
| Size | 0.004 | 0.001 | 4.52 | 0.000 | $2.53*10^{-6}$ |
| Size2 | $-1.44*10^{-7}$ | $3.23*10^{-8}$ | −4.46 | 0.000 | $-1.04*10^{-10}$ |
| Cap | −0.254 | 1.660 | −0.15 | 0.879 | $-6.10*10^{-4}$ |
| Age80 | 0.181 | 0.598 | 0.30 | 0.762 | $-3.99*10^{-4}$ |
| Profit | 1.725 | 2.026 | 0.85 | 0.394 | 0.002 |
| COMB. R&D | | | | | |
| Constant | −2.660 | 0.733 | −3.63* | 0.000 | |
| Size | 0.004 | 0.001 | 5.26* | 0.000 | $9.30*10^{-4}$ |
| Size2 | $-1.57*10^{7}$ | $-3.13*10^{-8}$ | −5.02* | 0.000 | $-3.65*10^{-8}$ |
| Cap | 0.670 | 1.209 | 0.55 | 0.579 | 0.156 |
| Age80 | 1.198 | 0.463 | 2.59* | 0.010 | 0.289 |
| Profit | −1.316 | 1.603 | −0.82 | 0.412 | −0.307 |

Number of observations: 333
Log likelihood function: −251.912
Pseudo $R^2$: 0.297

*Note:*  * denotes significance at the 5 percent level. ** denotes significance at the 10 percent level.

Before we summarize the empirical results and conclude the chapter, we shall take a closer look at the results for the industry-specific dummy variables, presented in tables 5A.4 and 5A.5, that were included in the multinomial logit model to control for differences between industries. Table 5.7 summarizes the industry dummy variables that were significant at the 5 and 10 percent levels 1999 for the choices PROD. R&D and COMB. R&D. The industries for which the industry dummy variables have negative marginal effects can be regarded as process oriented. Industries which have positive marginal effects can be expected to have a high technological content. These are usually considered to be innovative industries. Among the industry dummy variables that have significant marginal effects in 1997, a similar pattern is apparent. Most of these dummy variables were also significant in 1999. An exception is, for example, manufacturing of furniture, which had significant negative marginal effects for both PROD. R&D and COMB. R&D in 1997.

*Table 5.7  Summary of significant industry dummy variables, 1999*

|  | Positive sign | Negative sign |
|---|---|---|
| PROD. R&D | Manufacture of chemicals and chemical products (SIC 24) | Manufacture of food products and beverages (SIC 15) |
|  | Manufacture of machinery and equipment (SIC 29) | Manufacture of textiles (SIC 17) |
|  | Manufacture of office machinery and computers (SIC 30) | Manufacture of wearing apparel; dressing and dyeing of fur (SIC 18) |
|  | Manufacture of medical, precision and optical instruments (SIC 33) | Tanning and dressing of leather (SIC 19) |
|  |  | Manufacture of wood and of products of wood and cork (SIC 20) |
|  |  | Manufacture of pulp, paper and paper products (SIC 21) |
|  |  | Publishing, printing and reproduction of recorded media (SIC 22) |
|  |  | Manufacture of coke, refined petroleum products and nuclear fuel (SIC 23) |
| COMB. R&D | Manufacture of chemicals and chemical products (SIC 24) | Manufacture of wearing apparel; dressing and dyeing of fur (SIC 18) |
|  | Manufacture of rubber and plastic products (SIC 25) | Tanning and dressing of leather (SIC 19) |
|  | Manufacture of machinery and equipment (SIC 29) | Manufacture of wood and of products of wood and cork (SIC 20) |
|  | Manufacture of office machinery and computers (SIC 30) | Manufacture of pulp, paper and paper products (SIC 21) |
|  | Manufacture of electrical machinery and apparatus (SIC 31) | Publishing, printing and reproduction of recorded media (SIC 22) |
|  | Manufacture of radio, television and communication equipment (SIC 32) |  |
|  | Manufacture of medical, precision and optical instruments (SIC 33) |  |

# CONCLUSIONS AND SUGGESTIONS FOR FUTURE RESEARCH

The primary focus of this chapter has been to investigate the relationship between firm size and age and the probability of conducting process and product R&D. Increased knowledge about firms' decisions regarding these issues is of course of great interest to researchers and policy makers who want to understand the processes that underlie economic growth. A number of advantages and disadvantages of being a small or large and an old or new firm, as regards the decision to conduct process and product R&D, have been presented. The issue about complementarities between process and product R&D has also been discussed.

The empirical results show that we can expect substantial complementarities between the two. This synergy is apparent for process R&D since almost no firm chooses to concentrate only on process innovation. Another interpretation would be that there are very few industries where price competition is so important that the firms are able to focus on lowering the price, and therefore concentrate their innovative efforts on process R&D. In order to remain competitive, firms have to conduct product innovations, which also explains the more pronounced effect of size and age on the probability of firms conducting both process and product R&D.

The importance of continuous and combined product and process R&D discussed in this chapter has additional aspects that could be interesting to elaborate further. One possible issue in investigating further concerns how the firms' decision process regarding innovation can be expected to occur in more detail. Is the choice of conducting certain R&D dependent on previous choices? That is, does the firm first choose between conducting no R&D and conducting R&D and then in a second step choose between process, product or combined R&D? In order to investigate such conditional decisions, a nested multinomial model could be specified and estimated. In addition to the quantitative method used in this chapter it could also be interesting to combine the study with a qualitative study, in which the firms' decision makers are interviewed about the decision-making process regarding strategies for investing in product and process R&D.

It would, of course, also be interesting to study the patterns of product and process R&D over a longer time period than the two years that was possible to include in this study. It should be noted that 1997 and 1999 represent a period when the Swedish economy was expanding and still recovering from the very severe economic crisis experienced at the beginning of the 1990s.

## NOTES

1. Other measures frequently used as innovation indicators are, for example, patent applications, granted patents and innovation expenditures. See Kleinknecht et al. (2002) for a discussion on this issue.
2. Standard Industrial Classification.
3. The database 'Affärsdata' provides information from the Swedish Patent and Registration Office.
4. Special thanks to Martin Andersson at Jönköping International Business School, Sweden, for his assistance with the data.
5. See, for example, Greene (2003) for further details about this robust variance estimator.
6. The regression results of the choice PROC. R&D for 1999 and 1997 are presented in Tables 5A.2 and 5A.3.

## REFERENCES

Acs, Z.J. and D.B. Audretsch (1987), 'Innovation, Market Structure, and Firm Size', *Review of Economics and Statistics*, **69**, 567–74.

Acs, Z.J. and D.B. Audretsch (1989), 'Small Firm Entry in U.S. Manufacturing', *Economica*, **56**, 255–65.

Acs, Z.J. and D.B. Audretsch (1990), *Innovation and Small Firms*, MIT Press, Cambridge, MA.

Agarwal, R. and M. Gort (1996), 'The Evolution of Markets and Entry, Exit and Survival of Firms', *Review of Economics and Statistics*, **78**, 489–98.

Aghion P. and P. Howitt (1992), 'A Model of Growth through Creative Destruction', *Econometrica*, **60**, 323–51.

Arrow, K.J., (1962), 'Economic Welfare and the Allocation of Resources for Invention' in R.R. Nelson (ed.), *The Rate and Direction of Inventive Activity: Economic and Social Factors*, National Bureau of Economic Research, Princeton University Press, Princeton, NJ, pp. 609–26.

Audretsch, D., B. Bozeman, K.L. Combs, M. Feldman, A.N. Link, D.S. Siegel, P. Stephan, G. Tassey and C. Wessner (2002), 'The Economics of Science and Technology', *Journal of Technology Transfer*, **27**, 155–203.

Audretsch, D.B. and M.P. Feldman (1996), 'R&D Spillovers and the Geography of Innovation and Production', *American Economic Review*, **86**, 630–40.

Bain J.S. (1956), *Barriers to New Competition*, Harvard University Press, Cambridge, MA.

Baldwin J.R. and P.K. Gorecki (1987), 'Plant Creation versus Plant Acquisition: The entry Process in Canadian Manufacturing', *International Journal of Industrial Organization*, **5**, 27–41.

Cohen, W. (1995), 'Empirical Studies of Innovative Activity' in P. Stoneman (ed), *Handbook of the Economics of Innovation and Technological Change*, Blackwell, Cambridge, MA, pp. 182–264.

Cohen, W. and S. Klepper, (1996), 'Firm Size and the Nature of Innovation within Industries: The Case of Process and Product R&D', *Review of Economics and Statistics*, **78**, 232–43.

Cohen, W.M. and R.C. Levin (1989), 'Empirical Studies of Innovation and Market Structure', in R. Schmalensee and R.D. Willig (eds), *Handbook of Industrial Organization*, Vol. II, North-Holland, Amsterdam, pp. 1059–107.

Demsetz, H. (1969), 'Information and Efficiency: Another Viewpoint', *Journal of Law and Economics*, **12**, 1–22.

Fritsch, M. and M. Meschede (2001) 'Product Innovation, Process Innovation, and Size', *Review of Industrial Organization*, **19**, 335–50.

Geroski, P. (1995), *Market Structure, Corporate Performance and Innovative Activity*, Oxford University Press, Oxford.

Geroski, P. (1999), 'Innovation as an Engine of Competition' in D. Mueller, A. Haid and J. Weigand, (eds), *Competition Efficiency and Welfare*, Kluwer, Dordrecht, pp. 13–26.

Gort, M. and S. Klepper (1982), 'Time Paths in the Diffusion of Product Innovation', *Economic Journal*, **92**, 630–53.

Greene, W.H. (2003), *Econometric Analysis*, 5th edn,Prentice-Hall, Englewood Cliffs, NJ.

Griliches, Z. (1979), 'Issues in Assessing the Contribution of Research and Development to Productivity Growth', *Bell Journal of Economics*, **10**, 92–116.

Henreksson, M. (2003), 'Entreprenörskapet – Välfärdsstatens svaga länk?', *Ekonomisk Debatt*, **31**, 5–17.

Hoshi, T., A. Kashyap and D. Scharfstein (1991), 'Corporate Structure, Liquidity, and Investment: Evidence from Japanese Industrial Groups', *The Quarterly Journal of Economics*, **106**, 33–60.

Huergo, E. and J. Jaumandreu (2004), 'How Does Probability of Innovation Change with Firm Age?', *Small Business Economics*, **22**, 193–207.

Johansson, B., H. Lööf and A. Rader Olsson (2005), 'Firm Location, Corporate Structure, Firm R&D Investment, Innovation and Productivity', CESIS Working Paper Series No. 31, Royal Institute of Technology, Stockholm.

Karlsson, C. (1988), 'Innovation Adaption and the Product Life Cycle', Umeå Economic Studies No. 185, Umeå University.

Kleinknecht, A., K. van Montfort and E. Brouwer (2002), 'Non-Trivial Choice Between Innovation Indicators', *Economics of Innovation and New Technology*, **11**, 109–21.

Klepper, S. (1996), 'Entry, Exit and Growth over the Product Life Cycle', *The American Economic Review*, **86**, 562–83.

Link, A.N. (1982), 'A Disaggreggated Analysis of Industrial R&D: Product versus Process Innovation', in D. Sahal (ed.), *The Transfer and Utilization of Technical Knowledge*, Lexington Books, Lexington, MA.

Mansfield, E. (1963), 'The Speed of Response of Firms of new Techniques', *Quarterly Journal of Economics*, **77**, 290–311.

Mansfield, E. (1971), *Research and Innovation in the Modern Corporation*, Macmillan, London.

Mansfield, E. (1981), 'Composition of R&D Expenditures: Relationship to Size Concentration and Innovation Output', *Review of Economics and Statistics*, **62**, 610–14.

Milgrom, P. and J. Roberts (1990), 'The Economics of Modern Manufacturing: Technology, Strategy and Organization', *American Economic Review*, **80**, 511–28.

Miravete, E.J. and J.C. Pernias (2006), 'Innovation Complementarity and Scale of Production', *Journal of Industrial Economics*, **54**, 1–29.

Orr, D. (1974), 'The Determinants of Entry: A Study of the Canadian Manufacturing Industries', *Review of Economics and Statistics*, **56**, 58–66.

Pavitt, K., M. Robson and J. Townsend (1987), 'The Size Distribution of Innovating firms in the UK: 1945–1983', *Journal of Industrial Economics*, **35**, 297–316.

Scherer, F.M. (1991), 'Changing Perspectives on the Firm Size Problem', in Z.J. Acs and D.B. Audretsch (eds), *Innovation and Technological Change: An International Comparison*, Harvester Wheatsheaf, New York.

Schumpeter, J. (1934), *The Theory of Economic Development*, Harvard University Press, Cambridge, MA.

Schumpeter, J.A. (1942), *Capitalism, Socialism and Democracy*, Harper & Row, New York.

Siegfried, J.J. and L.B. Evans (1994), 'Empirical Studies of Entry and Exit: A Survey of the Evidence', *Review of Industrial Organization*, 9, 121–55.

Stoneman, P. (1995), 'Introduction' in P. Stoneman (ed.) *Handbook of the Economics of Innovation and Technological Change*, Blackwell, Cambridge, MA, pp.1–13.

Sutton, J. (1998), *Technology and Market Structure Theory and History*, MIT Press, Cambridge, MA.

Tirole, J. (1988), *The Theory of Industrial Organization*, MIT Press, Cambridge, MA.

Train, K.E. (1993), *Qualitative Choice Analysis: Theory Econometrics and an Application to Automobile Demand*, MIT Press, Cambridge, MA.

Train, K.E. (2003), *Discrete Choice Methods with Simulation*, Cambridge University Press, Cambridge.

Yip, G.S. (1982), *Barriers to Entry: A Corporate Strategy Perspective*, Lexington Books, D.C. Heath & Co., Lexington, MA.

## APPENDIX 5A

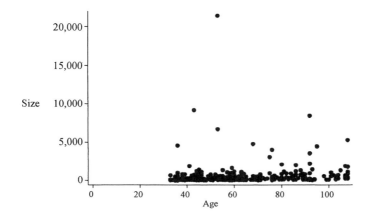

*Figure 5A.1  The relationship between firm age and size 1999*

*Table 5A.1  Correlation matrix, 1999*

|        | Size   | Size2  | Cap    | Age80 | Profit |
|--------|--------|--------|--------|-------|--------|
| Size   | 1.000  |        |        |       |        |
| Size2  | 0.861  | 1.000  |        |       |        |
| Cap    | 0.076  | −0.029 | 1.000  |       |        |
| Age80  | 0.111  | 0.011  | 0.120  | 1.000 |        |
| Profit | −0.000 | −0.020 | −0.006 | 0.029 | 1.000  |

*Table 5A.2  Results of the multinomial logit model, 1999 (the choice of PROC. R&D)* [a]

| Variable  | Coeff.          | Robust std err | $z$     | $p$   |
|-----------|-----------------|----------------|---------|-------|
| PROC. R&D |                 |                |         |       |
| Constant  | −29.694         | 1.611          | −18.43* | 0.000 |
| Size      | 0.003           | 0.001          | 2.74*   | 0.006 |
| Size2     | $3.01*10^{-7}$  | $2.06*10^{7}$  | 1.46    | 0.143 |
| Cap       | 4.268           | 3.451          | 1.24    | 0.216 |
| Age80     | −50.337         | 7.331          | −6.87*  | 0.000 |
| Profit    | 0.891           | 3.559          | 0.25    | 0.802 |

| Variable | Coeff. | Robust std err | $z$ | $p$ |
|---|---|---|---|---|
| Manufacture of food products and beverages (SIC 15) | 24.160 | 1.132 | 21.35* | 0.000 |
| Manufacture of textiles (SIC 17) | −12.997 | 1.215 | −10.69* | 0.000 |
| Manufacture of wearing apparel; dressing and dyeing of fur (SIC 18) | −12.019 | 1.360 | −8.84* | 0.000 |
| Tanning and dressing of leather (SIC 19) | −12.919 | 1.405 | −9.19* | 0.000 |
| Manufacture of wood and of products of wood and cork (SIC 20) | −13.197 | 1.170 | −11.28* | 0.000 |
| Manufacture of pulp, paper and paper products (SIC 21) | −16.966 | 4.151 | −4.09* | 0.000 |
| Publishing, printing and reproduction of recorded media (SIC 22) | −10.499 | 1.253 | −8.38* | 0.000 |
| Manufacture of coke, refined petroleum products and nuclear fuel (SIC 23) | −12.134 | 1.535 | −7.91* | 0.000 |
| Manufacture of chemicals and chemical products (SIC 24) | 24.399 | 2.084 | 11.71* | 0.000 |
| Manufacture of rubber and plastic products (SIC 25) | −12.729 | 1.042 | −12.22* | 0.000 |
| Manufacture of other non-metallic mineral products (SIC 26) | −13.712 | 1.775 | −7.72* | 0.000 |
| Manufacture of basic metals (SIC 27) | −25.502 | 5.881 | −4.34* | 0.000 |
| Manufacture of machinery and equipment (SIC 29) | −11.873 | 1.063 | −11.17* | 0.000 |
| Manufacture of office machinery and computers (SIC 30) | −11.994 | 2.169 | −5.53* | 0.000 |
| Manufacture of electrical machinery and apparatus (SIC 31) | −12.245 | 1.070 | −11.44* | 0.000 |
| Manufacture of radio, television and communication equipment (SIC 32) | −204.547 | 75.970 | −2.69* | 0.007 |
| Manufacture of medical, precision and optical instruments (SIC 33) | −11.638 | 1.1179 | −10.41* | 0.000 |
| Manufacture of motor vehicles (SIC 34) | −35.350 | 9.330 | −3.79* | 0.000 |
| Manufacture of other transport equipment (SIC 35) | 26.154 | | | |
| Manufacture of furniture (SIC 36) | −12.573 | 1.612 | −10.89* | 0.000 |

*Notes:*

a.   Note that the marginal effects from the choice PROC. R&D could not be calculated due to the very low number of firms choosing this outcome.
b.   *denotes significance at the 5 percent level. ** denotes significance at the 10 percent level.

*Table 5A.3  Results of the multinomial logit model, 1997 (the choice of PROC. R&D)* [a]

| PROC. R&D | Coeff. | Robust std err | z | p |
|---|---|---|---|---|
| Constant | −30.012 | | | |
| Size | 0.007 | 0.003 | 1.94** | 0.053 |
| Size2 | $-2.29*10^{-6}$ | $1.97*10^{6}$ | −1.16 | 0.245 |
| Cap | 2.638 | 1.634 | 1.61 | 0.106 |
| Age80 | −37.234 | 1.003 | −37.14* | 0.000 |
| Profit | 1.589 | 7.152 | 0.22 | 0.824 |
| Manufacture of food products and beverages (SIC 15) | 24.622 | 1.503 | 16.38* | 0.000 |
| Manufacture of textiles (SIC 17) | −14.390 | 1.288 | −11.17* | 0.000 |
| Manufacture of wearing apparel; dressing and dyeing of fur (SIC 18) | −15.206 | | | |
| Tanning and dressing of leather (SIC 19) | −16.373 | | | |
| Manufacture of wood and of products of wood and cork (SIC 20) | −16.693 | 2.417 | −6.91* | 0.000 |
| Manufacture of pulp, paper and paper products (SIC 21) | −14.244 | 2.230 | −6.39* | 0.000 |
| Publishing, printing and reproduction of recorded media (SIC 22) | 16.402 | | | |
| Manufacture of coke, refined petroleum products and nuclear fuel (SIC 23) | −16.291 | 2.075 | −7.85* | 0.000 |
| Manufacture of chemicals and chemical products (SIC 24) | 25.694 | 1.867 | 13.76* | 0.000 |
| Manufacture of rubber and plastic products (SIC 25) | −15.769 | 1.650 | −9.56* | 0.000 |
| Manufacture of other non-metallic mineral products (SIC 26) | −16.047 | 1.695 | −9.47* | 0.000 |
| Manufacture of basic metals | −13.558 | 1.612 | −8.41* | 0.000 |

(SIC 27)

| PROC. R&D | Coeff. | Robust std err | z | p |
|---|---|---|---|---|
| Manufacture of machinery and equipment (SIC 29) | −14.045 | 1.444 | −9.72* | 0.000 |
| Manufacture of office machinery and computers (SIC 30) | 20.247 | | | |
| Manufacture of electrical machinery and apparatus (SIC 31) | −14.771 | 1.571 | −9.40* | 0.000 |
| Manufacture of radio, television and communication equipment (SIC 32) | −11.192 | 1.398 | −8.01* | 0.000 |
| Manufacture of medical, precision and optical instruments (SIC 33) | −14.284 | 2.008 | −7.11* | 0.000 |
| Manufacture of motor vehicles (SIC 34) | −16.318 | 1.594 | −10.23* | 0.000 |
| Manufacture of other transport equipment (SIC 35) | −16.051 | 3.317 | −4.84* | 0.000 |
| Manufacture of furniture (SIC 36) | −16.527 | 1.190 | −13.89* | 0.000 |

*Notes:*
a.    Note that the marginal effects from the choice PROC. R&D could not be calculated due to the very low number of firms choosing this outcome.
b.    *denotes significance at the 5 percent level. ** denotes significance at the 10 percent level.

*Table 5A.4  Industry dummy results of the multinomial logit model, 1999*

| Variable | Coeff. | Robust std err | z | p | Marginal effect |
|---|---|---|---|---|---|
| PROD. R&D | | | | | |
| Manufacture of food products and beverages (SIC 15) | −2.356 | 1.435 | −1.64** | 0.100 | −0.042 |
| Manufacture of textiles (SIC 17) | −35.674 | 0.796 | −44.83* | 0.000 | −0.104 |
| Manufacture of wearing apparel; dressing and dyeing of fur (SIC 18) | −35.593 | 0.957 | −37.20* | 0.000 | −0.051 |

| Tanning and dressing of leather (SIC 19) | −35.833 | 1.106 | −32.39 | 0.000 | −0.047 |
|---|---|---|---|---|---|
| Variable | Coeff. | Robust std err | z | p | Marginal effect |
| Manufacture of wood and of products of wood and cork (SIC 20) | −2.996 | 1.949 | −1.54 | 0.124 | −0.042 |
| Manufacture of pulp, paper and paper products (SIC 21) | −3.105 | 1.278 | −2.43* | 0.015 | −0.047 |
| Publishing, printing and reproduction of recorded media (SIC 22) | −38.414 | 1.303 | −29.48* | 0.000 | −0.052 |
| Manufacture of coke, refined petroleum products and nuclear fuel (SIC 23) | −34.896 | 1.493 | −23.36* | 0.000 | −0.052 |
| Manufacture of chemicals and chemical products (SIC 24) | 1.391 | 0.820 | 1.75** | 0.090 | 0.031 |
| Manufacture of rubber and plastic products (SIC 25) | 0.993 | 0.911 | 1.09 | 0.275 | 0.024 |
| Manufacture of other non-metallic mineral products (SIC 26) | −0.806 | 1.085 | −0.74 | 0.458 | −0.023 |
| Manufacture of basic metals (SIC 27) | −0.626 | 1.143 | −0.55 | 0.584 | −0.022 |
| Manufacture of machinery and equipment (SIC 29) | 1.451 | 0.791 | 1.83** | 0.067 | 0.034 |
| Manufacture of office machinery and computers (SIC 30) | 3.614 | 1.169 | 3.09* | 0.002 | 0.129 |
| Manufacture of electrical machinery and apparatus (SIC 31) | 0.383 | 1.011 | 0.38 | 0.701 | −0.010 |
| Manufacture of radio, television and communication equipment (SIC 32) | 1.342 | 0.952 | 1.41 | 0.159 | 0.035 |
| Manufacture of medical, precision and optical instruments (SIC 33) | 1.656 | 0.952 | 1.74** | 0.082 | 0.027 |
| Manufacture of motor | 0.294 | 0.973 | 0.30 | 0.763 | 0.021 |

vehicles (SIC 34)

| Variable | Coeff | Robust std err | z | p | Marginal effect |
|---|---|---|---|---|---|
| Manufacture of other transport equipment (SIC 35) | 2.174 | 1.329 | 1.64 | 0.102 | 0.082 |
| Manufacture of furniture (SIC 36) | 0.006 | 1.206 | 0.01 | 0.996 | 0.004 |
| COMB. R&D | | | | | |
| Manufacture of food products and beverages (SIC 15) | −1.087 | 1.139 | −0.95 | 0.340 | −0.161 |
| Manufacture of textiles (SIC 17) | 0.659 | 0.814 | 0.81 | 0.418 | 0.181 |
| Manufacture of wearing apparel; dressing and dyeing of fur (SIC 18) | −35.068 | 0.832 | −42.13* | 0.000 | −0.331 |
| Tanning and dressing of leather (SIC 19) | −35.194 | 0.992 | −35.48* | 0.000 | −0.304 |
| Manufacture of wood and of products of wood and cork (SIC 20) | −3.905 | 1.583 | −2.47* | 0.014 | −0.230 |
| Manufacture of pulp, paper and paper products (SIC 21) | −1.343 | 0.779 | −1.72** | 0.085 | −0.189 |
| Publishing, printing and reproduction of recorded media (SIC 22) | −38.367 | 1.255 | −30.56* | 0.000 | −0.336 |
| Manufacture of coke, refined petroleum products and nuclear fuel (SIC 23) | 2.759 | 1.685 | 1.64 | 0.102 | 0.592 |
| Manufacture of chemicals and chemical products (SIC 24) | 1.718 | 0.644 | 2.67* | 0.008 | 0.366 |
| Manufacture of rubber and plastic products (SIC 25) | 1.240 | 0.729 | 1.70** | 0.089 | 0.267 |
| Manufacture of other non-metallic mineral products (SIC 26) | -0.275 | 0.883 | −0.31 | 0.755 | −0.046 |
| Manufacture of basic metals (SIC 27) | 0.221 | 0.739 | 0.30 | 0.765 | 0.053 |

| Variable | Coeff. | Robust std err | z | p | Marginal effect |
|---|---|---|---|---|---|
| Manufacture of machinery and equipment (SIC 29) | 1.779 | 0.603 | 2.95* | 0.003 | 0.369 |
| Manufacture of office machinery and computers (SIC 30) | 3.222 | 1.103 | 2.92* | 0.004 | 0.486 |
| Manufacture of electrical machinery and apparatus (SIC 31) | 1.474 | 0.729 | 2.02* | 0.043 | 0.339 |
| Manufacture of radio, television and communication equipment (SIC 32) | 1.514 | 0.771 | 1.96* | 0.049 | 0.321 |
| Manufacture of medical, precision and optical instruments (SIC 33) | 2.148 | 0.706 | 3.04* | 0.002 | 0.449 |
| Manufacture of motor vehicles (SIC 34) | −0.532 | 0.904 | −0.59 | 0.556 | −0.098 |
| Manufacture of other transport equipment (SIC 35) | 1.951 | 1.255 | 1.55 | 0.120 | 0.373 |
| Manufacture of furniture (SIC 36) | −0.332 | 1.139 | −0.29 | 0.771 | −0.062 |

*Note:* *denotes significance at the 5 percent level. ** denotes significance at the 10 percent level.

*Table 5A.5  Industry dummy results of the multinomial logit model 1997*

| Variable | Coeff. | Robust std err | z | p | Marginal effect |
|---|---|---|---|---|---|
| PROD. R&D | | | | | |
| Manufacture of food products and beverages (SIC 15) | −1.184 | 1.205 | −0.98 | 0.325 | $-7.64*10^{-4}$ |
| Manufacture of textiles (SIC 17) | −0.098 | 1.316 | −0.07 | 0.940 | $-9.20*10^{-5}$ |

| Variable | Coeff. | Robust std err | z | p | Marginal effect |
|---|---|---|---|---|---|
| Manufacture of wearing apparel; dressing and dyeing of fur (SIC 18) | −40.220 | 1.290 | −31.17 | 0.000 | −0.001 |
| Tanning and dressing of leather (SIC 19) | −40.720 | 1.255 | −32.47 | 0.000 | −0.001 |
| Manufacture of wood and of products of wood and cork (SIC 20) | −41.796 | 1.171 | −35.69 | 0.000 | −0.005 |
| Manufacture of pulp, paper and paper products (SIC 21) | −41.201 | 0.922 | −44.68 | 0.000 | −0.011 |
| Publishing, printing and reproduction of recorded media (SIC 22) | −42.819 | 1.440 | −29.74 | 0.000 | −0.001 |
| Manufacture of coke, refined petroleum products and nuclear fuel (SIC 23) | −40.465 | 1.071 | −37.77 | 0.000 | −0.001 |
| Manufacture of chemicals and chemical products (SIC 24) | 0.991 | 0.894 | 1.11 | 0.268 | $4.69*10^{-4}$ |
| Manufacture of rubber and plastic products (SIC 25) | 0.237 | 1.088 | 0.22 | 0.827 | $-3.37*10^{-4}$ |
| Manufacture of other non-metallic mineral products (SIC 26) | −1.177 | 1.120 | −0.98 | 0.327 | $-8.08*10^{-4}$ |
| Manufacture of basic metals (SIC 27) | −0.123 | 1.137 | −0.11 | 0.914 | $-3.64*10^{-4}$ |
| Manufacture of machinery and equipment (SIC 29) | 1.383 | 0.805 | 1.72** | 0.085 | 0.001 |
| Manufacture of office machinery and computers (SIC 30) | 40.260 | | | | 0.999 |

| Variable | Coeff. | Robust std err | z | p | Marginal effect |
|---|---|---|---|---|---|
| Manufacture of electrical machinery and apparatus (SIC 31) | −39.654 | 0.880 | −45.07 | 0.000 | −0.011 |
| Manufacture of radio, television and communication equipment (SIC 32) | 2.211 | 1.159 | 1.91 | 0.056 | 0.001 |
| Manufacture of medical, precision and optical instruments (SIC 33) | 1.341 | 1.007 | 1.33 | 0.183 | $6.58*10^{-5}$ |
| Manufacture of motor vehicles (SIC 34) | 1.023 | 1.132 | 0.90 | 0.366 | 0.001 |
| Manufacture of other transport equipment (SIC 35) | −1.044 | 3.559 | −0.29 | 0.769 | $−6.62*10^{-4}$ |
| Manufacture of furniture (SIC 36) | −40.864 | 0.953 | −42.87 | 0.000 | −0.002 |
| COMB. R&D | | | | | |
| Manufacture of food products and beverages (SIC 15) | −0.966 | 1.202 | −0.80 | 0.422 | −0.191 |
| Manufacture of textiles (SIC 17) | −0.0542 | 0.839 | −0.06 | 0.948 | −0.012 |
| Manufacture of wearing apparel; dressing and dyeing of fur (SIC 18) | −38.876 | 1.216 | −31.98* | 0.000 | −0.396 |
| Tanning and dressing of leather (SIC 19) | −39.975 | 1.185 | −33.73* | 0.000 | −0.397 |
| Manufacture of wood and of products of wood and cork (SIC 20) | −2.658 | 1.403 | −1.90** | 0.058 | −0.345 |
| Manufacture of pulp, paper and paper products (SIC 21) | −1.204 | 0.936 | −1.29 | 0.198 | −0.223 |

| Variable | Coeff. | Robust std err | z | p | Marginal effect |
|---|---|---|---|---|---|
| Publishing, printing and reproduction of recorded media (SIC 22) | −43.920 | 1.323 | −33.19* | 0,000 | −0.400 |
| Manufacture of coke, refined petroleum products and nuclear fuel (SIC 23) | 0.387 | 1.047 | 0.37 | 0.711 | 0.944 |
| Manufacture of chemicals and chemical products (SIC 24) | 1.313 | 0.735 | 1.79** | 0.074 | 0.316 |
| Manufacture of rubber and plastic products (SIC 25) | 1.129 | 0.862 | 1.31 | 0.191 | 0.274 |
| Manufacture of other non-metallic mineral products (SIC 26) | −0.517 | 0.878 | −0.59 | 0.556 | −0.111 |
| Manufacture of basic metals (SIC 27) | 0.527 | 0.816 | 0.65 | 0.518 | 0.128 |
| Manufacture of machinery and equipment (SIC 29) | 1.260 | 0.692 | 1.82** | 0.069 | 0.301 |
| Manufacture of office machinery and computers (SIC 30) | −3.590 | 0.941 | −3.82* | 0.000 | −0.384 |
| Manufacture of electrical machinery and apparatus (SIC 31) | 1.219 | 0.923 | 1.32 | 0.186 | 0.299 |
| Manufacture of radio, television and communication equipment (SIC 32) | 2.253 | 1.091 | 2.07* | 0.039 | 0.483 |
| Manufacture of medical, precision and optical instruments (SIC 33) | 2.160 | 0.829 | 2.61* | 0.009 | 0.761 |

| Variable | Coeff. | Robust std err | $z$ | $p$ | Marginal effect |
|---|---|---|---|---|---|
| Manufacture of motor vehicles (SIC 34) | 0.613 | 1.171 | 0.52 | 0.601 | 0.149 |
| Manufacture of other transport equipment (SIC 35) | −1.031 | 2.945 | −0.35 | 0.726 | −0.198 |
| Manufacture of furniture (SIC 36) | −40.732 | 0.905 | −45.00* | 0.000 | −0.519 |

*Note:*  * denotes significance at the 5 percent level. ** denotes significance at the 10 percent level.

# 6. University-educated Labour, R&D and Regional Export Performance

**Urban Gråsjö**

## INTRODUCTION

What are the major sources of knowledge in the innovation process? This is of course an important question to answer since there is an undisputable fact that innovation promotes economic growth. However, the answer is not obvious because it depends both on the measure used as an output of the innovation process as well as on the country under investigation. When the number of patents (granted as well as patent applications) is used as an output, the empirical evidence points towards company (private) R&D as the most important knowledge source. University R&D is also of some importance, but its importance varies considerably between different countries. Empirical studies performed on US and European data agree on the importance of company R&D, but differ when it comes to the effect from universities. In a general comparison, studies using US data (Jaffe, 1989; Feldman, 1994; Anselin et al., 1997) demonstrate larger effects of university R&D on patent production than comparable studies using data from different countries in Europe. For instance, the empirical findings in Gråsjö (2004) reveal that university R&D has no impact on the production of patents for Swedish municipalities. The same result can also be found for France (Ronde and Hussler, 2005). Furthermore, in a study conducted on data from West Gemany, Fritsch and Slavtchev (2005) show that the effect from university R&D is much smaller (although statistically significant) than the corresponding effect in the US studies.

In contrast to patents, literature-based innovation output measures provide a direct indicator of innovation (Acs et al., 2002; Kleinknecht et al., 2002). Screening the new product announcements in trade and technical journals generates literature-based innovation output indicators. The advantage of new innovations as indicators is that they document the actual commercialisation of technical ideas. Acs et al. (2002) use data based on 125 US metropolitan statistical areas (MSAs) in a knowledge production framework with patents and new product innovations as dependent variables. Their empirical findings show a dominance of company R&D over university research. However, this dominance is not so accentuated for new product innovations. This pattern is also replicated for research spillovers from surrounding areas; university R&D being more important for new product innovations and company R&D being the dominant factor for patents.

This raises a number of questions: is university R&D more effective if another output is used in the knowledge production process and is company R&D still the dominating explanatory variable? Is accessibility to R&D the appropriate input variable or is a university-educated labour force a better choice? Is there any evidence for productive knowledge flows between municipalities if variables other than patents and R&D efforts are used as outputs and inputs in the innovation process?

Although patents are commonly used as proxies for the output of the innovation process, they do not by themselves generate economic growth. The classical definition of an innovation stresses introduction on the market. Thus, market penetration (or commercialisation) distinguishes invention from innovation. If a firm also succeeds in introducing a product on the export market it implies a successful market penetration. Therefore export value or exports of high-value products could be useful measures of the innovative capacity in a region. Even though exports are not usually used as an output of an innovation process, it is widely agreed that knowledge is one of the crucial ingredients of innovation and in turn the main basis of international competitiveness and hence of successful export performance. Several empirical studies have tried to establish the link between export performance and innovation on a firm or a national level. Usually used measures for innovation in these studies are, for instance, R&D expenditures, R&D employment and number of patents (Soete, 1987). However, the studies at nation and firm level do not account for the role of geographical proximity. Proximity in space is a crucial factor when it comes to transmitting and absorbing technological and scientific knowledge.[1]

This chapter focuses on how knowledge and knowledge diffusion affect exports on a regional level and the main questions are:

- To what extent can accessibility to university and company R&D explain exports (measured by export value and exports of high-value products) in Swedish municipalities?
- Is it R&D effort or is it the presence of a well-educated population that best explains the exporting performance (measured by export value and exports of high-value products) of a municipality?

In order to answer these questions, a knowledge production function is estimated both on an aggregated and on an industry sector level. The explanatory variables are expressed as accessibility to R&D (company and university) and university-educated labour on three geographical levels (intra-municipal, intra-regional and inter-regional).

Such a specification makes it possible to reveal productive spatial knowledge flows. The estimations are conducted with quantile regressions, which enable an examination of the entire conditional distribution of the dependent variable. This is a desirable feature since municipalities in Sweden are very heterogeneous with respect to knowledge indicators and export performance.

The remaining sections of the chapter are organised as follows. In 'Theoretical background and previous research' the theoretical framework is presented. The accessibility concept used to model spatial spillovers is presented in 'Modelling spatial spillovers'. 'Data, empirical model and hypotheses' presents the data and the empirical model used for the knowledge production function, and 'Choice of estimation method' contains a discussion of the appropriate estimation method. In 'Regression results', the estimation results from the regressions are presented. The chapter ends with the main conclusions of the empirical findings.

## THEORETICAL BACKGROUND AND PREVIOUS RESEARCH

In recent decades a new theory of specialisation and trade has emerged with emphasis on differentiated competition, scale economies and the size of the home market. The new approach claims that economic specialisation is to a large extent based on increasing returns and that differences in resources (factor intensities) can explain only certain parts of the trade flows and the location of production (Krugman, 1979, 1980, 1981; Dixit and Norman, 1980; Lancaster, 1980; Helpman, 1981). In this framework, firms supply differentiated product varieties to a monopolistic competitive market. The trade specialisation is driven by economies of scale and customers' taste for variety, and generates intra-industry trade, where similar manufactured products are exchanged. The more similar countries are, the more important intra-industry trade becomes (Helpman and Krugman, 1985). Thus, with increasing returns as a basic explanation, trade develops due to advantages of specialisation also among economies and regions that are very similar to each other regarding resource endowments. The gains from trade arise because production costs fall as the scale of output increases. The traditional theory with resource-based advantages cannot explain why almost identical products are produced in different regions and then traded between these same regions. With increasing returns as a complementary basic explanation there is a much broader assortment of comparative advantages and trade flows (Johansson and Karlsson, 2001).

It is important to observe that scale economies imply a location advantage for large regions with regard to all kinds of products with a demand characterised by a set of potential customers representing a small share of the region's total set of customers (ibid.). The demand for variety in large regions increases the opportunities for individual companies to find their own varieties. Hence, large urban regions can specialise in diversity and rely on the strength of both internal and external scale economies and develop a number of different, often interacting, clusters. A counteracting force in large regions with a high economic density is high land values. Thus, firms in large regions must be more productive in order to be able to cover the extra costs for land and premises in such environments. However, the presence of internal and external scale economies offers the necessary cost savings.

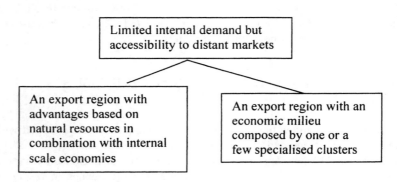

*Source:* Johansson and Karlsson (2001).

*Figure 6.1  Specialisation conditions for small and medium-sized regions*

Johansson and Karlsson (2001) stress that scale economies and specialisation are of importance for small or medium-sized functional regions. The specialisation in these regions can have two basic forms (see Figure 6.1). The first may be thought of as the classical Ricardian case, in which a small or medium-sized region hosts industries that are natural resource based and for which internal economies of scale are important. The second form of specialisation refers to the idea of localised external economies of scale discussed above. In this case, small or medium-sized functional regions may also develop a specialisation, that is, a cluster, in a self-organised way. In such a development it is possible to observe the agglomeration of a narrow set of industries within the same sector that are able to generate external economies of scale, that is, localisation economies.

Apart from differences in the relative availability of resources and the existence of economies of scale and product differentiation, dynamic changes in technology among nations or regions can be a determinant of international trade. These changes are examined by the technological gap and product cycle models. According to the technology gap model sketched by Posner (1961), a great deal of trade among industrialised countries is based on the introduction of new products and new production processes. These give the innovating firm and nation a temporary monopoly in the world market. Such a temporary monopoly is based on patents and copyrights, which are granted to stimulate the flow of inventions.

Many researchers have used different kinds of product cycle models in their empirical studies of economic activities, innovations and technological development. There are different versions of the theory to be found in the literature, but a common feature is that products go through phases in which innovative competition dominates the earlier stages and price and marketing competition dominates the latter. Vernon (1966) and Hirsch (1967) used the model in their efforts to explain the Leontief paradox. They also included a spatial dimension of the model and stressed that demand for different types of knowledge, skills and other inputs changes systematically over time and space (see also Norton and Rees, 1979).

The spatial product life cycle theory assumes that the need for R&D resources and knowledge intensity of the labour force is most important in the first phase of the product cycle, and the product is therefore developed and produced in regions that have a competitive advantage of these resources (Andersson and Johansson, 1984; Johansson and Karlsson, 1987). The new product is also gradually exported from these regions. During the next step, the growth phase, the production and the export volume increase due to product standardisation and rapidly increasing market demand. The production may start to relocate to other regions, because the need for knowledge-intensive production factors becomes less important. In the growth phase, skilled labour is still needed, but the need for sufficient space and accessibility to the goods transportation networks is now becoming urgent. Therefore, the most appropriate allocation is near large agglomerations (Cole, 1981; Batten, 1982; Karlsson, 1988). During the phase of maturity, when the product as well as the production methods are well defined, the initiating regions often lose their advantage and the production moves to regions with lower input costs. There is no extensive need for skilled labour and the most appropriate location tends to be in the periphery (Johansson and Karlsson, 1987).

Johansson and Andersson (1998) provide an answer as to where new product cycles are initiated by listing five properties which increase the region's probability of having a high-frequency product development:

1.    High accessibility to information about new product introductions.
2.    High accessibility to an educated workforce.
3.    High accessibility to R&D competence.
4.    High accessibility to customers prepared to try out new products.
5.    High accessibility to suppliers of specialised components and services.

Andersson (1985) refers to the regions that have these five characteristics as 'C-regions', stressing that their economic milieu has a rich endowment of communication, cognitive capacity and creativity. Andersson and Johansson (1984) classify metropolitan regions as the most important nodes for fostering and imitating innovations. Consequently, in such regions the variety of products in the market tends to be high. This also reflects the export pattern of the region. Generally speaking, the export is characterised by a large amount of high-priced (new) products. The prices tend to be high due to small initial production volumes and few competitors.

The relation between export competitiveness and innovation at both the nation and the firm level is explored in several empirical studies (Fagerberg, 1988; Greenhalgh et al., 1994; Wakelin, 1998; Basile, 2001). The general concluding results from these studies are that innovation, measured by proxies of input (e.g., R&D expenditure) or of output (e.g., number of patents) is an important factor in explaining export performance. What is lacking in the studies at nation and firm level is the role of geographical proximity in facilitating the transmission and the absorption of technological and scientific knowledge. Grossman and Helpman (1991) argue that the spatial concentration of knowledge spillovers may play an important role in shaping national and regional patterns of specialisation and comparative advantages. Hence, if the knowledge flows only take place within well-defined spatial boundaries, then the regions with the initial technological endowments will extend their technological advantages through cumulative processes. Developed regions with a longstanding tradition of research, marketing, entrepreneurial organisation, and so on have accumulated a stock of knowledge that allows them to be more dynamic in the creation of products with market potential. However, if much of the knowledge generated in one region can be enjoyed by other regions with similar characteristics, the capacity to export will be determined not only by the region's stock of knowledge but also by other regions' knowledge.

The importance of geographical proximity on knowledge diffusion has been revealed in several studies (e.g., Jaffe, 1989; Jaffe et al., 1993;

Feldman, 1994; Audretsch and Feldman, 1996; Anselin et al. 1997, 2000; Acs et al., 2002; Bottazzi and Peri, 2003; Fischer and Varga, 2003). Closeness between agents and other members in the regional innovation system is more likely to offer greater opportunities to interact face to face, which will develop the potential of the innovation system. The theoretical explanation is that a great deal of new economic knowledge relevant in different innovation processes is hard to codify and is therefore not perfectly available. Thus, in most cases, face-to-face contacts are necessary for transferring tacit (complex) knowledge.[2] The existence of knowledge diffusion has led to agglomeration in urban areas and industry clusters. The closer competing or complementary firms are to one another, the more likely it is that knowledge will be transferred either informally or formally.

There are several possible ways to measure geographical proximity. Karlsson and Manduchi (2001) have proposed an accessibility concept in order to incorporate geographical proximity (described in 'Modelling spatial spillovers' below). The accessibility measure is based on Weibull (1976) and is constructed according to two main principles. First, the size of attractiveness in a destination has a positive effect on the propensity to travel. Second, the time distance to a destination affects the propensity to travel negatively.

It is difficult to find any previous empirical work where export is used as an output in a knowledge-production process in a spatial context. One exception is Breschi and Palma (1999). They evaluate to what extent localised knowledge spillovers can affect trade performance in high-technology industries in Italy. Their empirical findings imply that local knowledge spillovers appear to positively affect the trade performance in the industrial automation and instruments sectors.

In the literature, there is some disagreement about the causality direction between knowledge and export performance. In this chapter the hypothesis is that high accessibility to university-educated labour and R&D has a positive effect on export performance. It is also possible to argue that exposure to international markets makes the exporting companies more innovative. Thus, the companies have to be committed in R&D activities in order to maintain or improve their competitive strength. The so-called 'learning-by-exporting' literature has been developed in that context (Clerides et al., 1998; Bernard and Jensen, 1999). On the other hand, one might expect the learning hypothesis to have more explanatory power for countries facing significant technological gaps regarding the foreign markets. This may be less relevant for companies in developed countries like Sweden.[3] Thus, the notion that causality runs from export performance to knowledge activities is beyond the scope of this chapter and is not investigated here.

## MODELLING SPATIAL SPILLOVERS

The conceptual framework for analysing geographic spillovers is based on the knowledge production function of Griliches (1979). In order to examine the influence of knowledge flows on the output of regional innovation systems, it is possible to use the number of patents in each region as an endogenous variable, regressed against the R&D effort from companies and universities (see Jaffe, 1989; Feldman and Florida; 1994; Fischer and Varga, 2003; among others).  In this chapter, the accessibility to both R&D and university-educated labour is used instead of R&D effort. Furthermore, instead of patents, total export value and number of high-value export products are used as outputs. The method with accessibilities in knowledge production has been used in a series of papers (see, e.g., Gråsjö, 2004; Andersson and Ejermo, 2004a,b; Andersson and Karlsson, 2005).

The accessibility of location $i$ to itself and to $n - 1$ surrounding locations is defined as the sum of its internal accessibility to a given opportunity $X$ and its accessibility to the same opportunity in other locations (not only neighbours),

$$A_i^X = x_1 f(c_{i1}) + ... + x_i f(c_{ii}) + ... + x_n f(c_{in}),$$  (6.1)

where $A_i^X$ is the total accessibility of location $i$. $x_i$ is a measure of an opportunity $X$, which can be an opportunity such as R&D efforts in universities and companies. $f(c)$ is the distance decay function that determines how the accessibility value is related to the cost of reaching the opportunity. A very common way of calculating an accessibility value when the accessibility is interpreted as potential of opportunity, is to use an exponential distance-decay function (see, e.g., Martellato et al., 1998), and then $f(c)$ takes the following form,

$$f(c_{ij}) = \exp\{-\omega t_{ij}\}$$  (6.2)

where $t_{ij}$ is the time distance between locations $i$ and $j$, and $\omega$ is a time sensitivity parameter. The value of $\omega$ in (6.2) depends on whether the interaction is local, intra-regional (between locations in a region), or inter-regional (locations $i$ and $j$ in different regions). It is apparent that the accessibility value may improve in two ways, either by an increase in the size of the opportunity, $x_j$, or by a reduction in the time distance between locations $i$ and $j$. If the total accessibility to a specific opportunity is decomposed into local, intra-regional and inter-regional, then:

$$A_i^X = A_{iL}^X + A_{iR}^X + A_{iOR}^X,$$  (6.3)

where:

$A_{iL}^{X} = x_i \exp\{-\omega_L t_{ii}\}$, local accessibility to opportunity $X$ for location $i$;

$A_{iR}^{X} = \sum_{r \in R, \, r \neq i} x_r \exp\{-\omega_R t_{ir}\}$, intra-regional accessibility to opportunity

$X$ for location $i$;

$A_{iOR}^{X} = \sum_{k \notin R} x_k \exp\{-\omega_{OR} t_{ik}\}$, inter-regional accessibility to opportunity

$X$ for location $i$; and

$j$ defines locations within the own region $R$, and $k$ defines locations in other regions.

The accessibility concept expressed in equation (6.3) has several advantages. First, it incorporates 'global' spillovers and does not only account for the impact from neighbours or locations within a certain distance band. Second, the separation of the total effect into local, intra-regional and inter-regional spillovers captures potential productive knowledge flows between locations and makes the inferential aspects more clear. Third, distance is often measured by the physical distance, but a better way to measure it is to use the time it takes to travel between different locations (Beckman, 2000). Time distances are also crucial when it comes to attending business meetings and also to spatial borders of labour markets (see Johansson and Klaesson, 2001, for the Swedish case). Thus, accessibility provides a connection between the functional and the spatial component of an urban system (Bertuglia and Occelli, 2000). It defines the range and temporal organisation of economic opportunities available in space as well the cost of overcoming space in order to explore the opportunities in different locations. Accessibility accounts for the size of an opportunity in a location and discounts the value of the opportunity with time distance in a way that reflects the willingness to explore that opportunity given its size and distance. Accessibility is also a robust operational measurement tool which makes spatial proximity operational (Karlsson and Manduchi, 2001).

In the accessibility calculations the time sensitivity parameter value $\omega_L$ is set to 0.02, $\omega_R$ to 0.1 and $\omega_{OR}$ to 0.05. Johansson et al. (2003) estimated these values by using data on commuting flows within and between Swedish municipalities in 1990 and 1998. It may look strange that the intra-regional accessibilities have the highest parameter value ($\omega_R = 0.1$). But the intra-regional commuting trips, which are in the time span from approximately 15 to 45 minutes, are the ones that are most time sensitive. That is, increased commuting time in this time span will hamper the propensity to travel the most (see Figure 6.2).

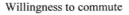

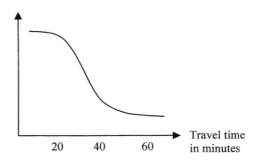

Source: Johanson et al. (2003).

*Figure 6.2  Willingness to commute to other municipalities*

When the accessibility variables have been calculated they can be entered in a knowledge production function. The standard choice of the functional form is often a version of Cobb–Douglas. However, it could be argued that the various accessibilities are most probably substitutes and hence the implication of Cobb–Douglas that one zero in inputs is enough for zero output does not make sense. Therefore an additive linear functional form is used to model the knowledge production,

$$y_i = \alpha\alpha \ A_{iL}^X \beta_1 - A_{iR}^X \beta_2 + A_{iOR}^X \beta_3 + u_i. \tag{6.4}$$

The marginal effect of the accessibility variables answers the question 'What is the effect on the dependent variable if the accessibility to an opportunity (R&D, university-educated labour) increases by 1?'. The obvious subsequent question is then: 'How can an accessibility increase of 1 be accomplished?'. It has already been stated in this chapter that the accessibility is affected by the size of the opportunity and commuting time within a location or between locations. Appendix 6A1 gives an example that shows the relation between accessibility and size of the opportunity. The example is intended to help the reader with the result interpretations in 'Regression results' (see below).

# DATA, EMPIRICAL MODEL AND HYPOTHESES

## Data and Descriptive Statistics

The variables used in the coming regressions are:

- Export value (in SEK) and number of export products with export price above 1000 SEK per kg, are yearly averages during 1997–99 for Swedish municipalities.
- Accessibility to university R&D and company R&D are computed using a yearly average of conducted R&D measured in man-years during 1993–99 for Swedish municipalities.[4]
- Accessibility to university-educated labour is computed using a yearly average of the number of people with at least three years of university studies for Swedish municipalities during 1993–99.
- Population dummy variables are based on an average of the populations in Swedish municipalities during 1993–99.

Statistics Sweden (SCB) collects data on companies' exports, performed R&D in universities and companies, level of education and population size in Swedish municipalities. The company R&D data disaggregated by industrial sector according to SNI92.[5] The data on university R&D are not divided into industrial sectors. Hence, when university R&D used in the following analysis, it is always on an aggregated level. Exports can be regionalised because each exporting firm is assigned to a municipality according to the location of its establishment. The exports are registered by product according to the Combined Nomenclature (CN) classification system (8-digit level). A concordance table between CN and SNI92 is used to couple the export data to the same industrial sectors.

The National Road Administration has data on commuting time between and within Swedish municipalities and these are used in the accessibility calculations. The descriptive statistics of the variables on the aggregated data set are presented in Table 6.1. The variable 'Large population' equals one if the population is greater than 100,000 and 'Medium population' equals one if the population is between 50 and 100,000. Note the large differences between the mean and the median for all variables. This is a particular difficulty for the variables that are treated as endogenous in the regressions. If the distribution of the dependent variable is skewed with a few very influential variables, an ordinarly least square (OLS) regression gives biased results.

*Table 6.1 Descriptive statistics for the 288 municipalities in Sweden*
        *(aggregated level)*

| Variable | Mean | Median | Std dev. | Min | Max |
|---|---|---|---|---|---|
| Export value ($10^9$ SEK) | 2.236 | 0.720 | 5.507 | 0.00086 | 48.43 |
| Number of high-value export products | 60.09 | 28.67 | 88.37 | 0.667 | 727.7 |
| Accessibility to university R&D, local | 52.53 | 0 | 320.8 | 0 | 3012 |
| Accessibility to university R&D, intra-regional | 114.9 | 1.726 | 301.0 | 0 | 1990 |
| Accessibility to university R&D, inter-regional | 96.49 | 22.64 | 164.1 | 0.00049 | 1023 |
| Accessibility to company R&D, local | 8.339 | 0.001 | 46.34 | 0 | 643.8 |
| Accessibility to company R&D, intra-regional | 19.47 | 0.641 | 50.91 | 0 | 383.3 |
| Accessibility to company, inter-regional | 13.89 | 7.390 | 19.34 | 0.00010 | 168.2 |
| Accessibility to university-educated labour, local | 1,755 | 477.3 | 5,699 | 1.562 | 82,442 |
| Accessibility to university-educated labour, intra-reg | 3,280 | 399.1 | 8,172 | 0 | 56,610 |
| Accessibility to university-educated labour, inter-reg | 2,948 | 2,166 | 2,954 | 0.031 | 20,611 |
| Access. to univ.-educ. labour, local, per 1,000 inhabitants | 53.42 | 44.26 | 35.81 | 0.080 | 312.8 |
| Access. to univ. R&D, local, per 1,000 employed | 0.892 | 0 | 4.325 | 0 | 39.35 |
| Access. to comp. R&D, local, per 1,000 employed | 0.251 | 0.00018 | 0.816 | 0 | 9.625 |
| Large population (>100, 000) | 0.038 | 0 | 0.192 | 0 | 1 |
| Medium population (50 to 100,000) | 0.125 | 0 | 0.331 | 0 | 1 |

Figure 6.3 shows the skewed spatial distribution of exports, university-educated labour and R&D in Sweden. Maps showing the spatial distribution of exports, university-educated labour and R&D in Sweden are presented in Figure 6.4. The main feature is that all used variables are concentrated in the

regions with the largest municipalities. As in Figure 6.3, it is evident that conducted R&D has the highest geographical concentration. Furthermore, note also the different geographical distribution of the number of high-value export products and export value. For example, the export value is relatively high (above 5 per cent of the total in Sweden) in regions (Gävle and Örebro) where the knowledge intensity is on a substantially lower level.

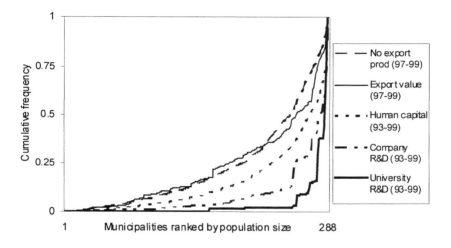

*Figure 6.3 Cumulative share of exports, human capital and R&D for Swedish municipalities*

## Empirical Model

The research unit in this chapter is Swedish municipalities. Thus, the locations referred to in equations (6.1)–(6.3) are municipalities. The regions are local labour market (LLM) regions. An LLM region consists, in most cases, of a number of municipalities that are connected through intensive commuting flows. In the sparsely populated areas, these regions often comprise single municipalities. There are 81 LLM regions, ensuring that firms have only short distances to travel between different locations within their LLM, in most cases taking less than 50 minutes to travel from one to another. The average time distance is 20–30 minutes (Johansson et al., 2002).

**Number of high-value export products**        **Export value**

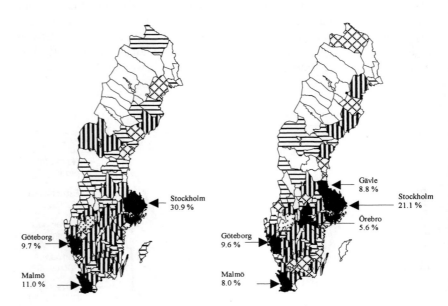

**Company R&D (man-years)**        **University R&D (man-years)**

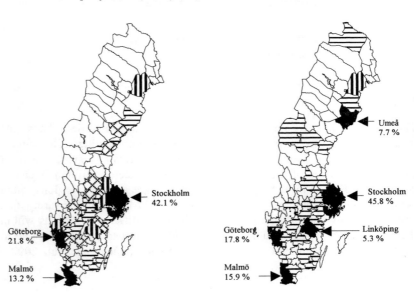

**University-educated labour**

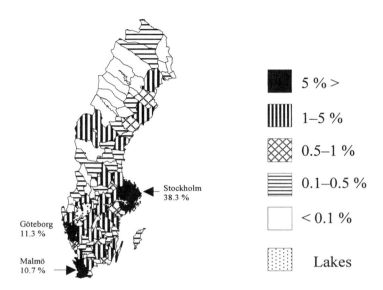

*Note:* The maps are based on classification LA2003 (Statistics Sweden), where LLM region Stockholm includes Uppsala, and LLM region Malmö includes Helsingborg.

*Figure 6.4    Distribution across LLM regions (percentage of the total in Sweden)*

LLM regions are delineated on the basis of intensity of intra-regional commuting flows are thus characterised by a high frequency of intra-regional interaction. The borders of an LLM region are distinguished by a sharp decline in the intensity of such flows. Hence, LLM regions can be conceived as arenas for face-to-face interaction and milieus for the generation and diffusion of innovation ideas. The opportunities are university-educated labour (at least three years of university studies) and conducted R&D work in universities and companies in Sweden.

In accordance with the discussion in 'Theoretical background and previous research', the following variables are used for municipality $i$ in the empirical model:

Dependent variables

- total export value;
- number of export products with a price greater than 1,000 SEK per kg.With 1,000 SEK per kg as a cut-off value, approximately 13 per cent of the products exported from the Swedish municipalities had a price that exceeded this limit.[6]

Explanatory variables     Local (intra-municipal), intra-regional and inter-regional accessibility to:

- university R&D;
- company R&D; and
- university-educated labour (at least three years of university studies).

In addition, two dummy variables measuring the size of the population in the municipalities are included in the model. These variables enable a comparison between municipalities with a large $(D_1)$, medium-sized $(D_2)$ and a small population.

The population dummy variables are used to control for high accessibility to information about new product introductions and high accessibility customers and suppliers (see the properties of an innovative region in 'Theoretical background and previous research').[7] The hypothesis is that municipalities with large populations have an economic activity that exceeds that of smaller municipalities, and this ought to affect the output.

In order to answer the questions outlined in the Introduction, the first choice would be to estimate equation (6.4) with a single regression using an export variable as the dependent variable and accessibility to university R&D, company R&D and university-educated labour on all three geographical levels as exogenous variables. This is not possible, however, because of problems with multicollinearity, especially between the intra-regional variables (VIF = 21.8) and also to some extent between the inter-regional variables (VIF = 13.8).[8] This is natural because R&D is to a large extent carried out by university-educated labour. Therefore two separate specifications are estimated, one with the R&D variables and the other with university-educated labour as exogenous variables.[9] The following equation is estimated for the R&D variables:

$$\text{Exp}_i = a + b_1 A_{iL}^{uR\&D} + b_2 A_{iOR}^{uR\&D} + b_3 A_{iL}^{cR\&D} + b_4 A_{iR}^{cR\&D} + b_5 D_1 + b_6 D_2 + u_i, \qquad (6.5)$$

where $\text{Exp}_i$ = total export value and number of export products with a price above 1,000 SEK per kg in municipality $i$, $uR\&D$ = university R&D in man-years and $cR\&D$ = company R&D in man-years. The other notations are as before. Any other combination of intra- and inter-regional variables would also accomplish a low degree of multicollinearity. I have chosen to keep the pair that has the highest correlation with the export variables. To estimate the relationship between exports and accessibility to university-educated labour the following equation is used:

$$\text{Exp}_i = a + b_1 A_{iL}^{ed} + b_2 A_{iR}^{ed} + b_3 A_{iOR}^{ed} + b_4 D_1 + b_5 D_2 + u_i, \qquad (6.6)$$

where *ed* is the notation for university-educated labour aged 16–74 with at least three years of university studies. In order to get a direct comparison of the importance of university-educated labour, company and university R&D on exports and to avoid the multicollinearity problem, one solution is to express the variables of interest with respect to some size variable. Therefore, the local accessibilities per capita are used in the specification:

$$\text{Exp}_i = \frac{A_{iL}^{ed}}{Pop_i} \beta_1 + \frac{A_{iL}^{cR\&D}}{Pope_i} / \beta_2 - \frac{A_{iL}^{uR\&D}}{Pope_i} / \beta_3 \vdash u_i, \qquad (6.7)$$

where $Pop_i$ = the number of people aged 16–74 in municipality *i* and $Pope_i$ = the number of people aged 16–64 gainfully employed with a place of work in municipality *i*.[10] The choice of $Pope_i$ as a scaling factor is motivated by the fact that company and university R&D are registered by workplace, while the people that constitute the university-educated labour are registered by the place where they live. The estimation results of (6.5), (6.6) and (6.7) are presented in 'Regression results'.

**Research Hypotheses**

In accordance with the discussion in 'Theoretical background and previous research', the hypothesis is that companies, which together produce a large number of high-value export products, are located in municipalities (in large functional regions) with high accessibility to R&D and university-educated labour. This means that the parameter estimates of the local and/or intra-regional accessibilities are supposed to be positive and statistically significant. High total export values are likely to be found in municipalities where the companies produce and export products in the growth or mature phase of the life cycle. When the products are in these phases, the companies may still need R&D and university-educated labour, but not to the extent that characterised the creativity phase. Thus, the local and/or intra-regional accessibilities may be of importance in order to explain the total export value in a municipality. However, the hypothesis is that the fit of the model is higher (resulting in higher $R^2$ values) when the number of high-value export products is used as the dependent variable.

Whether it is university R&D, company R&D or university-educated labour that best explains the variations in the municipalities' export performance is to some extent an open question. The theory does not give any hints, but the empirical findings in Gråsjö (2004) reveal that the effects of university R&D were completely crowded out by company R&D when the number of patent applications in Swedish municipalities was used as an output of the knowledge production process.

In order to test the hypotheses outlined above and to answer the questions in the Introduction, a discussion of the choice of a proper estimation method has to be conducted. The next section describes why the quantile regression technique is preferred to the OLS method.

## CHOICE OF ESTIMATION METHOD

In Appendix 6A2, the distributions of the dependent variables are analysed graphically. It is easy to see that the distributions are skewed and have outliers. One way of dealing with highly influential outliers is to use quantile regression as an alternative to OLS.[11] The quantile regression method has the important property that it is robust to distributional assumptions. The quantile regression estimator gives less weight to outliers of the dependent variable than OLS, which weakens the impact that outliers might have on the results.

There are also theoretical advantages with quantile regressions. The municipalities are most likely heterogeneous in their ability to export products. Thus, the effects of the variables explaining the abilities do not have to be and probably are not the same for all municipalities.[12] It could be the case that municipalities with low export values do not experience the same effect from an accessibility increase of highly skilled labour as municipalities with high export values. OLS cannot account for heterogeneity of this kind. OLS assumes that the conditional distribution of the export values, given the set of municipality characteristics, is homogeneous. This implies that no matter what point on the conditional distribution is analysed, the OLS estimates of the relationship between the dependent variable and the regressors are the same. OLS regression estimates the conditional mean of the dependent variable as a function of the explanatory variables. In contrast, quantile regression enables the estimation of any conditional quantile of the dependent variable as a function of the explanatory variables. By estimating the marginal effects of the explanatory variables for different quantiles, a more complete description of the relationship between dependent and explanatory variables is achieved.

Koenker and Bassett (1978) originally recommended quantile regressions as a robust alternative to OLS to solve the problem with errors that are not normally distributed. The regression technique may be viewed as a natural extension of least squares estimation of conditional mean models, to the estimation of a group of models for conditional quantile functions. The simplest case is the median regression estimator that minimises a sum of absolute residuals. The other conditional quantile functions are estimated by minimising an asymmetrically weighted sum of absolute residuals. Quantile regression is especially useful in the presence of heteroscedasticity, because the marginal effects of the covariates may differ for different quantiles. In the special case where the errors are homoscedastic, the marginal effects will be the same across quantiles, though the intercept will differ. Koenker and Bassett (1982) proposed a method to estimate the variance-covariance matrix. But Gould (1992) and Rogers (1992) argued that this method underestimates the standard errors if the residuals are heteroscedastic. Gould suggested a bootstrap re-sampling procedure to overcome this problem. The procedure is standardised in the Stata statistical package.[13] Needless to say, quantile regression is not the same as dividing the complete dataset into different quantiles of the dependent variable and then running OLS on these subsets. This action would truncate the dependent variable, introduce a sample selection bias and will result in a procedure where not all observations are being used for each estimate.

Although quantile regression has been widely used in the past decade in many areas of applied econometrics, applications concerning knowledge production are not that easily found. One exception is Audretsch et al. (2005) in their examination of locational choice as a firm strategy to access knowledge spillovers from universities, using a dataset of young high-technology start-ups in Germany.[14]

The regressions in the following section are conducted for every fifth quantile (Q5, Q10, Q15 etc.). If the parameter estimates of the accessibility variables are not statistically significant for any conditional quantile, then no graph is presented. The parameter estimates of the population dummy variables can be found in Appendix 6A3. In order to solve the heteroscedasticity problem for the quantile regressions, bootstrap procedures with 3,000 replications are conducted. The analyses are carried out both on an aggregated level and for the sector 'Manufacture of office machinery, electrical machinery and communication equipment'. This sector has the highest total export value and also the largest number of high-value export products. The multicollinerarity problem is less severe on the sector level, which enables the inclusion of the inter-regional accessibility to company

R&D variable in Equation (6.5). The export value or the number of high-value export products in sector $j$ is regressed against the accessibility measures for university R&D on an aggregated level and the three accessibility measures for company R&D in sector $j$. All the industrial sectors with some registered export are presented in Appendix 6A4. When modelling spatial inter-dependencies it is important to check whether there are any remaining effects in the error terms, that is, whether the chosen specifications in section 'Data, empirical model and hypotheses' model feasible spatial effects. In Appendix 6A5 pre-estimation tests are performed that rule out problems with spatial autocorrelation.

## REGRESSION RESULTS

### Export and Accessibility to R&D

Equation (6.5) is estimated in order to examine to what extent variations in accessibility to R&D explain variations in total export value and number of high-value export products. Figure 6.5 shows the marginal effects of accessibility to university and company R&D on export values for aggregated data. The 95 per cent confidence bands from bootstrapped estimation errors in the quantile regressions are shown as dotted lines. Consequently, given a specific quantile, if both the upper *and* the lower confidence limit are either above *or* below zero, then the parameter estimate is statistically significant for the quantile in question. As can be seen, it is only local accessibility to company R&D that can explain the variations in export value for Swedish municipalities. The parameter estimates are positive and significant for municipalities with total export values corresponding to the upper part of the conditional distribution (except for Q95). An accessibility increase raises the export value the most for municipalities corresponding to Q80. The quantile value for Q80 is 2.64 billion SEK and hence a municipality with this export value will increase its export value by approximately 0.15 billion SEK if the accessibility increases by one. Note also the large differences between the marginal effects for the different quantiles (although most of them are statistically insignificant).

In Figure 6.6, export value on the sector level is regressed against accessibility to R&D. As on the aggregated level, it is only local accessibility to company R&D that has an effect on export value. The quantile regression estimates are significant for municipalities in the middle part of the conditional distribution.

In Figure 6.7 the dependent variable is altered to the number of export products with a price above 1,000 SEK per kg. As expected and in accordance with the previous discussion ('Theoretical background and previous research'), the importance of accessibility to R&D increases (resulting in higher $R^2$ values) when this output measure is used. The intra-regional effect is positive and statistically significant over the whole conditional distribution, with the largest marginal effects in the upper tail of the distribution (from 0.2 to 0.7). As an example, a municipality corresponding to the median, that is, with approximately 28.7 high-value export products, will increase this number by 0.5 if the intra-regional accessibility to company R&D is raised by 1.

**Dependent variable:** Export value ($10^9$ SEK)

| Explanatory variables | Estimate |
|---|---|
| Local accessibilty to company R&D | see fig. |
| Intra-regional accessibilty to company R&D | ns |
| Local accessibilty to university R&D | ns |
| Inter-regional accessibilty to university R&D | ns |

ns = not statistically significant for any quantile

Local accessibility company to R&D

|  | Q5 | Q10 | Q15 | Q20 | Q25 | Q30 | Q35 | Q40 | Q45 | Q50 | Q55 | Q60 | Q65 | Q70 | Q75 | Q80 | Q85 | Q90 | Q95 |
|---|---|---|---|---|---|---|---|---|---|---|---|---|---|---|---|---|---|---|---|
| Quantile | 0.05 | 0.08 | 0.13 | 0.17 | 0.26 | 0.31 | 0.36 | 0.44 | 0.53 | 0.72 | 0.87 | 1.05 | 1.23 | 1.50 | 2.04 | 2.64 | 3.67 | 4.76 | 7.57 |
| Pse $R^2$ | 0.15 | 0.16 | 0.18 | 0.19 | 0.20 | 0.21 | 0.23 | 0.25 | 0.26 | 0.27 | 0.28 | 0.29 | 0.30 | 0.31 | 0.34 | 0.37 | 0.41 | 0.45 | 0.53 |

*Figure 6.5 Export value and accessibility to R&D (aggregated level)*

**Dependent variable:** Export value ($10^6$ SEK)

| Explanatory variables | Estimate |
|---|---|
| Local accessibilty to company R&D | see fig. |
| Intra-regional accessibilty to company R&D | ns |
| Inter-regional accessibilty to company R&D | ns |
| Local accessibilty to university R&D | ns |
| Inter-regional accessibilty to university R&D | ns |

ns = not statistically significant for any quantile

Local accessibility company to R&D

|  | Q5 | Q10 | Q15 | Q20 | Q25 | Q30 | Q35 | Q40 | Q45 | Q50 | Q55 | Q60 | Q65 | Q70 | Q75 | Q80 | Q85 | Q90 | Q95 |
|---|---|---|---|---|---|---|---|---|---|---|---|---|---|---|---|---|---|---|---|
| Quantile | 0.03 | 0.14 | 0.26 | 0.47 | 1.00 | 1.34 | 2.41 | 3.71 | 5.61 | 7.83 | 10.9 | 17.0 | 28.2 | 45.2 | 78.9 | 128 | 239 | 375 | 1180 |
| Pse $R^2$ | 0.12 | 0.12 | 0.12 | 0.12 | 0.13 | 0.14 | 0.15 | 0.16 | 0.17 | 0.18 | 0.19 | 0.20 | 0.21 | 0.22 | 0.23 | 0.24 | 0.24 | 0.25 | 0.25 |

*Figure 6.6 Export value and accessibility to R&D (manufacturing of office machinery, electrical machinery and communication equipment)*

There are also productive knowledge flows from municipalities outside the functional region. Inter-regional accessibility to university R&D affects the number of high-value export products positively for municipalities corresponding to quantiles above the median of the conditional distribution. In Figure 6.7 it can also be seen that increasing local accessibility to company R&D has a proven effect for municipalities with a number of export products below the median.

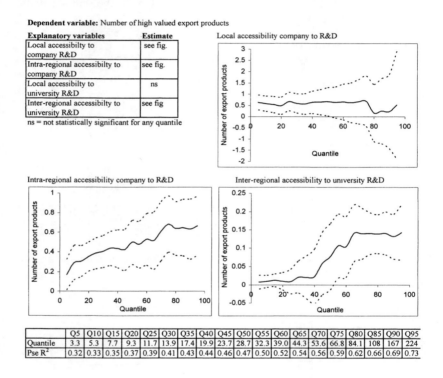

**Dependent variable:** Number of high valued export products

| Explanatory variables | Estimate |
|---|---|
| Local accessibilty to company R&D | see fig. |
| Intra-regional accessibilty to company R&D | see fig. |
| Local accessibilty to university R&D | ns |
| Inter-regional accessibilty to university R&D | see fig |

ns = not statistically significant for any quantile

| | Q5 | Q10 | Q15 | Q20 | Q25 | Q30 | Q35 | Q40 | Q45 | Q50 | Q55 | Q60 | Q65 | Q70 | Q75 | Q80 | Q85 | Q90 | Q95 |
|---|---|---|---|---|---|---|---|---|---|---|---|---|---|---|---|---|---|---|---|
| Quantile | 3.3 | 5.3 | 7.7 | 9.3 | 11.7 | 13.9 | 17.4 | 19.9 | 23.7 | 28.7 | 32.3 | 39.0 | 44.3 | 53.6 | 66.8 | 84.1 | 108 | 167 | 224 |
| Pse R² | 0.32 | 0.33 | 0.35 | 0.37 | 0.39 | 0.41 | 0.43 | 0.44 | 0.46 | 0.47 | 0.50 | 0.52 | 0.54 | 0.56 | 0.59 | 0.62 | 0.66 | 0.69 | 0.73 |

*Figure 6.7   Number of high-value export products and accessibility to R&D (aggregated level)*

According to Figure 6.8, intra-regional accessibility to company R&D is the variable that best explains the variations of the dependent variable in the industrial sector 'Manufacture of office machinery, electrical machinery and communication equipment'. Once again the largest marginal effects can be found in the upper part of the distribution. The values range from 0.4 for Q5 to 1.3 for Q90.

Before exploring the importance of university-educated labour on exports, a summary of the main results might be in order:

- The total value of exported products is affected only by local accessibility to company R&D. The effects are positive and significant for municipalities where the values of the aggregated export are high (Q75 to Q90). Knowledge flows between and within functional regions are of no importance.

- The intra- and inter-regional accessibilities play a more important role for the number of high-value products in Swedish municipalities. This is the case both on an aggregated level and on a sector level.

**Dependent variable:** Number of high valued export products

| Explanatory variables | Estimate |
|---|---|
| Local accessibilty to company R&D | ns |
| Intra-regional accessibilty to company R&D | see fig. |
| Inter-regional accessibilty to company R&D | ns |
| Local accessibilty to university R&D | ns |
| Inter-regional accessibilty to university R&D | ns |

ns = not statistically significant for any quantile

Intra-regional accessibility to company R&D

|  | Q5 | Q10 | Q15 | Q20 | Q25 | Q30 | Q35 | Q40 | Q45 | Q50 | Q55 | Q60 | Q65 | Q70 | Q75 | Q80 | Q85 | Q90 | Q95 |
|---|---|---|---|---|---|---|---|---|---|---|---|---|---|---|---|---|---|---|---|
| Quantile | 0.3 | 0.7 | 1.3 | 1.7 | 2.3 | 3.3 | 4.0 | 4.7 | 5.7 | 7.3 | 9.3 | 10.8 | 12.3 | 15.1 | 20.2 | 27.4 | 37.7 | 56.7 | 77.7 |
| Pse R² | 0.22 | 0.26 | 0.28 | 0.30 | 0.32 | 0.34 | 0.36 | 0.38 | 0.40 | 0.42 | 0.43 | 0.45 | 0.47 | 0.50 | 0.52 | 0.54 | 0.56 | 0.58 | 0.59 |

*Figure 6.8   Number of high valued export products and accessibility to R&D (manufacturing of office machinery, electrical machinery)*

**Export and Accessibility to University-educated Labour**

Equation (6.6) is estimated to establish to what extent accessibility to university-educated labour affects exports in Swedish municipalities. The estimation results of equation (6.6) presented in Figure 6.9 indicate positive effects of increased local accessibility to university-educated labour. In contrast to R&D (see Figure 6.5), well-educated labour also appears to have significant positive effects for municipalities with export values in the lower part of the distribution. Furthermore, there are negative impacts of intra-regional accessibility to university-educated labour. The interpretation is that an increased number of well-educated people in a municipality have a positive (local) effect on the export value of the municipality but a negative (intra-regional) effect on the other municipalities' export values in the region.

**Dependent variable**: Export values ($10^9$ SEK)

| Explanatory variables | Estimate |
|---|---|
| Local accessibilty to university educated labour | see fig. |
| Intra-regional accessibilty to university educated labour | see fig. |
| Intra-regional accessibilty to university educated labour | ns |

ns = not statistically significant for any quantile

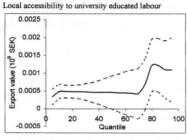

| | Q5 | Q10 | Q15 | Q20 | Q25 | Q30 | Q35 | Q40 | Q45 | Q50 | Q55 | Q60 | Q65 | Q70 | Q75 | Q80 | Q85 | Q90 | Q95 |
|---|---|---|---|---|---|---|---|---|---|---|---|---|---|---|---|---|---|---|---|
| Q, mean | 0.05 | 0.08 | 0.13 | 0.17 | 0.26 | 0.31 | 0.36 | 0.44 | 0.53 | 0.72 | 0.87 | 1.05 | 1.23 | 1.50 | 2.04 | 2.64 | 3.67 | 4.76 | 7.57 |
| Pse $R^2$ | 0.15 | 0.18 | 0.21 | 0.23 | 0.24 | 0.24 | 0.25 | 0.26 | 0.27 | 0.28 | 0.29 | 0.29 | 0.30 | 0.31 | 0.32 | 0.34 | 0.36 | 0.39 | 0.48 |

*Figure 6.9    Export value and accessibility to university-educated labour (aggregated level)*

**Dependent variable**: Export values ($10^6$ SEK)

| Explanatory variables | Estimate |
|---|---|
| Local accessibilty to university educated labour | see fig. |
| Intra-regional accessibilty to university educated labour | ns |
| Intra-regional accessibilty to university educated labour | ns |

ns = not statistically significant for any quantile

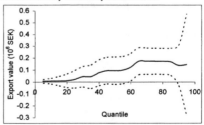

| | Q5 | Q10 | Q15 | Q20 | Q25 | Q30 | Q35 | Q40 | Q45 | Q50 | Q55 | Q60 | Q65 | Q70 | Q75 | Q80 | Q85 | Q90 | Q95 |
|---|---|---|---|---|---|---|---|---|---|---|---|---|---|---|---|---|---|---|---|
| Q, mean | 0.03 | 0.14 | 0.26 | 0.47 | 1.00 | 1.34 | 2.41 | 3.71 | 5.61 | 7.83 | 10.9 | 17.0 | 28.2 | 45.2 | 78.9 | 128 | 239 | 375 | 1180 |
| Pse $R^2$ | 0.009 | 0.01 | 0.02 | 0.02 | 0.03 | 0.04 | 0.05 | 0.06 | 0.08 | 0.10 | 0.11 | 0.13 | 0.15 | 0.17 | 0.18 | 0.20 | 0.21 | 0.22 | 0.24 |

*Figure 6.10   Export value and accessibility to university-educated labour (manufacturing of office machinery, electrical machinery and communication equipment)*

From Figure 6.9 it is also evident that there are no beneficial (inter-regional) knowledge flows from municipalities outside the own region. On the sector level (see Figure 6.10), the only statistically significant effects can be found from local accessibility. This is the case for quantiles in the upper part of the distribution (except Q95).

When the number of high-value export products is used as an output, the results are quite different (see Figure 6.11). The local accessibility to university-educated labour seems to matter only for the municipalities with few high-value export products (Q5 and Q10). Figure 6.11 also shows that it is not necessary to have well-educated people living in the municipality where the number of high-value export products is registered. Hence, both intra-regional and inter-regional accessibility to university-educated labour have positive and statistically significant parameter estimates over the whole conditional distribution.

Figure 6.12 shows the marginal effects of accessibility to university-educated labour in the industrial sector 'Manufacture of office machinery, electrical machinery and communication equipment'. The number of

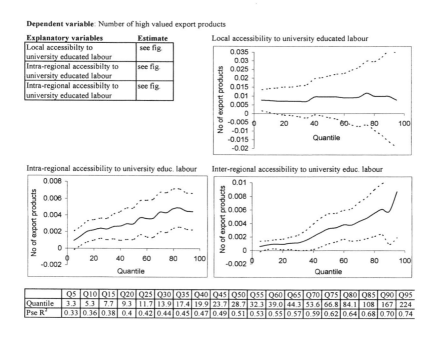

*Figure 6.11 Number of high-value export products and access to university-educated labour (aggregated level)*

**Dependent variable**: Number of high valued export products

| Explanatory variables | Estimate |
|---|---|
| Local accessibilty to university educated labour | ns |
| Intra-regional accessibilty to university educated labour | see fig. |
| Intra-regional accessibilty to university educated labour | see fig. |

ns = not statistically significant for any quantile

Intra-regional accessibility to university educ. labour　　　Inter-regional accessibility to university educ. labour

| | Q5 | Q10 | Q15 | Q20 | Q25 | Q30 | Q35 | Q40 | Q45 | Q50 | Q55 | Q60 | Q65 | Q70 | Q75 | Q80 | Q85 | Q90 | Q95 |
|---|---|---|---|---|---|---|---|---|---|---|---|---|---|---|---|---|---|---|---|
| Quantile | 0.3 | 0.7 | 1.3 | 1.7 | 2.3 | 3.3 | 4.0 | 4.7 | 5.7 | 7.3 | 9.3 | 10.8 | 12.3 | 15.1 | 20.2 | 27.4 | 37.7 | 56.7 | 77.7 |
| Pse R² | 0.26 | 0.29 | 0.32 | 0.35 | 0.36 | 0.39 | 0.4 | 0.42 | 0.44 | 0.46 | 0.47 | 0.49 | 0.5 | 0.53 | 0.55 | 0.56 | 0.58 | 0.59 | 0.59 |

*Figure 6.12　Number of high-value export products and access to university-educated labour (manufacturing of office machinery, electrical machinery and communication equipment)*

exported products in a municipality is above all affected by the accessibility to well-educated labour within the region but outside the own municipality. The largest effects can be found for the municipalities with an export performance corresponding to the largest quantiles.

The figures displaying the marginal effects of R&D and university-educated labour show that there is a much smaller magnitude of the marginal effects of university-educated labour. The explanation is that the magnitudes of the accessibilities to university-educated labour are much higher (see Table 6.1).[15]

### University-educated Labour or R&D: Which Is Most Important?

Equation (6.7) is estimated in order to answer the question whether it is accessibility to R&D or accessibility to university-educated labour that best explains the variations in municipalities' exports. The regression results are presented in Figures 6.13–6.14 and 6.15–6.16.

**Dependent variable**: Export value ($10^9$ SEK)

| Explanatory variables | Estimate |
|---|---|
| Local accessibilty to university educated labour per 1000 inhabitants | see fig. |
| Local accessibilty to university R&D per 1000 employed | ns |
| Local accessibilty to company R&D per 1000 employed | ns |

ns = not statistically significant for any quantile

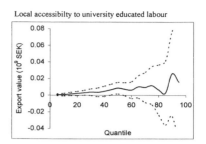

Local accessibilty to university educated labour

| | Q5 | Q10 | Q15 | Q20 | Q25 | Q30 | Q35 | Q40 | Q45 | Q50 | Q55 | Q60 | Q65 | Q70 | Q75 | Q80 | Q85 | Q90 | Q95 |
|---|---|---|---|---|---|---|---|---|---|---|---|---|---|---|---|---|---|---|---|
| Quantile | 0.05 | 0.08 | 0.13 | 0.17 | 0.26 | 0.31 | 0.36 | 0.44 | 0.53 | 0.72 | 0.87 | 1.05 | 1.23 | 1.50 | 2.04 | 2.64 | 3.67 | 4.76 | 7.57 |
| Pse R² | 0.00 | 0.01 | 0.02 | 0.03 | 0.04 | 0.05 | 0.06 | 0.07 | 0.08 | 0.08 | 0.09 | 0.11 | 0.12 | 0.13 | 0.14 | 0.15 | 0.17 | 0.21 | 0.32 |

*Figure 6.13 Export value: university-educated labour vs. R&D (aggregated level)*

**Dependent variable**: Export value ($10^6$ SEK)

| Explanatory variables | Estimate |
|---|---|
| Local accessibilty to university educated labour per 1000 inhabitants | see fig. |
| Local accessibilty to university R&D per 1000 employed | ns |
| Local accessibilty to company R&D per 1000 employed | see fig. |

ns = not statistically significant for any quantile

Local accessibilty to university educated labour    Local accessibilty to company R&D

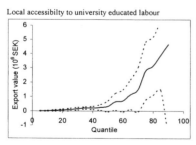
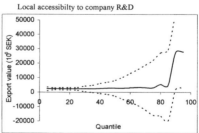

| | Q5 | Q10 | Q15 | Q20 | Q25 | Q30 | Q35 | Q40 | Q45 | Q50 | Q55 | Q60 | Q65 | Q70 | Q75 | Q80 | Q85 | Q90 | Q95 |
|---|---|---|---|---|---|---|---|---|---|---|---|---|---|---|---|---|---|---|---|
| Quantile | 0.03 | 0.14 | 0.26 | 0.47 | 1.00 | 1.34 | 2.41 | 3.71 | 5.61 | 7.83 | 10.9 | 17.0 | 28.2 | 45.2 | 78.9 | 128 | 239 | 375 | 1180 |
| Pse R² | 0.04 | 0.06 | 0.07 | 0.07 | 0.07 | 0.08 | 0.08 | 0.08 | 0.08 | 0.09 | 0.09 | 0.09 | 0.10 | 0.10 | 0.11 | 0.11 | 0.12 | 0.14 | 0.17 |

*Figure 6.14 Export value: university-educated labour vs. R&D (manufacturing of office machinery, electrical machinery and communication equipment)*

**Dependent variable**: Number of high valued export products

| Explanatory variables | Estimate |
|---|---|
| Local accessibility to university educated labour per 1000 inhabitants | see fig. |
| Local accessibility to university R&D per 1000 employed | ns |
| Local accessibility to company R&D per 1000 employed | ns |

ns = not statistically significant for any quantile

Local accessibility to university educated labour

| | Q5 | Q10 | Q15 | Q20 | Q25 | Q30 | Q35 | Q40 | Q45 | Q50 | Q55 | Q60 | Q65 | Q70 | Q75 | Q80 | Q85 | Q90 | Q95 |
|---|---|---|---|---|---|---|---|---|---|---|---|---|---|---|---|---|---|---|---|
| Quantile | 3.3 | 5.3 | 7.7 | 9.3 | 11.7 | 13.9 | 17.4 | 19.9 | 23.7 | 28.7 | 32.3 | 39.0 | 44.3 | 53.6 | 66.8 | 84.1 | 108 | 167 | 224 |
| Pse R$^2$ | 0.05 | 0.08 | 0.10 | 0.12 | 0.16 | 0.18 | 0.19 | 0.20 | 0.22 | 0.24 | 0.26 | 0.28 | 0.30 | 0.33 | 0.36 | 0.40 | 0.44 | 0.49 | 0.53 |

*Figure 6.15    Number of high-value export products: university-educated labour vs. R&D (aggregate level)*

**Dependent variable**: Number of high valued export products

| Explanatory variables | Estimate |
|---|---|
| Local accessibility to university educated labour per 1000 inhabitants | see fig. |
| Local accessibility to university R&D per 1000 employed | ns |
| Local accessibility to company R&D per 1000 employed | ns |

ns = not statistically significant for any quantile

Local accessibility to university educated labour

| | Q5 | Q10 | Q15 | Q20 | Q25 | Q30 | Q35 | Q40 | Q45 | Q50 | Q55 | Q60 | Q65 | Q70 | Q75 | Q80 | Q85 | Q90 | Q95 |
|---|---|---|---|---|---|---|---|---|---|---|---|---|---|---|---|---|---|---|---|
| Quantile | 0.3 | 0.7 | 1.3 | 1.7 | 2.3 | 3.3 | 4.0 | 4.7 | 5.7 | 7.3 | 9.3 | 10.8 | 12.3 | 15.1 | 20.2 | 27.4 | 37.7 | 56.7 | 77.7 |
| Pse R$^2$ | 0.04 | 0.07 | 0.08 | 0.10 | 0.13 | 0.15 | 0.16 | 0.18 | 0.20 | 0.22 | 0.24 | 0.25 | 0.28 | 0.30 | 0.33 | 0.38 | 0.42 | 0.46 | 0.48 |

*Figure 6.16    Number of high-value export products: university-educated labour vs. R&D (manufacturing of office machinery, electrical machinery and communication equipment)*

The results indicate a clear dominance for accessibility to university-educated labour both on aggregated data and sector level. Thus, both total export value and the number of high-value export products are primarily determined by the accessibility to university-educated labour. The clearest picture is given when the number of high-value export products is used as the dependent variable (Figures 6.15–6.16), with marginal effects being statistically significant for the whole conditional distribution. This is also manifested with considerably higher[2] values. Accessibility to company R&D and university R&D is obviously to a large extent crowded out by accessibility to university-educated labour.

## CONCLUSIONS

This chapter promotes the use of exports as an output measure of a knowledge production process in a regional setting. In spite of theoretical advances regarding knowledge and international competitiveness, there are still very few empirical works that attempt to verify the relationship between localised knowledge spillovers and regional export performance.

The purpose of this chapter has been to investigate the importance of accessibility to university R&D, company R&D and university-educated labour, on export performance in Swedish municipalities. Two different output measures have been used in a knowledge-production framework: export value and number of export products with a price above 1,000 SEK per kg. In accordance with the hypotheses outlined in 'Data, empirical model and hypotheses' and the theory discussion in 'Theoretical background and previous research', the estimations show that the fit of the model is higher when the latter is used as an output. Thus, accessibility to different kinds of knowledge sources is first of all important when the export pattern in a municipality is characterised by a diversity of high-priced products.

Although it is hard to separate the effects of the explanatory variables, due to multicollinearity problems, the empirical findings indicate that accessibility to university-educated labour is the factor that drives the export performance the most. Both accessibility to company R&D and accessibility to university-educated labour affect exports in separate estimations. On the other hand (as in Gråsjö, 2004), accessibility to university R&D seems to have very little impact on export performance. It could be the case that university R&D affects the investigated outputs indirectly through its feasible impact on conducted company R&D. The relation between university and company R&D and their combined effect on the knowledge output needs further study and is a question for future research. Furthermore, the supply of students and graduates that constitutes the base of the university-educated labour is certainly large in regions where university R&D is large. Recent studies (e.g., Faggian and McCann, 2006) also indicate that university R&D is mainly accessed indirectly via labour-market transactions.

How about the importance of geographical proximity? The answer to this question differs with respect to the output measure used. By using the accessibility concept on three geographical levels it is apparent that the effects are very local when total export value in municipalities is the dependent variable. Local (within the municipality) accessibility to university-educated labour or company R&D is the only variable that has a positive statistically significant effect. However, when the output measure is the number of high-value export products, the intra-regional and to some extent the inter-regional knowledge flows, appear to be more influential. The result shows that intra-regional accessibility to company R&D and university-educated labour is positive and statistically significant for the whole conditional distribution. The largest effects can be found in the upper tail, that is, the intra-regional knowledge flows are especially productive for municipalities with an export characterised by many high-value products.

All estimations are conducted with quantile regression. The chapter emphasizes the appropriateness of this regression technique, especially when the dependent variable has influential outliers and the distribution is skewed. However, quantile regression is also a suitable method when the research unit is heterogeneous with respect to the explanatory variables and an investigation over the entire conditional distribution is desired.

One dimension that has not been taken into consideration in this chapter is the potential impact from abroad. However, due to lack of data it has not been possible to include international accessibility to R&D in the analysis. One way to account for this is to include import flows in the analysis. For instance, accessibility to high-value import products or to special import groups could be useful measures that affect knowledge production. This is a natural extension of the work presented in this chapter.

## ACKNOWLEDGEMENT

An earlier version of this paper was published in the *Intenational Regional Science Review*, 31 (3), July 2008, 211-56, Sage Publications.

## NOTES

1. See, e.g., Jaffe (1989); Jaffe et al. (1993); Feldman (1994); Audretsch and Feldman (1996); Anselin et al. (1997, 2000); Acs et al. (2002); Bottazzi and Peri 2003; Fischer and Varga (2003).
2. According to Polanyi (1966), knowledge can be divided into two categories: codified (explicit) knowledge and tacit (implicit) knowledge. Codified knowledge is transmittable in a formal, systematic way and does not require direct experience of the knowledge that is

being acquired. On the other hand, tacit knowledge is context dependent, often deeply embedded into an 'organisational culture', and difficult to codify.

3. Arnold and Hussinger (2005) examine the causal relationship between productivity and exporting in German manufacturing. The authors find that causality runs from productivity to exporting, and not vice versa. Similar evidence is found in Yamada (1998) for several developed countries (with Italy as an exception). On the other hand, Bigsten et al. (2004) find evidence for learning effects for several sub-Saharan African countries.

4. I have not considered using panel data techniques because the data on exports are only available for three years (1997, 1998 and 1999) and the R&D data are available for 1993, 1995, 1997 and 1999.

5. SNI92 ('Standard för svensk näringsgrensindelning', established 1992) is the Swedish equivalent of the NACE (Nomenclature Générale Activités Économiques dans les Communautés Européennes) classification system used in the European Union. SNI92 was employed in 1993 to make Swedish statistics correspond to the statistics of the European Union.

6. The number of exported products depends of course on how disaggregated the data are. The exports are registered by product according to the Combined Nomenclature (CN) classification system (8-digit level). The table in Appendix 6A4 reports the number of possible different products in each industrial sector.

7. In order to avoid problems with multicollinearity, dummy variables are used instead of a continuous population variable. Employment or wage sum are other measures that account for economic activity. However, the correlation between population, employment and wage sum are very high, approximately 0.98 for Swedish municipalities.

8. The variance inflation factor, $VIF = 1/(1-R^2)$, where $R^2$ is the goodness of fit measure for the auxillary regressions. For instance 'Access to univ R&D, municip' on the LHS and the other explanatory variables on the RHS (Greene, 1993, p. 267).

9. Breschi and Palma (1999) have estimated a similar function. As a dependent variable they used share of exports of region $i$ in high-tech sector $j$ and as explanatory variables (i) share of patents in region $i$ in high-tech sector $j$ and (ii) share of patents in neighbouring regions in high-tech sector $j$, where neighbouring regions mean regions sharing a boundary with region $i$.

10. Equation (4.3) gives no indication of multicollinearity ($VIF = 1.29$).

11. Another alternative is to run OLS on the logarithmic values of the variables with skewed distributions. This is an option if the variables never take the value zero. In this chapter estimations are conducted both on an aggregated level and for three industrial sectors, and several municipalities do not have any high-value export on the sector level.

12. In Varga (1998, 2000a, 2000b, 2001) the heterogeneous economic activity in US metropolitan areas is emphasised. Varga stresses that a 'critical mass' of economic agglomeration, which mainly can be found in big municipalities, is needed in order to expect substantial effects of university research on regional innovation.

13. The procedure is called the design matrix bootstrap (see Gould, 1992, for further details).

14. See also Gråsjö (2004).

15. In order to compare the magnitudes of the marginal effects (and as a clarification), elasticity calculations evaluated at the median reveal the following result:Aggregated level, intra-regional accessibility to company R&D on no. of high-value export products: 0.011; and Aggregated level, intra-regional access. to univ. educated labour on no. of high valued export products: 0.014

# REFERENCES

Acs, Z.J., Anselin, L. and Varga, A. (2002), 'Patents and Innovation Counts as Measures of Regional Production of New Knowledge', *Research Policy*, **31**, 1069–85.

Andersson, M. and Ejermo, O. (2004a), 'How Does Accessibility to Knowledge Sources Affect the Innovativeness of Corporations? Evidence from Sweden', *Annals of Regional Science*, **39**, 741–65.

Andersson, M. and Ejermo, O. (2004b), 'Sectoral Knowledge Production in Swedish regions 1993–1999', in Karlsson, C., Flensburg, P. and Hörte, S.Å. (eds), *Knowledge Spillovers and Knowledge Management*, Edward Elgar, Cheltenham, UK and Northampton, MA, USA.

Andersson, Å.E. (1985) *Kreativitet: Storstadens framtid* (Creativity: The Future of the Metropolis), Prisma, Stockholm.

Andersson, Å.E. and Johansson, B. (1984), 'Knowledge Intensity and Product Cycles in Metropolitan Regions', WP–84–13, International Institute for Applied Systems Analysis A–2361, Laxenburg, Austria.

Andersson, M. and Karlsson, C. (2005), 'Knowledge Accessibility and Regional Economic Growth', Working Paper Series in Economics and Institutions of Innovation, **40**, Royal Institute of Technology, CESIS, Stolkhom.

Anselin, L,. Varga, A. and Acs, Z. (1997), 'Local Geographic Spillovers between University Research and High Technology Innovations', *Journal of Urban Economics*, **42**, 422–48.

Anselin, L., Varga, A. and Acs, Z. (2000), 'Geographic spillovers and university research: a spatial econometric perspective', in Nijkamp, P. and Stough, R. (eds), *Special Issue on Endogenous Growth: Models and Regional Policy, Growth and Change*, **31**, 501–16.

Arnold, J.M. and Hussinger, K. (2005), 'Export Behavior and Firm Productivity in German manufacturing: A Firm-level Analysis', *Review of World Economics*, **141**, 219–43.

Audretsch, D.B. and Feldman, M.P. (1996), 'R&D Spillovers and the Geography of Innovation and Production', *American Economic Review*, **86**, 630–40.

Audretsch, D.B., Lehman, E.E. and Warning, S. (2005), 'University Spillovers and New Firm Location', *Research Policy*, **34**, 1113–22.

Basile, R. (2001), 'Export Behaviour of Italian Manufacturing Firms over the Nineties: The Role of Innovation', *Research Policy*, **30**, 1185–201.

Batten, D.F. (1982), 'On the Dynamics of Indusrtial Evolution', *Regional Science and Urban Economics*, **12**, 449–62.

Beckman, M. (2000), 'Interurban Knowledge Networks', in Batten, D., Bertuglia, C., Martellato, D. and Occelli, S. (eds), *Learning, Innovation and the Urban Evolution*, Kluwer Academic, London, pp. 127-35.

Bernard, A.B. and Jensen, B. (1999), 'Exceptional Exporter Performance: Cause, Effect, or Both?', *Journal of International Economics*, **47**, 1–25.

Bertuglia, C. and Occelli, S. (2000), 'Impact of New Information Technologies on Economic–Spatial Systems: Towards an Agenda for Future Research', in Batten, D. et al. (eds), *Learning, Innovation and the Urban Evolution*, Kluwer Academic, London, pp. 237-54.

Bigsten, A., Collier, P., Dercon, S., Fafchamps, M., Gauthier, B., Gunning, J.W., Haraburema, J., Oduro, A. Ooestendrop, R., Patillo, C., Söderblom, T.F. and Zeufack, A. (2004), 'Do African manufacturing firms learn from exporting?', Centre for the study of African Economics Working Paper. *Journal of Development Studies* **40** (3) 115-41.

Bottazzi, L. and Peri, G. (2003), 'Innovation and spillovers in regions: Evidence from European patent data', *European Economic Review*, **47**, 687–710.

Breschi, S. and Palma, D. (1999), 'Localised knowledge spillovers and trade competitiveness: the case of Italy', in Fischer, M., Suarez, L. Villa and Steiner, M. (eds), *Innovation, Networks and Localities*, Springer Verlag, Berlin.

Clerides, S.K., Lach, S. and Tybout, J. (1998), 'Is Learning-by-Exporting Important? Micro-Dynamic Evidence from Colombia, Morocco, and Mexico', *Quarterly Journal of Economics*, **113**, 903–47.

Cole, S. (1981), 'Income and Employment Effects in a Model of Innovation and Transfer of Technology', in Cole, S. (ed.) *Methods for Development Planning. Scenarios, Models an Micro Studies*, Unesco Press, Paris, pp. 236–57.

Dixit, R. and Norman, V. (1980), *Theory of International Trade*, Cambridge University Press, Cambridge.

Fagerberg, J. (1988), 'International Competitiveness', *Economic Journal*, **98**, 355–74.

Faggian, A. and McCann, P. (2006), 'Human Capital Flows and Regional Knowledge Assets: A Simultaneous Equation Approach', *Oxford Economic Papers*.

Feldman, M.P., (1994), *The Geography of Innovation*, Kluwer Academic, Boston, MA.

Feldman, M.P. and Florida, R. (1994), 'The geographic sources of innovation: Technological infrastructure and product innovation in the United States', *Annals of the Association of American Geographers*, **84**, 210–29.

Fischer, M.M. and Varga, A. (2003), 'Spatial knowledge spillovers and university research: evidence from Austria', *Annals of Regional Science*, **37**, 303–22.

Fritsch, M. and Slavtchev, V. (2005), 'The Role of Regional Knowledge for Innovation', ERSA conference paper, Amsterdam.

Gould, W.W. (1992), 'Quantile regression with bootstrapped standard errors', *Stata Technical Bulletin*, **9**, 19–21.

Gråsjö, U. (2004), 'The Importance of Accessibility to R&D on Patent Production in Swedish Municipalities', Working Paper Series in Economics and Institutions of Innovation, **19**, Royal Institute of Technology, CESIS.

Greene, W.H. (1993), *Econometric Analysis*, 2nd edn, Macmillan, Basingstoke.

Greenhalgh, C., Taylor, P. and Wilson, R. (1994), 'Innovation and Export Volumes and Prices, a Disaggregated Study', *Oxford Economic Papers*, **46**, 102–34.

Griliches, Z. (1979), 'Issues in Assessing the Contribution of R&D to Productivity Growth', *Bell Journal of Economics*, **10**, 92–116.

Grossman, G.M. and Helpman, E. (1991), *Innovation and Growth in the Global Economy*, MIT Press, Cambridge, MA.

Helpman, E. (1981), 'International Trade in the Presence of Product Differentiation, Economies of Scale and Monopolistic Competition: A Chamberlain–Heckscher–Ohlin Approach', *Journal of International Economics*, **11**, 305–40.

Helpman, E. and Krugman, P. (1985), *Market Structure and Foreign Trade*, MIT Press, Cambridge, MA.

Hirsch, S. (1967), *Location of Industry and International Competitiveness*, Clarendon Press, Oxford.

Jacobs, J. (1961), *The Death and Life of Great American Cities*, Vintage Books, New York.

Jaffe, A.B. (1989), 'Real effects of academic research', *American Economic Review*, **79**, 957–70.

Jaffe, A.B., Trajtenberg, M. and Henderson, R. (1993), 'Geographic localization of knowledge spillovers as evidenced by patent citations', *Quarterly Journal of Economics*, **108**, 577–98.

Johansson, B. and Andersson, Å.E. (1998), 'A Schloss Laxenburg Model of Product Cycle Dynamics', in Beckmann, M.J., Johansson, B., Snickars, F. and Thord, R. (eds), *Knowledge and Networks in a Dynamic Economy*, Springer-Verlag, Berlin and Heidelberg, pp. 181–219.

Johansson, B. and Karlsson, C. (1987), 'Processes of Industrial Change: Scale, Location and Type of Job', in Fischer, M. and Nijkamp, P. (eds), *Regional Labour Market Analysis*, North-Holland, Amsterdam.

Johansson, B. and Karlsson, C. (2001), 'Geographic Transaction Costs and Specialisation Opportunities of Small and Medium-Sized Regions: Scale Economies and Market Extension', in Johansson, B., Karlsson,C. and Stough, R. (2001) (eds), *Theories of Endogenous Growth: Lessons for Regional Policies*, Springer-Verlag, Berlin, pp. 150-80.

Johansson, B. and Klaesson, J. (2001), Förhandsanalys av Förändringar i Transport- och Bebyggelsesystem, JIBS.

Johansson B., Klaesson, J. and Olsson, M. (2002), 'Time Distances and Labor Market Integration', *Papers in Regional Science*, **81**, 305–27.

Johansson, B., Klaesson, J. and Olsson, M. (2003), 'Commuters' Non-Linear Response to Time Distances', *Journal of Geographical Systems*, **5 (3)**, 315-29..

Karlsson, C. (1988), 'Innovation Adoption and the Product Life Cycle', *Umeå Economic Studies*, No. 185, University of Umeå.

Karlsson, C. and Manduchi, A. (2001), 'Knowledge Spillovers in a Spatial Context', in Fischer, M. and Fröhlich, J. (eds), *Knowledge, Complexity and Innovation Systems*, Springer-Verlag, Berlin.

Kleinknecht, A., Van Montfort, K. and Brouwer, E. (2002), 'The Non-trivial Choice Between Innovation Indicators', *Economics of Innovation and New Technology*, **11**, 109–21.

Koenker, R. and Bassett, G. (1978), 'Regression Quantiles', *Econometrica*, **46**, 33–50.

Koenker, R. and Bassett, G. (1982), 'Robust tests for heteroscedasticity based on regression quantiles', *Econometrica*, **50**, 43–61.

Krugman, P. (1979), 'Increasing Returns, Monopolistic Competition, and International Trade', *Journal of International Economics*, **9**, 469–79.

Krugman, P. (1980), 'Scale Economies, Product Differentiation and the Pattern of Trade', *American Economic Review*, **70**, 950–59.

Krugman, P. (1981), 'Trade, Accumulation and Uneven Development', *Journal of Development Economics*, **8**, 149–61.

Lancaster, K. (1980), 'Intra-Industry Trade under Perfect Monopolistic Competition', *Journal of Regional Science*, **33**, 129–44.

Martellato, D., Nijkamp, P. and Reggiani, A. (1998), 'Measurement and Measures of Network Accessibility: economic perspectives', in Button, K., Nijkamp, P. and Priemus, H. (eds), *Transport Networks in Europe; Concepts, Analysis and Policies*, Edward Elgar, Chettenhan, UK and Lyme, USA, pp. 161–80.

Norton, R.D. and Rees, J. (1979), 'The Product Cycle and the Spatial Decentralization of American Manufacturing', *Regional Studies*, **13**, 141–51.

Polanyi, M. (1966), *The Tacit Dimension*, Routledge & Kegan Paul, London.

Posner, M.V. (1961), 'International Trade and Technical Change', *Oxford Economic Papers*, **13**, 323–41.

Rogers, W.H. (1992), 'Quantile regression standard errors', *Stata Technical Bulletin*, **9**, 16–9.

Ronde, P. and Hussler, C. (2005), 'Innovation in Regions: What Does Really Matter', *Research Policy*, **34**, 1150–72.

Soete, L. (1987), 'The Impact of Technological Innovation on International Trade Patterns: The Evidence Reconsidered', *Research Policy*, **16**, 101–30.

Varga, A. (1998), *University Research and Regional Innovation: A Spatial Econometric Analysis of Academic Technology Transfers*, Kluwer Academic, Boston, MA.

Varga, A. (2000a), 'Local Academic Knowledge Spillovers and the Concentration of Economic Activity', *Journal of Regional Science*, **40**, 289–309.

Varga, A. (2000b), 'Universities in Local Innovation Systems', in Acs, Z. (2000), *Regional Innovation, Knowledge and Global Change*, Pinter, New York, pp. 139-52.

Varga, A. (2001), 'Universities and Regional Economic Development: Does Agglomeration Matter?', in Johansson B., Karlsson C. and Stough, R.R. (eds), *Theories of Endogenous Growth*, Springer-Verlag, Berlin, pp. 345-67

Vernon, R. (1966), 'International Investment and International Trade in the Product Cycle', *Quarterly Journal of Economics*, **80**, 190–207.

Wakelin, K. (1998), 'Innovation and export behaviour at the firm level', *Research Policy*, **26**, 829–41.

Weibull, J. (1976), 'An Axiomatic Approach to the Measurement of Accessibility', *Regional Science and Urban Economics*, **6**, 357–79.

Yamada, H. (1998), 'A note on the causality between export and productivity: An empirical re-examination', *Economics Letters*, **61**, 111-114.

## APPENDIX 6A1

Suppose that commuting time between and within locations is according to Table 6A1.1.

*Table 6A1.1  Interpretation of accessibilities*

| Time sensitivity values and assumed time distances | | |
|---|---|---|
| Accessibility | $\omega$ | t (min) |
| Local | 0.02 | 15 |
| Intra-regional | 0.1 | 30 |
| Inter-regional | 0.05 | 90 |

With values from Table 6.A1.1, a local accessibility increase by 1 is accomplished if the opportunity increases by 1.35. The computation is straightforward:

$$\Delta A_{iL}^{X} = \exp(-\omega_{L}t_{L})\Delta x_{i} = \exp(-0.02 \cdot 15) \cdot \Delta x_{i} = 1,$$

and then solving for $\Delta x_{i}$,

$$\Delta x_{i} = \frac{1}{\exp(-0.02 \cdot 15)} = 1.35.$$

The intra-regional accessibility increase equals 1 if the sum of all opportunity changes,

$$\sum_{r \in R, r \neq i} \Delta x_{r},$$

is 20 according to:

$$\Delta A_{iR}^{X} = \exp(-\omega_{R}t_{R})\sum_{r \in R, r \neq i} \Delta x_{r} = \exp(-0.1 \cdot 30) \cdot \sum_{r \in R, r \neq i} \Delta x_{r} = 1$$

$$\sum_{r \in R, r \neq i} \Delta x_{r} = \frac{1}{\exp(-0.1 \cdot 30)} = 20.$$

The corresponding calculation for the inter-regional accessibility is as follows:

$$\Delta A_{iOR}^{X} = \exp(-\omega_{OR}t_{OR})\sum_{k \notin R} \Delta x_{k} = \exp(-0.05 \cdot 90) \cdot \sum_{k \notin R} \Delta x_{k} = 1$$

$$\sum_{k \notin R} \Delta x_k = \frac{1}{\exp(-0.05 \cdot 90)} = 90 \ .$$

Thus, if commuting time between location $i$ in region $R$ and all locations outside $R$ is 90 minutes, then the sum of all opportunities in municipalities outside region $R$ has to increase by 90 in order to achieve an inter-regional accessibility increase by 1.

## APPENDIX 6A2

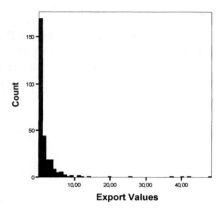

*Figure 6A2.1    Distribution of export values (dependent variable)*

*Figure 6A2.2    Distribution of number of export products (dependent variable)*

Table 6A3.1 Parameter estimates for population dummy variables. Exports and accessibility to university-educated labour, Eq. (2.5), D1 = 1 if population > 100,000, D2 = 1 if population between 50,000 and 100,000

| | Export value ($10^9$ SEK), aggregated level | | | | Export value ($10^6$ SEK), sector level | | | | No. of export products, aggregated level | | | | No. of export products, sector level | | | |
|---|---|---|---|---|---|---|---|---|---|---|---|---|---|---|---|---|
| | d1 | t | d2 | t | d1 | t | d2 | t | d1 | t | d2 | t | d1 | t | d2 | t |
| q5 | 3.05 | 2.10 | ns | | ns | | ns | | ns | | 36.2 | 6.90 | ns | | 10.0 | 4.00 |
| q10 | ns | | ns | | ns | | ns | | 123 | 3.36 | 35.0 | 3.96 | ns | | 11.4 | 3.56 |
| q15 | 3.42 | 2.03 | 0.75 | 3.20 | ns | | ns | | 126 | 3.76 | 43.3 | 3.72 | ns | | 14.6 | 3.41 |
| q20 | ns | | 0.90 | 3.71 | ns | | ns | | 132 | 4.33 | 50.4 | 3.89 | ns | | 16.6 | 3.06 |
| q25 | ns | | 0.89 | 3.07 | ns | | ns | | 140 | 4.93 | 55.7 | 4.03 | ns | | 22.4 | 3.83 |
| q30 | ns | | 0.87 | 2.50 | ns | | ns | | 136 | 5.13 | 70.4 | 5.10 | 36.3 | 2.01 | 25.1 | 4.42 |
| q35 | 4.14 | 2.23 | 1.20 | 3.11 | ns | | ns | | 136 | 4.73 | 73.5 | 5.52 | 34.2 | 1.97 | 28.0 | 5.54 |
| q40 | 4.20 | 2.13 | 1.30 | 3.06 | ns | | ns | | 133 | 4.11 | 71.6 | 5.46 | 38.0 | 2.18 | 30.0 | 6.62 |
| q45 | 4.17 | 2.02 | 1.31 | 2.64 | ns | | ns | | 138 | 3.28 | 72.1 | 5.83 | 37.5 | 2.26 | 29.7 | 6.84 |
| q50 | 5.08 | 2.30 | 1.60 | 2.46 | ns | | ns | | 136 | 3.28 | 80.0 | 5.83 | 47.5 | 2.67 | ns | |
| q55 | 5.01 | 2.04 | 1.59 | 1.97 | ns | | ns | | 133 | 2.49 | 83.0 | 5.63 | ns | | ns | |
| q60 | ns | | 2.15 | 2.21 | ns | | ns | | 132 | 2.07 | 81.3 | 4.98 | 49.2 | 2.28 | 33.1 | 5.54 |
| q65 | ns | | 2.98 | 2.69 | ns | | 257 | 2.23 | ns | | 91.9 | 5.33 | 51.0 | 1.98 | 31.4 | 4.77 |
| q70 | ns | | 2.97 | 2.37 | ns | | ns | | ns | | 101 | 5.63 | ns | | 33.4 | 4.23 |
| q75 | ns | | 3.80 | 2.82 | ns | | ns | | ns | | 101 | 5.62 | ns | | 32.0 | 3.45 |
| q80 | ns | | 3.55 | 2.14 | ns | | ns | | 334 | 3.14 | 107 | 5.83 | ns | | 33.4 | 3.12 |

| | Export value (10⁹ SEK), aggregated level | | | | Export value (10⁶ SEK), sector level | | | | No. of export products, aggregated level | | | | No. of export products, sector level | | | |
|---|---|---|---|---|---|---|---|---|---|---|---|---|---|---|---|---|
| | d1 | t | d2 | t | d1 | t | d2 | t | d1 | t | d2 | t | d1 | t | d2 | t |
| q85 | ns | | ns | 1.88 | ns | | ns | | 327 | 3.16 | 121 | 6.62 | 98.8 | 2.50 | 50.1 | 4.65 |
| q90 | ns | | ns | 0.69 | ns | | ns | | 326 | 3.44 | 117 | 6.57 | 96.4 | 2.31 | 49.4 | 4.73 |
| q95 | ns | | ns | 0.93 | ns | | ns | | 323 | 3.39 | 112 | 5.93 | 113 | 2.59 | 51.6 | 4.89 |

Table 6A3.2  *Parameter estimates for population dummy variables. Exports and accessibility to university-educated labour, Eq. (2.6), D1 = 1 if population > 100,000, D2 = 1 if population between 50,000 and 100,000*

| | Export value (10⁹ SEK), aggregated level | | | | Export value (10⁶ SEK), sector level | | | | No. of export products, aggregated level | | | | No. of export products, sector level | | | |
|---|---|---|---|---|---|---|---|---|---|---|---|---|---|---|---|---|
| | d1 | t | d2 | t | d1 | t | d2 | t | d1 | t | d2 | t | d1 | t | d2 | t |
| q5 | ns | | ns | | ns | | ns | | 82.9 | 2.55 | 19.1 | 2.11 | ns | | ns | |
| q10 | ns | | ns | | ns | | ns | | 83.8 | 2.26 | ns | | ns | | ns | |
| q15 | ns | | ns | | ns | | ns | | 100.0 | 2.49 | 34.6 | 2.24 | 27.7 | 2.36 | 10.56 | 2.24 |
| q20 | ns | | ns | | ns | | ns | | 99.3 | 2.42 | ns | | 27.3 | 2.23 | ns | |
| q25 | ns | | ns | | ns | | ns | | 105.0 | 2.67 | 56.7 | 3.09 | 28.1 | 2.07 | 20.43 | 3.08 |
| q30 | ns | | ns | | ns | | ns | | 104.0 | 2.48 | 60.7 | 3.30 | ns | | 21.00 | 3.26 |
| q35 | ns | | ns | | ns | | ns | | 101.0 | 2.42 | 64.1 | 3.44 | ns | | 24.21 | 3.90 |

Table 6A3.3 Parameter estimates for population dummy variables. Exports and accessibility to university-educated labour, (eq. 2.6), D1 = 1 if population > 100,000, D2 = 1 if population between 50,000 and 100,000

| | Export value (10⁹ SEK), aggregated level | | | | Export value (10⁶ SEK), sector level | | | | No. of export products, aggregated level | | | | No. of export products, sector level | | | |
|---|---|---|---|---|---|---|---|---|---|---|---|---|---|---|---|---|
| | d1 | t | d2 | t | d1 | t | d2 | t | d1 | t | d2 | t | d1 | t | d2 | t |
| q40 | ns | | ns | | ns | | ns | | 94.4 | 2.18 | 60.4 | 3.09 | ns | | 23.61 | 3.74 |
| q45 | ns | | ns | | ns | | ns | | ns | | 64.5 | 3.14 | ns | | 26.26 | 3.81 |
| q50 | ns | | ns | | ns | | ns | | ns | | 73.6 | 3.39 | 43.0 | 2.51 | 26.58 | 3.68 |
| q55 | ns | | ns | | ns | | ns | | ns | | 75.0 | 3.30 | 41.1 | 2.30 | 29.44 | 3.89 |
| q60 | ns | | ns | | ns | | ns | | ns | | 82.9 | 3.51 | 38.8 | 1.98 | 29.10 | 3.63 |
| q65 | ns | | ns | | ns | | ns | | ns | | 84.6 | 3.31 | ns | | 28.35 | 3.27 |
| q70 | ns | | ns | | ns | | ns | | ns | | 75.7 | 2.89 | ns | | 25.36 | 2.63 |
| q75 | ns | | 3.74 | 2.09 | ns | | ns | | ns | | 69.6 | 2.58 | ns | | 23.93 | 2.17 |
| q80 | ns | | ns | | ns | | ns | | ns | | 86.5 | 3.07 | ns | | 29.31 | 2.13 |
| q85 | ns | | ns | | ns | | ns | | ns | | 81.7 | 2.67 | ns | | 47.87 | 2.88 |
| q90 | ns | | ns | | ns | | ns | | ns | | 98.0 | 2.87 | ns | | 46.24 | 2.43 |
| q95 | ns | | 30.6 | 2.21 | ns | | ns | | ns | | 93.6 | 2.62 | ns | | ns | |

APPENDIX 6A4

Table 6A4.1 Description and statistics of the industrial sectors

| Group | Export value per year, bSEK (1997–1999) | No. of export products with price > 1000 SEK/kg (1997–1999) | Company R&D, man-year (1993–1999) | Description | SNI codes | No. of possible different products (CN classification system) |
|---|---|---|---|---|---|---|
| G1 | 3.60 | 54.00 | 26.2 | Agriculture, forestry and fishing | 1, 2, 5 | 784 |
| G2 | 5.95 | 14.00 | 8.6 | Mining | 10, 11, 12, 13, 14 | 133 |
| G3 | 14.45 | 55.67 | 26.2 | Manufacture of food and tobacco products | 15, 16 | 1,881 |
| G4 | 11.36 | 1,045.33 | 3.6 | Manufacture of textiles, clothing an leather products | 17, 18, 19 | 1,458 |
| G5 | 24.59 | 33.67 | 1.9 | Manufacture of wood and wood products, except furniture | 20 | 216 |
| G6 | 68.49 | 432.67 | 105.9 | Manufacture of paper, paper products, publishing and printing | 21, 22 | 271 |
| G7 | 70.30 | 783.33 | 996.3 | Manufacture of coke, refined petroleum products and nuclear fuel, chemicals and chemical products | 23, 24 | 1,581 |
| G8 | 16.45 | 389.33 | 19.1 | Manufacture of rubber and plastics products | 25 | 266 |
| G9 | 6.16 | 255.00 | 5.4 | Manufacture of other non-metallic mineral products | 26 | 320 |
| G10 | 44.41 | 296.00 | 57.6 | Manufacture of basic metals | 27 | 803 |
| G11 | 20.85 | 1,010.67 | 34.9 | Manufacture of fabricated metal products, except machinery and equipment | 28 | 372 |

| Group | Export value per year, bSEK (1997–1999) | No. of export products with price > 1000 SEK/kg (1997–1999) | Company R&D, man year (1993–1999) | Description | SNI codes | No. of possible different products (CN classification system) |
|---|---|---|---|---|---|---|
| G12 | 88.60 | 2961.00 | 133.0 | Manufacture of machines and equipment | 29 | 1030 |
| G13 | 127.29 | 5,315.33 | 438.7 | Manufacture of office machinery, electrical machinery and communication equipment | 30, 31, 32 | 678 |
| G14 | 18.82 | 3,550.33 | 125.4 | Manufacture of medical, precision and optical instruments, watches and clocks | 33 | 347 |
| G15 | 106.49 | 417.00 | 161.6 | Manufacture of motor vehicles and other transport equipment | 34, 35 | 309 |
| G16 | 13.69 | 563.67 | 0.3 | Manufacture of furniture | 36 | 292 |
| G18 | 2.20 | 3.00 | 13.4 | Distribution of water and electricity | 40 | 3 |
| G27 | 0.06 | 71.33 | 67.7 | Other business activities | 74 | 9 |
| G30 | 0.24 | 58.33 | 8.5 | Other community, social and personal service activities | 90, 91, 92, 93 | 18 |
| Total | 643.99 | 1,7309.67 | 2,234.3 | | | |

## APPENDIX 6A5

Anselin (2003) distinguishes between:

1. unmodelled effects (with spatially lagged error terms);
2. modelled effects (with spatially lagged explanatory variables); and
3. unmodelled and modelled effects (with spatially lagged dependent variables)

The model specifications (6.5 and 6.6), derived in 'Data, empirical model and hypotheses', are examples of the second category. To test that spatially lagged explanatory variables are the right choice, that is, that it is not the error terms or the dependent variables that should be spatially lagged, three different test statistics for spatial dependence have been calculated. Moran's *I* is probably the most used test statistic, but it does not indicate how to proceed (which alternative spatial model to use) if it signals presence of spatial autocorrelation.[1] Therefore, two Lagrange Multiplier tests, *LM-err* and *LM-lag*, are also performed (see, e.g., Burridge, 1980; Anselin, 1988; Anselin and Florax, 1995). The three test statistics have been calculated using three different weight matrices *W1*, *W2* and *W3*. *W1* is a row standardised binary weight matrix and *W2* and *W3* are inversed time distance matrices with the following weights:

- *W1*, with weights $w_{ij} \neq 0$ if municipality *i* and *j* are in the same region;
- *W2*, with $w_{ij} = 1/t_{ij} \neq 0$ if $t_{ij} < 30$ minutes, zero otherwise ; and
- *W3*, with $w_{ij} = 1/t_{ij} \neq 0$ if $t_{ij} < 60$ minutes, zero otherwise.

In Table 6A5.1 the results of the tests are presented. The tests are performed with different dependent variables on equation (6.5)–(6.7).

Equation (6.7) is without spatially lagged explanatory variables, that is, without intra- and inter-regional accessibilities. Hence, this specification might experience a higher risk of having spatially auto-correlated errors. As can be seen from the table, Moran's *I*, *LM-err* or *LM-lag* indicate spatially auto-correlated errors for any model specification at the 5 per cent significance level. The lowest *p*-value can, not surprisingly, be found for Equation (6.7) (*LM-err* with weight matrix *W2*).

**Note**

1. Moran's *I* was originally adopted only on single variables, but Cliff and Ord (1972) and Hordijk (1974) applied the principle for spatial autocorrelation to the residuals of regression models for cross-sectional data.

# References

Anselin, L. (1988), 'Lagrange Multiplier Test Diagnostics for Spatial Dependence and Spatial Heterogeneity', *Geographical Analysis*, **20**, 1–17.

Anselin, L. (2003), 'Spatial Externalities, Spatial Multipliers and Spatial Econometrics', *International Regional Science Review*, **26**, 153–66.

Anselin, L. and Florax, R. (eds) (1995), *New Directions in Spatial Econometrics*, Springer-Verlag, Berlin.

Burridge, P. (1980), 'On the Cliff–Ord Test for Spatial Autocorrelation', *Journal of the Royal Statistical Society B*, **42**, 107–8.

Cliff, A. and Ord, J.K. (1972), 'Testing for Spatial Autocorrelation among Regression Residuals', *Geographical Analysis*, **4**, 267–84.

Hordijk, L. (1974), 'Spatial Correlation in the Disturbances of a Linear Interregional Model', *Regional and Urban Economics*, **4**, 117–40.

Table 6A5.1  Pre-estimation tests for spatial dependence

| Equation, Dependent variable | Moran's I | | | LM-err | | | LM-lag | | |
|---|---|---|---|---|---|---|---|---|---|
| | W1 | W2 | W3 | W1 | W2 | W3 | W1 | W2 | W3 |
| Eq. 6.1, Export value | -0.019 | -0.044 | -0.015 | 0.144 | 0.646 | 0.253 | 0.005 | 0.033 | 0.027 |
| | (0.88) | (0.68) | (0.92) | (0.70) | (0.42) | (0.62) | (0.95) | (0.86) | (0.87) |
| Eq. 6.1, No. of export products | -0.014 | 0.035 | 0.022 | 0.073 | 0.404 | 0.532 | 8.1E-8 | 0.0004 | 0.0001 |
| | (0.94) | (0.64) | (0.74) | (0.79) | (0.53) | (0.47) | (1.00) | (0.99) | (0.99) |
| Eq. 6.2, Export value, | -0.013 | -0.021 | -0.002 | 0.064 | 0.141 | 0.006 | 0.0005 | 0.002 | 0.0003 |
| | (0.96) | (0.90) | (0.96) | (0.80) | (0.71) | (0.94) | (0.98) | (0.97) | (0.99) |
| Eq. 6.2, No. of export products | -0.002 | 0.006 | -0.0002 | 0.248 | 0.012 | 6.4E-5 | 0.0002 | 6.1E-7 | 1.8E-8 |
| | (0.84) | (0.88) | (0.94) | (0.62) | (0.91) | (0.99) | (0.99) | (1.00) | (1.00) |
| Eq. 6.3, Export value | -0.039 | 0.085 | 0.045 | 0.620 | 2.38 | 2.20 | 0.022 | 0.003 | 0.051 |
| | (0.70) | (0.38) | (0.64) | (0.43) | (0.12) | (0.14) | (0.88) | (0.96) | (0.82) |
| Eq. 6.3, No. of export products | -0.003 | 0.027 | 0.026 | 0.004 | 0.141 | 0.718 | 2.0E-4 | 5.1E-4 | 0.001 |
| | (0.99) | (0.72) | (0.72) | (0.95) | (0.71) | (0.37) | (0.99) | (0.98) | (0.97) |

*Note:* p-values in parenthesis.

# 7. Magnitude and Destination Diversity of Exports: The Role of Product Variety

## Martin Andersson

## INTRODUCTION

The relationship between product variety and exports is emphasized in a vast amount of research on international trade. In the seminal work by Krugman (1980), for instance, larger countries have larger export sales because they produce a broader spectrum of varieties than smaller countries. Gains from trade arise because consumers' preferences are characterized by 'love-for-variety' and imports expand the set of product varieties available for consumption. Scale economies in the production of each variety and limited domestic resources prevent a single country from producing all possible varieties. One of several merits of this type of framework is that it offers an explanation for intra-industry (or two-way) trade.

With reference to the new trade theory, a growing literature aims at quantifying the relationships between product variety, trade and welfare. For instance, Hummels and Klenow (2005) investigate whether larger economies export more by exporting more of a common set of goods (the intensive margin) or by exporting a larger set of goods to more markets (the extensive margin).[1] They find that about 60 percent of the bigger exports of larger countries are accounted for by the extensive margin. Broda and Weinstein (2004a,b) test the prediction that a major gain from trade is the expansion of varieties through imports on US data, 1972–2001. Their results suggest that the welfare gains from variety growth in imports are about 2.8 percent, (2004b) of US GDP. Moreover, in a series of papers, Funke and Ruhwedel (2001, 2002) have examined the link between export variety and export performance in East Asian and OECD countries, respectively. Their findings suggest that production of differentiated export products allows for export market penetration and growth.

A separate literature focuses on micro-level data (most often firm- or plant-level data) to analyze how different characteristics of individual firms affect their export activities.[2] In this literature an extensive amount of research has analyzed the relationship between firm-level productivity, entry and survival in export markets. A major conclusion of these studies is that a combination of sunk costs of entry and heterogeneity in the underlying characteristics of firms explain why not all firms export (Greenaway and Kneller, 2007). Likewise, heterogeneity across exporters in terms of the extent of penetration of geographic markets can be explained by market-specific sunk costs of entry and heterogeneity among exporters. In view of these observations, theoretical models that adhere to individual firms have been developed. For instance, Bernard et al. (2003) present a model that builds on Eaton and Kortum (2002) with Ricardian differences in technological efficiency between producers. Melitz (2003) develops a dynamic monopolistic competition model with heterogeneous firms and fixed costs of exporting and derives intra-industry reallocation effects of trade. In a model with the same market structure, Chaney (2008) introduces fixed entry costs and transport cost per geographic market. Moreover, Eaton et al. (2005) develop a model with heterogeneous firms, entry costs for each market and transport costs. Their model allows for both monopolistic and 'head-to-head' competition as the range of possible goods depends on a distinct parameter in the model.

This chapter adheres to both sets of literature and analyzes the relationship between the variety in export supply and exports at the firm level. The existing literature on the role of variety for exports is, without exception, focused on the aggregate national level. To the author's knowledge, no paper related to this literature has studied the relationship between variety in export supply and exports at the level of the individual firm. Similarly, the literature analyzing the characteristics of individual firms and their export behavior has not yet considered variety in supply as a pertinent characteristic of exporting firms, in neither empirical nor theoretical work. However, a basic observation is that product differentiation applies to the supply of individual firms in the sense that most firms supply a *product line*, that is, a set of related products (see Brander and Eaton, 1984; Katz, 1984). In fact, modern manufacturing firms are often 'multi-variety' firms.

## Product Variety in Modern Manufacturing Firms

Milgrom and Roberts (1990) and Milgrom et al. (1991) remark that a characteristic feature of 'modern (or lean) manufacturing' firms is broad product lines coupled with frequent updates of the product lines. According to the authors, this is a response to the development of flexible machine tools and programmable multitask production equipment in the late twentieth century. These technical innovations lowered the cost of realizing demand advantages of having broader product lines, by implying a higher extent of economies of scope. Moreover, in his acclaimed book *The Modern Firm*, Roberts (2004) emphasizes that there is complementarity between flexibility and variety in supply at the level of the individual firm in the sense that 'it will be worthwhile to bear the costs of flexibility only if the desired variety is high, and a high level of variety will be worthwhile only if the production system is flexible', (ibid, p.38).

Many firms do indeed supply a set of related products (see, e.g., Dunne et al., 1988). Even though they may produce a single basic product, they typically offer several varieties of that product. Firms such as Nikon and Pentax, for instance, supply a wide range of different cameras with associated accessories. Similarly, the product lines of firms in the mobile-phone industry, such as Ericsson, Nokia, Motorola, and so on, typically consist of a number of differentiated mobile-phones. The same principle applies to the majority of car manufacturers around the globe and producers of intermediate goods, such as subcontractors. In fact, limited competitiveness of firms is often partly explained by limited variety in supply.[3]

**Purpose and Outline**

Against the background above, this chapter analyzes the relationship between the variety in export supply and exports at the level of individual manufacturing firms, and assesses how the size of the export sales (in terms of export value) is related to the variety in export supply across individual exporters. The chapter applies a decomposition methodology akin to Hummels and Klenow (2005), such that the relative contribution of the extensive and intensive margins, respectively, can be revealed. This decomposition allows for an inclusive assessment of the structure and composition of firms' export flows. A case is made that multi-product firms can potentially penetrate a larger set of export markets through the materialization of economies of scope. For instance, if entry costs associated with geographic markets are firm specific – as they are typically modeled – rather than product specific, multi-product firms have a natural potential cost advantage compared to single-product firms, since the entry cost per volume unit is likely to be lower for multi-product firms.

The chapter makes use of highly detailed firm-level export data from Sweden. For each firm, these data provide information on export value (SEK) and export volume (kilogram) across destinations and products. The product categories are the finest possible according to the CN[4] classification system, which is common for EU member countries.

The rest of the chapter is organized as follows: 'Theoretical background' starts by presenting the basic relationship between variety and exports in Krugman (1980), which motivates an overall positive relationship between variety and the size of export sales. Then, the chapter uses a model set-up by Johansson (2005) to introduce multi-product firms – that is, firms that produce more than one variety – in the basic Krugman framework. This provides a theoretical motivation for multi-product with larger export sales than single-product firms. 'Export variety at the level of the individual firm' presents the data and reports some stylized facts about export variety at the firm level as regards Swedish firm-level export data. The empirical analysis is presented in the same section. Conclusions are given in 'Summary and discussion'.

## THEORETICAL BACKGROUND

By using the model of monopolistic competition developed by Dixit and Stiglitz (1977), Krugman (1980) provided a simple illustration of the relationship between the size of a country's exports and the number of differentiated goods (varities) produced within that country. This section derives the basic result in the Krugman model and then uses a set-up in Johansson (2005) to introduce and motivate multi-product firms in Krugman's model.

### Variety and Exports at the Country Level

Consider a case in which consumers derive utility among a set of $K=\{1, \ldots, n\}$ different product groups. Each product group $k$ can be thought of as the selection of differentiated products belonging to a distinct industry. Every consumer shares the same Cobb–Douglas preferences for the different product groups:

$$U = \prod_{k \in K} C_k^{\beta_k} \qquad \sum_{k \in K} \beta_k = 1 \qquad (7.1)$$

where $\beta_k$ denotes the constant budget share of goods in product group $k$, $0 < \beta_k < 1 \ \forall k \in K$. Since each product group $k$ consists of a number of products, each $C_k$ represents a composite index of the consumption of products in product group $k$. Thus, $C_k$ is a sub-utility function defined over the set $N^k = \{1, \ldots, n\}$ of products belonging to product group $k$. $C_k$ is a constant elasticity of substitution (CES) aggregator over the varieties available in product group $k$:

$$C_k = \left( \sum_{j \in N^k} x_j^{\theta} \right)^{\frac{1}{\theta}} \qquad \forall k \in K, \qquad (7.2)$$

which implies 'love-for-variety' for the products within every product group $k$, $0 < \theta < 1$. A consumer is better off the larger the set of products available for consumption in each product group. The specification in (7.2) implies that the demand for a product in product group $k$ is given by:

$$x_j = p_j^{-\varepsilon} \left( P_k^{\varepsilon-1} \beta_k Y \right) \qquad \forall j \in N^k$$

$$P_k \equiv \left( \sum_{j \in N^k} p_j^{1-\varepsilon} \right)^{\frac{1}{1-\varepsilon}} \qquad (7.3)$$

where $\varepsilon \equiv (1-\theta)^{-1}$ denotes the price elasticity of demand, $Y$ is the consumer income, $p_j$ is the price of variety $j$ and $P_k$ denotes the price index of the products in product group $k$.

Every product in product group $k$ is produced according to the following cost function:

$$c(x_j) = \lambda + \mu x_j \qquad \forall j \in N^k \qquad (7.4)$$

where $c(x_j)$ denotes the total cost of producing $x_j$. Equation (7.4) implies (internal) scale economies in production and each product will thus be produced by a single firm.

Given (7.3) and (7.4), each firm will obey the following pricing rule:

$$p_j = \left( \frac{\varepsilon}{\varepsilon-1} \right) \mu . \qquad (7.5)$$

Since each product enters in the utility function in (7.2) in a symmetric fashion, $x_j = x$ and $p_j = p$ for all $j \in N^k$. This means that the equilibrium number of products available for consumption in product group $k$, $n_k$, is given by $n_k = \beta_k Y / \lambda \varepsilon$.

By denoting an identical foreign country with (*) and assuming that the two countries trade in product group $k$, the total amount of products in this product group available for consumption becomes $(n_k + n_k^*)$. The home country's share of world exports in product group $k$ can then be formulated as:

$$\frac{n_k}{n_k + n_k^*} = \frac{\beta_k Y}{\varepsilon \lambda (n_k + n_k^*)} \qquad \forall k \in M. \qquad (7.6)$$

This equation states that if the home country's expenditure on product group $k$ increases relative to foreign, then the home country will increase its share of world exports in the same product group simply because it increases the number of products produced in that product group. According to this framework then, the size of the total exports in a specific product group and the number of products produced in the same product group are inseparable phenomena.

## Multi-product Firms and Economies of Scope

In the former model each product is produced by a single firm. However, as stated in the introduction, many firms can be characterized as 'multi-product' firms in the sense that they produce a range of products, often within a specific product group. Multi-product firms can be motivated by economies of scope on the production side.[5] Formally, such scope economies obtains when the following condition is satisfied (Bailey and Friedlaender, 1982):

$$c(x_1, x_2) < c(x_1, 0) + c(0, x_2),  \qquad (7.7)$$

that is, when the joint production of $x_1$ and $x_2$ results in lower total costs than separate production. A cost function which contains an input common for a set of products (or varieties) satisfies the criteria in (7.7) (Panzar and Willig, 1981).

In order to allow for multi-product firms through economies of scope in the former model, the cost function for a typical firm in a product group $k$ in (7.4) is rewritten:

$$c(x_j) = \alpha + \lambda + \mu x_j;  \qquad (7.8)$$

where $\lambda$ is a product-specific fixed cost and $\alpha$ is a fixed cost that can be shared among a subset $n^k \subset N^k$ of the total amount of possible varieties in product group $k$ (see Johansson, 2005). $\mu$ remains the marginal cost of production. $\lambda$ and $\mu$ are assumed to be the same for all products. Equation (7.8) satisfies the condition in (7.7). There are several types of investments that give rise to a fixed cost such as $\alpha$, for example, flexible production technologies and distribution centers, and so on. However, the most general common input is certainly knowledge and information. Knowledge and information gained by producing and selling one product is usually applicable for a set of related products.[6]

In association with the cost function in (7.8), three sets of simplifying assumptions are introduced:

1. The introduction of (differentiated) products requires product ideas, which arrive in firms in a random process.
2. The number of products produced by a multi-product firm is always small in relation to the total number of products in the market.
3. There are no possibilities for mergers.[7]

As will be evident below, assumption (1) motivates the coexistence of single- and multi-product firms in the market. The second assumption discourages strategic behavior, such as cross-subsidizing, and keeps the pricing decision of multi-product firms as simple as possible.[8] Specifically, like single-product firms, multi-product firms consider the price index in (7.3) as given in their pricing decision. This is valid due to (2) and implies that a multi-product firm prices its respective products just like single-product firms do. The CES preference structure in (7.2) implies that the cross-price elasticity of demand is the same between all products. Thus, (7.5) holds for all firms and products. A consequence of this is that no firm has strategic control such that it is products rather than firms that compete with each other.

Consider now a firm $s$ with multiple product ideas $j \in n^k$, that is, ideas for products that jointly can rely on firm $s$'s fixed cost $\alpha$. If firm $s$ produces $n_s$ products $j \in n^k$, it follows from the above assumptions that $x_i = x_j$ for all products $i, j$. Thus, the total cost of firm $s$ can be expressed as:

$$c(n_s) = \alpha + n_s \lambda + n_s \mu x_j. \tag{7.9}$$

From (7.9) it is evident that a multi-product firm like $s$ has a cost advantage over a single-product firm because:

$$\frac{c(1)}{x} - \frac{c(n_s)}{n_s x} = \frac{\alpha}{x}\left(1 - \frac{1}{n_s}\right), \tag{7.10}$$

where $c(1)$ applies to single-product firms and $x$ denotes the level of supply of a product.

According to the outline above, a (temporary) equilibrium in which both single- and multi-product firms operate on the market is possible. The model approaches equilibrium as additional products are introduced on the market. An incumbent firm that receives a product idea that can rely on $\alpha$ needs only to pay $\lambda$ to introduce the product on the (export) market. A non-incumbent firm needs to pay $(\lambda + \alpha)$. Let $n^e$ denote the number of products in the market for which the operating profits of firms that remain single-product firms is just enough to cover the fixed costs $(\lambda + \alpha)$, which means that the market is saturated for single-product firms. In such a situation, the following condition thus holds for a single-product firm:

$$p = \left(\frac{\varepsilon}{\varepsilon-1}\right)\mu = \frac{(\alpha+\lambda)}{x}. \qquad (7.11)$$

However, a multi-product firm that has received multiple ideas for products that jointly can rely on the fixed cost $\alpha$, the following holds at $n^e$, where $n$ denotes the number of products produced by the firm:

$$p = \left(\frac{\varepsilon}{\varepsilon-1}\right)\mu > \frac{\alpha/n+\lambda}{x} \qquad \text{if } n > 1 \qquad (7.12)$$

Equations (7.11) and (7.12) imply that in a market which there exist single-product firms that make zero profits, multi-product firms can make positive profits. The reason is that such firms are able to spread the fixed cost $\alpha$ over a larger of products. Since (7.8) applies to all firms, it means that all firms have a potential to exploit scope economies. In the present framework, whether this potential is materialized for a given firm depends on whether it receives multiple ideas for products that jointly can rely on $\alpha$.

The framework above provides a rationale for multi-product firms as well as a basis for the coexistence of single- and multi-product firms in a given market. It also predicts that multi-product firms will have larger export sales than single-product firms. Specifically, a firm which supplies twice as many export varieties will have twice the export value, since $x$ and $p$ are the same for all varieties in the (global) market. Thus, the elasticity of export sales with respect to the number of products would be unity.

However, if the penetration of export markets is associated with fixed entry costs (as is typically found in the literature[9]), the above framework suggests that multi-product firms are potentially capable of paying a larger set of such entry costs than single-product firms via their cost advantage. Likewise, if entry costs are firm- rather than product-specific, multi-product firms have a cost advantage over single-product firms since the entry cost per volume unit would be lower for multi-product firms. This would translate into an elasticity of export sales with respect to the number of products larger than unity.

In the model below, gains from producing a number of products arise because all consumers buy a limited amount of *each* variety. An alternative approach to product variety is to assume that the benefit of product variety arise from the presence of heterogeneous consumers. Lancaster (1990, p.

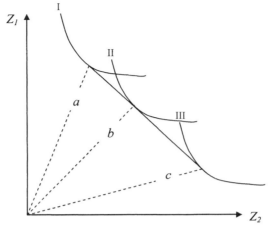

*Figure 7.1   Perfect product differentiation in Lancaster's 'characteristics approach'*

189) points out that 'demand for variety may arise from a taste for diversity in individual consumption and/or from diversity in tastes *even* when each consumer chooses a single variant'. The formulation in (7.2) is an example of the former, that is, taste for diversity in individual consumption. If there is diversity in tastes when each consumer buys a single product, returns from supplying a set of products arise from heterogeneous preferences among consumers. In this case, multi-product firms discriminate between consumers with different preferences and develop a product line accordingly. Such product differentiation can be illustrated with the 'characteristic-approach' developed in Lancaster (1966a,b). Figure 7.1 illustrates the principle. In the figure, consumers are assumed to derive utility from two characteristics, $Z_1$ and $Z_2$. There are three products available on the market with different densities of the two characteristics. This gives rise to three product vectors $a$, $b$ and $c$. The straight and negatively sloped line that joins these vectors is the characteristics frontier, which is the same for all consumers. Consumers choose a point on the characteristics frontier according their preferences. There are three groups of consumers (I, II, III) with different preferences over the two characteristics. The figure describes 'perfect' product differentiation as each group of customers would consume a single product and there is a perfect match between the preferences of the consumers and the density in terms of the characteristics of the products.

The subsequent section provides an empirical assessment of the returns to variety in export supply at the firm level. The section also describes the data and presents an overall picture of the extent of variety in export supply among exporting firms.

## EXPORT VARIETY AT THE LEVEL OF THE INDIVIDUAL FIRM

### Presentation of Data

Highly detailed firm-level export data are used, including data for Swedish exporting firms in 2003. For each firm, product category and export destination (country) information is provided on (i) export value (SEK) and (ii) export volume (kilogram). A firm is defined as a legal entity. The product categories are the finest possible according to the CN classification system, which is standard for EU member countries. In 2003, Swedish firms exported well over 9,000 different product categories according to this classification. Since each firm may produce a number of products that are each exported to a set of destinations, the database is very large. For example, for the year 2003 there are over 640,000 entries in the database. The structure of these data makes it possible to measure a firm's export variety along two dimensions: (i) export product categories and (ii) export destinations.

The exports of each firm are recorded in export categories according to the 8-digit CN classification scheme. In this chapter, each such 8-digit category is referred to as an export product.[10] Variety in the export supply of a firm then manifests itself in that a firm exports a set of such categories (products). This means that a higher number of export categories is interpreted as a higher variety in export supply.[11] Moreover, a destination (country) will be referred to as a market.

Table 7.1 presents descriptive statistics of the extent of export variety among all Swedish exporting firms with a total export value larger than 50,000 SEK (approx. €5,000) in 2003. All firms were categorized into seven classes according to the number of export products. For each class, the table presents (i) the mean number of export products per firm, (ii) the mean number of markets penetrated by the firms, (iii) the number of firms belonging to the class, (iv) each class's share of the total number of export firms and (v) each class's share of Sweden's total export value.

The table shows that most firms export a very limited number of products to a very limited number of markets. In fact, the typical firm with an aggregate export value of €5, 000 exports 1–5 products to 1–4 markets market. However, these firms (60 percent) constitute less than 7 percent of Sweden's total export value. In the 7th category we find the firms with the highest variety in their exports. On average, these firms export about 42 products to a total of about 20 markets and constitute over 80 percent of total exports.[12] This illustrates strong concentration to a few firms.

*Table 7.1   Descriptive statistics for 7 categories of firms in 2003, categories constructed based on the number of export products)*

| Class | Mean no. products | Mean no. of markets | Number of firms | Share of firms (%) | Share of export value (%) |
|-------|------|------|-------|------|------|
| 1 | 1.0 (0.0) | 1.4 (1.5) | 3,668 | 19.3 | 1.1 |
| 2 | 2.0 (0.0) | 2.3 (2.9) | 2,736 | 14.4 | 1.1 |
| 3 | 3.0 (0.0) | 3.2 (3.7) | 2,063 | 10.9 | 1.1 |
| 4 | 4.4 (0.5) | 4.3 (5.1) | 2,884 | 15.2 | 3.3 |
| 5 | 6.9 (0.8) | 6.3 (7.1) | 2,457 | 12.9 | 4.4 |
| 6 | 11.4 (1.9) | 9.6 (9.8) | 2,488 | 13.1 | 8.1 |
| 7 | 41.9 (57.5) | 19.5 (19.1) | 2,690 | 14.2 | 80.9 |

*Note:* Standard deviations are presented within brackets. Only firms with an aggregate export value > 50, 000 SEK (approx. €5,000) are included.

Figures 7.2 and 7.3 provide an illustration of the frequency by which Swedish exporting firms export a different number of products and serve a different number of markets, respectively. The horizontal axis measures the number of products and number of markets, respectively. In each figure the vertical axis measures the number of firms. An observation then shows the number of firms which exports to a given number of products (markets). The relationships in each figure are summarized by the corresponding equations, where $f$ denotes number of firms, $n$ number of products and $m$ number of markets. These figures are analogous to those presented in Eaton et al. (2004) on French firm-level export data.

No. of firms

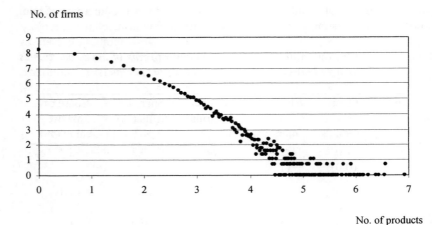

No. of products

*Figure 7.2    Frequency by which Swedish exporting firms export a different number of products (logarithmic scales) f*

No. of firms

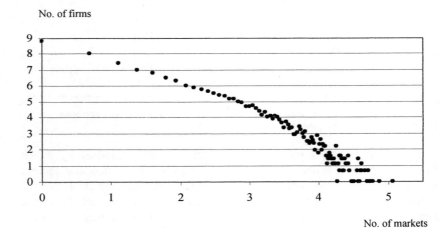

No. of markets

*Figure 7.3    Frequency by which Swedish exporting firms serve a different number of markets (logarithmic scales)*

$$\ln f = 9.13 - 1.65 \ln n \qquad\qquad (7.13)$$

$$\ln f = 10.58 - 2.13 \ln m. \qquad\qquad (7.14)$$

Figures 7.2 and 7.3 show that the frequency by which more export products are supplied and more markets are penetrated declines smoothly with the number of firms until a few firms export a large number of products and have penetrated a large number of markets, respectively. Equation (7.13) shows that the number of firms falls off with the number of export products, that is, the extent of export variety, with an elasticity of 1.6. The corresponding elasticity for the number of markets amounts to 2.13 (see 7.14). The latter elasticity is in the neighborhood of that reported in Eaton et al. (2004) who estimate an identical elasticity of 2.50 on French firm-level export data. The distribution reported in Figure 7.3 lends support to the claim that the penetration of individual geographic markets is associated with fixed entry costs.

In summary, as in previous studies, the data show a strong heterogeneity in terms of the number of export products across firms and the extent of export market penetration across firms. Most firms export a limited set of products to a limited set of markets. Firms with higher variety in export supply tend to serve more markets. Moreover, there is also heterogeneity across export products in the sense that most products are exported to a limited number of markets.

## Export Variety and Exports across Individual Firms

The theoretical framework 'Theoretical background' implies that firms with greater export variety should have larger export sales. Moreover, the corresponding discussion suggested that multi-product firms can theoretically use cost advantages to penetrate a larger set of export markets. This subsection aims at empirically examining the relationship between variety in export supply and exports at the firm level using a cross-section of exporting firms in the manufacturing sector[13], (a list of the industries included in the manufacturing sector is presented in Appendix 7A). A decomposition methodology akin to Hummels and Klenow (2005) is applied to estimate how large a share of the estimated relationships are accounted for by the 'extensive' and the 'intensive' margin, respectively.

The relationship between export variety and the size of export sales for individual firms is estimated by regressing the total export value of a firm $i$, $x_i$, on the number of export products of the same firm, $n_i$, while controlling for inter-industry heterogeneity through industry dummies $D_j$ (1 if firm $i$ is in industry $j$; 0 otherwise) :

$$\ln x_i = \varphi + \beta \ln n_i + \sum_{j=1}^{J} \gamma_j D_j + \varepsilon_i \tag{7.15}$$

which yields an estimated elasticity of the export value with respect to the extent of export variety.

A decomposition of the total exports of each firm $i$, $x_i$, can be made by observing that $x_i$ can be expressed as:

$$x_i = \sum_{r \in m^i} \sum_{s \in n^i} p_{i,sr} q_{i,sr} \qquad (7.16)$$

where $m^i$ denotes the set of markets firm $i$ exports to and $n^i$ denotes the set of products that the firm is exporting, $p_{i,sr}$ is the price of product $s$ in market $r$ and $q_{i,sr}$ is the volume (kilogram) exported of product $s$ to market $r$. Equation (7.16) can readily be rewritten to read:

$$x_i = \sum_{r \in m^i} P_{i,r} Q_{i,r} \qquad P_{i,r} Q_{i,r} \equiv \sum_{s \in n^i} p_{i,sr} q_{i,sr} \qquad (7.17)$$

which simply states that the total export of firm $i$ is the sum of the total export value to each market. The right-hand side in (7.17) can now be decomposed into:

$$x_i = M_i \left( P_{i,r}^* Q_{i,r}^* \right) \qquad P_{i,r}^* Q_{i,r}^* \equiv \left( M_i \right)^{-1} \sum_{r \in m^i} P_{i,r} Q_{i,r} \qquad (7.18)$$

where $M_i$ denotes the number of markets firm $i$ has entered and $P_{i,r}^* Q_{i,r}^*$ denotes the average value of the shipments to a market. In Hummel and Klenow's (2005) terminology, $M_i$ can be interpreted as the 'extensive' margin whereas $P_{i,r}^* Q_{i,r}^*$ can be interpreted as the 'intensive' margin. Equation (7.18) implies that a firm's total exports is the sum of the extensive and the intensive margins:

$$\ln x_i = \ln M_i + \ln(P_{i,r}^* Q_{i,r}^*) \qquad (7.19)$$

The intensive margin can further be decomposed by distinguishing between average export prices per kilogram and average export volumes (in kilograms):

$$P_{i,r}^* Q_{i,r}^* = \frac{\sum_{r \in m^i} P_{i,r} Q_{i,r}}{\sum_{r \in m^i} Q_{i,r}} \frac{\sum_{r \in m^i} P_{i,r} Q_{i,r}}{M_i} = \hat{P}_i^* \hat{Q}_{i,r}^* \qquad (7.20)$$

which means that:

$$\ln(P_{i,r}^* Q_{i,r}^*) = \ln \hat{P}_i^* + \ln \hat{Q}_{i,r}^* \qquad (7.21)$$

The described decomposition methodology implies that the relative contribution of each of the components to the relationship between variety in export supply and exports can be revealed. It allows us to explore, for example, whether larger export sales of a firm with export variety are primarily due to larger export sales per market (the intensive margin) or are due to the larger number of export markets served (the extensive margin)? It also allows for an assessment of whether the effect of the intensive margin is first and foremost due to (average) prices or (average) quantities.

In order to achieve this, (7.15) is first estimated by means of ordinary least squares (OLS). This gives an estimate of the $\beta$-parameter in (7.15), that is, an estimated elasticity of the export value of firms with respect to the variety in export supply. Then each of the components described in (7.19) and (7.21) is regressed separately on the variables on the right-hand side (7.15). Since OLS is a linear operator, the estimated coefficients of these components sum to the original estimated $\beta$-parameter obtained from the OLS estimation of (7.15). This means in turn that the contribution of each component to the estimated $\beta$-parameter in (7.15) can be calculated.

The results of the procedure described above are presented in Table 7.2. The estimations are based on a cross-section of 18,986 export firms in the manufacturing sector in 2003. All standard errors are calculated using White's (1980) heteroskedasticity-consistent covariance matrix.

The results suggest a positive and significant correlation between the variety in export supply and the size of export sales at the firm level. The estimated $\beta$-parameter in (7.15) amounts to 1.24 and is statistically significant at the 0.01 level. This suggests that a firm with 10 percent higher export variety in general has 12.4 percent larger export sales, which is a clear indication that there are gains from variety in export supply in terms of the size of export sales. The estimates imply increasing returns to variety in export supply at the level of the individual firm. Is this primarily due to larger export sales per export product or rather that firms with larger variety in export supply export to a larger set of markets? The estimates show that the relationship between variety in export supply and exports can be attributed to the extensive and intensive margins, roughly on a 50–50 basis. As seen in the table, 54 percent of the larger export sales can be ascribed to the extensive margin, whereas 46 percent can consequently be ascribed to the intensive margin. Although the estimates in Table 7.2 cannot be interpreted with reference to causality, the results are consistent with the claim that firms which export a set of products are potentially able to penetrate a larger set of export markets by realizing scope economies. Moreover, the effect of the intensive margin is solely due to larger export volumes per market. The contribution from the price component is negative but small, that is, –2 per cent. Thus, firms with higher variety in export supply tend to have marginally lower average prices per kilogram which has a negative effect on their total export value.

*Table 7.2  The relationship between export variety and the size of export sales at the firm level*

|  |  | $\ln n_i$ | Share of the estimated β-parameter in (7.15) | $R^2$ |
|---|---|---|---|---|
| $\ln x_i$ | Export value (size of export sales) | 1.24 (0.012) | – | 0.40 |
| $\ln M_i$ | Extensive margin | 0.66 (0.006) | 54% | 0.48 |
| $\ln(P^*_{i,r}Q^*_{i,r})$ | Intensive margin | 0.58 (0.01) | 46% | 0.21 |
|  |  |  | Share of intensive margin |  |
| $\ln \hat{P}^*_i$ | Price | −0.02 (0.011) | −2% | 0.29 |
| $\ln \hat{Q}^*_{i,r}$ | *Volume* | 0.59 (0.015) | 102% | 0.26 |

*Note:* * standard errors in brackets (calculated according to White's (1980) covariance matrix.

Two robustness tests of the results in Table 7.2 were carried out.[14] First, to test whether the results are sensitive to particular observations, the relationships were re-estimated by excluding one observation at a time. This produced negligible changes to estimated parameters and the share of the respective margins remained unchanged. Second, the relationships were estimated by the quintile (or robust) regression technique (see Koenker and Bassett, 1978), using the 50th quintile (median) with bootstrapped standard errors to avoid underestimation due to heteroskedasticity. Also with this method, the changes in the parameter estimates were negligible and the share of the respective margins remained unchanged.

## SUMMARY AND DISCUSSION

New trade theory suggests an important link between product variety and international trade and a growing literature is devoted to empirical assessments of the relationship between product variety, trade and welfare. Empirical studies suggest a strong link between product differentiation and comparative advantages and that variety growth is associated with welfare expansion. In addition, as micro-data on individual exporters have become available in different countries, several studies of how different characteristics of individual firms affect their export activities have emerged.

Existing studies on the role of product variety for trade and comparative advantages are focused on the aggregate national level. Likewise, the literature analyzing the characteristics of individual firms and their export behavior has not yet considered variety in supply as a pertinent characteristic of exporting firms, either in empirical or in theoretical work. However, if consumers value variety, the variety in supply is likely to be a significant attribute of firms.

This chapter has contributed to the literature by studying the relationship between variety in export supply and exports at the firm level, using highly detailed Swedish firm-level export data. Variety in export supply was measured as the number of export products of a given firm.

The data reveal that the typical firm exports a limited set of products to a limited set of markets. Although firms with a large variety in export supply are relatively few in number, they constitute a substantial share of Sweden's total exports. Firms with greater variety indeed have larger export sales (in terms of export value). An analysis of a cross-section of exporting firms shows that 1 percent greater variety in export supply is typically associated with a 1.24 percent larger export sales. Some 54 percent of this relationship is explained by the extensive margin, that is, that firms with larger export variety serve a larger set of markets. A potential explanation for this is that multi-product firms can realize economies of scope, which is certainly valid if entry costs are firm-specific rather than product specific.

Admittedly, the methodology applied does not reveal causative relationships. The results of this chapter should therefore be regarded as suggestive rather than conclusive. Nevertheless, the results suggest that variety is a pertinent attribute of a firm's exports. The results do indeed indicate that the variety in export supply is a pertinent characteristic of exporters. The present research can, however, be extended along a number of lines. One relevant question is to what extent is there endogeneity between export variety and exports, which can potentially be addressed by controlling for the variety in supply of the firms as they enter export market(s). However, such an analysis remains a subject for future research. We could examine the dynamics between exports and product variety if a panel dataset could be constructed and the change of product variety over time could be captured. Moreover, one would assume that a significant proportion of the exporting firms also supply products to the domestic market. Since product variety is not determined by the international market alone, future studies could consider this factor in the models and empirical analyses. This, however, requires data on domestic deliveries.

## NOTES

1.  A large intensive margin is consistent with models building on Armington's (1969) assumption of differentiation by origin, whereas a large extensive margin is consistent with the monopolistic competition framework in Krugman (1980).
2.  See Tybout (2003) and Greenaway and Kneller (2007) for surveys of this literature. Stylized facts about exporters contra non-exporters are reported in *inter alia* Bernard and Jensen (1995, 1999), Clerides et al. (1998), Bernard et al. (2003) and Eaton et al. (2004). In these studies it is shown that exporters are a small subset of all producers and tend to be larger and more productive. Moreover, a small fraction of the exporters exports to a large set of countries (see, in particular, Eaton et al., 2004 and 2005).
3.  Roberts (2004) discusses Ford versus Toyota as regards flexibility, variety and performance (see also Gerwin, 1993 and MacDuffie et al., 1996).
4.  CN = combined nomenclature.
5.  Alternatively, multi-product firms can be explained by purchasing economies of scope on the demand side, which are obtained when consumers value variety but incur switching costs if they change supplier (see, e.g., Klemperer, 1995).
6.  With respect to knowledge being a common input, it should be noted that Teece (1980, 1982) forcefully argued that economies of scope does not imply that it is more efficient to produce two goods by one firm unless the market for the common input is imperfect. The market for knowledge and information certainly tends to be imperfect (see Arrow, 1962).
7.  This assumption is introduced to keep the analysis simple, although there is an obvious incentive for mergers in the present set-up. Eaton and Schmitt (1994) and Norman and Thisse (1999), for instance, show that scope economies tend to promote concentration of industries via, for example, mergers and preemption.
8.  See Brander and Eaton (1984) and Katz (1984) for an extensive analysis of pricing decisions of multi-product firms.
9.  See, e.g., Tybout (2003) and Greenaway and Kneller (2007).
10.  A similar definition of products can be found in Schott (2004) and Broda and Weinstein (2004a, b).
11.  This way of measuring variety in export supply does not account for the distribution of export sales across different products. Other measures, such as an entropy measure, could be used to account for the distribution of sales across products. However, adding a product to the export supply is a more significant expansion of the variety than changing the distribution of sales across a (given) set of products.
12.  However, the standard deviations reveal that there is a large dispersion within the category.
13.  The cross-section dataset applied here only covers exporting firms with an aggregate export value larger than 50,000 SEK (approx. €5,000). A selection problem due to the fact that firms may self-select into export markets because of productivity thresholds associated with exports (see Tybout, 2003), potentially exists but is not addressed here. The analysis is confined to exporting firms.
14.  The results of the robustness tests are available from the author upon request.

# REFERENCES

Armington, P.S. (1969), 'A Theory of Demand for Products Distinguished by Place of Production', *International Monetary Fund Staff Papers*, **16**,159-178

Arrow, K.J. (1962), 'Economic Welfare and the Allocation of Resources for Invention', in NBER, *The Rate and Direction of Economic Activity: Economic and Social Factors*, Princeton University Press, Princeton

Bailey, E. and A. Friedlaender, (1982), 'Market Structure and Multiproduct Industries', *Journal of Economic Literature*, XX, 1024–48.

Ben-Akiva, M.E. and S.R. Lerman (1985), *Discrete Choice Analysis*, MIT Press, Cambridge, MA.

Bernard, A.B and J.B. Jensen (1995), 'Exporters, Jobs and Wages in US Manufacturing 1976–1987', *Brookings Papers on Economic Activity*, 67–119.

Bernard, A.B. and J.B. Jensen (1999), 'Exceptional Exporter Performance: cause, effect or both?', *Journal of International Economics*, **47**, 1–25.

Bernard, A.B. J. Eaton, J.B. Jensen and S. Kortum (2003), 'Plants and Productivity in International Trade', *American Economic Review*, **93**, 1268–90.

Brander, J.A., J. Eaton (1984), 'Product Line Rivalry', *American Economic Review*, **74**, 323–34.

Broda, C. and D.E. Weinstein, (2004a), 'Variety Growth and World Welfare', *American Economic Review*, **94**, 139–44.

Broda, C. and D.E. Weinstein (2004b), 'Globalization and the Gains from Variety', NBER Working Paper, 10314.

Chaney, T. (2008), 'Distorted Gravity – the intensive and extensive margins of international trade', forthcoming in *American Economic Review*.

Clerides, S., S. Lach and J. Tybout (1998), 'Is Learning by Exporting Important: micro-dynamic evidence from Colombia, Mexico and Morocco', *Quarterly Journal of Economics*, **113**, 903–47.

Dixit, A.K and J.E. Stiglitz (1977) 'Monopolistic Competition and Optimum Product Diversity', *American Economic Review*, **67**, 297-308.

Dunne, T., J. Roberts and L. Samuelson (1988), 'Patterns of Firm Entry in US Manufacturing Industries', *Rand Journal of Economics*, **19**, 495–515.

Eaton, J. and S. Kortum (2002), 'Technology, Geography and Trade', *Econometrica*, **70**, 1741–80.

Eaton, J., S. Kortum and F. Kramarz (2004), 'Dissecting Trade: firms, industries and export destinations', *American Economic Review*, **94**, 150–54.

Eaton, J., S. Kortum and F. Kramarz (2005), 'An Anatomy of International Trade: evidence from French firms', Mimeograph, University of Minnesota, MN,

Eaton, B. and N. Schmitt (1994), 'Flexible Manufacturing and Market Structure', *American Economic Review*, **84**, 875–88.

Funke, M. and R. Ruhwendel (2001), 'Export Variety and Export Performance: evidence from East Asia', *Journal of Asian Economics*, **12**, 493–505.

Funke, M. and R. Ruhwendel (2002), 'Export Variety and Export Performance: empirical evidence for the OECD countries', *Review of World Economics*, **138**, 97–114.

Gerwin, D. (1993), 'Manufacturing Flexibility: a strategic perspective', *Management Science*, **39**, 395–410.

Greenaway, D. and R. Kneller (2007), 'Firm Heterogeneity, Exporting and Foreign Direct Investment', *Economic Journal*, **117**, 134-161

Hummels, D. and P.J. Klenow (2005), 'The Variety and Quality of a Nation's Exports', *American Economic Review*, **95**, 704–23.

Johansson, B. (2005), 'Diversity and Superiority in Local and Global Innovation Processes', Jönköping International Business School.

Katz, M.L. (1984), 'Firm-Specific Differentiation and Competition among Multiproduct Firms', *Journal of Business*, **57**, 149–66.

Klemperer, P. (1995), 'Competition when Consumers have Switching Costs: an overview with applications to industrial organization, macroeconomics and international trade', *Review of Economic Studies*, **62**, 515–39.

Koenker, R. and G. Bassett (1978), 'Regression Quantiles', *Econometrica*, **46**, 33–50.

Krugman, P. (1980), 'Scale Economies, Product Differentiation and the Pattern of Trade', *American Economic Review*, **70**, 950–59.

Lancaster, K. (1966a), 'A New Approach to Consumer Theory', *Journal of Political Economy*, **74**, 132–57.

Lancaster, K. (1966b), 'Change and Innovation in the Technology of Consumption', *American Economic Review*, **56**, 14–23.

Lancaster, K. (1990), 'The Economics of Product Variety: A Survey', *Marketing Science*, **9**, 189–206.

MacDuffie, J.P., K. Sethuraman and M.L. Fischer (1996), 'Product Variety and Manufacturing Performance: evidence from the international automotive assembly plant study', *Management Science*, **42**, 350–69.

Melitz, M.J. (2003), 'The Impact of Trade on Intra-Industry Reallocations and Aggregate Industry Productivity', *Econometrica*, **71**, 1695-1725

Milgrom, P., Y. Qian and J. Roberts (1991), 'Complementarities, Momentum and the Evolution of Modern Manufacturing', *American Economic Review*, **81**, 84–8.

Milgrom, P. and J. Roberts (1990), 'The Economics of Modern Manufacturing: technology, strategy and organization', *American Economic Review*, **80**, 511–28.

Norman, G. and J.F. Thisse (1999), 'Technology Choice and Market Structure: strategic aspects of flexible manufacturing', *Journal of Industrial Economics*, **47**, 345–72.

Panzar, J. and R. Willig (1981), 'Economies of Scope', *American Economic Review*, **71**, 268–72.

Roberts, J. (2004), *The Modern Firm – Organizational Design for Performance and Growth*, Oxford University Press, Oxford.

Schott, P. (2004), 'Across-Product versus Within-Product Specialization in International Trade', *Quarterly Journal of Economics*, **119**, 647–78.

Teece, D. (1980), 'Economies of Scope and the Scope of the Enterprise', *Journal of Economic Behavior and Organization*, **1**, 223–47.

Teece, D. (1982), 'Towards an Economic Theory of the Multiproduct Firm', *Journal of Economic Behavior and Organization*, **3**, 39–63.

Tybout, J. (2003), 'Plant and Firm Level Evidence on "New" Trade Theories', in E.K. Choi, E.K and J. Harrigan (eds), *Handbook of International Trade*, Blackwell, Oxford, 388-415

White, H. (1980), 'A Heteroscedasticity-Consistent Covariance Matrix Estimator and Direct Test for Heteroscedasticity', *Econometrica*, **48**, 817–38.

## APPENDIX - INDUSTRIES IN THE MANUFACTURING SECTOR

| Sector | Name |
|---|---|
| 1 | Wood products |
| 2 | Paper |
| 3 | Publishing, printing |
| 4 | Petroleum products, nuclear fuel |
| 5 | Basic chemical |
| 6 | Pesticides, agro-chemical products |
| 7 | Paints, varnishes |
| 8 | Pharmaceuticals |
| 9 | Soaps, detergents, toilet preparations |
| 10 | Other chemicals |
| 11 | Man-made fibers |
| 12 | Rubber and plastics products |
| 13 | Non-metallic mineral products |
| 14 | Basic metals |
| 15 | Fabricated metal products |
| 16 | Energy machinery |
| 17 | Non-specific purpose machinery |
| 18 | Agricultural and forestry machinery |
| 19 | Machine-tools |
| 20 | Special-purpose machinery |
| 21 | Weapons and ammunition |
| 22 | Domestic appliances |
| 23 | Office machinery and computers |
| 24 | Electric motors, generators, transformers |
| 25 | Electric distribution, control, wire, cable |
| 26 | Accumulators, battery |
| 27 | Lightning equipment |
| 28 | Other electrical equipment |
| 29 | Electronic components |
| 30 | Signal transmission, telecommunications |
| 31 | Television and radio receivers, audiovisual electronics |
| 32 | Medical equipment |
| 33 | Measuring instruments |
| 34 | Optical instruments |
| 35 | Watches, clocks |
| 36 | Motor vehicles |
| 37 | Other transport equipment |
| 38 | Furniture, consumer goods |

# 8. Differences in Survivor Functions according to Different Competitive Strategies

## Raquel Ortega-Argilés and Rosina Moreno

## INTRODUCTION

Among the models based on industrial dynamics, the most influential is by Jovanovic (1982), who concludes that the longer a firm operates within a market, that is, the more experience it acquires, the more efficient it becomes. As a firm becomes less efficient, its competitors will step in and encroach on its position in the market. Jovanovic's model is of 'passive learning'. This occurs because firms concentrate their efforts on making themselves more efficient solely by modifying their behavior. They do not consider high risks. Other authors, including Klepper (1993, 1996a and 1996b), have introduced the concept of 'capacity' into industrial dynamics. This term refers to the capacity of entrepreneurs to adopt innovations in their operations so as to make them more competitive than their competitors. It is a type of learning similar to that formulated by Ericson and Pakes (1995), known as 'active learning'. It is based on the capacity of firms to become more competitive thanks to the adoption of innovations both in their products (Jovanovic and McDonald, 1994) and in their methods of production and organization (Klepper, 1993).

Therefore, a company's behavior is dictated by the decisions made over the course of its life. These decisions will determine its efficiency and, in turn, its survival. The main decisions that a firm makes are related to prices, production levels and its investments choices. The firm can improve its products, that is, it can introduce new products or make modifications to existing ones (incremental innovations) which would give it greater leverage in the market *vis-à-vis* its direct competitors. These would even include the firm's capacity to diversify, in other words, to operate in different markets or different industries. On the other hand, the firm can improve its processes which are linked to a reduction in costs and an increase in productivity. These improvements would make the firm more efficient and would translate into a reduction in prices (price competition). Factors of this type are closely linked with process innovations and the implementation of new technologies. Additionally, internal improvements, which are linked to firms' organizational capacity (innovations in organization), are improvements that would modify firms' corporate structure. Therefore, they include factors related to internal organization, such as management, ownership and the capacity to expand the number of establishments.

In this chapter, we analyze whether the adoption of a competitive behavior is a determinant for firms' survival in Spanish manufacturing industries. We also investigate and examine the most important type of strategies used. Thus, we first construct a summary of the different competition strategies that impact on the rate of growth and the ability of firms to survive in the market. Through the use of non-parametric tests and proportional hazard models, we then assess the extent to which each strategy signaled or implied in the theoretical literature is a significant determinant for the firm's survival.

The chapter is structured in six sections. Following the introduction, the second and third sections review both the theoretical and conceptual literature related to firm survival. In the fourth section, we describe the methodology including both a critique and a discussion of the advantages of the method chosen. The fifth section describes the database and the variables used in the analysis. We then describe the main results in the sixth section. The final section presents the main conclusions and discusses directions for future research on this topic.

## THEORETICAL ASSUMPTIONS

This chapter, like many others conducted within the field of industrial dynamics, is based on Schumpeter's model of 'creative destruction' (1942) in which firms of a certain size and in a context of a split market need to adopt new processes and behaviors in order to maintain themselves and to grow. Most studies that analyze the problem of a firm's life are focused on two principal factors: the size and the age of the firm (Mansfield, 1962). Studies of this type find no correlation between the size of the firm and its rate of growth.

In order to explain deviations from the law of proportional growth, Jovanovic (1982) proposed a theory of business selection ('noisy selection model') with incomplete information. According to this theory, firms learn from their efficiency as they acquire experience of operating in the industrial sector. The main premise of the model is that the most efficient firms grow throughout their lifetime and, therefore, survive the different stages of the cycle, that is, they sustain their competitiveness. On the other hand, those that do not grow will eventually fail. Jovanovic's model confirms the results obtained by authors who followed Schumpeterian theory. The main conclusions or results can be summarized as follows: the size of the firm seems to be positively related to the rate of firm output, profit and earnings; the variability of the rates of business results at any specific time is greater in the industries with higher density; and finally, a high concentration of businesses is associated with greater profits for the large but not for the small firms. Thus, the conclusion seems to be that small firms grow more rapidly than large firms and show a greater propensity for failure.

Hopenhayn (1992), Ericson and Pakes (1995) and Pakes and Ericson (1998) followed a similar line of reasoning. However, they build on Jovanovic's postulates and recognize that a firm has the capacity to accelerate the process of acquired learning through research and development (R&D) investment. Hopenhayn develops a dynamic stochastic model for a competitive industry that endogenously determines processes for entry and exit and for an individual firm's output and employment. Hopenhayn, following the preliminary work by Jovanovic (1982) and Ericson and Pakes (1995), provides a simple framework in order to address questions related to the process of job and firm reallocation, thus, complementing the previous related research. Hopenhayn argued that the only dynamic decision faced by firms is the exit decision, that is, a stopping time problem. However, from his point of view it is possible to introduce investment decisions and some other competitive strategies, which expand the state vector in the dynamic problem solved by firms.[1] Finally, the works by Ericson and Pakes consider two models of firm behavior that allow for heterogeneity among firms, idiosyncratic (or firm-specific) sources of uncertainty, and discrete outcomes (exit and/or entry). In their model developed in 1995, focus was on the impact of uncertainty arising from investments in research and exploration-type processes. The manager acts as an optimizing agent who makes entry decisions incurring sunk costs. The stochastic outcome of a firm's investment, the success of other firms in the industry and competitive pressure from outside the industry (both in the market and through entry) determine the profitability and value of the firm. They have improved the model developed by Jovanovic in the sense that their model permits the acceleration of the acquired learning process by means of R&D investments.

We should not, however, ignore the theoretical studies that examine the business skills that ensure business survival and growth. The authors of these studies, based on the theory of competitive advantage, employ Klepper (1993, 1996a, 1996b) as the main reference. The main sources of survival are those that stress the importance of accumulative economies of scale in R&D. This characteristic provides an advantage to firms that enter an industry early versus entering later. The literature based on the life cycle of the industry has a series of clearly established factors that are related to the different stages of a firm's life cycle. Thus, we find economies of scale, learning curves, and barriers to entry and financial resources that are combined with maturity and technological change. These factors determine the competitive behavior of the firm and thus should be considered as the fundamental factors in industrial evolution. The principal results are the existence of a positive relationship between the probability of survival and the size and age of the firm. Further, Jovanovic and McDonald's (1994) study is based on a shakeout focus. They present a model in which the earliest entrants employ a common technology that after a certain time is replaced by a new one. This new technology ensures low unit costs and, therefore, a higher level of output per firm. The transition to the new technology generates an exit or shakeout of the first generation of firms and the survival of a small number of firms which now employ this new, large-scale technology.

Finally, it is important to highlight the fact that knowledge and technological progress are the main engines of economic dynamics in most endogenous growth models and thinking (Romer, 1986). In these models innovation is not given, but rather determined by other factors such as productivity, investment and savings. So, although it is beyond the scope of the present chapter, we should, therefore, bear in mind that all the strategies related to innovation would in turn generate economic growth.

## CONCEPTUAL FRAMEWORK

Audretsch (1995) and Geroski (1995) state that the existence of survival barriers is more important than entry barriers. Firms can enter the market relatively easily, but they will encounter many difficulties when it comes to continuing their activities in the market. It is assumed that the survival barriers vary between industries, thus taking into account that huge differences exist in product differentiation strategy adopted by the sector, the technological conditions or the market power of the established firms, among other important aspects (Segarra et al. 2002).

Bain (1956) identified four elements in the market structure that affect the capacity of established firms to avoid losses in their extraordinary benefits due to new firm entries. In his view there are four entry or survival barriers:

1. *Scale economies* (fixed costs) If the minimum efficient scale is a significant proportion of industry demand, the market can be composed of a small number of firms without the stimulation of the entry of new firms.

2. *Absolute cost advantages* Established firms can have highly qualified production techniques that can be learned through a learning-by-doing process or by the R&D internal process. Capital accumulation can reduce the production costs and can impede access to new inputs by the new entrants.
3. *Product differentiation advantages* Established firms can patent product innovations or can find the correct market share and enjoy the consumer's loyalty.
4. *The required capital* Potential entrants may have financial problems due to the high risk of their project in a highly competitive market.

Another theoretical trend with regard to entry barriers is illustrated by Bain (1956), Modigliani and Miller (1958) and Sylos Labini (1962) and is known as the 'limit-price model'. This model shows that established firms can maintain a low price to discourage the entry of new firms into the market. However, some authors (Jovanovic, 1982; Milgrom and Roberts, 1982; Segarra et al., 2002) argue that in the industries in which scale economies are not relevant, small size firms can operate at a level lower than the minimum efficient scale of production without experiencing cost disadvantages.

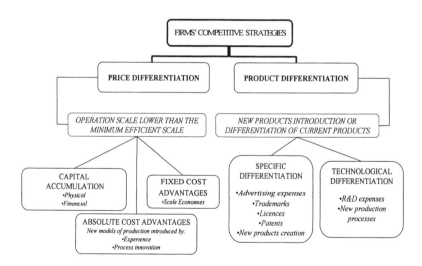

*Figure 8.1 Firm competitive strategies*

Taking into account the previous literature, Figure 8.1 summarizes the different concepts presented above. As indicated, the different competitive strategies adopted by the firms can be classified into two groups: price and product competition strategies. In this chapter, we focus on the latter. The price competition strategy (called 'price differentiation strategy') encompasses a type of strategy that helps firms operate at a lower level than the minimum efficient scale. This lower scale of operation in the majority of cases is the result of the accumulation of financial and knowledge resources. A product competition strategy establishes market niches and allows firms to obtain concrete market power with their customers. Among the diverse tactics that firms can adapt within a product competition strategy context are those related to 'specific differentiation' (advertising expenses and the introduction of new products, among others) and 'technological differentiation' (R&D) expenses as well as the use of new production processes). The specific differentiation strategy is developed in markets with a standard technology and with high importance placed on the design strategy. On the other hand, a technological differentiation strategy is crucial in non-standard product markets with a high level of substitution elasticity.

The general hypothesis of this chapter is that the introduction of some type of product competition strategy gives the firm a greater probability of survival. Based on this notion and on the theoretical literature already discussed, the firm wins a greater market share in the industry when it uses strategies to differentiate its product from that of its competitors, thereby increasing the likelihood of survival. Simultaneously, firms that adopt strategies that support a more flexible production process obtain cost savings. This means that their likelihood of survival is greater than those that do not adopt such strategies.

## METHODOLOGY

The methodology used in analyzing a firm's behavior throughout its life, specifically the survival of a particular event, is related to the science of biometry. This science was developed to explain the evolution of a number of patients who presented a pathology and the probability of these patients surviving this condition in a given period. Survival can, therefore, be defined as the analysis of the time that passes until the failure occurs. In the case of the patient, this is the analysis of the time following the diagnosis until death occurs. In our case, it is the time from the moment in which a firm is established in a market until an exit occurs.

The empirical literature has analyzed business dynamics and, more specifically, firm exit behavior using various techniques. Some of the literature uses logit or probit models of a discrete choice form (Audretsch, 1995; Colombo and Delmastro, 2000, 2001; Littunen, 2000; Heshmati, 2001;

Headd, 2002), in which the dependent variable is the probability of exit. Another type of modeling used is that of models for censored data. The dependent variable always takes a positive value and is constituted by the months that have passed since the firm's establishment (Audretsch et al., 1999). Finally, some authors have used simple least squares regression methods (Karlsson and Nyström, 2003; Van Praag, 2003). However, the use of such models fails to consider the vast amount of information and, in most cases, depends on data from cohorts of firms, thus subjecting such studies to the limitations of the representativeness of the sample. In order to solve the problems presented by these models, econometric techniques were adopted (parametric and non-parametric) for the estimation of duration models. Indeed, many authors are convinced by the efficiency of econometric duration models for the analysis of firm survival (Mata and Portugal, 1994; Mata et al., 1995; Segarra et al., 2002).

The variable of interest in duration analysis is the length of time that passes between the moment at which the phenomenon begins and the moment in which either the phenomenon terminates or the measurement is taken. This might occur before the termination of the phenomenon. Thus, when the measurement is taken, the phenomenon might not have finished. Therefore, both the use of conventional statistical methods and estimation by minimum or least squares are not adequate for examining the duration of a process. This is because they fail to consider the censor problem in the data. These methods use the information in an incomplete manner, so that the estimation by ordinary least squares provides biased and inconsistent estimates. Furthermore, in such cases the likelihood of the event occurring (the firm exiting the market) will not be conditioned on the evolution of the individual throughout the period being analyzed (having remained in the market until the moment immediately before deciding to exit), but rather will be centered on the mean probability that the event will occur during the period under observation.

Econometric duration models consider the dynamics of the whole process, that is, they take into consideration the evolution of a firm's life over time. Thus, it is not only relevant whether or not a firm decides to exit a market during the period of study, but it is also important to see the evolution of the risk of exit and the determinants of this event over time. Most studies that analyze growth following entrance using these techniques analyze only a cohort of firms (Audretsch, 1991; Mahmood, 1992; Mata and Portugal, 1994; Audretsch and Mahmood, 1995; Agarwal, 1997; Agarwal and Audretsch, 2001; Segarra and Callejón, 2002; Segarra et al., 2002). The use of a cohort of firms reduces the study to an analysis of a series of firms that have many characteristics in common and, therefore, information is lost. The loss could be due to different characteristics that arise when firms enter the market at different times, or if the event begins before or after the moment chosen as the initial point in the period analyzed. Furthermore, as Mata et al. (1995) point out, most studies take into consideration only the conditions affecting the firm at the moment in which it is established. Thereby, they assume that the conditions at establishment will determine its likelihood of survival during its life. However, as a firm operates, it is quite likely that the relative importance of variables under investigation will change or vary over time, and it is probable that the most recent observations of these variables will have more influence in predicting the survival versus those recorded at the beginning of the period. The use of different cohorts of entrants allows an analysis of the effect of a firm's age on the probability of its survival. This is something that cannot be achieved when only one cohort of firms is analyzed, since they all have the same age.

Taking the above discussion into consideration, in this chapter we use the most efficient techniques derived from biometry. First, we start with an analysis of the factors determining the survival rates in the case of Spanish manufacturing firms. This is done through the use of a representative sample of data of firms founded before 1990 and that have survived beyond 2001, in order to obtain the maximum amount of information. The comparison of the determinants of the survival is carried out by a graphical analysis of the behavior of the differentiated groups defined by different firm determinants. Specifically, the literature advises using this kind of analysis before deploying a hazard model with variables that vary over time with the aim of ensuring that the variables fulfill the proportional hazard assumptions that are required in semi-parametric hazard models.

This analysis takes the following assumptions into account. For a simple covariate, $x$, the Cox proportional hazard model reduces to:

$$h(t; x) = h_0(t)\exp(x\beta) \tag{8.1}$$

where $h_0(t)$ is known as the baseline hazard function and $\beta$ is the vector of the regression parameters from the Cox model. We can define $S_0(t)$ and $H_0(t)$ as being representative of the survival functions and baseline cumulative hazard function in the model, respectively. The proportional risk assumption implies:

$$H(t) = H_0(t)\exp(x\beta) \tag{8.2}$$

or

$$\ln H(t) = \ln H_0(t) + x\beta \tag{8.3}$$

where $H(t)$ is the accumulated hazard function. Thus, under the proportional hazard assumption, the logarithms of the cumulative hazard functions at each level of the explanatory variable have an equal slope. This is the basic assumption of the first stage of the implementation.

Additionally, the proportional hazard assumption implies that:

$$S(t) = S_0(t)^{\exp(x\beta)} \tag{8.4}$$

If $S(t)$ is the estimation made with the reference survivor function of the Cox model, this is a step function, like the Kaplan–Meier estimate, and, in fact, reduces to the Kaplan–Meier estimate when $x = 0$. Therefore, for each level of the explanatory variable of interest, we can assess non-fulfillment of the proportional hazard assumptions making comparisons between the two estimations of survival with estimates calculated independently from the model (Kalbfleisch and Prentice, 1980).[2]

Second, differences in the survivor functions of the observed subgroup are tested for statistical significance. For this reason, we use a variety of non-parametric tests of equality of the survival functions for some of the variables. The tests analyzed, all based on the $\chi^2$ test, are the Peto–Peto–Prentice, the Wilcoxon–Breslow–Gehan, the Long-rank and the Tarone–Ware. These tests compare two or more distributions and comprise the weighted sum of the differences between the actual number of firm exits and the expected value for each of the groups being compared. The difference between the tests lies in the weighting method. The tests can be used with the following situations in mind. The Long-rank test should be used if it is believed that the survival functions are proportional between the groups being compared; the Wilcoxon–Breslow–Gehan test when the survival function may be disproportional and when the patterns are believed to be equal between groups. Finally, if the function varies in a non-proportional manner and there is a requirement to control for possible differences in the patterns of the various groups, of the Peto-Peto-Prentice test is the most appropriate.

# DATABASE AND DEFINITION OF VARIABLES[3]

The database used is the Survey of Business Strategies (*Encuesta sobre Estrategias Empresariales* (ESEE)) produced by the SEPI Foundation and partly financed by the Ministry of Industry, Tourism and Trade and the ICO foundation. The ESEE is a statistical research project that conducts an annual survey of a number of companies representing manufacturing industries in Spain. Its design is relatively flexible and it has two applications. On the one hand, it provides in-depth knowledge of the sector's evolution over time by means of multiple data concerning business development and company decisions. The ESEE is also designed to generate microeconomic information that enables specification and testing of econometric models. As far as its coverage is concerned, the reference population of the ESEE consists of companies with ten or more workers in what is usually classified as a manufacturing industry. The geographical area of reference is Spain and the variables have a timescale of one year. One of the most outstanding characteristics of the ESEE is its high degree of representativeness. It examines the production activity of firms aggregated to a 2-digit level corresponding to the manufacturing sector. This aggregation in 20 industries corresponds to the NACE–CLIO classification. [4]

In order to analyze the effect that the competitive innovative strategy adopted by the firm has on its survival, the following explanatory variables have been included and drawn from the leading theoretical and empirical studies conducted in the field. In the case of product competition strategies, we consider both technological and specific differentiation strategies.

The variables that seek to proxy *technological differentiation strategies* are R&D expenses and process innovations introduced in the firm. The first is a dichotomous variable that takes the value of 1 when the firm incurs R&D costs and null otherwise (*RDC*). This variable was constructed in line with the work of Heshmati (2001). The effect of investment in innovation on the probability of market survival has been analyzed by several authors (Mahmood, 2000; Segarra and Callejón, 2002).

A dichotomous variable that reflects whether or not the firm makes or introduces process innovations[5] (*PROC*) is also introduced to proxy whether the competition strategy adopted by the firm is based on production flexibility. To complement this, in order to analyze what type of modification in the production process has more impact on survival, two additional variables are introduced. First, we construct a dichotomous variable that takes a value of 1 when the modification involves the introduction of new machinery (*MACH*). Another dichotomous variable takes a value of 1 when the firm has adopted new methods in its organization of production (*ORG*) and null otherwise.

As for *specific differentiation strategies*, we construct a dichotomous variable that takes the value of 1 when the firm makes any investment in advertising in the year under review and zero when no investments are made (*ADV*). The effect of advertising on industrial dynamics has been analyzed elsewhere for the case of Spain (Lafuente and Lecha, 1988; Aranguren, 1999; Segarra and Callejón, 2002; Segarra et al., 2002). Following the theory of active learning and the specific differentiation strategy (Klepper, 1993; Jovanovic and McDonald, 1994), a number of variables have been introduced to reflect the impact of the expenses incurred in innovation as well as those attributable to the type of innovation made by the firm on the probability of a firm's survival. An initial focus of the analysis involves analyzing the influence that product innovations may have.[6] This requires the introduction of a dichotomous variable that describes whether or not the firm introduces new products into the market in a given year (PROD). Finally, as we continue to focus on a firm's product competition strategies, our chapter introduces a series of variables that allow us to identify the strategies that favor the probability of market survival in the Spanish manufacturing industry. Thus, we introduce variables that define the type of product innovation with respect to the products that were previously produced. *MAT* is a dichotomous variable that takes a value of 1 when the product is considered new because of the use of new materials in its production. *COMP* takes a value of 1 when the new product incorporates new components or intermediate products, and *DES* takes a value of 1 when the product incorporates a new design or means of presentation. Finally, *FUNC* is a dichotomous variable that takes a value of 1 when the new product fulfills a different function or functions.

## RESULTS

First, we develop a graphical analysis to help analyze the differences in the survivor functions between different groups defined by means of different competitive strategies. In this graphical analysis, we first show the figure that offers the differences in the cumulative hazard survivor function between small- and large- firm samples (Figure 8.2) showing that an important difference exists in the survival function between them. Large firms (firms with more than 200 employees) appear to have a higher survival probability than smaller firms (firms with less than 200 employees). This provides us with a reason for developing a differentiated comparative analysis between the survival functions of small and large firms. Although we have developed a separate analysis for the small and large firm samples, we show the results only for the whole sample. However, some comments will refer to this differentiation and the results can be displayed upon request.

First, we analyze the technological differentiation competition strategy. We consider the survival functions of the firms that incur R&D expenses and firms that develop process innovations.

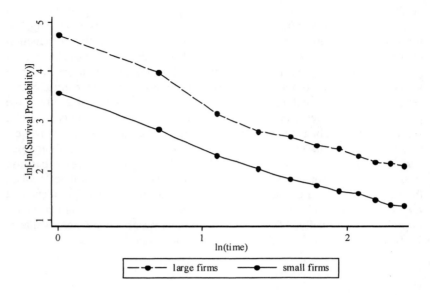

*Figure 8.2  Cumulative hazard survivor functions-size effect*

The individual comparisons for the variable that classifies firms into the group that develops an R&D investment and those that do not are shown in Figures 8.3 and 8.4. Figure 8.3 shows the comparison between the logs of the cumulative hazard function for the two groups of the R&D investment covariate. The figure displays lines that are parallel, implying that the proportional hazards assumption for the R&D investment variable has not been violated. To be more concise, we performed a second graphical method for evaluating the proportional hazard assumption. This method consists of plotting the Kaplan–Meier observed survival curves and compares them with the Cox predicted curves for the same variable. When the predicted and observed curves are close together, the proportional hazard assumption has not been violated. Thus, Figure 8.4 confirms the fulfillment of the proportional hazard assumption for this variable. The observed values and predicted values are close together. Therefore, the assumption of the proportional risk is inviolate for R&D costs. In the light of the results obtained in these figures, we can conclude that firms that incur R&D expenses have a longer life than firms that do not. Audretsch (1995) and Audretsch et al. (2000) also report a positive effect of R&D expenditures on the survival probability for the US and Italian cases, respectively. However, although not provided in the chapter, the plots made separately for small and large firms show that this effect appears to be determinant in small firms but not to have any important effect for the large firms' sample. One possible explanation is that in large firms, R&D investments are implemented as an ordinary activity.

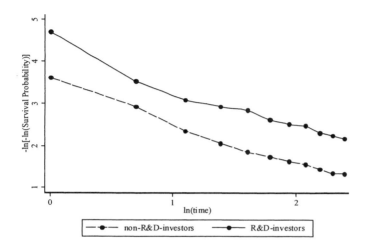

*Figure 8.3  Analysis for the R&D cost effect*

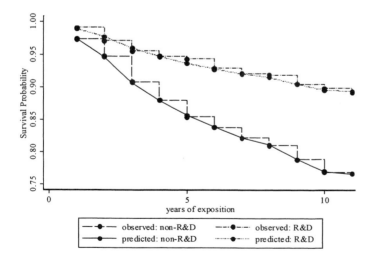

*Figure 8.4  Comparative analysis for the R&D cost effect*

The other competition strategy based on technological differentiation is the introduction of process innovations. As we can see in Figures 8.5 and 8.6, the development of process innovations has a positive effect on the firms' survival. Improving production techniques has a direct effect on the reduction of costs both in personnel (with the introduction of computerized techniques) and in production costs, which in turn imply longer survival rates. Few studies include a similar variable to this one. As far as we know, only Colombo and Delmastro (2001) analyze the role that the differences play in productivity based on the adoption of advanced manufacturing technologies on the closure of Italian manufacturing firms. In their study, the cost structure and the possibility of incurring irretrievable expenses are found to influence exit behavior. Technologies of this type affect design and engineering as well as the manufacturing area of the activity. These authors claim that while the adoption of new basic equipment directly affects production costs, the adoption of more advanced categories of production equipment might be a sign of a firm's greater ability to differentiate its product and making some innovation on it as well as alleviating cost competition. Firms that have used this type of advanced technology present a lower closure (exit or termination) rate because of the technical change implemented in the production processes. Similarly, for the Dutch case, Cefis and Marsili (2005) concluded that being a process innovator implies possession of greater innovative capabilities. This, thereby, enables the firm to adapt more readily and quickly to radical changes in technologies and markets. This enhanced ability to adapt to changes is the key contributor to increasing the chances of survival.

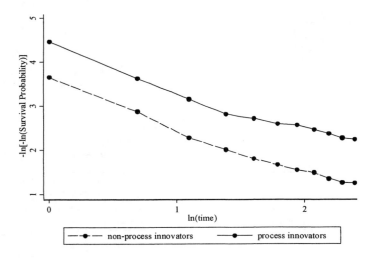

*Figure 8.5  Analysis for the introduction of new processes*

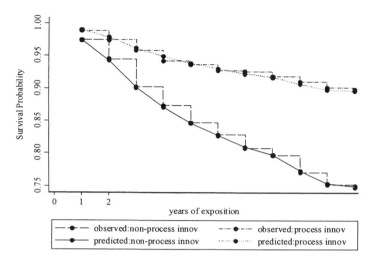

*Figure 8.6 Comparative analysis for the introduction of new processes*

In this stage of the analysis, we evaluate differences of different strategies within the technological differentiation competition strategy. In this case, we evaluate the introduction of new machinery and the development of any type of organizational innovation. The corresponding figures are provided in Appendix 8A1. We found that in the first case, firms that introduce a new type of machinery in the production process have a higher probability of survival than firms that do not. Nevertheless, the implementation of organizational innovations does not appear to present any particular effect on the survival of the Spanish manufacturing firms in either of the analyzed samples.

Regarding the specific differentiation strategy, we analyze the strategies based on advertising investments as well as the introduction of product innovations in the market. Figures 8.7 and 8.8 provide evidence that investment in advertising as a factor of product differentiation, contributes to the reduction of risk of failure in Spanish firms. Although not provided in the chapter, the separate analysis for small and large firms shows that this effect is a determining factor in the case of small firms, but not in that of large firms. In most cases, large firms understand this set of costs as a part of their ordinary activity and, therefore, it is not a determining factor in their survival. Caves and Porter (1977) claim that the theory of strategic groups operating in an industry, in which mobility barriers exist and the scale of returns is small, suggests that a strategy based on product differentiation would facilitate

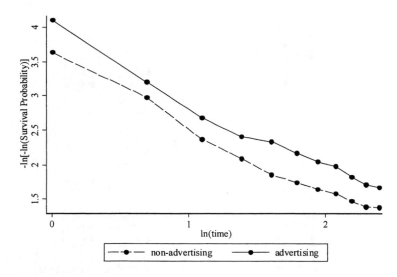

*Figure 8.7   Analysis for investments in advertising*

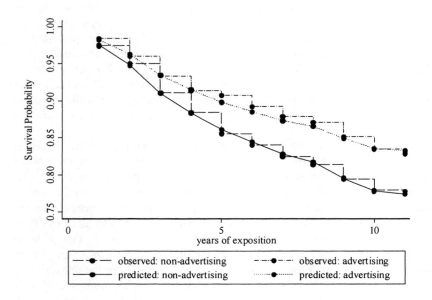

*Figure 8.8   Comparative analysis for investments in advertising*

viability. Segarra and Callejón (2002) report that the greater the intensity of investment in advertising in an industry, the higher the failure rate will be among those entering the sector. They claim that in markets where the customer information and the salesperson's reputation are important, start-up firms face greater entry barriers. This reasoning corresponds to our result that advertising implies longer survival for smaller firms but not for their larger counterparts. This effect of advertising costs on Spanish firm survival has been analyzed by other authors who arrive at the same conclusion (Lafuente and Lecha, 1988; Aranguren, 1999; Segarra et al., 2002).

Finally, we analyze the impact of the introduction of new or improved products in the market (Figures 8.9 and 8.10). As observed, the introduction of product innovations implies an important reduction in the risk of failure of Spanish manufacturing firms. For the case of Finnish manufactures, Littunen (2000) reported that the introduction of products on the market increases the probability of the firm remaining in the market. However, Cefis and Marsili (2005) failed to find any particular effect for the product innovation strategy in the survival rate for the Dutch case.

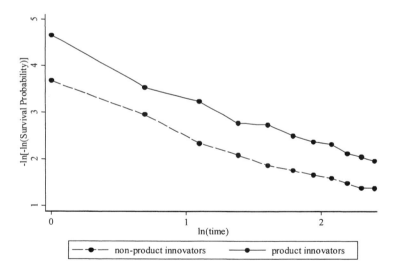

*Figure 8.9 Analysis for product innovation*

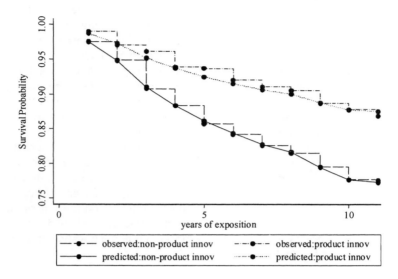

*Figure 8.10  Comparative analysis for product innovation*

Additionally, going deeper into the analysis of the type of product innovations introduced, we develop the same analysis for the different competitive strategies involving the incorporation of new products in the market. The required plots are given in Appendix 8A2. We analyze the effect on the survivor function of the introduction of new components, the development of new design, and the implementation of new functions of the products. In all the cases, the fact of introducing improved products according to these different aspects implies a higher rate of survival.

In the second stage, Table 8.1 shows the results of the non-parametric tests of homogeneity for the variables that we consider relevant in the explanation of a firm's survival. These tests are extensions of non-parametric rank tests which allow the comparison of two or more distributions for censored data. Data may contain completed or right-censored spells, and late entry (left truncation) can also be handled with this type of methodology.[7] As can be seen, given the characteristics of the database and in order to reduce the heterogeneity, we proceeded to conduct a differentiated analysis with the firms grouped according to their size. This differentiation allowed us to observe in detail the differences between the competitive strategies that the firms adopted in relation to their size.

Table 8.1  The results of non-parametric tests

| | ALL FIRMS | | | | SMALL FIRMS | | | | LARGE FIRMS | | | |
|---|---|---|---|---|---|---|---|---|---|---|---|---|
| | Longrank | Peto–Peto–Prentice | Wilcoxon–Breslow | Tarone–Ware | Long rank | Peto–Peto–Prentice | Wilcoxon–Breslow | Tarone–Ware | Long rank | Peto–Peto–Prentice | Wilcoxon–Breslow | Tarone–Ware |
| RDC | **36.87** | **36.67** | **33.66** | **36.08** | **15.14** | **14.60** | **11.37** | **13.49** | **5.25** | **5.45** | **7.29** | **6.38** |
| | (0.0000) | (0.0000) | (0.0000) | (0.0000) | (0.0001) | (0.0001) | (0.0007) | (0.0002) | (0.0220) | (0.0196) | (0.0069) | (0.0115) |
| PROC | **62.09** | **60.94** | **51.91** | **57.93** | **27.54** | **26.41** | **20.46** | **24.23** | **17.03** | **17.15** | **17.11** | **17.39** |
| | (0.0000) | (0.0000) | (0.0000) | (0.0000) | (0.0000) | (0.0000) | (0.0000) | (0.0000) | (0.0000) | (0.0000) | (0.0000) | (0.0000) |
| MACH | **27.17** | **27.91** | **29.08** | **28.98** | **20.41** | **20.85** | **20.69** | **21.25** | **5.15** | **5.38** | **6.94** | **6.21** |
| | (0.0000) | (0.0000) | (0.0000) | (0.0000) | (0.0000) | (0.0000) | (0.0000) | (0.0000) | (0.0232) | (0.0204) | (0.0084) | (0.0127) |
| ORG | 0.03 | 0.02 | 0.02 | 0.00 | 0.18 | 0.24 | 0.62 | 0.42 | 0.58 | 0.58 | 0.59 | 0.59 |
| | (0.8585) | (0.9024) | (0.8897) | (1.0000) | (0.6726) | (0.6223) | (0.4295) | (0.5167) | (0.4463) | (0.4467) | (0.4416) | (0.4410) |
| ADV | **10.90** | **11.08** | **11.07** | **11.36** | **10.67** | **10.55** | **8.95** | **10.18** | 1.10 | 1.03 | 0.42 | 0.74 |
| | (0.0010) | (0.0009) | (0.0009) | (0.0008) | (0.0011) | (0.0012) | (0.0028) | (0.0014) | (0.2939) | (0.3107) | (0.5147) | (0.3912) |
| PROD | **24.40** | **24.87** | **24.94** | **25.42** | **11.35** | **11.24** | **9.77** | **10.83** | 0.99 | 1.13 | 2.32 | 1.64 |
| | (0.0000) | (0.0000) | (0.0000) | (0.0000) | (0.0008) | (0.0008) | (0.0018) | (0.0010) | (0.3197) | (0.2878) | (0.1280) | (0.2003) |
| MAT | **4.51** | **4.38** | 2.92 | 3.75 | **6.10** | **5.65** | 3.15 | **4.57** | 2.03 | 1.93 | 1.32 | 1.66 |
| | (0.0337) | (0.0364) | (0.0873) | (0.0527) | (0.0135) | (0.0175) | (0.0760) | (0.0325) | (0.1546) | (0.1649) | (0.2501) | (0.1982) |
| COMP | **5.26** | **5.26** | **4.31** | **4.89** | **6.12** | **5.95** | **4.36** | **5.34** | 1.85 | 1.80 | 1.44 | 1.64 |
| | (0.0218) | (0.0218) | (0.0379) | (0.0270) | (0.0133) | (0.0147) | (0.0367) | (0.0209) | (0.1739) | (0.1793) | (0.2294) | (0.2008) |
| DES | **15.77** | **15.85** | **14.39** | **15.37** | **9.54** | **9.26** | **7.00** | **8.36** | 0.40 | 0.47 | 1.01 | 0.71 |
| | (0.0001) | (0.0001) | (0.0001) | (0.0001) | (0.0020) | (0.0023) | (0.0081) | (0.0038) | (0.5258) | (0.4937) | (0.3139) | (0.4009) |
| FUNC | **8.03** | **8.28** | **7.75** | **8.07** | **5.92** | **5.96** | **4.88** | **5.56** | 0.00 | 0.00 | 0.03 | 0.00 |
| | (0.0046) | (0.0040) | (0.0054) | (0.0045) | (0.0150) | (0.0147) | (0.0272) | (0.0184) | (0.9464) | (0.9784) | (0.8591) | (0.9537) |

Note: p-values are reported in brackets. Statistically significant results are presented in bold.

The tests vary according to the samples used. In the samples which include all the firms, all the tests were significant and, therefore, the hypothesis of homogeneity was rejected. The only exception is the case of those firms that base their product innovations on improvements to their internal organization. Likewise, all the hypotheses regarding no differences in survivor functions across subgroups (e.g., to account for R&D expenditures vs. not accounting for them) were rejected in the case of small firms, with the exception again of the variable that proxies organizational changes. Differences between groups were not significant in most cases for the large firm group, except in the cases related to the incursion on R&D costs, the implementation of process innovations and the introduction of new machinery in the production process.

Overall, our results have highlighted that firm survival is influenced by the product competition strategies followed by the firm both in relation to technological as well as specific differentiation. The survival rate of small firms depends very much on all of the strategies considered in the chapter: R&D and advertising expenses, product and process innovations, with the only exception of the adoption of new methods in the organization of production, which does not have a significant impact. However, in the case of large firms, not all of the strategies are relevant for a firm's survival, being significant only for those with R&D investments and process innovations, specially the ones whose modification involves the introduction of new machinery.

## CONCLUSIONS

In this chapter, we have conducted a detailed analysis of the principal strategies that have determined the competitive behavior of firms operating in the Spanish manufacturing sector since the 1990s. We based our analysis on the importance of the innovations made within these firms as a vehicle for their business survival.

The theory underpinning industrial dynamics today is rich and abundant but it continues to base its main arguments on the theory of market selection formulated by Jovanovic (1982), who devised a model in which market selection is considered to be based on business efficiency acquired by a firm operating within the market. In many cases, because of a lack of efficiency, firms are forced to abandon the market, leaving the firms that know how to be efficient as the market's sole survivors. Over the years, it has been shown that in addition to the experience that a firm might acquire, other factors might also be significant in determining its competitive strategies. These are noted in the theory that relates improvements in competitiveness with business innovation (Ericson and Pakes, 1995; Klepper, 1996b). In this chapter, basing our analysis on Jovanovic's theory and the improvements made to it by Ericson, Pakes and Klepper, we have selected the principal strategies adopted by firms to become as competitive as possible.

Regarding the main results of the chapter, we conclude that the effect of implementing constant innovations, as both an innovative effort through expenses in R&D and the results of these investments in new products or production processes, has a determining role in a firm's probability of survival. In fact, especially for the case of small firms, we conclude that their ability to innovate will determine the likelihood of their survival. More generally speaking, the adoption of competitive strategies based on innovation in the Spanish manufacturing industries play a determining role in firms' survival, given the high number of determinants that do not violate the proportional hazard assumption and when the predicted and the observed values are similar. This effect is higher for smaller firms. Following this conclusion, we can say that the evidence from the analysis supports a conclusion that innovative strategies in small and medium-sized firms act as a barrier for survival in Spanish manufacturing industries.

Another important point to be drawn from our results, bearing in mind the different samples analyzed, is that the results obtained when considering the whole sample of firms are more similar to those obtained when only the sample of small firms is used. This is due to the fact that Spain's industrial sectors are, mainly, composed of small and medium-sized firms. They tend to adopt very different strategies from those of their larger counterparts which compete with them in the market. The survival rate of small firms depends on all of the strategies considered in the chapter: R&D and advertising expenses, product and process innovations, with the only exception being the adoption of new methods in the organization of production. This factor does not have a significant impact. However, in the case of large firms, not all the strategies are relevant for firms' survival, being significant only for those related to R&D investments and process innovations, especially those whose modification involves the introduction of new machinery.

## NOTES

1. A version of the model is used in Hopenhayn and Rogerson (1991), with the focus on the study of the effect of labour firing costs on job turnover, productivity and welfare.
2. For more information about this type of model, see the pioneering study that gave the name to this type of model (Cox, 1972).
3. For further information concerning the data, see Fariñas and Huergo (1999) and Fariñas and Jaumandreu (1994, 1999).

4. NACE is a general industrial classification of economic activities within the European Union and CLIO is the Classification and Nomenclature of the Input–Output table. Both classifications are officially recognized by the Accounting Economic System.
5. Process innovations are defined as major modifications in the production process.
6. Product innovations are defined as completely new products or modifications, meaning that the new product is quite different from the product previously being produced.
7. Simply, at each distinct failure time in the data, the contribution to the test statistic is obtained as a weighted standardized sum of the difference between the observed and expected number of deaths in each of the groups. The expected number of deaths is obtained under the null hypothesis of no differences between the survival experiences of the different groups.

# REFERENCES

Agarwal, R. (1997), 'Survival of Firms over the Product Life Cycle', *Southern Economic Journal*, **63**, 571–84.
Agarwal, R. (1998), 'Small Firm Survival and Technological Activity', *Small Business Economics*, **11**, 215–24.
Agarwal, R. and D.B. Audretsch (2001), 'Does Entry Size Matter? The Impact of the Life Cycle and Technology on Firm Survival', *The Journal of Industrial Economics*, **49**, 21–43.
Aranguren, M.J. (1999), 'Determinants of Economic Units Creation in the Period 1985-93: The Case of Manufacturing Industry in CAPV', *Small Business Economics*, **12**, 203–15.
Audretsch, D.B. (1991), 'New-Firm Survival and the Technological Regime', *The Review of Economics and Statistics*, **72**, 441–50.
Audretsch, D.B. (1995), 'Innovation, Growth and Survival', *International Journal of Industrial Organization*, **13**, 441–57.
Audretsch, D.B. and T. Mahmood (1995), 'New Firm Survival: New Results Using a Hazard Function', *The Review of Economics and Statistics*, **77**, 97–103.
Audretsch, D.B., P. Houweling and A.R. Thurik (2000), 'Firm Survival in the Netherlands', *Review of Industrial Organization*, **16**, 1–11.
Audretsch, D.B., E. Santarelli and M. Vivarelli (1999), 'Start-up Size and Industrial Dynamics: Some Evidence from Italian Manufacturing', *International Journal of Industrial Organization*, **17**, 965–83.
Bain, D. (1956), *Barriers to New Competition. Their Character and Consequences in Manufacturing Industries*, Cambridge, MA: Harvard University Press.
Becchetti, L. and G. Trovatto (2002), 'The Determinants of Growth for Small and Medium Sized Firms. The Role of the Availability of External Finance', *Small Business Economics*, **19**, 291–306.
Caves, R.E. and M. Porter (1977), 'From Entry Barriers to Mobility Barriers: Conjectural Decisions and Contrived Deterrence to New Competition', *Quarterly Journal of Economics*, **91**, 241–61.
Cefis, E. and O. Marsili (2005), 'A Matter of Life and Death: Innovation and Firm Survival', *Industrial and Corporate Change*, **14**, 1167-92.
Colombo, M.G. and M. Delmastro (2000), 'A Note on the Relation between Size, Ownership Status and Plant's Closure: Sunk Costs vs. Strategic Size Liability', *Economics Letters*, **69**, 421–27.
Colombo, M.G. and M. Delmastro (2001), 'Technology Use and Plant Closure', *Research Policy*, 30, 21–34.

Comanor, W.S. and T.A. Wilson (1979), 'The Effect of Advertising on Competition: A Survey', *Journal of Economic Literature*, **17**, 453–76.
Cox, D.R. (1972), 'Regression Models and Life Tables', *Journal of the Royal Statistics Society*, **34**, 187–220.
Ericson, R. and A. Pakes (1995), 'Markov-Perfect Industry Dynamics: A Framework for Empirical Work', *Review of Economic Studies*, **62**, 53–82.
Esteve, S.A. and J.A. Sanchis (2004), 'The Determinants of Survival of Spanish Manufacturing Firms', *Review of Industrial Organization*, **25**, 251–73.
Fariñas, J.C. and E. Huergo (1999), 'Tamaño empresarial, innovación y políticas de competencia', *Economía Industrial*, **329**, 67–80.
Fariñas, J.C. and J. Jaumandreu (1994), 'La Encuesta sobre Estrategias Empresariales: Características y usos', *Economía Industrial*, Sept.–Oct., 109–19.
Fariñas, J.C. and J. Jaumandreu (1999), 'Diez años de Encuesta sobre Estrategias Empresariales (ESEE)', *Economía Industrial*, **329**, 29–42.
Fariñas, J.C. and L. Moreno (2000), 'Firms' Growth, Size and Age: A Nonparametric Approach', *Review of Industrial Organization*, **17**, 249–65.
Geroski, P. (1995), 'What Do We Know About Entry?', *International Journal of Industrial Organization*, **13**, 421–40.
Görg, H. and E. Strobl (2003), 'Multinational Companies, Technology Spillovers and Plant Survival', *Scandinavian Journal of Economics*, **105**, 581–95.
Harris, R.I.D. and P. Hassaszadeh (2002), 'The Impact of Ownership Changes and Age Effects on Plant Exits in UK Manufacturing, 1974–1995', *Economics Letters*, **75**, 309–17.
Headd, B. (2002), 'Redefining Business Success: Distinguishing between Closure and Failure', *Small Business Economics*, **21**, 51–61.
Heshmati, A. (2001), 'On the Growth of Micro and Small Firms: Evidence from Sweden', *Small Business Economics*, **17**, 213–28.
Hopenhayn, H.A. (1992), 'Entry, Exit, and Firm Dynamics in Long Run Equilibrium', *Econometrica*, **60**, 1127–50.
Hopenhayn, H.A., and R. Rogerson (1991), 'Job Turnover and Policy Evaluation: A General Equilibrium Analysis', Unpublished manuscript, University of Minnesota.
Jovanovic, B. (1982), 'Selection and the Evolution of Industry', *Econometrica*, **50**, 649–70.
Jovanovic, B. and G.M. McDonald (1994), 'The life cycle of a competitive industry', *Journal of Political Economy*, **102**, 322–47.
Kalbfleisch, J.D. and R.L. Prentice (1980), *The Statistical Analysis of Failure Time Data*, New York: John Wiley & Sons.
Karlsson, C. and K. Nyström (2003), 'Exit and Entry Or the Product Life Cycle: Evidence from the Swedish Manufacturing Industry', *Small Business Economics*, **21**, 135–44.
Klepper, S. (1993), 'Entry, Exit and Innovation over the Product Life Cycle: The Dynamics of First Movers Advantages, Declining Product Innovation and Market Failure', Mimeo, Carnegie Mellon University.
Klepper, S. (1996a), 'Entry, Exit, Growth, and Innovation over the Product Life Cycle', *American Economic Review*, **86**, 562–83.
Klepper, S. (1996b), 'Evolution, Market Concentration and Firm Survival', Mimeo, Carnegie Mellon University, Pittsburg, PA.
Lafuente, A. and G. Lecha (1988), 'Determinantes Sectoriales Del Nacimiento De Empresas En La Industria Española', *Investigaciones Económicas*, **12**, 329–35.
Littunen, H. (2000), 'Networks and Local Environmental Characteristics in the Survival of New Firms', *Small Business Economics*, **15**, 59–71.

Mahmood, T. (1992), 'Does the Hazard Rate for New Plants Vary between Low- and High-Tech Industries?', *Small Business Economics*, **4**, 201–09.

Mahmood, T. (2000), 'Survival of Newly Founded Businesses: A Log-Logistic Model Approach', *Small Business Economics*, **14**, 223–37.

Mansfield, E. (1962), 'Entry, Gibrat's Law, Innovation, and the Growth of Firms', *The American Economic Review*, **52**, 1023–1051.

Mata, J. and P. Portugal (1994), 'Life Duration of New Firms', *Journal of Industrial Economics*, **42**, 227–45.

Mata, J. and P. Portugal (1999), 'Technology Intensity, Demand Conditions, and the Longevity of Firms', in D.B. Audretsch, and A.R. Thurik (eds), *Innovation, Industry Evolution, and Employment*, Cambridge: Cambridge University Press.

Mata, J. and P. Portugal (2004), 'Patterns of Entry, Post-Entry Growth and Survival', *Small Business Economics*, **22**, 283–98.

Mata, J., P. Portugal and P. Guimaraes (1995), 'The Survival of New Plants: Start-up Conditions and Post-Entry Evolution', *International Journal of Industrial Organization*, **13**, 459–81.

Milgrom, P. and M.J. Roberts (1982), 'Limit Pricing and Entry under Incomplete Information', *Econometrica*, **50**, 443–50.

Modigliani, F. and M.H. Miller (1958), 'The Cost of Capital, Corporate Finance, and the Theory of Investment', *American Economic Review*, **48**, 261–97.

Pakes, A. and R. Ericson (1998), 'Empirical Implications of Alternative Models of Firm Dynamics', *Journal of Economic Theory*, **79**, 1–45.

Romer P.M. (1986), 'Increasing Returns and Long-run Growth', *Journal of Political Economy*, **94**, 1002–37.

Schumpeter, J. (1942), *Capitalism, Socialism and Democracy*, New York: Harper & Row.

Segarra, A.D., J.M. Arauzo, N. Gras, M. Manjón, F. Mañé, M. Teruel and B. Theilen (2002), *La Creación Y La Supervivencia De Las Empresas Industriales*, Madrid: Civitas Ediciones S.L.

Segarra, A. and M. Callejón (2002), 'New Firms' Survival and Market Turbulence: New Evidence from Spain', *Review of Industrial Organization*, **20**, 1–14.

Sylos Labini, P. (1962), *Oligopoly and Technical Progress*, Cambridge, MA: Harvard University Press.

Van Praag, C.M. (2003), 'Business Survival and Success of Young Small Business Owners', *Small Business Economics*, **21**, 1–17.

# APPENDIX 8A1 TECHNOLOGICAL DIFFERENTIATION BUSINESS COMPETITIVE STRATEGY

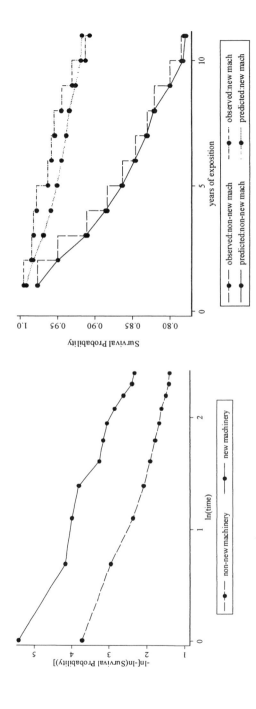

*Figure 8A1.1  Comparative analysis for the new machinery strategy*

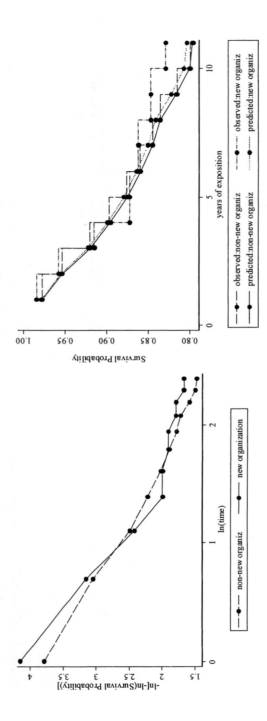

*Figure 8A1.2 Comparative analysis for the new organization strategy*

# APPENDIX 8A2 SPECIFIC DIFFERENTIATION BUSINESS COMPETITIVE STRATEGY

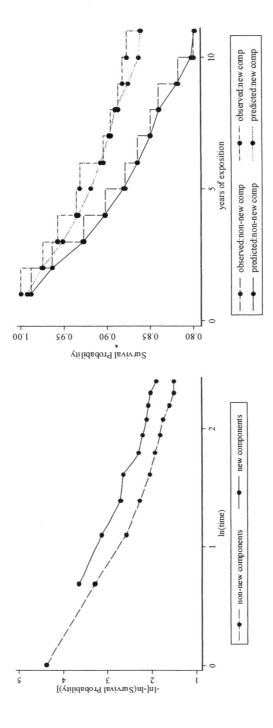

*Figure 8A2.1  Comparative analysis for the new components strategy*

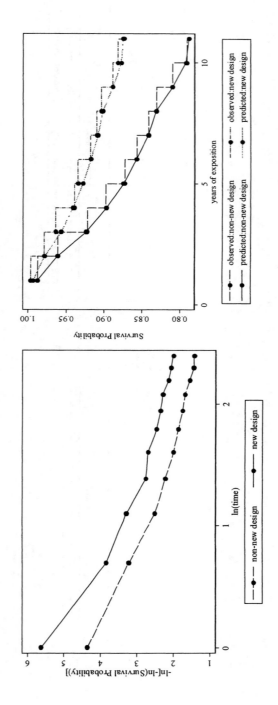

*Figure 8A2.2 Comparative analysis for the new design strategy*

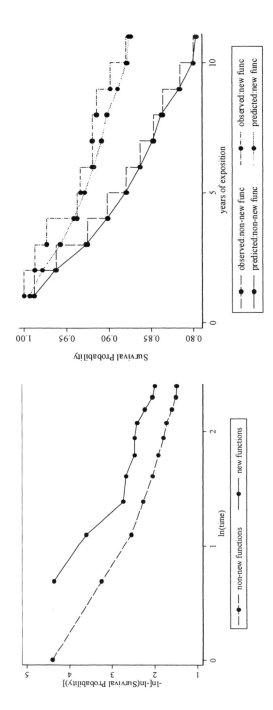

*Figure 8A2.3  Comparative analysis for new functions strategy*

# 9. A Resource-based Analysis of Bankruptcy Law, Entrepreneurship and Corporate Recovery

## Gary A.S. Cook, Naresh R. Pandit and Keith Pond

## INTRODUCTION

There are three main ways that bankruptcy[1] law can affect entrepreneurship. First, a legal regime that makes bankruptcy expensive can deter potential entrepreneurs by punishing failure too severely. Second, a regime that stigmatizes bankruptcy can discourage failed entrepreneurs from trying again. Third, a badly designed bankruptcy regime can affect Schumpeterian (1942) 'creative destruction' by hindering the quick and efficient elimination of non-viable firms. This last point is emphasized in Franks and Torous's (1992) classic examination of the desirable features of a bankruptcy regime. Employing a cost–benefit framework, they argue that financially distressed firms should not be allowed to limp on when more value could be realized by immediate closure. Equally, when firms are worth more alive than dead they should not be broken up. Particular bankruptcy regimes may be biased one way or another (Gertner and Scharfstein, 1991) an issue under-researched in the area of small and medium-sized enterprises (SMEs) (Ravid and Sundgren, 1998). The *Global Entrepreneurship Monitor*'s conceptual model (Reynolds et al., 2002) concurs on the importance of efficient bankruptcy, with business 'churning' clearly related to both entrepreneurial dynamism and enhanced growth prospects for the economy.

Because of these relationships between bankruptcy law, entrepreneurship, and economic growth, many countries have been attempting to improve their bankruptcy regimes (Audretsch, 2002), many within collective frameworks provided by the IMF (1999), the OECD (1998) and the European Union (European Commission, 2000, 2003, 2004). And there is much to improve. Reynolds et al. (2001), commenting on key issues facing entrepreneurship in 25 countries, find that poor cultural attitudes, reflected in a country's bankruptcy law, are a high priority for action for 13 countries, with severity of punishment for failed entrepreneurs and/or social stigmatization being specifically mentioned for seven of these.[2]

This chapter contributes to our understanding of this topic by analyzing a particular bankruptcy procedure within an entrepreneurship promoting regime, the UK Company Voluntary Arrangement (CVA), which was specifically designed to promote the rehabilitation of bankrupt *but viable* SMEs. It will provide evidence on the circumstances in which the balance of probability favors a rehabilitation attempt. In so doing it addresses the gap in the literature on the success and failure of entrepreneurial ventures regarding the question of how to spot bankrupt but viable enterprises. It goes further in arguing that the Resource-based View (RBV) provides the appropriate framework within which to consider success and failure of entrepreneurial firms, both in the context of financial distress and more generally. It does not attempt to develop a usable 'failure prediction' model, or a 'how to' guide to rescuing insolvent SMEs.

Resources are increasingly acknowledged within the entrepreneurship field as important influences on survival, strategy and performance (Brush and Chaganti, 1998). What is largely missing from this growing literature is anything on resources and the prospect of failure. This chapter addresses that gap. The broad aims of the chapter are expressed in terms of two research questions. First, what factors discriminate between those bankrupt SMEs that can be saved and those that cannot? In respect of this question, what we think we know about success and failure of all firms, but especially SMEs, is based on an incoherent and ill-fitting mosaic of research based on differing samples and included variables, lacking a unifying conceptual framework (Pandit, 2000). This state of affairs urges the second research question. Can the firm's RBV be used to explain the factors that discriminate between bankrupt SMEs that can be saved and those that cannot?

The chapter is structured as follows. The next section provides the study's context by providing a very brief overview of bankruptcy law and entrepreneurship in the UK. This is followed by a review of the relevant literature which leads to the generation of six hypotheses. Next the study's research design is elucidated and this is followed by a presentation and discussion of results. The results are used to inform discussion on the UK insolvency regime. A final section concludes.

## BANKRUPTCY LAW AND ENTREPRENEURSHIP IN THE UK

The *Global Entrepreneurship Monitor* (Reynolds et al., 1999, 2000, 2001, 2002, 2004 and Acs et al., 2005) finds that despite favorable *conditions*, entrepreneurial *activity* is only mediocre in the UK. In 2004 the UK ranked 16th out of 34 countries in terms of total entrepreneurial activity (TEA). In the face of these and similar findings, the UK government has repeatedly asserted that SMEs and, by extension, the entrepreneurial culture which supports their formation and development, are vital to the success of the UK economy (HM Treasury/DTI, 2001, 2002; Small Business Service, 2003) and require policy support to tackle current underachievement. The two key issues that need to be addressed are, first, negative attitudes towards business failure (Ernst & Young, 2001; Michaelis et al., 2001; Harding, 2002; IFF Research, 2002; Shurry et al., 2002; Small Business Service, 2003) and second, the unnecessary failure of viable SMEs experiencing temporary difficulties (Moorcroft et al., 2004).

The main way that these issues have been tackled is via new legislation. Legislative changes have been based on two main arguments. First, that the traditional approach in the UK, which has been strongly secured creditor-oriented[3] (Franks and Torous, 1992; Insolvency Service, 2000, 2001, 2002), has led to the unnecessary termination of viable businesses as secured creditors have enforced their collateral through a process known as 'administrative receivership'. Second, that the law has been too punitive towards honest failure, with the stigma and hardship which attend bankruptcy in the UK acting as a disincentive both to setting up in business in the first place and also attempting to start a new business following the experience of bankruptcy.

In the UK, the serious promotion of viable business rescue and entrepreneurship through bankruptcy procedures dates back to 1982, when the influential Cork Report (Cork Committee, 1982) was produced. Legislation based on the recommendations of this report was enacted in 1985–86. The legislative changes saw the advent of two customized business rescue procedures. Of these, the administration order was the more formal, requiring a petition to the court for the making of an administration order and the *removal* of the directors from control of the company. Administration is now less formal under the Enterprise Act 2002 but its scope is undiminished. By way of contrast, the second procedure, the CVA, the focus of this study, was intentionally designed to be more informal, being both an out-of-court and a *debtor-in-possession* procedure (i.e., the firm's management remain in place during the course of the procedure). A CVA is initiated by the directors of a financially troubled company making a written proposal to creditors, which typically contains an agreed schedule of repayment of a proportion of debt. This proposal must identify a 'nominee', who must be licensed to act as an insolvency practitioner (IP).[4] The nominee is responsible for both reporting the debtor's proposal to the court and ultimately for overseeing the implementation of the voluntary arrangement, should a CVA be agreed upon. The nominee summons meetings of the company and all its known creditors and a high threshold of support (75 percent by value of claims) from creditors present and voting is required for approval. An approved voluntary arrangement is binding upon all creditors who had notice of the meeting and were entitled to vote. However, secured creditors and preferential creditors[5] cannot have an arrangement foisted upon them without their agreement. Once the scheme has been approved, the nominee, who is transformed into the 'supervisor', must see that the arrangement is put into effect and may petition for the winding up of the company if payments are not made in line with the plan. The supervisor is not expected to run the business during the CVA, and the debtor is allowed to remain in possession. Moreover the debtor is free to make any decisions (except regarding monies paid into the creditors' fund) without reference either to the supervisor or to a court. A CVA is terminated either by satisfaction of debts or by the supervisor initiating an administration or liquidation. One very important feature of a CVA is that it only provides a stay on actions brought by existing creditors at the time the arrangement is voted on. New creditors post-agreement can petition for winding up without hindrance, therefore it is imperative that a firm in CVA both meets its agreed schedule of payments into the creditors' fund under the CVA and avoids incurring any new bad debts.

## LITERATURE REVIEW AND HYPOTHESIS GENERATION

The first research question of this study is how to tell which among bankrupt firms are viable and so warrant an attempt at rehabilitation and which do not and so warrant termination. This is a question that neither the vast failure prediction literature (Altman, 1968; Taffler, 1982) nor that on 'success and failure' addresses directly. One thing on which many researchers agree, is that it is very difficult to predict success and failure, whichever way these terms are defined (Cooper, 1993; Dickinson et al., 1984; Gartner et al., 1998; Westhead, 1995). One reason for this is that most signals of failure are given out by firms that actually manage to survive (Piesse and Wood, 1992). Greater understanding is therefore needed in order to make better-informed decisions regarding which firms to try to rehabilitate. Another consideration is that success and failure may be governed by the complex interaction of a set of factors (Duchesneau and Gartner, 1990). Chrisman et al. (1998) suggest almost 200 relevant variables collected under the general headings of entrepreneurial characteristics, industry structure, business strategy, resources and organizational structure, processes and systems. This is a useful typology, but as with all typologies, it falls short of constituting a coherent theoretical framework. This is also a general problem of the existing literature on entrepreneurial failure, small-firm failure and corporate failure

(Pandit, 2000). The current study attempts to improve on this by framing the analysis within the RBV (Wernerfelt, 1984; Barney, 1991), which has rapidly become influential in the strategy and international business literatures and which is also becoming important within the entrepreneurship field (Barney et al. 2001; Schoemaker and Amit, 1994; Shrivastava et al., 1994; Wernerfelt, 1995).

What may be said about resources and failure? Following Franks and Torous (1992), an intuitive starting-point would be to argue that failing firms that do not have the resource base necessary to earn a normal return on capital should be closed down and those which do, should be subject to a rehabilitation attempt. However, this is simplistic as it neglects the fact that firm performance may be only weakly related to its resource base. Adopting this thought, we can identify four types of underperformance leading to bankruptcy: *Type 1*: a firm whose bankruptcy is entirely due to an inadequate resource base; *Type 2*: a firm which has an inadequate resource base but is surviving in the shortrun until an adverse environmental factor pushes it into bankruptcy; *Type 3*: a firm that has made a big mistake in believing it had spotted a viable commercial opportunity which in fact did not exist (a failure of entrepreneurial vision), in which case there is no corresponding criterion of adequate or inadequate resources (Shane and Venkataraman, 2000); and *Type 4*: a firm which does have an adequate resource base but which is pushed into bankruptcy by an adverse temporary factor. On this basis, it is possible to reason that companies of the last type should be rehabilitated if possible and other types should be wound up. Following on from this, we have the study's central proposition which informs six hypotheses that are subsequently developed:

> A firm which has resource strength or lacks resource weakness but is pushed into bankruptcy by adverse temporary factors will be more likely to succeed in a CVA.

A number of specific resources have been identified as being important to entrepreneurial firms, although there is little detail on the precise type of firm or context in which each type of resource will be more or less critical, a weakness also of the more general strategy-related RBV literature (Schultze, 1994; Rouse and Daellenbach, 1999; Barney, 2001; Priem and Butler, 2001a, 2001b). Much of the literature on RBV and entrepreneurship places high importance on the quality of top management as a resource (Mosakowski, 1993; Dollinger, 1995; Brush and Chaganti, 1998; Chandler and Hanks, 1998; Shane and Venkataraman, 2000). In the entrepreneurial firm, the entrepreneur has a vital role in seeing opportunities, assembling resources and coordinating resources to bring to bear capabilities within the market (Chandler and Hanks, 1994; Dollinger, 1995; Alvarez and Buzenitz, 2001; Barney et al., 2001; Brush et al., 2001; Phan, 2004). This sits with Bozner et al.'s (1998) emphasis on the importance of mental models and cognitive capacities as inimitable resources.

H1: CVA success will be less likely when poor management is the primary resource weakness.

No matter what resources the company may possess, unless they are effectively marshaled it will be to little avail (Thomas and Pollock, 1999). By the same token, even the most brilliant entrepreneur needs good resources to work with (Pringle and Kroll, 1997). The quality of the resource base both at inception and as it is developed over time is seen to have a crucial influence on the degree of success of the company (Lichtenstein and Brush, 2001). Hunt (1997) places high importance on the ability to identify and serve customer segments, implying a premium on marketing management. Chandler and Hanks (1994) conclude that the ability to organize and harness human resources is of critical importance for firm performance. Likewise, Brush and Chaganti (1998) find that HRMhas a positive influence on performance. Brush et al. (2001) argue that some resources, of which financial resources are the chief example, simply allow access to other resources. Insolvent firms by definition lack financial resources. Poor financial management over time will inhibit the development of other resource strengths and is indicative of weak management.

H2: CVA success will be less likely when poor marketing management is an important resource weakness.

H3: CVA success will be less likely when poor HRMis an important resource weakness.

H4: CVA success will be less likely when poor financial management is an important resource weakness.

Good relationships with suppliers can be an important resource-based advantage (Rangone, 1999; Brush et al., 2001). Where creditors are unsupportive during difficult times (e.g., in a CVA), this indicates that the company concerned has a poor 'relationship' resource. In this respect all classes of creditor can be important, but for different reasons. Secured creditors, generally banks, have a very strong position in the UK bankruptcy system and they can make life very difficult for a firm which does not have their favor. Similarly, preferential creditors, especially the Inland Revenue (which collects corporation tax) and HM Customs and Excise (which collects sales taxes) have a very strong position. They also generally ask for strong terms to be imposed such as 100 percent repayment of the original debt plus statutory interest. This may saddle the company in a CVA with an impossible burden. Unsecured creditors often have little choice but to go along with a CVA proposal. In other types of bankruptcy regime they will almost certainly receive nothing, whereas in a CVA they have at least some prospect of a return. Nevertheless, they can be both hostile and awkward during the course of the CVA where they judge the directors of the company to have been either reckless or dishonest in the course of running up their debts. Moreover, some dissenting unsecured creditors may have been bound into the plan under the majority voting rules (discussed above). In short, supportive creditor attitudes indicate the existence of relationship capital, unsupportive creditor attitudes the opposite.

H5: CVA success is positively related to the strength of 'relationship' resources.

Chandler and Hanks (1994) argue that a critical feature of the firm's task environment is the other firms with which it must interact in order to survive and grow. What this implies is that the strength of competing firms and the intensity of rivalry will influence survival and performance prospects (see also Porter, 1980, 1985). In a RBV what matters is not the *absolute* quality of the resources, but rather the quality (and breadth) of the resources a firm controls *relative to competitors*.

H6: CVA success is positively related to relative resource strength and negatively to relative resource weakness.

**Control Variables**

There are a number of important control variables which have been included in the extant literature on small-firm success and failure which are worthy of inclusion in this study. In studies examining the relationship between resources and performance, size and age are the two most common, being consistently positively associated with firm survival (Mosakowski, 1993; Chandler and Hanks, 1994, 1998; Brush and Chaganti, 1998; Audretsch, 2002; Zahra et al., 2004). Controls for broad line of activity, manufacturing, services, distribution and construction are included, although they seldom emerge as being significant in the literature. This is in line with RBV, which is predicated on the assumption that variability in performance is greater *within* industries than *between* them.

Three further control variables, worthy of inclusion in this study but not addressed in the extant literature, are whether or not the CVA is carried out in conjunction with another bankruptcy procedure, the experience of the IP charged with implementing the CVA and the size of the company that the IP belongs to.  Regarding the first of these further control variables, one important feature of UK bankruptcy law is that it provides for a CVA to be carried out in conjunction with an administration order as well as allowing each procedure to be carried out independently.  The administration order provides far greater powers of control and investigation to the administrator (who will often be the same individual as the CVA supervisor) as well as providing a strong moratorium against hostile creditor actions.  The administrator has the important power to dismiss and appoint directors. One would expect, therefore, that CVAs conducted in conjunction with an administration order would be more likely to succeed, since the administrator/supervisor has a better chance both to assess the prospects of the company and to remedy any senior management deficiencies.  Regarding the number of cases the IP had previously supervised, the simple expectation is that the more experienced the IP, the higher the probability of a successful outcome.  By the same token, the larger the accounting firm to which the IP belongs, the higher the probability of success, as the IP has a greater wealth of expertise within the firm to lean on.

## RESEARCH DESIGN AND OPERATIONALIZATION OF HYPOTHESES

Data to test the six hypotheses were collected from a  postal questionnaire sent to all 1,522 names appearing on the HMSO[6] list of licensed IPs in 2002. The questionnaire appears as Appendix 9A.  A total of 435 replies were received, a response rate of 28.6 percent.  Of these, 350 indicated that they had no experience of CVAs and therefore could not complete the questionnaire, itself an interesting finding.  The fact that many IPs have no experience of CVAs helps explain the modest response rate.  It is difficult to assess the response rate regarding IPs who do have experience of CVAs because there is no list of such IPs to compare with.  Inspection of the responses reveals a mix of small- and large-firm practitioners and a reasonable geographic spread, and therefore no obvious gross bias.  In some cases, the IP, having conducted more than one CVA, was able to fill in more than one questionnaire and so our final sample consisted of questionnaires on 97 different CVAs.

CVA success or failure was measured on the basis of the rating given by the CVA supervisor of the extent to which the CVA plan had been realized. It could be argued that the supervisor may be disposed to assess the performance of a CVA that s/he had personally implemented too favorably. Two points may be made to counter this argument. First, success as rated by the supervisor is found to be strongly correlated with more objective measures of success such as total dividends paid and the proportion of promised dividends actually paid to preferential and unsecured creditors (secured creditors are almost always promised and paid 100 percent of their debt). Moreover, analysis of a previous cohort of companies in CVA (Milman and Chittenden, 1995) revealed that the assessment of the IP is significantly correlated with eventual survival free of insolvency. Second, responding supervisors did in several cases acknowledge that performance against plan had been very poor.

In line with the discussion above, the main results come from an ordered probit analysis of supervising IP ratings of how the CVA performed against plan. The categories of performance against plan were condensed into three since there were comparatively few cases which had been judged to have been 'unsuccessful' or to have performed 'just below plan'. Accordingly the 'very unsuccessful' and 'unsuccessful' categories were aggregated into an 'unsuccessful' category, those performing 'in line with' or 'just below' plan as 'satisfactory' and those performing 'above plan' as being 'very successful'.

Independent variables were coded 1 (important) where respondents ranked them as being 'important' or 'very important' in the questionnaire, as 0 (not important) otherwise. Robustness tests were conducted by adding 'moderately important' cases to the 'important' category and repeating all analyses. Robustness was also checked by using alternative groupings of outcomes in the ordered probit analysis. These robustness tests led to no substantive differences in the conclusions reached.

In terms of factors indicating resource strength or weakness, causes of bankruptcy and reasons for attempting rehabilitation, respondents were asked to rate each possible factor on a Lickert scale ranging from 1 (not at all important) to 5 (very important). The most important indicators of resource weakness were when respondents judged the bankruptcy to have occurred due to poor marketing management, poor human resource management (HRM) and poor financial management (hypotheses 2–4). In addition, a new variable was constructed which indicated where the firm's problems were solely attributable to poor management (hypothesis 1). This was a dichotomous variable which took the value 1 when any of the specific types of poor management was rated as being either an important or very important reason for the firm's bankruptcy and no other reason was given for the bankruptcy. Also, when it was indicated that the arrival of new management was a reason for attempting the CVA, this was taken to indicate an existing resource weakness in the company.

The strength of relationship resources was measured in terms of the attitudes of each class of creditors. Respondents were asked to rate these attitudes as positive, negative or neutral (hypothesis 5). Similarly, to test hypothesis 6, we simply related CVA success to the importance attached to increased competition as a cause of a company's bankruptcy. The existence or otherwise of resource-based strength was derived by proxy from the reasons for implementing the CVA by assessing: (a) the willingness of the shareholders to commit new capital; (b) the identification of turnaround potential by the supervising IP; and (c) the identification of the company's problems as being temporary. Finally, measured factors which might lead to firm failure which did not relate to resource weakness were: (a) the failure of one major contract; (b) one bad debt; (c) sheer bad luck; (d) a general downturn in the market; and (e) adverse macroeconomic conditions.

## RESULTS

The results presented in Table 9.1 shed considerable light on the central proposition and theoretical hypotheses. Due to strong collinearity between the variable indicating that bad management was the sole cause of a company's problems and the three variables indicating weakness with financial management, HRM and marketing, results are reported only for the models which included the three specific causes of management failure, as dropping the composite variable had very marginal effect on coefficients and was data admissible according to a likelihood ratio test. The converse was true of dropping the three separate variables indicating weak management. A set of regressions was run with just the composite variable indicating a problem with management and those indicating problems with financial management, HRM and marketing excluded and there was little substantive difference in either the full or restricted models. The full model reported in Table 9.1 is highly significant, yet few of the individual variables appear as significant. This is due in part to limited degrees of freedom with 36 variables and only 78 observations (some cases had to be dropped as they did not have data available for all variables) and also some multicollinearity, the age variables in particular being quite strongly correlated. Comparison of the coefficients between the full and restricted models in the table reveals fair stability in most of the coefficients, with only very few sign changes discussed below. The full model was tested down to the restricted model by eliminating those variables which either appeared least significant based on *t*-

ratios or which appeared least important from a theoretical point of view. These variable deletions were data admissible as evidenced by a likelihood ratio test. As a robustness check, the sequence of deletions was altered, however the same model was arrived at and none of the principal conclusions reported below were altered.

In a separate regression (not reported), the composite variable indicating poor management variable took the expected negative sign, but was far from significant. In a univariate contingency table test, cases where bad management was the only important cause of the company's problems did have a significantly lower chance of success ($\chi^2(1) = 3.634$, $p = 0.057$). This confirms the findings of Cook et al. (2001) that poor management is significantly associated with a lower chance of survival free from insolvency of firms in CVAs. Therefore H1 receives modest support.

The three management failings all emerge with negative signs as expected, with poor marketing emerging as the strongest influence, significantly reducing the chances of a successful CVA. In a univariate contingency table test, poor financial management as an important cause of the company's difficulties was significantly associated with a lower incidence of CVA success ($\chi^2(1) = 3.665$, $p = 0.056$) and the influence of problems of financial management on chances of success was stronger than that of problems with HRM in all specifications. The difficulty experienced in CVAs of dealing with poor management is underscored by the negative coefficient on new or improved management being an important rationale for attempting the CVA. This evidence therefore supports hypotheses 2-4.

Regarding creditor attitudes, the results indicate that chances of success are significantly higher where unsecured creditors are supportive of the CVA. Support from secured and preferential creditors is not influential. A somewhat different picture emerges when the dummy indicating supportive creditor attitudes is replaced by one indicating unsupportive creditor attitudes (not reported in the table). Here it is unsupportive secured creditors who exert the most important and significant negative influence on the chance of a successful outcome. This evidence provides support for hypothesis 5.

The importance of the strategic position of the firm, which relates to hypothesis 6, is indicated by the significant influence of increased competition as a cause of the company's problems. This factor has a consistently negative influence as expected and is statistically significant in the restricted model. On the other hand, the positive, and in some specifications significant, coefficient on the variable indicating the company's problems stemmed from a general decline in demand for the type of product or service the firm sells, indicates that the company's prospects are not as badly impaired by general difficulties facing all firms as in cases where its problems stem from the fact that it is at some disadvantage relative to its rivals. The fact that poor marketing management has a consistently negative coefficient is also consistent with hypothesis 6, as poor positioning in the market will place a company at a competitive disadvantage. CVAs are simply not designed to deal with this kind of strategic failure.

One variable runs counter to the hypothesis. Where the company is not able to compete as normal due to the fact of being in a bankruptcy procedure appears to significantly increase the chance of success. However, in a sub-sample regression (not reported) of cases where the aim was to preserve the company, not just the business, this variable took a negative, though insignificant sign. This makes sense. Where being known to be in an insolvency regime itself causes problems, it is better to wind up the company and make a fresh start with the business preserved as a going concern.

Where turnaround potential was an important reason for the CVA, success is more likely, significantly so in the restricted model. The fact that the company's problems were temporary in nature and that the shareholders were prepared to invest additional funds were also positive influences as expected, but were far from conventional significance. The arrival of new management, indicating an important resource weakness, was a negative influence as expected.

Table 9.1 *Ordered probit analysis results*

| Variable | Full Model | | Restricted Model | |
|---|---|---|---|---|
| | Coeff. | *t*-ratio | Coeff. | *t*-ratio |
| Poor marketing management was an important cause of the bankruptcy | −2.659 | −1.541 | −1.960 | −1.750* |
| Poor human resource management was an important cause of the bankruptcy | −0.822 | −0.389 | −0.732 | −0.666 |
| Poor financial management was an important cause of the bankruptcy | −0.445 | −0.423 | −0.353 | −0.972 |
| The arrival of new management was an important reason for the CVA | −0.804 | −0.649 | −0.767 | −1.073 |
| Secured creditors were supportive of the CVA | −0.077 | −0.078 | | |
| Preferential creditors were supportive of the CVA | 0.237 | 0.408 | | |
| Unsecured creditors were supportive of the CVA | 1.435 | 1.218 | 1.391 | 2.440** |

| | | | | |
|---|---|---|---|---|
| Increased competition was an important cause of the bankruptcy | −1.295 | −1.435 | −1.363 | −2.186 ** |
| A general demand in decline for the company's type of product was an important cause of the bankruptcy | 1.141 | 1.138 | 0.852 | 1.635 |
| The company had difficulty acting as a normal competitor due to the CVA | 1.524 | 1.379 | 1.086 | 1.926 * |
| The company's turnaround potential was an important reason for the CVA | 1.017 | 0.705 | 1.052 | 1.924 * |
| The fact that the company's problems were temporary in nature was an important reason for the CVA | 0.120 | 0.110 | | |
| Shareholders willing to invest additional funds | 0.004 | 0.002 | | |
| A single bad debt was an important cause of the bankruptcy | 0.401 | 0.191 | | |
| The failure of one big project was an important cause of the bankruptcy | 0.614 | 0.856 | | |
| Bad luck was an important cause of the bankruptcy | 0.392 | 0.189 | 1.004 | 0.875 |
| Poor macroeconomic conditions were an important cause of the bankruptcy | −0.880 | −0.695 | | |
| Failure of another company was an important cause of the bankruptcy | −0.298 | −0.187 | −1.019 | −0.988 |
| Problems with a major contract was an important cause of the bankruptcy | −0.749 | −0.631 | | |
| Amount of debt owed to secured creditors | −0.0003 | −0.693 | −0.0001 | −0.709 |
| Amount of debt owed to preferential creditors | 0.0006 | 0.214 | | |

| Variable | Full Model | | Restricted Model | |
|---|---|---|---|---|
| | Coeff. | *t*-ratio | Coeff. | *t*-ratio |
| Amount of debt owed to unsecured creditors | 0.0001 | 0.526 | | |
| Age of the company | 0.194 | 0.953 | 0.026 | 2.238** |
| $Age^2$ | −0.008 | −0.960 | | |
| $Age^3$ | 0.00008 | 1.002 | | |
| Firm belongs to manufacturing sector | 0.318 | 0.251 | | |
| Firm belongs to distribution sector | −0.479 | −0.377 | | |
| Firm belongs to service sector | −1.048 | −0.740 | −0.980 | −2.169** |
| CVA done in conjunction with administration order | −0.550 | −0.733 | | |
| The IP's accounting practice has between 10 and 50 partners | 2.573 | 1.802* | 1.617 | 3.866*** |
| The IP's accounting practice has more than 50 partners | 3.033 | 2.133** | 2.016 | 3.643*** |
| Years of experience of the insolvency practitioner | 0.016 | 0.474 | | |
| The IP's accounting practice has supervised between 5 and 25 CVAs | 0.138 | 0.150 | | |
| The IP's accounting practice has supervised more than 25 CVAs | −1.081 | −0.728 | | |
| The major purpose of the CVA was to rehabilitate the company | −0.296 | −0.854 | −0.374 | −0.760 |
| CONSTANT | −1.977 | −1.053 | −0.964 | −1.524 |
| Log-likelihood | −45.164 | | −51.083 | |
| $\chi^2$ | 74.524*** | | 62.685*** | |
| % correct predictions | 68 | | 71 | |
| LR test of restriction $\chi^2(18)$ | | | 11.838 | |

*Note:* *** indicates significant at 1 percent; ** significant at 5 percent; and, * significant at 10 percent.

Those causes of failure which did not imply a resource weakness of the firm generally took positive signs as expected. A general decline in demand for the type of product the company sold was positive and not far from significance in the restricted model. Other positive influences on the chances of success that were some way further from being statistically significant were a single bad debt, the failure of one big project and sheer bad luck. Poor macroeconomic conditions takes a negative sign and the most obvious interpretation here is that a firm which becomes bankrupt at such a time is more likely to struggle to trade free of incurring further debts and also to make contributions to the creditors' fund. Less easy to explain are the negative signs on the failure of another company and problems with a major contract, although again the latter could be related, somewhat tenuously, to poor management. Both point to the classic prescription for SMEs not to become too reliant on just one customer. In sum, the balance of evidence indicates support for hypothesis 6 and our central proposition.

Results regarding the control variables are somewhat mixed. There is little evidence that size (measured in terms of debt owed to creditors) is a significant influence on chance of success, yet neither does it appear to exert a counter-intuitive influence. In the full model, none of the polynomial terms for age is close to statistical significance. This is due to the high degree of collinearity between the variables. As can be seen, when the squared and cubed terms are removed, age emerges as a positive and significant influence on the chance of success. The industry sector dummies for manufacturing and distribution were a long way from statistical significance, therefore there is no meaningful difference between chance of success for firms in these sectors compared to the default category of construction.

Implementing a CVA in conjunction with an administration order, which is negative and far from significant in the model, does have a moderately large positive coefficient in a model run on the subset of cases where the objective was to preserve the company as a whole (and in some alternative specifications was significant). This makes sense. A period in administration, where the administrator takes effective control of the company and has the power to dismiss directors, may help correct management failings in a way which is much less easy in a CVA alone. In cases where the objective is to trade the company on in preparation for sale as a going concern, then the management will be changed via the market for corporate control and the possibility of doing so under an administration order is irrelevant.

The size of the accounting practice to which the IP belongs is a positive and significant influence on the chance of success, while the years of experience of the IP is positive but not significant. Somewhat against expectation is the result that where a large number of CVAs had previously been managed by the IP's company, the chances of success were lower. One possible interpretation of this result is that it is common knowledge in the bankruptcy world that there are 'ambulance chasers' who will push a CVA on desperate directors with the promise that they will retain control of their company, taking a fee for acting as nominee and supervisor and then mopping up by taking another fee as liquidator when the CVA fails.

## CONCLUSION

There are a number of findings regarding the factors that influence success within CVAs. Where problems are due to poor management, then chances of successful delivery of the CVA plan are lower. This reflects the difficulties of correcting poor management within the CVA, where the debtor remains in possession and the CVA supervisor has no powers to direct management or investigate the company. This is borne out in the finding that a CVA done in conjunction with administration, which does grant the administrator such powers, enjoys a higher degree of success, at least where the purpose of the CVA is to preserve the company as opposed to trading the company on until a suitable sale of the business can be arranged. The singular importance of the quality of management is entirely consistent with the RBV which has been proposed in this chapter as a useful framework within which to analyze bankrupt SMEs.

The utility of the resource-based framework is also attested to by the support for hypotheses 2, 3 and 4, which indicate that firms with important resource weaknesses are unlikely to be associated with a successful CVA process. Resource weaknesses which leave the firm at a competitive disadvantage relative to rivals (hypothesis 6) are particularly problematic, while strong relationship resources in terms of relationships with key creditors emerge as having a fundamental bearing on the chance of success within a CVA. Ultimately, we find that a successful outcome following bankruptcy is likely when a firm has resource *strength* and became bankrupt for *non*-resource-related reasons. In short, we find strong support for this study's central proposition, that a firm which has resource strength or lacks resource weakness but is pushed into bankruptcy by adverse temporary factors will be more likely to succeed in a CVA.

What does this evidence imply about the utility of the UK government's attempts to use bankruptcy law reform to promote entrepreneurship? First, the procedure does allow the problems of bankrupt SMEs to be addressed, resulting in good rates of business survival and orderly wind-up in those cases where the company cannot be saved. Thus CVAs can help avoid failure or, if not, mitigate its effects. One important aspect of the CVA in this regard is the high degree of flexibility it allows in negotiations between the company and its creditors, while avoiding high direct and indirect costs of drawn-out court procedures. A series of R3/SPI[7] surveys (1996a, 1996b, 1997, 1999, 2000) have shown the CVA to outperform other bankruptcy regimes in terms of business survival, preservation of employment and recovery of debts by creditors. To that extent, the CVA deserves to be more strongly promoted. It is a mature regime which can work well in the hands of a good IP and has the potential to make a larger contribution if used more widely. One aspect which is particularly important is that CVAs pay better returns to trade creditors than other types of regime, thus helping to avoid a domino effect where the failure of one company can lead to the failure of its suppliers. Nevertheless, policy makers have to be realistic. The CVA is not, nor could it be, a panacea. Moreover, the CVA took around a decade to bed down in the UK bankruptcy system, therefore patience is warranted before harvesting the fruits of legislative change.

In terms of specific implications, the nature of a debtor-in-possession regime requires careful consideration. The results presented here indicate that such a regime can present problems where poor management cannot be either directed or replaced, nor can the managerial resources of a turnaround agent easily be brought to bear. Designing a bankruptcy procedure which is capable of correcting senior management and strategic deficiencies would appear extremely difficult. The UK experience indicates that a strong stay on creditors' actions and strong powers to direct the affairs of the company and to appoint and dismiss directors are basic requirements. The belief that a debtor-in-possession regime would encourage earlier reporting of financial difficulties by directors has been flatly contradicted by experience in the UK and presents no valid offsetting benefit.

One issue that policy makers still need to address satisfactorily is how to get directors of failing companies to come forward sooner. Doing so will increase the chance of a successful turnaround and limit the extent to which directors dissipate their personal wealth in what may prove to be a doomed attempt to keep a company afloat. This, however, is likely to prove a tough nut to crack, as is the problem of changing attitudes towards failure and entrepreneurship more generally. Policy makers also need to address more fully how to support failed entrepreneurs. They are unlikely to learn where they went wrong or improve their skills as a result of going through a CVA *per se*. Training and support might be provided to encourage those who fail to try again, while lessening the risk that they will repeat the same mistakes. Provision of information is also called for (Moorcroft et al., 2004) but this fails to recognize the overconfidence often associated with the entrepreneur.

What are the implications for entrepreneurs or would-be entrepreneurs? This research indicates that poor management and in particular poor marketing management, failing to keep up with the competition and poor financial management are all associated with lower degrees of CVA success. These can all be influenced by the entrepreneur, for example through appropriate training or taking professional advice and being vigilant about competitive position. The research also indicates the importance of managing customer and supplier relationships. The attitude of creditors can make or break an attempt at survival when problems emerge. An important element of this is being candid with lenders and trade creditors. The evidence regarding the poorer chances of success where the cause of the firm's financial problems was the failure of another firm or problems with a major contract support the traditional advice to avoid over-reliance on a single customer. Additionally, the quality of the IP has been seen to influence outcomes, therefore entrepreneurs need to choose their advisers with care. Finally, entrepreneurs also need to be realistic. There will be some companies which no bankruptcy regime will be able to make viable. In those cases it is better to arrange as smooth an exit as possible.

What of directions for future research? This research is a small step beset by limitations. It has been based on a small sample, selected by the IPs who chose to respond to the survey. Ideally a larger random sample would be drawn from a more comprehensive sampling frame of completed CVAs. This is currently out of reach, as there does not exist even a database of completed CVAs, let alone one which contains anything like the detail on the companies involved as has been achieved in the current study. It has been based on broad measures of resource advantage and disadvantage and not on in-depth research carried out within the organization where many complex resources abide (Rouse and Daellenbach, 1999). Nor has attention been given to how firms construct their own understandings of their resource strengths and weaknesses. Nevertheless, the chapter suggests from both a theoretical and empirical standpoint that RBV is a useful and potentially powerful framework within which to explain the success and failure of entrepreneurial enterprises. In so doing, it builds on a small but growing body of literature which is advancing the use of RBV within the field of entrepreneurship. It also suggests, together with this growing body of work, that the RBV offers a promising research program within entrepreneurship which over time will measure key resources with greater sophistication and lead to a greater understanding of what the key resources in different contexts are. This chapter has suggested some ways in which the nature of the bankruptcy regime may affect entrepreneurship and there is an urgent need for further work, particularly given the plethora of policy initiatives that are being implemented and mooted around the globe based on little apparent solid research evidence.

## ACKNOWLEDGEMENT

The authors acknowledge the support of the Institute of Chartered Accountants in England and Wales, grant number 5-403.

## NOTES

1.  In the UK the correct term to apply to *companies* is 'insolvency'. Bankruptcy applies only to individuals. However, throughout this chapter the more usual international term is used.
2.  The 13 in question were Australia, Belgium, Finland, France, Hungary, Japan, New Zealand, Norway, Portugal, South Africa, Spain, Sweden and the UK. Of these, the seven with severe punishment for failed entrepreneurs and/or social stigmatization of failure were Australia, Belgium, France, New Zealand, Portugal, Sweden and the UK.
3.  Secured creditors, of whom by far the most important examples are banks in the UK, have traditionally had a very high degree of power in UK bankruptcy law and have rights over some or all of the company's assets in the event of bankruptcy. These rights are enforced through the appointment of an administrative receiver whose sole duty is to realize assets and satisfy the appointer's claim.
4.  An insolvency practitioner is authorized by one of the chartered accountancy bodies, the law societies, the Insolvency Practitioners' Association, or the Department of Trade and Industry to implement a bankruptcy proceeding.
5.  A preferential creditor is defined in Schedule 6 of the Insolvency Act 1986 and has priority when funds are distributed by a liquidator, administrative receiver or trustee in a bankruptcy. Crown preferential debt has been abolished by the Enterprise Act 2002.
6.  Her Majesty's Stationery Office (HSMO) provides information services for the government, industry and the general public.
7.  R3/SPI is a trade association for insolvency practitioners. The original acronym stood for Society of Practitioners of Insolvency. The name was changed to the Association of Business Recovery Professionals, abbreviated to R3, standing for Rescue, Recovery, Renewal, reflecting the priority given to rescue within bankruptcy.

## REFERENCES

Acs, Z.J., Arenius, P., Hay, M. and Minniti, M. (2005), *Global Entrepreneurship Monitor*, 2004 Executive Report, Babson College / London Business School.

Altman, E. I. (1968), 'Financial Ratios, Discriminant Analysis and the Prediction of Corporate Bankruptcy', *Journal of Finance*, 23, 589–609.

Alvarez, S.A. and Buzenitz, L.W. (2001), 'The Entrepreneurship of Resource-Based Theory', *Journal of Management*, 27, 755–75.

Audretsch, D.B. (2002), 'Entrepreneurship: A Survey of the Literature', Commission of the European Communities, Brussels.

Barney, J.B. (1991), 'Firm Resources and Sustained Competitive Advantage', *Journal of Management*, 17, 99–120.

Barney, J.B. (2001), 'Is the Resource-Based "View" A Useful Perspective for Strategic Management Research? Yes', *Academy of Management Review*, 26, 41–56.

Barney, J., Wright, M. and Ketchen, D.J. (2001), 'The Resource-Based View of the Firm: Ten Years after 1991', *Journal of Management*, 27, 625–41.

Bozner, W.C., Maloney, J.T. and Thomas, H. (1998), 'Paradigm Shift: The Parallel Origins, Evolution and Function of Strategic Group Analysis within the Resource-Based Theory of the Firm', In Baum, J.A.C. (ed.), *Advances in Strategic Management*, 15, JAI, Greenwich, CT.

Brush, C.G. and Chaganti, R. (1998), 'Business without Glamour? An Analysis of Resources on Performance by Size and Age in Small Service and Retail Firms', *Journal of Business Venturing*, 14, 233–57.

Brush, C.G., Greene, P.G. and Hart, M.M. (2001), 'From Initial Idea to Unique Advantage: The Entrepreneurial Challenge of Constructing A Resource Base', *Academy of Management Executive*, 15, 64–78.

Chandler, G.H. and Hanks, S.H. (1994), 'Market Attractiveness, Resource-Based Capabilities, Venture Strategies, and Venture Performance', *Journal of Business venturing*, 9, 331–49.

Chandler, G.H. and Hanks, S.H. (1998), 'An Examination of the Substitutability of Founders' Human and Financial Capital in Emerging Business Ventures', *Journal of Business Venturing*, 13, 353–69.

Chrisman, J.J., Bauerschmidt, A. and Hofer, C.W. (1998), 'The Determinants of New Venture Performance: An Extended Model', *Entrepreneurship, Theory and Practice*, 13, 5–29.

Cook, G.A.S., Pandit, N.R. and Milman, D. (2001), 'Formal Rehabilitation Procedures and Insolvent Firms: Empirical Evidence on the British Company Voluntary Arrangement Procedure', *Small Business Economics*, 17, 255–71.

Cooper, A.C. (1993), 'Challenges in Predicting New Firm Performance', *Journal of Business Venturing*, 8, 241–53.

Cork Committee (1982), *Insolvency Law and Practice*, Cmnd 8558, HMSO, London.

Dickinson, R.A., Ferguson, C.R. and Sircar, S. (1984), 'Critical Success Factors and Small Business', *American Journal of Small Business*, 8, 49–58.

Dollinger, M.J. (1995), *Entrepreneurship: Strategies and Resources*, Irwin, Boston, MA.

Duchesneau, D.A. and Gartner, W.B. (1990), 'A Profile of New Venture Success and Failure in an Emerging Industry', Journal of Business Venturing, 5, 297–312.

Ernst & Young (2001), *Global Entrepreneurship Monitor 2001*, UK Executive Report, London Business School, London.

European Commission (2000), 'Towards Enterprise Europe. Work Programme for Enterprise Policy 2000–2005', Commission Staff Working Paper, SEC (2000) 771.

European Commission (2003), 'Creating an Entrepreneurial Europe. The Activities of the European Union for Small and Medium-Sized Enterprises', Commission Staff Working Paper, SEC (2003), 58.

European Commission (2004), *Action Plan: The European Agenda for Entrepreneurship*, COM (2004) 70 final, Commission of the European Communities, Brussels.

Franks, J.R. and Torous, W.N. (1992), 'Lessons from a Comparison of US and UK Insolvency Codes', *Oxford Review of Economic Policy*, 8, 70–82.

Gallagher, C.C. and Stewart, H. (1985), 'Business Death and Firm Size in the UK', *International Small Business Journal*, 4, 42–57.

Gartner, W.B., Starr, J.A. and Bhat, S. (1998), 'Predicting New Venture Survival: An Analysis of "Anatomy of A Start-up" Cases from Inc. Magazine', *Journal of Business Venturing*, 14, 215–32.

Gertner, R. and Scharfstein, D. (1991), 'Theory of Workouts and the Effects of Reorganization Law', *Journal of Finance*, 46, 1189–222.

Harding, R. (2002), *Global Entrepreneurship Monitor*, United Kingdom 2002, London Business School, London.

HM Treasury/DTI (2001), *Productivity in the UK: Enterprise and the Productivity Challenge*, HM Treasury, London.

HM Treasury/DTI (2002), *Enterprise Britain: A Modern Approach to Meeting the Enterprise Challenge*, HMSO, London.

Hunt, S.D. (1997), 'Resource Advantage Theory: An Evolutionary Theory of Competitive Firm Behavior?', *Journal of Economic Issues*, 31, 59–77.

IFF Research (2002), *Household Survey of Entrepreneurship: Follow-Up Survey*, Small Business Service, London.

Insolvency Service (2000), *Review of Company Rescue and Business Reconstruction Mechanisms*, Insolvency Service, London.

Insolvency Service (2001), *Productivity and Enterprise-Insolvency: A Second Chance*, HMSO Cm 5234, London.

Insolvency Service (2002), *An Update on the Corporate Insolvency Proposals, Insolvency Service, London* (available at www.insolvency.gov.uk).

International Monetary Fund (IMF) (1999), *Orderly and Effective Insolvency Procedures. Key Issues*, International Monetary Fund, Washington, DC.

Lichtenstein, B.M.B. and Brush, C.G. (2001), 'How do "Resource Bundles" Develop and Change in New Ventures? A Dynamic and Longitudinal Exploration', *Entrepreneurship Theory and Practice*, 15, 37–58.

Michaelis, C., Smith, K. and Richards, S. (2001), *Regular Survey of Small Business Opinions. First Survey-Final Report*, Small Business Service, London.

Milman, D. and Chittenden, F.C. (1995), *Corporate Rescue: CVAs and the Challenge of Small Companies*, Certified Accountants Educational Trust, London.

Moorcroft, T., Telling, G. and Corney, R. (2004), *Companies Cannot Do It Alone: An Investigation into UK Management Attitudes to CVAs*, CSFI, No. 66.

Mosakowski, E. (1993), 'A Resource-Based Perspective on the Dynamic Strategy-Performance Relationship: An Empirical Examination of the Focus and Differentiation Strategies in Entrepreneurial Firms', *Journal of Management*, 19, 819–39.

Organization for Economic Cooperation and Development (OECD) (1998), *Fostering Entrepreneurship, Organization for Economic Cooperation and Development*, Paris.

Pandit, N.R. (2000), 'Some Recommendations for Improved Research on Corporate Turnaround', *M@n@gement*, 3, 31–56.

Phan, P.H. (2004), 'Entrepreneurship Theory: Possibilities and Future Directions', *Journal of Business Venturing*, 19, 617–20.

Piesse, J. and Wood, D. (1992), 'Issues in Assessing MDA Models of Corporate Failure: A Research Note', *British Accounting Review*, 24, 33–42.

Porter, M.E. (1980), *Competitive Strategy: Techniques for Analyzing Industries and Competitors*, Free Press, New York.

Porter, M.E. (1985), *Competitive Advantage: Creating and Sustaining Superior Performance*, Free Press, New York.

Priem, R.L. and Butler, J.E. (2001a), 'Is the Resource-Based "View" a Useful Perspective for Strategic Management Research?', *Academy of Management Review*, 26, 22–40.

Priem, R.L. and Butler, J.E. (2001b), 'Tautology in the Resource-Based View and the Implications of Externally Determined Resource Value: Further Comments', *Academy of Management Review*, 26, 57–65.

Pringle, C.D. and Kroll, M.J. (1997), 'Why Trafalgar Was Won before It Was Fought: Lessons from Resource–Based Theory', *Academy of Management Executive*, 11, 73–89.

R3 (2000), *9th Survey of Company Insolvency*, R3, London.

Rangone, A. (1999), 'A Resource-Based Approach to Strategy Analysis in Small-Medium-Sized Enterprises', *Small Business Economics*, 12, 233–48.

Ravid, S.A. and Sundgren, S. (1998), 'The Comparative Efficiency of Small-Firm Bankruptcies: A study of US and Finnish Bankruptcy Codes', *Financial Management*, 27, 28–40.

Reynolds, P.D., Bygrave, W.D. and Autio, E. (2004), *Global Entrepreneurship Monitor*, 2003 Executive Report, Babson College, Wellesley, MA.

Reynolds, P.D., Bygrave, W.D. Autio, E., Cox, L.W. and Hay, M. (2002), *Global Entrepreneurship Monitor*, 2002 Executive Report, Babson College, Wellesley, MA.

Reynolds, P.D., Camp, S.M., Bygrave, W.D., Autio, E. and Hay, M. (2001), *Global Entrepreneurship Monitor*, 2001 Executive Report, Babson College, Wellesley, MA.

Reynolds, P.D., Hay, M., Bygrave, W.D., Camp, S.M. and Autio, E. (2000), *Global Entrepreneurship Monitor*, 2000 Executive Report, Babson College, Wellesley, MA.

Reynolds, P.D., Hay, M. and Camp, S.M. (1999), *Global Entrepreneurship Monitor*, 1999 Executive Report, Babson College, Wellesley, MA.

Rights of Priority Committee (1999), Nya förmånsrättsregler, SOU 1999:1.

Rouse, M.J. and Daellenbach, U.S. (1999), 'Rethinking Research Methods for the Resource-Based Perspective: Isolating Sources of Sustainable Competitive Advantage', *Strategic Management Journal*, 20, 487–94.

Schoemaker, P.J.H. and Amit, R. (1994), 'Investment in Strategic Assets: Industry- and Firm-Level Perspectives', In Shrivastava, et al., (eds), pp. 3-33.

Schulze, W.S. (1994), 'The Two Schools of Thought in Resource-Based Theory: Definitions and Implications in Research', in Shrivatsava et al. (eds), pp. 127-51.

Schumpeter, J. (1942), *Capitalism, Socialism and Democracy*, Harper, New York.

Shane, S. and Venkataraman, S. (2000), 'The Promise of Entrepreneurship as a Field of Research', *Academy of Management Review*, 25, 217–26.

Shrivastava, P., Huff, A. and Dutton, J. (eds) (1994), *Advances in Strategic Management*, 10, JAI Press, Greenwich, CT.

Shurry, J., Lomax, S. and Vyakarnam, S. (2002), *Household Survey of Entrepreneurship 2001*, Small Business Service, London.

Small Business Service (2003), *Small Firms: Big Business! A Review of Small and Medium-Sized Enterprises in the UK*, HMSO, London.

SPI (1996a), *5th Survey of Company Insolvency*, SPI, London.

SPI (1996b), *6th Survey of Company Insolvency*, SPI, London.

SPI (1997), *7th Survey of Company Insolvency*, SPI, London.

SPI (1999), *8th Survey of Company Insolvency*, SPI, London.

Taffler, R.J. (1982), 'Forecasting Company Failure in the UK Using Discriminant Analysis and Financial Ratio Data', *Journal of the Royal Statistical Society*, 145, 342–58.

Thomas, H. and Pollock, T. (1999), 'From I-O Economics' S-C-P Paradigm through Strategic Groups to Competence-Based Competition: Reflections on the Puzzle of Competitive Strategy', *British Journal of Management*, 10, 127–40.

Wernerfelt, B. (1984), 'A Resource-Based View of the Firm', *Strategic Management Journal*, 5, 171–80.

Wernerfelt, B. (1995), 'The Resource-Based View of the Firm: Ten Years After', *Strategic Management Journal*, 16, 171–74.

Westhead, P. (1995), 'Survival and Employment Growth Contrasts between Types of Owner-Managed High-Technology Firms', *Entrepreneurship, Theory and Practice*, 9, 5–27.
Zahra, S.A., Hayton, J.C. and Salvato, C. (2004), 'Entrepreneurship in Family vs. Non-Family Firms: A Resource-Based Analysis of the Effect of Organizational Culture', *Entrepreneurship Theory and Practice*, 18, 363–81.

# APPENDIX 9A  STUDY QUESTIONNAIRE

## COMPANY VOLUNTARY ARRANGEMENTS

Guidance Notes:

- Please fill out the questionnaire for each CVA completed after 1.1.95 which you have personally supervised.
- If you have supervised more than one CVA and are able to complete further questionnaires please either photocopy this form as required or request additional copies from Joyce Tuson on 01509 223132 or e-mail J.Tuson@lboro.ac.uk.
- The data collected for this survey is strictly confidential and will not be used for commercial purposes.

## PART 1: ABOUT YOU

Q1.1    For how long have you been a practising Insolvency Practitioner? _____ Years

Q1.2    How many partners does your firm have? *(please tick)*

☐ Less than 10    ☐ Between 10 and 50    ☐ Greater than 50

Q1.3    Estimated total number of CVAs administered by your company since 1985 *(please tick)*

☐ Less than 5    ☐ Between 5 and 25    ☐ Greater than 25

PART 2: ABOUT THE COMPANY

Q2.1    Company Name and Company Number (*required only for the purposes of secondary data collection*)

[   ]

Q2.2    How would you describe the company's <u>major</u> business activity? (*please tick only one*)

☐ Construction        ☐ Financial and Business Services   ☐ Manufacturing   ☐ Hotel and Catering
☐ Other Services      ☐ Property   ☐ Retail               ☐ Transport/Distribution   ☐ Wholesale

Other (*please specify*): _____

Q2.3    At the date of your appointment, what was:

a) the turnover of the company (£m)              _____        (*exact figures are not required*)

b) number of employees                           _____        (*exact figures are not required*)

c) the age of the company (years)                _____        (*exact figures are not required*)

d) total amount due to secured creditors (£000's) _____       (*exact figures are not required*)

e) total amount due to preferential creditors (£000's) _____ (exact figures are not required)

f) total amount due to unsecured creditors (£000's) _____ (exact figures are not required)

Q2.4 Which of the following best describes the company at the date of your appointment? (please tick one)

☐ Holding company that was not trading ☐ Dormant or defunct company (not trading)

☐ Property, investment or other asset-owning company (not trading) ☐ Active trading company

Q2.5 What caused the company's financial difficulties? (please tick one box per cause)

Rate in terms of importance on a scale from 1 to 5, where 1=not important and 5=very important; 0=not applicable

|  | 1 | 2 | 3 | 4 | 5 | 0 |
|---|---|---|---|---|---|---|
| A significant bad debt | ☐ | ☐ | ☐ | ☐ | ☐ | ☐ |
| Adverse macroeconomic conditions (e.g., interest/exchange rates) | ☐ | ☐ | ☐ | ☐ | ☐ | ☐ |
| Decline in demand for the type of product the company sells | ☐ | ☐ | ☐ | ☐ | ☐ | ☐ |
| Increased competition | ☐ | ☐ | ☐ | ☐ | ☐ | ☐ |
| Knock-on from failure of another company | ☐ | ☐ | ☐ | ☐ | ☐ | ☐ |
| One big project that failed | ☐ | ☐ | ☐ | ☐ | ☐ | ☐ |
| Poor financial management | ☐ | ☐ | ☐ | ☐ | ☐ | ☐ |
| Poor marketing | ☐ | ☐ | ☐ | ☐ | ☐ | ☐ |
| Poor human resource management | ☐ | ☐ | ☐ | ☐ | ☐ | ☐ |
| Problems with one major contract | ☐ | ☐ | ☐ | ☐ | ☐ | ☐ |
| Sheer bad luck | ☐ | ☐ | ☐ | ☐ | ☐ | ☐ |

Other ☐

*If other please specify:*

_____

_____

_____

**Q2.6**  a) How would you describe the attitude of the creditors to the proposed CVA? *(please tick one box per creditor type)*

| | Unsupportive | Neutral | Supportive | N/A |
|---|---|---|---|---|
| Secured creditors | ☐ | ☐ | ☐ | ☐ |
| Preferential creditors | ☐ | ☐ | ☐ | ☐ |
| Unsecured creditors | ☐ | ☐ | ☐ | ☐ |

b) If any of the above creditors were supportive, to what extent was this because: *(please tick one box per creditor type)*

| | Their claim was well covered so they were not at risk anyway | The assets were inadequate to meet their claim and the CVA offered the prospect of a better dividend | Other |
|---|---|---|---|
| Secured creditors | ☐ | ☐ | ☐ |
| Preferential creditors | ☐ | ☐ | ☐ |

Unsecured creditors ☐

☐

☐

*If other please specify:*

_____

_____

_____

## PART 3: ABOUT THE ARRANGEMENT

Q3.1 Were you initially employed by the company's secured creditors as an investigating accountant and then subsequently asked to supervise the CVA?

☐ Yes   ☐ No

Q3.2 Why was the CVA implemented? *(please tick one box per reason)*

*Rate in terms of importance on a scale from 1 to 5, where 1=not important and 5=very important; 0=not applicable*

|  | 1 | 2 | 3 | 4 | 5 | 0 |
|---|---|---|---|---|---|---|
| New or improved management was or would soon be in place | ☐ | ☐ | ☐ | ☐ | ☐ | ☐ |
| The most efficient way to wind up the business and distribute funds | ☐ | ☐ | ☐ | ☐ | ☐ | ☐ |
| The problems facing the business were only temporary | ☐ | ☐ | ☐ | ☐ | ☐ | ☐ |
| The shareholders were prepared to invest extra capital | ☐ | ☐ | ☐ | ☐ | ☐ | ☐ |
| The business had turnaround potential | ☐ | ☐ | ☐ | ☐ | ☐ | ☐ |
| Other | ☐ | ☐ | ☐ | ☐ | ☐ | ☐ |

*If other please specify:*

_____

_____

_____

Q3.3    How long did it take to secure approval for the arrangement?  _____  months

Q3.4    On what date was the CVA established? (mm/yy)  _____

Q3.5    On what date was the CVA concluded? (mm/yy)  _____

Q3.6    a) Did the CVA follow another insolvency procedure?    ☐ Yes    ☐ No

        b) If 'Yes' please specify the procedure _____

Q3.7    When the CVA was established what percentage return (pence in £ of original debt) was expected to be paid to the following groups of creditors?

        Secured _____    Preferential _____    Unsecured _____

Q3.8    When the CVA was completed what returns (pence in £) were actually paid?

        Secured _____    Preferential _____    Unsecured _____

Q3.9    During the course of the CVA, how would you describe the company's operation?

☐ Similar to a healthy competitor    ☐ Difficult because stakeholders were aware    ☐ Other
                                        of the company's involvement in a CVA

*If other please specify:*

_____
_____
_____

Q3.10   a) In terms of the following, how would you rate the CVA's success? *(please tick one box per item)*

*Rate on a scale from 1 to 5, where 1=very unsuccessful; 2=unsuccessful; 3=just below plan; 4=according to plan; 5=surpassed plan; 0=not applicable*

|                                                        | 1 | 2 | 3 | 4 | 5 | 0 |
|--------------------------------------------------------|---|---|---|---|---|---|
| Efficient winding up of company and distribution of funds | ☐ | ☐ | ☐ | ☐ | ☐ | ☐ |
| Rehabilitation of whole company as a viable business   | ☐ | ☐ | ☐ | ☐ | ☐ | ☐ |
| Rehabilitation of part of company as a viable business | ☐ | ☐ | ☐ | ☐ | ☐ | ☐ |

b) If you judge the CVA to have been unsuccessful (i.e., a score of 1 or 2 above), what were the reasons? *(please tick one box per reason)*

*Rate in terms of importance on a scale from 1 to 5, where 1=not important and 5=very important; 0=not applicable*

| | 1 | 2 | 3 | 4 | 5 | 0 |
|---|---|---|---|---|---|---|
| Adverse actions of secured creditors during the course of the CVA | ☐ | ☐ | ☐ | ☐ | ☐ | ☐ |
| Adverse actions of preferential creditors during the course of the CVA | ☐ | ☐ | ☐ | ☐ | ☐ | ☐ |
| Adverse actions of unsecured creditors during the course of the CVA | ☐ | ☐ | ☐ | ☐ | ☐ | ☐ |
| Business incapable of restoration to profitability | ☐ | ☐ | ☐ | ☐ | ☐ | ☐ |
| Defection of customers | ☐ | ☐ | ☐ | ☐ | ☐ | ☐ |
| Defection of employees | ☐ | ☐ | ☐ | ☐ | ☐ | ☐ |
| Defection of suppliers | ☐ | ☐ | ☐ | ☐ | ☐ | ☐ |
| Lack of security for additional lending | ☐ | ☐ | ☐ | ☐ | ☐ | ☐ |
| The CVA procedure proved too complicated and time consuming | ☐ | ☐ | ☐ | ☐ | ☐ | ☐ |
| The CVA procedure proved too expensive for the company to bear | ☐ | ☐ | ☐ | ☐ | ☐ | ☐ |
| Other | ☐ | ☐ | ☐ | ☐ | ☐ | ☐ |

*If other please specify:*

_____

_____

_____

Q3.11  With the benefit of hindsight, do you think that the CVA plan was:

☐ Too pessimistic          ☐ About right          ☐ Too optimistic

Q3.12 How do you think the interested parties have been affected by the CVA relative to an alternative insolvency procedure? *(please tick one box per party)*

*Rate in terms of importance on a scale from 1 to 5, where 1=not favourably and 5=very favourably; 0=not applicable*

|  | 1 | 2 | 3 | 4 | 5 | 0 |
|---|---|---|---|---|---|---|
| The company's directors | ☐ | ☐ | ☐ | ☐ | ☐ | ☐ |
| The secured creditors | ☐ | ☐ | ☐ | ☐ | ☐ | ☐ |
| The preferential creditors | ☐ | ☐ | ☐ | ☐ | ☐ | ☐ |
| The unsecured creditors | ☐ | ☐ | ☐ | ☐ | ☐ | ☐ |
| The company's employees | ☐ | ☐ | ☐ | ☐ | ☐ | ☐ |

*Please return your completed questionnaire in the enclosed pre-paid envelope*

IF YOU WOULD LIKE TO RECEIVE A SUMMARY OF THE RESEARCH FINDINGS AND/OR ARE ABLE TO PARTICIPATE FURTHER IN THIS RESEARCH PROGRAMME PLEASE LET US KNOW BY E-MAILING JOYCE TUSON: J.TUSON@LBORO.AC.UK

*THANK YOU FOR YOUR CO-OPERATION*

# 10. Agglomeration Economies, Learning Processes, and Patterns of Firm Spatial Clustering

**Vito Albino, Francisco Alvarez and Ilaria Giannoccaro**

## INTRODUCTION

Among different types of spatial concentration of related industries and firms, geographical clusters (GCs) are geographical concentrations of interconnected companies and institutions operating in a particular field. They include: suppliers of specialized inputs such as components, machinery, and services, providers of specialized infrastructures, manufacturers of complementary products, companies in related industries, and customers. Many clusters may also include governmental and other institutions such as universities and research centers (Porter, 1998). Thus, GCs may assume different configurations. For example, Markusen (1996) defines four types of GCs, namely: new industrial districts, satellite platforms, hub and spokes, and state-anchored districts.

In this chapter we consider GCs as geographical concentrations of firms, featuring the co-localization of a large number of firms involved in various phases of production of a homogeneous product family. These firms are generally highly specialized in a few phases of the production process, and integrated through a complex network of inter-organizational relationships (Becattini, 1990; Pouder and St John, 1996).

Geographical clusters have been extensively investigated in the literature. Different notions and models have been developed to explain their success, such as the agglomeration economies concept introduced by Marshall (1920) and further formalized by Krugman (1991); the flexible specialization production model conceptualized by Piore and Sabel (1984); the industrial atmosphere notion conceived by Marshall (1919); and the innovative milieu concept developed by the GREMI (Groupe de Recherche Europeen sur les Milieux Innovatours) (Maillat et al., 1993).

Agglomeration economies are positive externalities (benefits) resulting from the spatial clustering of economic activities and motivating firms to form geographical clusters. In traditional studies on the topic, it is argued that agglomeration economies are driven by production externalities, namely how co-locating affects the cost of productions and firms' production technologies. In fact, the benefits for co-located firms include production cost reductions and/or an increased production efficiency. For Marshall (1920), the industry localization may generate production externalities deriving from the existence of an industry demand that creates a pool of specialized labour and a pool of specialized input providers. For Krugman (1991), the benefits of agglomeration in essence depend on three factors: (i) substantially increasing returns to scale, at the level of both single firms (internal economies) and the industry (external economies); (ii) lower transportation costs; and (iii) a large local demand. A further benefit is the reduction of transaction costs due to the development of trust and cooperation among firms within the GCs (Dei Ottati, 1994; Powell, 1987; Porter, 1998).

Several formal models have been developed to examine agglomeration economies: some examples include those by David and Rosenbloom (1990), Krugman (1991), and Rauch (1993). Moreover, a number of empirical studies confirm that firms are more likely to locate new plants in regions with greater levels of similar industrial activity (e.g., Carlton, 1983; Bartik, 1985; Head et al., 1995).

The effect of production externalities is that the GCs become cost-efficient spatial configurations and that their source of competitive advantage is mainly based on cost. However, current strategic management literature points out that in today's economy the source of a sustainable competitive advantage for firms can no longer be limited to cost. Firms cannot simply pursue static efficiency to be competitive. A competitive advantage based on cost is, in fact, difficult to sustain in the long term due to the increased competitive pressure and faster development of innovations nowadays. In the modern economy, dynamic sources of competitive advantage need to be found. The knowledge-based strategic theory argues that knowledge is the fundamental factor that creates an economic value and competitive advantage for firms (Leonard-Barton, 1995; Spender, 1996; Grant, 1997). This knowledge-based view of competitive advantage is anchored in the resource-based theory of the firm (Barney, 1991), which suggests that firms' resources that are valuable, rare and inimitable will determine a long-term competitive advantage (Winter, 1987; Reed and Defillippi, 1990). The consequent attention paid to firms' intangible resources has led to the recognition that knowledge is the most strategically important of a firm's resources and plays a critical role in gaining and keeping the competitive advantage. What a firm knows, how it uses what it knows, and how fast it can develop new knowledge are key aspects for the firm's success (Hamel and Prahalad, 1994; Prusak, 1997). Competitive success is thus more closely related to the ability of firms to create and increase their internal knowledge. Learning is a key strategic process because it yields enhancements of the knowledge stock and technological capabilities of firms, thereby generating continuous change and innovation and not just simple average cost reductions (Malerba, 1992).

The acknowledgment of the importance of knowledge and learning has led scholars to rethink the logic of agglomeration economies and to pay renewed attention to knowledge externalities, namely the benefits that co-located firms receive in terms of knowledge. This concept was originated by Marshall (1920), who identified in knowledge spillovers a further factor motivating firms to form geographical clusters, and has been investigated by distinct schools of thought, adopting various perspectives: economic geographers have studied the relationship between localized knowledge spillovers and innovation (Romer, 1986; Krugman, 1991; Audretsch and Feldman, 1996); regional economists have developed the concept of collective learning (Baptista, 2000; Capello and Faggian, 2005); the French school of proximity has placed emphasis on the influence of distinctive dimensions of proximity on learning (see Boschma, 2005 for an interesting review); management scholars have investigated the nature of knowledge circulating in GCs, the knowledge transfer and creation processes embedded in GCs and the learning processes (Albino and Schiuma, 2003; Pinch et al., 2003; Tallman et al., 2004; Albino et al., 2006).

The shared idea of the foregoing studies is that the ability of firms to learn and develop new knowledge is a key factor for long-term competitive success and that the GC is a spatial configuration that enhances learning and knowledge creation. Thus, in GCs, knowledge externalities affect agglomeration economies and motivate firms to form GCs so as to gain knowledge benefits. Firms can gain benefits from co-location not only in terms of lower costs or improved efficiency in production but also in terms of increased knowledge stocks. Knowledge externalities are relevant to justify why knowledge-intensive industries (e.g., biotechnology) are geographically clustered. However, some scholars have also argued that the knowledge-based theory of GCs explains their nature better than traditional ones (Malmberg and Maskell, 2004). Even though knowledge externalities have recently received dramatic attention in the economic literature and despite the number of different schools of thought that have analyzed the topic adopting diverse perspectives, the concept remains ambiguous and is considered as a 'black box' (Breschi and Lissoni, 2001). Investigation of the black box is thus required. Our approach is to focus on the learning processes and how learning affects the geographical clustering of firms.

A further limitation of the literature is the prevailing adoption of a system-level perspective. In GC studies, the whole system is considered as the unit of analysis (Maskell, 2001b; Giuliani, 2005), and their phenomena and dynamics are observed at the macro level, devoting little attention to the internal mechanisms at a micro level that have determined the macro behavior of the system.

Our chapter follows this alternative direction, considering the single firm as the unit of analysis and analyzing the geographical clustering process in terms of the result of independent firms' location choices. Our contribution to the literature is thus twofold, consisting of an examination of the geographical clustering process (i) adopting the firm perspective and (ii) focusing on knowledge externalities associated with the learning processes.

The research methodology we have adopted is agent-based simulation (ABS), that is, a computational technique that originated in complexity science to examine complex adaptive systems (CASs) and has recently been applied to economic studies (Kauffman, 1993; Axelrod, 1997; Weiss, 2000). The term 'agent-based computational economics' (ACE) refers to the study of economic processes modeled as complex adaptive systems of interacting agents (Tesfatsion and Judd, 2006). In ABS, agents interact with each other in a non-linear manner with little or no central direction. The large-scale effects determined by the locally interacting agents are called the 'emergent properties' of the system. They are thus the spontaneous result of the interactions among agents according to a bottom-up, rather than a top-down approach. The main goal of ABS is to enrich our understanding of the fundamental processes regulating and determining the dynamics of CASs (Axelrod, 1997). Furthermore, it is a valuable tool for theory building and theory testing (ibid.; Carley and Gasser, 2000).

We consider GCs as CASs (Lane, 2002; Albino et al., 2006, 2007a) and study the geographical clustering process of firms as an emergent behavior. The ABS is used to modeling the geographical clustering of firms based on learning processes. We consider that firms can benefit from knowledge externalities produced thanks to two specific interactive learning processes, namely, learning by imitation and learning by interaction. The extent to which the learning processes develop knowledge stock is influenced by various dimensions of proximity, that is, geographical and cognitive proximity. Firms can modify their location in order to benefit from enhanced learning opportunities.

The proposed agent-based simulation model consists of agents (the firms) located on a grid (the geographical space), which interact, and develop their knowledge stocks thanks to learning. The goal of each agent is to maximize the value of its competitive advantage based on knowledge. To pursue this goal, the agent can move around the grid looking for new positions that could increase the competitive advantage.

Using the simulation model, we are interested in observing the resulting spatial configuration of the agents, in order to understand whether firms tend to cluster geographically when knowledge externalities associated with interactive learning processes are present. Furthermore, simulation is utilized to analyze the influence of the degree of heterogeneity of knowledge stocks and the existence of knowledge sources on the geographical clustering of firms.

This chapter is organized as follows. In the second section, the theoretical background of the research is presented. Then, the agent-based simulation is briefly presented and the main models of the GCs developed in the literature are reviewed in the third section. The model of the geographical clustering process based on knowledge externalities is discussed in the next section. A simulation analysis is carried out to study the emergence of GCs of agents in different scenarios in the fifth section. The conclusion summarizes the findings of the research and highlights the limitations of the study as well as the directions of further research.

## THEORETICAL BACKGROUND

### Learning Processes in Geographical Clusters

Learning is a dynamic and cumulative process of production of knowledge. It is linked to different sources of knowledge that may be either internal or external to the firm (Malerba, 1992). External learning processes are particularly significant in GCs because they create an environment conducive to innovation (Aydalot and Keeble, 1988; Pouder and St John, 1996; Keeble et al., 1999; Baptista, 2000).

The main external learning processes activated in GCs are: learning by localizing, learning by imitation, and learning by interaction (Albino et al., 2006). Learning by localizing (or collective learning) allows GC firms to develop their knowledge stocks thanks to their sense of belonging to the area, their capability of interacting and their sharing of common values. The internal cohesion promotes the introduction of new products or production techniques and reduces the uncertainty associated with innovations (Camagni, 1995; Gertler, 1995).

Learning by imitation occurs as a result of imitation and emulation processes among firms. The focused environment of the GCs, the sharing of common conditions and the transparent circulation of information makes it easy to observe successful and failed strategies adopted by each individual firm. In this way firms can learn from the experiences of other firms, emulating the success of others and adding something new of their own (Belussi and Arcangeli, 1998). Learning by imitation can also take place without any explicit interaction between local agents. In fact, even in the absence of close contacts and interactions, firms can monitor one another constantly, closely, and almost without effort or cost (Maskell, 2001b).

Learning by interaction derives from the interactions among firms belonging to networks of formal and established business relationships. It takes place when firms interact with their suppliers and customers. In the first case, information and knowledge are embedded in the components and semi-finished products supplied, and in subcontracting technical specifications. Interactions with customers can stimulate exploitation of the firm knowledge and creativity to develop product innovations that are able to satisfy customer needs (Piore and Sabel, 1984; Lipparini and Lorenzoni, 1996; Lipparini, 1998).

**Proximity and Learning**

Regional economy researchers have in recent years investigated the relationship between proximity, innovation, and learning. In particular, the French school of proximity has highlighted that different and intertwined dimensions of proximity affect the interactive learning processes. Five dimensions can be recognized: geographical, cognitive, organizational, social, and institutional (Boschma, 2005). We focus herein on geographical and cognitive proximity.

Geographical proximity is defined as the spatial or physical distance between two firms. It has recently been claimed that firms that are spatially concentrated benefit from knowledge externalities (Maskell, 2001a). Short distances, in fact, enable information contacts to be created and facilitate the exchange of tacit knowledge. The larger the distance between firms, the less the intensity of these positive externalities (Boschma, 2005). This may even be true for the exchange of codified knowledge, because its interpretation and assimilation may still require tacit knowledge and, thus, spatial closeness (Howells, 2002). Too much geographical proximity may also have a negative impact on interactive learning and innovation due to the problem of lock-in, meaning a lack of openness and flexibility (Boschma, 2005).

However, some authors have noticed that for interactive learning to take place, some level of cognitive proximity is required. The term 'cognitive proximity' refers to the similarity of the knowledge stocks of two firms (ibid.). Firms sharing the same knowledge stock and expertise may learn from each other. However, too much cognitive proximity may also have a negative impact on learning and innovation. In fact, some cognitive distance should be maintained to enhance interactive learning because knowledge building often requires dissimilar, complementary bodies of knowledge (Cohendet and Llerena, 1997).

Cognitive proximity also influences the firm's absorptive capacity, namely the firm's ability to absorb new knowledge. In their widely recognized theory on absorptive capacity, Cohen and Levinthal (1990) argue that the simple access to new knowledge is not a sufficient condition for acquiring it. The effective transfer of new knowledge requires the firm to be able to identify, interpret, and exploit it. The authors also recognize that the extent to which a firm is able to absorb new knowledge is a function of the prior level of knowledge the firm possesses. This prior knowledge confers a theoretical framework (cognitive map) in which to interpret the new knowledge, that otherwise cannot be understood. Therefore, the cognitive distance between the knowledge stock of the firm and the new knowledge matters. For the learning process to be effective, interacting firms need to be close enough in terms of knowledge stocks. In fact, cognitive proximity permits them to communicate and understand each other (Boschma, 2005).

# METHODOLOGY

## Agent-based Simulation

ABS is a simulation technique offered by the complexity science domain and aims at enriching our understanding of the fundamental processes regulating and determining the dynamics of CASs (Axelrod, 1997). ABS is characterized by a collection of autonomous, heterogeneous, intelligent, and interacting agents, which operate and exist in an environment (Epstein and Axtell, 1996). Agents are active goal-oriented entities that possess certain capabilities to perform tasks and communicate with other agents. To pursue their goals, they accomplish a given set of actions and interact with each other in a non-linear manner with little or no central direction. The dynamics of the locally interacting agents determine emergent behaviors in the system, known as 'emergent properties'.

ABS differs from traditional simulation because it adopts a bottom-up approach: the dynamics under investigation spontaneously emerge from the local interactions of the agents rather than being directly imposed by the modeler (top-down approach). As a research methodology, ABS is a valuable tool both for theory building and theory testing (Axelrod, 1997; Carley and Gasser, 2000). This approach thus seems appropriate to study the agglomeration process of GCs, because it has recently been recognized that

GCs are CASs, demonstrating the benefits deriving from the use of complexity science tools in the study of GCs (Lane, 2002; Albino et al., 2005, 2006).

## A Brief Review of Agent-based Models of Geographical Clusters

A small number of studies have recently applied ABS to study GCs (see Fioretti, 2006 for a review). They cover various topics: the formation process of the GCs (Brenner, 2001; Fioretti, 2001; Zhang, 2002) the importance of specific GC features for competitive success, such as the contemporary presence of competition and cooperation among firms, the organizational structure, and intensive information and knowledge sharing (Albino et al., 2007a, 2007b); the innovation capability (Albino et al., 2006); and the process of adaptation to technological developments (Boero and Squazzoni, 2002).

Referring to the formation process, Zhang (2002) studies the formation of high-tech industrial clusters, such as Silicon Valley, showing that such clusters can spontaneously emerge as a result of specific dynamics. He emphasizes that high-tech industrial clusters are characterized by concentrated entrepreneurship. The cluster can thus be explained by the social effect, according to which the appearance of one or a few entrepreneurs may inspire many followers locally. Once a cluster comes into existence, it tends to be reinforced by attracting more firms. The author proposes a Nelson–Winter model with an explicitly defined landscape and uses agent-based computational modeling to show the cluster's dynamics.

Fioretti (2001) develops a spatial agent-based computational model to study the formation and the evolution of the Prato industrial district. He focuses on the structure of the information flows that underlie the creation of production chains within the district and on the role of the middlemen. Brenner (2001) develops a cellular automata model of the spatial dynamics of entry, exit, and growth of firms within a region. He first identifies the mechanisms that modify a firm's state and then carries out a simulation analysis to investigate the influence of all the mechanisms on the geographic concentration.

While these studies have analyzed the GC formation process as the result of the existence of specific actors such as entrepreneurs, institutions, middlemen, and venture capitalists, our model, described in the next section, provides a study of the GC formation process arising from agglomeration economies based on knowledge externalities.

# THE AGENT-BASED MODEL OF GEOGRAPHICAL CLUSTERS

To investigate the process of geographical clustering of firms based on knowledge externalities, we have developed an agent-based model. The model aims to study the process of geographical clustering of firms as an emergent behavior of the system. This means that GCs will emerge as the spontaneous result of the firms' decisions and of interactions among firms.

The computational implementation of the model is made using *Free Pascal 1.0.10* software (Van Canneyt and Klampfe, 2005). More information on the software is available on the website *http://www.freepascal.org.* It combines the use of Pascal for mathematical programming with that of Java for the graphical interface. This general purpose language has been preferred to a specialized agent-based simulation software (e.g., Swarm), because it does not require too much programming sophistication and takes less time to achieve the simulation (Axelrod, 1997).

**Main Assumptions**

Our model is built upon the knowledge-based theory of the firm, which considers firms as knowledge users and producers (Grant, 1997). Firms' knowledge is conceptualized as knowledge stocks, in the sense of accumulated knowledge assets that are applied to produce goods and service (Decarolis and Deeds, 1999). In this first step of the research, only the knowledge stocks are modeled, thus herein knowledge is the only good produced and transferred. We do not consider different kinds of knowledge and do not distinguish between tacit and codified knowledge.

Firms are involved in location choices. Geographical relocation is costless and instantaneous. The location decision depends on the incentives caused by agglomeration externalities. Agglomeration economies are based only on knowledge externalities. They consist in the development of knowledge stocks to enhance learning processes. In this work two learning processes are taken into account, that is, learning by imitation and learning by interaction. Thus, no other sources of knowledge creation are considered, such as research and development (R&D) activities, for example, or external (to the GCs) sources of knowledge. These assumptions fit the features of the traditional Marshallian industrial districts, where the innovation carried out by firms is the result of learning processes based on the information and knowledge flows circulating inside the district in the form of learning by imitation and by interaction, whereas improved learning mechanisms based on R&D activities and links with external knowledge sources are less commonly used (Albino et al., 2006). Learning processes are affected by only two dimensions of proximity, namely geographical and cognitive proximity. Their influence is measured in terms of increases of the knowledge stock. The spatial lock-in effect is not considered.

### Agents and Environment

The agent of the model corresponds to a single firm. It is modeled as an object located in a rectangular grid (the geographical space). The grid is a matrix measuring 200 x 200. The number of agents ($N$) in the grid is defined as the population. Each agent $i$ is characterized by two dynamic attributes:

1. the value of accumulated knowledge stock at a given instant in time $K_{i,i}$, and
2. the spatial position occupied at a given instant in time on the grid $P_{i,t}$ $(x, y)$.

Given that we do not consider different kinds of knowledge stock, agents differ only in regard to the amount of knowledge stock they possess.

The goal of each agent is to maximize its fitness which, is influenced by the agent's position on the grid. Therefore, the agents move around looking for new positions with higher fitness during the simulation. The fitness measures the net benefits in terms of enhanced knowledge stocks that the agent receives in a given position. The net benefits are the difference between the knowledge stocks that agent $i$ learns from other agents $j$

$$( \sum_{\substack{j=1 \\ j \neq i}}^{N} \Delta K_{ij} ),$$

and the knowledge stocks that other agents $j$ learn from agent $i$

$$( \sum_{\substack{j=1 \\ j \neq i}}^{N} \Delta K_{ji} ).$$

In fact, note that when a firm locates near others, it benefits from geographical proximity by receiving knowledge stock but it also contributes to increasing the knowledge stock of the nearby firms (Shaver and Flyer, 2000). If the net result is negative, the co-location is not beneficial for the firm because it will lose competitive advantage with respect to the other firms. Thus, the firm will prefer to relocate at a distance from the others. Consider a start-up firm in the high-tech industry; it will prefer to locate in Silicon Valley where it can benefit from watching, discussing, and comparing solutions with related firms located in the GCs. It could exploit the other firms' mistakes and successes, identify the top performers and imitate their 'good' capabilities. In contrast, the top performers, having superior capabilities, will learn very much less from the less-capable firm as compared with what the latter can learn from the more-capable one. Thus, in terms of competitive advantage, the start-up firm will gain a positive net benefit, whereas the sum is negative for the top performer. As a result, the top performer will not have the incentive to co-locate but, on the contrary, to locate at a distance from the less-capable firm.

The fitness function, as defined, is a measure of the competitive advantage of the firm and is computed as follows:

$$\text{Fitness} = CA_i = \sum_{\substack{j=1 \\ j \neq i}}^{N} \Delta K_{ij} - \sum_{\substack{j=1 \\ j \neq i}}^{N} \Delta K_{ji}. \tag{10.1}$$

The agent possesses a mental model that represents its view of the external world, in the sense of what the agent knows about the other agents. Each agent knows the knowledge stock accumulated by the other agents and their position in the grid. In this first work we assume that agents know these values correctly, and we do not take errors into account.

Based on the agent attribute, we also define attributes characterizing the population. These are: the level of knowledge, its heterogeneity, and the presence of knowledge centers. The level of knowledge is computed as the mean of the agent knowledge stocks. Heterogeneity measures how different the agent knowledge stocks are. The more they differ, the more heterogeneous the population is. This attribute is calculated as the standard deviation of the agent knowledge stocks. The population may also be characterized by the existence of knowledge centers, namely agents with a higher knowledge stock than the general level of knowledge characterizing the population.

## Actions

### Learning
Agents are continuously engaged in interactive learning activities, that is, learning by imitation and learning by interaction with all the other agents of the population. The interactive learning activity is a one-to-one relation, in the sense that each agent activates $N-1$ learning relations at each step. Each learning relation between agent $i$ and agent $j$ determines a development of the knowledge stock of agent $i$ due to imitation ($\Delta K_{ij,imitation}$) and interaction ($\Delta K_{ij,interaction}$).

The effectiveness of the learning processes is influenced by geographical and cognitive proximity between the two interacting agents. Geographical proximity is assumed to enhance learning processes. This assumption is coherent with a large body of literature claiming that agents that are spatially concentrated will benefit from knowledge externalities (see 'Proximity and learning' above). Hence, $\Delta K_{ij,imitation}$ and $\Delta K_{ij,interaction}$ decrease with the increasing geographical distance between agents. Moreover, learning by interaction is assumed to develop higher knowledge stocks than learning by imitation, given the geographical distance. Since learning by interaction requires both parts to be intentionally involved in the relations and to cooperate to develop new knowledge and, on the contrary, learning by imitation occurs without any explicit interaction and coordination between firms (Maskell, 2001b), it is reasonable to assume that the development of knowledge stocks is less in the absence of cooperation and commitment, that is, when the learning process is by imitation.

Cognitive proximity influences the two learning processes in different ways. Effective learning by interaction is accomplished by maintaining a sufficient cognitive distance while securing some cognitive proximity. Consider a highly erudite person who talks with an unknowledgeable person: the interaction is not fruitful because they do not understand each other. Again, think of two historians with knowledge of the same period (say, Ancient Rome); even though they work together, they cannot learn from each other. But if one is experienced in history, while the other is an engineer, the interaction is more likely to develop new knowledge, for example, about how the ancient Romans would build an aqueduct. The same holds true for firms: the interaction between two consulting firms both providing software solutions in accounting is not fruitful because they have similar capabilities and nothing new to be shared. In contrast, the interaction between the consulting firm and a firm providing intelligent information and communication technologies (ICTs) solutions may create new knowledge such as a decision support system for accounting. Therefore, an inverted 'U' relationship is used to model the relationship between learning by interaction ($\Delta K_{ij,interaction}$) and cognitive distance. This relationship is coherent with the literature review, as presented in 'Proximity and learning' above.

Learning by imitation takes place when there is a cognitive distance. In particular, the knowledge stock due to learning by imitation is assumed to increase as the cognitive distance rises. This particular relationship is considered, given that imitation can potentially occur even if firms' knowledge stocks are different. What the firm will learn will depend on the firm's absorptive capacity (Cohen and Levinthal, 1990).

In particular, we use the following functions:

$$\Delta K_{ij\,imitation} = \frac{\left|K_j - K_i\right|}{K_i} \cdot \frac{1}{(d)^\alpha} \qquad , \text{if } K_j > K_i, \qquad (10.2)$$

otherwise $\Delta K_{ij\ imitation} = 0$.

$$\Delta K_{ij\ interaction} = \left\{ \frac{\beta |K_j - K_i|}{K_i} - \left( e^{\frac{\delta |K_j - K_i|}{K_i}} - 1 \right) \right\} \cdot \frac{1}{(d)^\gamma} \quad \text{if } \Delta K_{ij,\ interaction} > 0, \qquad (10.3)$$

otherwise, $\Delta K_{ij,interaction} = 0$.

Note that $d$ is the geographical distance between the agents $i$ and $|K_j - K_i|$ is the cognitive distance $(d_c)$ between the agents $i$ and $j$. Figures 10.1 and 10.2 depict the two functions where $\alpha = 1/2$, $\beta = 3$, $\delta = 1.2$, $\gamma = 1/4$ and $K_i = 1,000$.

The absorptive capacity of agent $i$ when he/she interacts with $j$ $(A_{ij})$ is computed the following:

$$A_{ij} = \frac{K_i}{K_i + K_j} . \qquad (10.4)$$

According to this function, the absorptive capacity is a number between 0 and 1 and is highest for the agent with the highest knowledge stock. In fact, we assume that an agent with a minor knowledge stock (e.g., a novice in a given area) will absorb less than a more knowledgeable and experienced agent, because the novice does not have an already assimilated mental map with which to interpret the new incoming information.

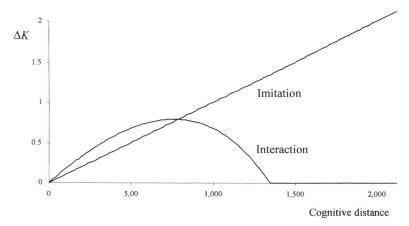

*Figure 10.1 The influence of the cognitive distance on $\Delta K$*

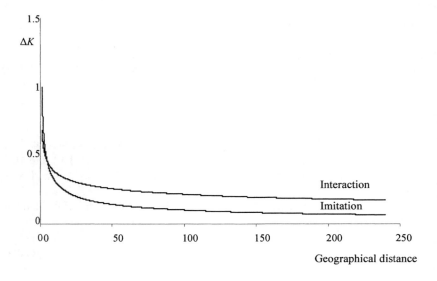

*Figure 10.2   The influence of the geographical distance on ΔK*

The final expression of the development of the knowledge stock for agent *i* when it interacts with *j* is the result of learning by imitation, learning by interaction, and the agent's absorptive capacity. It is calculated as follows:

$$\Delta K_{ij} = A_{ij} \cdot \Delta K_{ij,imitation} + A_{ij} \cdot \Delta K_{ij,interaction} \qquad (10.5)$$

**Developing knowledge stock**
As a consequence of learning activities, each agent increases its knowledge stock. At each step the value of $K_i$ is updated by adding the quantity of knowledge stock resulting from the learning by imitation and learning by interaction. Thus, the knowledge stock of agent *i* is updated as follows:

$$K_i(t+1) = K_i(t) + \sum_{\substack{j=1 \\ j \neq i}}^{N} \Delta K_{ij} \qquad (10.6)$$

**Choosing a new position**
Each agent *i* selects a position in the grid among the possible adjacent cells at each step (Figure 10.3). The agent will choose the position  (g) that maximizes his/her $CA_i$. Therefore, the agent computes the $CA_i$ for every new position including the current one and then chooses the position that ensures the highest value. Therefore, the new position is determined as follows:

$P_{i,t+1}(x, y) = g$ such that $CA_i(g) = \text{Max} \{CA_i(1), \dots, CA_i(8), CA_i(P_{i,t})\}$. (10.7)

| | | | |
|---|---|---|---|
| 1 | 2 | 3 | |
| 8 | $P_{i,t}$ | 4 | |
| 7 | 6 | 5 | |
| | | | |

*Figure 10.3 Possible new positions of the agent in the grid*

**Moving to the selected position**
At each step the agent moves into a new selected position.

**Measures**

**The emergence of spatial clusters**
Spatial clusters of agents will emerge from a random spatial distribution of agents when the agents that move on the grid searching for their preferred position assume a stable position, and are arranged in groups of two or more agents. In this situation, agents have no incentive to change their position. On the contrary, a clustering behavior does not emerge when agents continuously move around on the grid and/or assume a stand-alone stable position.

**Description of the pattern of spatial clusters**
Once spatial clusters have emerged, we can rely on measures that describe the emergent pattern of the clusters. The characteristics of the pattern are assessed using the following measures:

1. number of clusters;
2. average cluster size;
3. standard deviation of cluster size;
4. largest cluster size; and
5. smallest cluster size.

**Knowledge development**
We compute the following measures:

1. level of knowledge of the population (equal to the average of the knowledge stocks of agents);
2. highest knowledge stock; and
3. lowest knowledge stock.

**Sequencing of the Events and Simulation Steps**

At the start of the simulation, it is necessary to establish a specified number of agents and to assign characteristics to each agent, namely the starting position in the grid (randomly assigned) and the starting value of the knowledge stock (drawn at random from a uniform distribution). Subsequently, the simulation is updated according to the following steps:

1.  compute for the agent $i$ the value of $CA_i$ for all possible new positions including the current one;
2.  choose the position that maximizes $CA_i$;
3.  move agent $i$ into the new position;
4.  update the value of $K_i$;
5.  repeat actions (1) through (4) until all agents have gone through that process;
6.  repeat steps (1) through (4) for as many simulated time steps as specified; and
7.  compute the measures.

The number of simulation time steps is defined by assuming a value great enough to ensure the emergence of spatial clusters of agents.

## SIMULATION ANALYSIS

The model above is used to study the process of firms' geographical clustering based on knowledge externalities. First, we are interested to observe whether agents tend to cluster. Then, we shall provide answers to the following research questions:

1.  How does the starting heterogeneity of the population influence the geographical clustering process?
2.  Does the existence of knowledge centers affect the geographical clustering process?

To address the first issue, we ran the model with 30 agents. These are randomly positioned on the grid and have the starting knowledge stock ($K_{i,0}$), which is drawn at random from a uniform distribution with mean 1,000 and standard deviation 5.8 (i.e., Uniform (990; 1,010)).

To answer the first research question, we ran the model with a higher starting value for the population heterogeneity. To model this, the starting knowledge stocks ($K_{i,0}$) are drawn at random from a uniform distribution with the same mean (1,000) but a higher standard deviation (115.5). The considered distribution is the Uniform (800; 1,200). To answer the second research question, we ran the model with the existence of one agent characterized by a higher starting knowledge stock ($K_c$) than the population mean. The starting knowledge stock of the remaining 29 agents was drawn at random from the uniform distribution (990; 1,010). In particular, we considered three different configurations with three increasing $K_c$ , that is, 5, 000; 12,500; and 100,000.

In all the experiments the simulation time was equal to 1,000 and the number of replications was 30. The replications differed with regard to the starting spatial configurations of the agents on the grid. The simulation results are shown in Table 10.1, where the mean and standard deviation of the measures are calculated over the 30 replications.

In all the experiments, spatial clusters of agents emerged within the simulation time. The results were influenced by the starting spatial configuration of the agents. However, the important point about this and similar models is not that they generate a particular pattern of clusters, but that in every case, for a specific set of parameters, some degree of clustering always emerges (Gilbert, 2005).

Therefore, the results show that knowledge externalities motivate firms to form GCs. Agents prefer to be co-located rather than scattered, because in clusters they can improve their competitive advantage based on knowledge stock. Note that clusters emerge as the spontaneous results of each individual agent's decisions, so agents form clusters because this spatial configuration enhances their learning and consequently their knowledge stocks.

**The Influence of Heterogeneity**

To analyze the influence of heterogeneity, we compared the results of the experiments with $K_{i,0}$ = Unif (990; 1,010) and $K_{i,0}$ = Unif (800; 1,200). Heterogeneity influences the emergent pattern of clusters. In particular, the number of clusters increases by more than 30 percent, the average cluster size decreases (26 percent), and the standard deviation of cluster size also reduces (38 percent). Furthermore, the values of the smallest and the largest cluster size diminish (28 and 23 percent, respectively)[1]. Agents tend to form more groups of smaller sizes.

This outcome suggests that when there is greater heterogeneity, agents are less willing to co-locate. A similar behavior has been studied by Shaver and Flyer (2000), who found that when agents differ in terms of technology, human capital and other assets, those with a higher knowledge stock will

Table 10.1 Simulation results

| Heterogeneity | $K_{i,0}$ = Unif [990; 1,010] | | $K_{i,0}$ = Unif [800; 1,200] | | $K_{i,0}$ = Unif [990; 1,010] | | $K_{i,0}$ = Unif [990; 1,010] | | $K_{i,0}$ = Unif [990; 1,010] | |
|---|---|---|---|---|---|---|---|---|---|---|
| Knowledge center agent ($K_c$) | Absent | | Absent | | $K_c$ = 5,000 | | $K_c$ = 12,500 | | $K_c$ = 100,000 | |
| | Mean | Std | Mean | Std | Mean | Std | Mean | Std | Mean | Std |
| Number of clusters | 6.0 | 1.3 | 8.0 | 1.1 | 3.4 | 1.4 | 3.1 | 1.4 | 2.8 | 1.1 |
| Average cluster size | 5.3 | 1.3 | 3.9 | 0.6 | 11.2 | 7.1 | 12.9 | 8.2 | 13.4 | 7.3 |
| Std deviation of cluster size | 3.4 | 1.5 | 2.1 | 0.9 | 9.9 | 3.0 | 10.8 | 3.2 | 12.3 | 3.5 |
| Largest cluster size | 10.9 | 3.0 | 7.8 | 2.2 | 22.3 | 4.4 | 23.7 | 4.7 | 24.6 | 3.6 |
| Smallest cluster size | 2.6 | 1.3 | 2.0 | 0.3 | 2.5 | 2.3 | 2.1 | 2.2 | 2.3 | 2.2 |
| Average knowledge stock | 1,544.1 | 170.1 | 2,271.2 | 157.9 | 3,384.8 | 564.2 | 3,871.7 | 556.8 | 6,953.5 | 521.8 |
| Highest knowledge stock | 4,218.2 | 1,301.9 | 5,197.7 | 1,315.6 | 18,882.0 | 2,797.8 | 27,676.8 | 2,806.4 | 116,590.9 | 2,721.3 |
| Lowest knowledge stock | 1,218.4 | 51.2 | 1,697.1 | 57.8 | 1,577.7 | 293.5 | 1,646.9 | 336.8 | 1,648.7 | 323.9 |

prefer to locate at a distance from other firms, while those with less knowledge stock will tend to agglomerate. With regard to knowledge development, the average, the highest, and the lowest value of knowledge stock all increase with the heterogeneity of population.

**The Role of Knowledge Clusters**

To study the influence of the existence of a knowledge center, we compared the results of the first experiments with those of the last three. Regarding the characteristics of the pattern of clusters, the results show that as $K_c$ increases, the number of clusters tends to decrease, and the average cluster size, the standard deviation of cluster size, and the largest and the smallest values of cluster size increase. Agents tend to group in few clusters: one of them is very much bigger than the others. The knowledge center is then able to attract a large number of agents. Most agents find that it is beneficial to be close to the knowledge center. This outcome is consistent with the empirical evidence of GCs near universities, research centers, scientific parks, and firms with a highly innovative capacity.

The existence of the knowledge center also influences the knowledge development process. In particular, the average, the highest, and the lowest values of knowledge stock increase. We also computed the average of the knowledge stock without considering the agent $K_c$, because its value strongly affects the average.[2] The same trend of results was achieved. With the existence of $K_c$, the population is able to develop a greater knowledge stock that increases with the $K_c$ value.

## CONCLUSIONS

This chapter examined the concept of knowledge externalities in agglomeration economies, namely the knowledge-based benefits that co-located firms can gain and that motivate them to form GCs. These are now receiving renewed attention because in a knowledge-based economy, competitive success is related to the ability of firms to create and increase their knowledge, rather than pursuing static efficiency.

Knowledge externalities have been associated with two specific learning processes, and have been analyzed by adopting a firm-level perspective. Therefore, this chapter fills two gaps in the literature, namely the study of the central role of learning in the clustering process and a prevailing tendency to adopt a system-level perspective. We have considered that firms can benefit due to learning by imitation and learning by interaction. The extent to which these learning processes develop knowledge stocks is influenced by two dimensions of proximity: geographical and cognitive.

In particular, we have developed an ABS model of the geographical clustering of firms to investigate whether such clustering results from the existence of knowledge externalities. This approach is particularly valuable because it permits GCs to be studied as complex adaptive systems of interacting agents. In particular, we consider that it is the agent's individual decisions and the interactions among the agents that determine the emergence of the geographical cluster itself.

Agents have to maximize their competitive advantage by choosing their location in the environment that assures them the highest net benefits in terms of knowledge stock. The development of the knowledge stock depends on both the interactive learning processes and the agent's absorptive capacity. The effectiveness of learning by imitation and interaction in terms of increased knowledge stock is influenced by geographical and cognitive distances among agents. The aim of the simulation has been to observe the emergence of spatial clusters of agents.

The simulation results showed that agents tend to cluster geographically when knowledge externalities exist. The characteristics of the emergent pattern of clusters are mainly influenced by the starting spatial configuration of the agents. The influences of the heterogeneity of firms' knowledge stocks and of the existence of knowledge centers have also been investigated using the simulation. The results have shown that the geographical clustering process is largely influenced in terms of the emergent pattern of clusters. When there is notable heterogeneity, agents tend to form more groups of smaller sizes. When a knowledge center is located in the geographical space, agents tend to be attracted by it, so forming a big cluster and leaving out a very few agents arranged in small groups. This outcome is consistent with the birth of GCs around universities, research centers or firms with a highly innovative capacity.

Our model presents some limitations. It considers knowledge externalities associated with two specific GC learning processes. In some industries, however, collective learning may be more representative of innovation diffusions than the considered learning processes. Therefore, we should also introduce this learning process in the agent-based model. Furthermore, we do not distinguish between tacit and codified knowledge even though the transfer process of the two kinds of knowledge may differ. For example, the tacit knowledge to be transferred requires a geographical proximity much more than does codified knowledge. The various dimensions of proximity may influence the learning of tacit and codified knowledge in different ways. Investigating in this direction could be an interesting successive step of the research. The knowledge stock of firms also needs to be better modeled.

Different kinds of knowledge stocks should be introduced to distinguish agents not only in terms of the amount of knowledge stock but also of the kind of knowledge stock they possess (for example, in manufacturing, in marketing, and so on). Further attributes characterizing the firm should be added, for example, the resources, the products, and the markets. This would allow the strategic behavior of the firm to be better modeled.

Further limitations concern the proximity included in the model. We consider only geographical and cognitive proximities but we are aware that organizational, social and institutional proximity also play a key role in interactive learning. In particular, we think that the influence of organizational proximity should be much more closely investigated because it could be useful to explain some recent changes that GCs are undergoing, such as the emergence of firms taking a leader position. In the next step of the research we shall include the influence of organizational proximity on the learning processes. In this regard, a further extension of our model will be to introduce the different dimensions of proximity and examine which out of the possible combinations of proximity determine geographical clustering. The relationships between the various proximities can also be investigated.

Finally, we use specific relationships between learning and proximity. Most have been based on the literature but others have been assumed because to our knowledge there is no evidence in the literature. Thus, the assumed relationships should be validated by empirical research.

## NOTES

1. Differences in results are significant with $p < 0.001$.
2. The following values are obtained: 2,857.8; 3,050.9; and 3,172.8 for $K_c$ equal to 5,000, 12,500 and 100,000, respectively.

## REFERENCES

Albino, V. Carbonara, N. and Giannoccaro, I. (2005), 'Industrial Districts as Complex Adaptive Systems: Agent-Based Models of Emergent Phenomena', in Karlsson, C., Johansson, B., and Stough, R. (eds), *Industrial Clusters and Inter-firm Networks*, Cheltenham, UK and Northampton, MA, USA: Edward Elgar, pp. 73–82.

Albino, V., Carbonara, N. and Giannoccaro, I. (2006), 'Innovation within Industrial Districts: An Agent-Based Model', *International Journal of Production Economics*, **194** (1), 30–45.

Albino, V., Carbonara, N. and Giannoccaro, I. (2007a), 'Competitive Advantage of Geographical Clusters: A Complexity Science Approach and an Agent-based Simulation Study', in Rennard, J.P. (ed.), *Handbook of Research on Nature Inspired Computing for Economy and Management*, France: Idea Group, pp. 317–34.

Albino, V., Carbonara, N. and Giannoccaro, I. (2007b), 'Supply Chain Cooperation within Industrial districts: A Simulation Analysis', *European Journal of Operational Research*, **177** (1), 261–80.

Albino, V. and Schiuma, G. (2003), 'New Forms of Knowledge Creation and Diffusion in the Industrial District of Matera–Altamura–Santeramo', in Belussi, F., Gottardi, G. and Rullani, E. (eds), *The Technological Evolution of Industrial Districts*, Boston, MA: Kluwer Academic.

Audretsch, D.B. and Feldman, M.P. (1996), 'R&D Spillovers and the Geography of Innovation and Production', *American Economic Review*, **86** (3), 630–40.

Axelrod, R. (1997), 'Advancing the Art of Simulation in Social Sciences', in Conte, R., Hegselmann, R. and Terna, P. (eds), *Simulating Social Phenomena*, Berlin: Springer, pp. 21–40.

Aydalot, P. and Keeble, D. (eds) (1988), *High Technology Industry and Innovative Environments: The European Experience*, London: Routledge.

Baptista, R. (2000), 'Do Innovations Diffuse Faster Within Geographical Clusters?', *International Journal of Industrial Organization*, **18**, 515–35.

Barney, J.B. (1991), 'Firm Resources And Sustained Competitive Advantage', *Journal of Management*, **17**, 99–120.

Bartik, T.J. (1985), 'Business Location Decisions in the United States: Estimates of the Effects of Unionization, Taxes, and Other Characteristics of States', *Journal of Business and Economic Statistics*, **3** (1), 14–22.

Becattini, G. (1990), 'The Marshallian industrial district as a socio-economic notion', in Becattini, G., Pyke, F. and Sengenberger, W. (eds), *Industrial Distircts and Inter-firm co-operation in Italy*, Geneva: International Institute for Labour Studies, pp. 37-52.

Belussi, F. and Arcangeli, F. (1998), 'A Typology of Networks: Flexible and Evolutionary Firms', *Research Policy*, 27 (4), 415–28.

Boero, R. and Squazzoni, F. (2002), 'Economic Performance, Inter-Firm Relations and Local Institutional Engineering in a Computational Prototype of Industrial Districts', *Journal of Artificial Societies and Social Simulation*, **5**, (1), http://jasss.soc.surrey.ac.uk/5/1/1.html.

Boschma, R. (2004), 'Does Geographical Proximity Favour Innovation?', Paper presented at the 4th Congress on Proximity Economics, Marseilles, June 17–18.

Boschma, R. (2005), 'Proximity and Innovation: A Critical Assessment', *Regional Studies*, **39** (1), 61–75.

Brenner, T. (2001), 'Simulating the Evolution of Localised Industrial Clusters – An Identification of the Basic Mechanism', *Journal of Artificial Societies and Social Simulation*, **4** (3), http://www.soc.surrey.ac.uk/JASSS/4/3/4.html>.

Breschi, S., and Lissoni, F. (2001), 'Knowledge Spillovers and Local Innovation Systems: A Critical Survey', *Industrial and Corporate Change*, **10**, 975–1005.

Brusco, S. (1990), 'The Idea of the Industrial District: Its Genesis', in Becattini, G., Pyke, F. and Sengenberger, W. (eds), *Industrial Districts and Inter-Firm Co-Operation in Italy*, Geneva: International Institute for Labour Studies, pp.10–19.

Brusco, S., Minerva, T., Poli, I. and Solinas, G. (2002), 'Un Automa Cellulare per lo Studio del Distretto Industriale', *Politica Economica*, **18** (2), 147–92.

Camagni, R.P. (1989), 'Cambiamento Tecnologico, Milieu Locale e Reti di Imprese: Una Teoria Dinamica dello Spazio Economico', *Economia e Politica Industriale*, **64**, 209–36.

Camagni, R. (1995), 'Global Network and Local Milieu: Towards a Theory of Economic Space', in Conti, S., Malecki, E. and Oinas, P. (eds), *The Industrial*

*Enterprise and Its Environment: Spatial Perspectives*, Aldershot: Avebury, pp. 195–214.

Capello, R. and Faggian, A. (2005), 'Collective Learning and Relational Capital in Local Innovation Processes', *Regional Studies*, **39** (1), 75–87.

Carley, K.M. and Gasser, L. (2000), 'Computational Organizational Theory', in Weiss, G. (ed.), *Multi-Agent Systems. A Modern Approach to Distributed Artificial Intelligence*, Cambridge, MA: MIT Press, pp. 299–330.

Carlton, D.W. (1983), 'The Location and Employment Choices of New Firms: An Econometric Model with Discrete and Continuous Endogenous Variables', *Review of Economics and Statistics*, **65**, 440–49.

Cohen, W. and Levinthal, D. (1990), 'Absorptive Capacity: A New Perspective on Learning and Innovation', *Administrative Science Quarterly*, **35**, 128–52.

Cohendet, P. and Llerena, P. (1997), 'Learning, Technical Change, and Public Policy: How to Create and Exploit Diversity', in Edquist, C. (ed.), *Systems of Innovation. Technologies, Institutions and Organizations*, London: Pinter, pp. 223–41.

David, P. and Rosenbloom, J. (1990), 'Marshallian Factor Market Externalities and the Dynamics of Industrial Location', *Journal of Urban Economics*, **28**, 349–70.

Decarolis, D.M. and Deeds, D.L. (1999), 'The Impact of Stocks and Flows of Organizational Knowledge on Firm Performance: An Empirical Investigation of the Biotechnology Industry', *Strategic Management Journal*, **20**, 953–68.

Dei Ottati, G. (1994), 'Trust, Interlinking Transactions and Credit in the Industrial District', *Cambridge Journal of Economy*, **18** (6), 529–46.

Epstein, M.E., Axtell R. 1996, *Growing Artificial Societies: Social Science from the Bottom-up*, Washington, DC: Brookings Institution Press and Cambridge, MA: MIT Press.

Ernst, D. (2002), 'Global Production Networks and the Changing Geography of Innovation Systems: Implications for Developing Countries', *Economic Innovation and New Technology*, **11** (6), 497–523.

Fioretti, G. (2001), 'Information Structure and Behaviour of a Textile Industrial District', *Journal of Artificial Societies and Social Simulation*, **4** (4), http://www.soc.surrey.ac.uk/JASSS/4/4/1.html.

Fioretti, G. (2006), 'Agent-Based Models of Industrial Clusters and Districts', in Tavidze, A. (ed.), *Progress in Economics Research*, New York: Nova Science, pp. 125–42.

Gertler, M.S. (1995), 'Being There: Proximity, Organisation and Culture in the Development and Adoption of Advanced Manufacturing Technologies', *Economic Geography*, **71**, 1–26.

Gilbert, N. (2005), 'Agent-Based Simulation: Dealing with Complexity', http://cress.soc.surrey.ac.uk/resources/ABSS%20%20dealing%20with%20complexity-1-1.pdf.

Giuliani, E. (2005), 'The Structure of Cluster Knowledge Networks: Uneven and Selective, not Pervasive and Collective', DRUID Working Papers 05–11, Copenhagen Business School, Department of Industrial Economics and Strategy/Aalborg University, Department of Business Studies.

Giuliani, E. and Bell, M. (2005), 'The Micro-Determinants of Meso-Level Learning and Innovation: Evidence from a Chilean Wine Cluster', *Research Policy*, **34** (1), 47–68.

Grant, R.M. (1997), 'The Knowledge-Based View of the Firm: Implications for Management in Practice', *Long Range Planning*, **30** (3), 450–54.

Hamel, G. and Prahalad, C.K. (1994), *Competing for the Future*. Boston, MA: Harvard Business School Press.

Head, K., Ries, J. and Swenson, D. (1995), 'Agglomeration Benefits and Location Choice: Evidence from Japanese Manufacturing Investment in the United States', *Journal of International Economics*, **38**, 223–47.

Howells, J.R.L. (2002), 'Tacit Knowledge, Innovation and Economic Geography', *Urban Studies*, **39**, 871–84.

Jaffe, A.B., Trajtenberg, M. and Henderson, R. (1993), 'Geographic Localization and Knowledge Spillovers as Evidence by Patent Citations', *Quarterly Journal of Economics*, **108**, 577–98.

Kauffman, S.A. (1993) *The Origins of Orders: Self-Organization and Selection in Evolution*. New York/Oxford: Oxford University Press.

Keeble, D., Lawson, C., Moore, B. and Wilkinson, F. (1999), 'Collective Learning Processes, Networking and "Institutional Thickness" in the Cambridge Region', *Regional Studies*, **33**, 319–31.

Krogh, G. and Vicari, S. (1992), 'L'Approccio Autopoietico All'Apprendimento Strategico Sperimentale', *Economia e Politica Industriale*, **74/76**, 67–87.

Krugman, P.R. (1991), *Geography and Trade*, Cambridge, MA: MIT Press.

Lane, D. (2002), 'Complexity and Local Interactions: Towards a Theory of Industrial Districts, Complexity and Industrial Districts', in Curzio, A.Q. and Fortis, M. (eds), *Complexity and Industrial Clusters*, Heidelberg: Physica-Verlag, pp. 65–82.

Leonard-Barton, D. (1995), *Wellsprings of Knowledge*, Boston, MA: Harvard Business School Press.

Lipparini, A. (1998), 'L'apprendimento relazionale', *Sviluppo & Organizzazione*, **66**, 75–89.

Lipparini, A. and Lorenzoni, G. (1996), 'Le Organizzazioni ad Alta Intensità Relazionale. Riflessioni sui Processi di Learning by Interacting nelle Aree ad Alta Concentrazione di Imprese', *L'Industria*, **4**, 817–39.

Maillat, D., Quevit, M. and Senn, L. (eds) (1993), *Réseaux d'Innovation et Milieux Innovateurs: Un Pari pour le Développement Régional*, Neuchâtel: EDES.

Malerba, F. (1992), 'Learning by Firms and Incremental Technical Change', *Economic Journal*, **102**, 845–59.

Malmberg, A. and Maskell, P. (1999), 'The Competitiveness of Firms and Regions. "Ubiquitification" and the Importance of Localized Learning', *European Urban and Regional Studies*, **6**, 9–25.

Malmberg, A. and Maskell, P. (2004), 'The Elusive Concept of Localization Economies: Towards a Knowledge-Based Theory of Spatial Clustering', in Grabher, G. and Powell, W.W. (eds), *Networks,* Edward Elgar Series Critical Studies in Economic Institutions, Cheltenham, UK and Northampton, MA, USA: Edward Elgar, pp. 429–49.

Markusen, A. (1996), 'Sticky Places in Slippery Space: A Typology of Industrial Districts', *Economic Geography*, **72** (3), 293–313.

Marshall, A. (1919), *Industry and Trade*, London: Macmillan.

Marshall, A. (1920) *Principles of Economics*, London: Macmillan.

Maskell, P. (2001a), 'Knowledge Creation and Diffusion in Geographical Clusters', *International Journal of Innovation Management*, **5** (2), 213–37.

Maskell, P. (2001b), 'Towards a Knowledge-Based Theory of the Geographical Cluster', *Industrial and Corporate Change*, **10**, 921–43.

Pinch, S., Henry, N., Jenkins, M. and Tallman, S. (2003), 'From "Industrial Districts" to "Knowledge Clusters": A Model of Knowledge Dissemination and Competitive

Advantage in Industrial Agglomerations', *Journal of Economic Geography*, **3**, 373–88.

Piore, M. and Sabel, C.F. (1984), *The Second Industrial Divide*, New York: Basic Books.

Porter, M. (1998), 'Clusters and the New Economics of Competition', *Harvard Business Review*, **76** (6), 77–90.

Pouder, R. and St John, C.H. (1996), 'Hot Spots and Blind Spots: Geographical Clusters of Firms and Innovation', *Academy of Management Review*, **21** (4), 1192–225.

Powell, W.W. (1987), 'Hybrid Organizational Arrangements: New Form or Transitional Development', *California Management Review*, **19** (4), 67–87.

Prusak, L. (1997), *Knowledge in Organizations*, Washington, DC: Butterworth-Heinemann.

Rauch, J.E. (1993), 'Does History Matter Only when It Matters Little? The Case of City-Industry Location', *Quarterly Journal of Economics*, **108**, 843–67.

Reed, R. and Defillippi, R.J. (1990), 'Causal Ambiguity, Barriers to Imitation, and Sustainable Competitive Advantage', *Academy of Management Review*, **15** (1), 88–102.

Romer, P.M. (1986), 'Increasing Returns and Long-Run Growth', *Journal of Political Economy*, **94** (5), 1002–37.

Saviotti, P.P. (1996), *Technological Evolution, Variety and the Economy*, Cheltenham, UK and Brookfield, US: Edward Elgar.

Shaver, M.J. and Flyer, F. (2000), 'Agglomeration Economies, Firm Heterogeneity, and Foreign Direct Investment in the United States', *Strategic Management Journal*, **21**, 1175–93.

Spender, J.C. (1996), 'Making Knowledge the Basis of a Dynamic Theory of the Firm', *Strategic Management Journal*, **17**, 45–62.

Tallman, S., Jenkins, M., Henry, N. and Pinch, S. (2004), 'Knowledge, Clusters, and Competitive Advantage', *Academy of Management Review*, **29** (2), 258–71.

Tesfatsion, L. and Judd, K. (eds) (2006), *Handbook of Computational Economics*, Vol. 2: *Agent-based Computational Economics*, North-Holland: Elsevier.

Van Canneyt, M. and Klampfe, F. (2005), *User's Manual of Free Pascal*, http://www.freepascal.org.

Weiss, G., 2000. Multiagent Systems. A modern approach to distributed artificial intelligence. Cambridge, MA: The MIT Press.

Winter, S.G. (1987), 'Knowledge and Competence as Strategic Assets', in Teece, D.J. (ed.), *The Competitive Challenge: Strategies for Industrial Innovation and Renewal*, New York: Harper & Row, pp. 159–184.

Zhang, J. (2002), 'Growing Silicon Valley on a Landscape: An Agent-Based Approach to High-Tech Industrial Clusters', *Journal of Evolutionary Economics*, **13** (5), 529–48.

# 11. Assiduous Firms in a 'Learning Region': The Case of East Württemberg, Germany

## Waldemar Pfoertsch and Reha Tözün

## INTRODUCTION

'[Software is] far more like lettuce sitting in a warehouse than gold bars in a safe':[1] in other words, each technology has a shelf life and technological superiority is a temporary feat that wanes in the face of competition. This process is driven by the incessant search for fresh products and processes that inspire new technologies, often independently of any demand signals from customers (Marx, 1976). In such an environment, the effort invested by firms in technology and knowledge development, which may appear to a casual observer as an issue of choice, manifests itself as an imperative for economic survival and success – technology is the primary determinant of competitive advantage (Porter, 1998).

A region's economic well-being, on the other hand, is dependent on the performance of its resident enterprises and thereby, locations are economically influenced by the competition among technologies and ensuing technological change (Storper and Walker, 1989). This reciprocity between economy and technology was recognized as a fundamental trait of capitalist economy by Schumpeter, who famously christened the end-effect thereof as 'creative destruction' (Schumpeter, 1942). New technologies change the boundary conditions of competition, causing a state of flux through which the winners of the game are redefined. Naturally, this state of continuous change is of great interest for economics, management and economic geography literatures. Yet, in spite of the emphasis the authors so very often put on high-technology industries, tech-based competition is independent of the end products' complexity, and creation, renewal and absorption of knowledge are dictated to all industries in equal measure (Maskell, 1998; Porter, 1998; Gertler, 2003).

Through a geographical lens, attention converges on how to identify and explain spatiality of innovativeness; for there is little need to question the fact that a locality's rise and fall is clearly linked to its capacity for knowledge production (OECD, 1999). Economic geographers thereby have dealt with technological change in connection with the spatiality of innovation, knowledge creation and dissemination mechanisms. An influential insight of Alfred Marshall's writings on the industrial districts of England was how knowledge was shared ('knowledge was in the air') and (re)produced ('if one man starts a new idea, it is taken up by others and combined with suggestions of their own') in a location (Marshall, 1925 p. 271). Similarly and not surprisingly, collective learning processes were also an important aspect of the industrial districts model that was developed after the 1980s, especially for incremental innovation, and the systems of innovation models that followed, eloquently discussed the theoretical aspects of the social dimension of knowledge production (Asheim, 1996). The primary factor of existence and survival for regional agglomerations in innovation systems was declared to be the innovative capacity that is driven by relational and collective learning mechanisms (Malmberg, 1997; Cooke, 1998; Lundvall, 1998; Lundvall and Maskell, 2000). All this is naturally a step away from the neoclassical writings on economic geography, as it renounces the idea that individuals are solely profit-maximizing actors, and embraces the fact that economic relations are in fact socially embedded (Granovetter, 1985). Innovations are thus seen as more than mere products of personal or enterprise resources and capabilities alone, but are outcomes of interactions among actors in formal and informal exchanges.

The spatiality of social relations affects the innovation-inducing relations, as well. The knowledge-production processes that incorporate exchanges of non-codifiable, tacit information have a social dimension, which requires geographical proximity in order to function at its best or even to exist at all. To begin with, a shared cultural basis – shared language, values, norms – that lubricates the relational mechanisms can be developed and reproduced in groups where there is regular personal contact and shared experience. Furthermore, the personal contacts that embed exchanges of tacit information are more effective and efficient with face-to-face (F2F) interaction, which demands geographical proximity (Storper and Venables, 2004). This basic postulate – geography enables the mechanisms that produce knowledge, hence it is indispensable – is the core of the learning regions' literature that developed through the 1990s. Here the onus is on spatially embedded mechanisms of knowledge-producing relationships and their role in regions' continued economic vitality (Asheim, 1996; Maskell and Malmberg, 1999). Florida (1995 p. 528) defines learning regions as locations that 'function as collectors and repositories of knowledge and ideas, and provide an underlying environment or infrastructure which facilitates the flow of knowledge, ideas and learning'. These infrastructures are of soft (shared cognitive and social basis) and hard type (research establishments, regional networks), which help enterprises blend the contextual and codified types of knowledge. In this sense, a functional learning region is a socially embedded melting pot for the local and global for intra- and inter-firm cooperation and exchange (Asheim, 1996, 2006). If and when a region manages to build effective infrastructures to learning ends, the cumulative causality of enterprises' technological dynamism and resulting commercial success can potentially cause windfall effects and a self-sustaining system by attracting new customers, incoming investment and talented individuals (Myrdal, 1957; Saxenian et al., 2002). Furthermore, learning is instrumental in achieving sustenance and survival by helping a location to avoid lock-in situations (Asheim, 1996). Although the starting-point was geographical proximity in a learning regions concept, some authors soon acknowledged that the knowledge-producing contacts are not solely of local character, but have, in fact, a crucial supra-regional dimension in order to avoid cognitive dead-end situations (Bathelt et al., 2004).

The categories of knowledge are important elements of the relational learning literature. Two main groups are identified: one with a codifiable nature, where knowledge can be effectively expressed in common structural terms and hence is transferable and less location dependent. The second is of the so-called 'tacit' type, diffused in the actions (doings) of individuals and which has not been converted into explicit expressions – people know but cannot tell – at that point in time (Polanyi, 1983; Nonaka and Takeuchi, 1995; Gertler, 2003). It is preserved and nurtured at a level deeper than the conscious and often incorporates the latest knowledge that is not codified yet (Storper and Venables, 2004). Tacit knowledge has its 'social content' in habits, routines and values shared by groups of people that take part in 'doing'. Akin to oral histories, it is largely carried across time and space by the members of a community, and the formal and informal institutional structures in a region establish conditions that enable its sharing and re-creation (Storper, 1997). The intended and unintended meetings of the actors with the same or related specializations are perceived as enablers of upgrading and reproducing tacit knowledge and sources of additional innovation possibilities (Malmberg and Maskell, 2002).

Regional demand, that is, the customers in geographical proximity, has an overwhelming and deterministic effect on the competitiveness and development paths of regional economies (Porter, 1998). Whether originating from large private or public enterprises, or from small and medium-sized firms, the demand achieves more than just triggering the spatial augmentation of supply functions. For example, large enterprises can often be found at the center of these regional universes, facilitating the flows of products, services and knowledge through the supply chains that feed their operations and their effect can go deeper than the sum of the yearly regional purchasing volume, inasmuch as creating and shaping entire regional economic spheres (Scott, 1988). Their inputs into the knowledge pools of regions can be substantial, although the exact mechanisms that give way to dissemination of this know-how is dependent on corporate strategies and practices, plus other social and institutional factors. Even when the regional demand they generate is weak, the presence of large firms can be felt through different means. It is a common phenomenon for new businesses to be started by the employees of large firms or through spin-offs,[2] which enable the transfer of especially tacit knowledge outside of large firms' legal and operational boundaries and pave the way for fresh possibilities of interaction and learning, which otherwise could not have existed so unrestrictedly.

The interaction between firms and academic institutions is another potential channel of interactive learning for regions. These institutions often offer a substitute capacity for internal research and development (R&D) and pools of knowledge that the firms can tap in at need. The increasing technological complexity and volatility increase the demand for partners in research who can quickly bring necessary knowledge and skills on board. Small and medium-sized enterprises (SMEs), for example, often utilize their relations with these institutions to deal with shorter timelines and to get assistance with market-bound ideas. The learning path between enterprises and academic institutions is not a one-way street but interactive, and respective knowledge bases and learning capacities play a crucial role in the outcome and continuity of these relations. Institutional mechanisms play their role in causing national and regional disparities, with some regions better endowed with institutionalized relations between enterprises and research establishments (Heidenreich and Krauss, 1998).

Leaning on the preceding theoretical background, the starting premise of this chapter is that all regions host activities that stimulate learning, albeit with regional and industrial differentials. Each enterprise in each region produces or accumulates knowledge, yet there are disparities, in terms of rate of accumulation and utilization. First, for both the enterprises and the academic (or research) establishments, their core knowledge basis and internal knowledge-production skills are their springboard; and knowledge-production is driven as an interplay between internal resources and contacts with 'others'. Indeed, this basis and internal mechanisms equip the enterprise to interact with and to learn from (and with) others. These interactions can be intentional or serendipitous, traded or non-traded, at enterprise level or personal-relations based, transaction based or otherwise; and they can result from interaction with suppliers or customers, private and public research centers, enterprises from related industries and networking institutions. They incorporate exchange of market-, product- or process-related information of varying forms and degrees and the knowledge production in these relations could be the main target or a byproduct. It is unrealistic to seek superiority in one of these aims or mechanisms over others, largely because the variety of examples 'out there' would easily negate it. The enterprises apprehend, requite, process and respond to the various signals received during these interactive processes, which is one of the reasons for different learning and innovation potentials among firms in the same industry and the same location.[3]

Considering the heterogeneous compositions of industrial agglomerations in terms of enterprises, academic and research capacities, public and networking functions and the varied character of enterprise behavior to interaction, regions and regional industries have unevenly knit learning fabrics and divergent innovation paths. For sophisticated high-technology sectors, the air gets even thinner at the regional level in terms of potential partners for learning-inducing relations. Yet, the distances are still important; the knowledge-intensive interactions have a considerable amount of tacitness and they function more effectively and affordably through F2F contacts, whose costs increase with distance (Storper and Venables, 2004). Especially for SMEs, given their limited resources, these costs are a make-or-break type of barrier, but insufficient local resources can still send firms to seek out supra-regional contacts (Porter, 1998; Bathelt et al., 2004). Hence, it is expected that smaller firms choose their busiest 'global pipelines' over short distances, given the condition that desired learning relations are available. At this point, due to their nature as depositories of dense, multifaceted knowledge bases and loci of innovativeness, metropolitan urban regions emerge as likely locations for smaller enterprises to tap into for knowledge (Feldman and Audretsch, 1999). In this context, knowledge links deserve a more rigorous investigation in studies dealing with functional regions, in addition to commuting patterns or supply relations (OECD, 2002).

In the following sections, these hypotheses will be compared to data collected on the optics industry located in the East Württemberg region of Germany (EW). The empirical evidence presented here, which has been collected during the field research conducted for the Economic Development Corporation of East Württemberg (WiRO), deals chiefly with the grouping of SMEs in the optics industry in EW. The qualitative data collected though expert interviews are complemented with secondary resources about the region in general and its optics industry. Fifteen qualitative interviews with manager-owners and high-ranking managers of optics firms, faculty members of Allen University of Applied Sciences, Steinbeis Institute and the PhotonicsBW initiative were conducted in order to sample the relevant parties in the region. The WiRO databank was used as the primary resource to select interview candidates, and the selection process was carried out by considering fields of interest for faculty members and respective product and service sophistication, completed projects and reputation in respective niches for enterprises. The reputation factor was evaluated on the basis of the inputs of WiRO experts and faculty members, who provided up-to-date information about the regional industry. The need to unearth the workings of the relational dimension of learning shifted the emphasis to qualitative inputs and had the aforementioned statistical records been the sole resource of data, very little would have been achieved, since the optics industry is very opaquely represented at the NUTS3 level. The inherent openness and potentiality of expert interview methodology allows a glimpse behind the bare numbers and helps to identify the nature and workings of the relational links. The methodology was especially crucial to understand the motivation behind the enterprises' search for supra-regional links.

Referring back to the learning region premise presented earlier, it is interesting at this point to know the means by which smaller firms seek complementary relational learning channels to access their region's offering, and the geographical scale on which they build these supplementary channels. It is claimed that some SMEs, designated as 'assiduous' in the title of this chapter, seek supra-regional resources to expand their knowledge and skills, in response to insufficient learning resources in their region. Understanding the behavior of these enterprises and the role played by geography in their decisions can provide a more detailed insight into enterprise behavior and regional economic change. Because firms use a mixture of local and global resources to expand their knowledge base, this chapter will examine the range between these two spatial extremes and the solutions devised by firms.

## THE OPTICS INDUSTRY IN THE EW REGION

East-Württemberg (EW) is a relatively less talked about part of the Baden-Württemberg state of Germany (BW), which is a much discussed location in economic geography literature (Figure 11.1). EW covers an area of 2,138 sq. km. and as of 2005 had a population of 452,595. It is composed of two districts, Heidenheim and Ostalbkreis, the latter being the larger of the two. The economy in the region has an industrial focus with a mixture of larger enterprises and SMEs, which has been a familiar pattern in the German economy since the early days of its industrialization (Herrigel, 1996). Other than optics, metal working and treatment, machine building and automotive industries play important economic roles for EW. The optics industry can be divided into two main groups: smaller enterprises and the firms belonging to Carl Zeiss AG, who can claim to have started the industry in EW.

*Figure 11.1    East-Württemberg region, located in Baden-Württemberg state of Germany*

**Carl Zeiss Group**

Carl Zeiss was founded in Jena in 1846 and after a long, successful and innovative period, it was divided into two separate enterprises during the cold war years due to political polarization. For more than four decades the original operation continued in the German Democratic Republic (GDR) as VEB Carl Zeiss JENA, while the new establishment ran as Carl Zeiss AG in the Federal Republic of Germany.[4] The inauguration of the latter was also the starting-point of optics in EW. After the Second World War, Allied Forces decided to relocate a group of Carl Zeiss employees from Jena, which had become East German territory, to Heidenheim – a small town located east of BW state. Eventually, a suitable and empty factory building lured the new Carl Zeiss to nearby Oberkochen, where it is located today (Kogut and Zander, 2000). The unification of Germany triggered the merging process which, starting in 1991, was completed by the total acquisition of the Jenoptik GmbH operations by the Carl Zeiss Group in 1995. The company eventually settled on the Oberkochen location as its sole corporate headquarters after a period when Oberkochen and Jena shared the management responsibilities. Today, the firm operates through a global network, which consists of 14 global manufacturing sites, and various research units and sales companies (Carl Zeiss, 2005). Carl Zeiss representatives clearly state that the firm operates as a global enterprise and decisions regarding EW are taken purely according to good business practice.

At the time of the research, Carl Zeiss operations in EW consisted of several individual units in addition to the extensive Oberkochen premises, where a broad span of research and production activity is carried out in the following fields: camera/cine lenses, display technologies, semiconductor and nanotechnology, industrial metrology, microscopy, surgical and ophthalmology, eyeglasses and lenses and planetariums. Having displayed marked swings during the late 1990s, the total number of Carl Zeiss employees in EW has been relatively stable in the last five years (Table 11.1). The total number of persons employed in the industrial sectors in EW in 2004 was 77,187, of which 5,605 were in Oberkochen and 13,581 in Aalen. Oberkochen being the small municipality it is, the 4,298 Carl Zeiss jobs in 2004 made up 77 percent of all industrial employment. In Aalen, this ratio for the same year was nearly 12 percent.

*Table 11.1    Total employment at Carl Zeiss*

| Date | Oberkochen | Aalen | Total |
| --- | --- | --- | --- |
| 01.10.1994 | 4,329 | 1,449 | 5,778 |
| 01.10.1995 | 3,707 | 1,358 | 5,065 |
| 01.10.1996 | 3,491 | 1,377 | 4,868 |
| 01.10.1997 | 3,514 | 1,519 | 5,033 |
| 01.10.1998 | 3,779 | 1,554 | 5,333 |
| 01.10.1999 | 3,656 | 1,612 | 5,268 |
| 01.10.2000 | 4,092 | 1,772 | 5,864 |
| 01.10.2001 | 4,151 | 1,775 | 5,926 |
| 01.10.2001 | 4,384 | 1,638 | 6,022 |
| 01.10.2002 | 4,151 | 1,775 | 5,926 |
| 01.10.2002 | 4,384 | 1,638 | 6,022 |
| 01.10.2003 | 4,298 | 1,603 | 5,901 |
| 01.10.2004 | 4,316 | 1,613 | 5,929 |

*Source:* E-mail correspondence with Carl Zeiss AG.

Of the 38 optics firms identified in the region, 10 belong to the Carl Zeiss Group. In employment and turnover numbers, they account for the bulk of the output of the regional optics industry.

## Small and Medium-sized Optics Enterprises

Considering that there was no optics expertise in the region before Carl Zeiss arrived, the whole optics industry in EW is the result of a huge knowledge spillover. Other than Carl Zeiss Group firms, 28 SMEs[5] comprise the rest of the optics industry. Most have been founded by FH Aalen graduates who were born in or around the region. A prior career with the Carl Zeiss Group is also common among the entrepreneurs and employees of SMEs.

Figure 11.2 displays the specializations of the optics and optoelectronics firms identified in EW, together with the respective number of Carl Zeiss enterprises therein. The Carl Zeiss Group enterprises that would technically fall in the SME definition are listed in the Carl Zeiss Group's numbers.

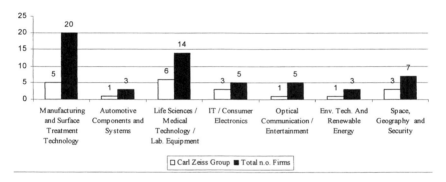

*Figure 11.2   Specializations of firms located in EW region*

As shown in Figure 11.2, 20 of the 38 firms offer solutions and services in the manufacturing-related applications. According to the statements of interviewees, the significant presence of metal working and machinery industries in EW and BW (Table 11.2) are the primary drivers, which exemplifies the importance of regional demand (Porter, 1998). The nature of the products and processes in this segment reflects an artisanship tradition, incorporating expert workmanship, and the firms have a tendency to keep the tasks in-house to the best of their ability, organizing their internal operations to allow swift reactions to their clients' demands. Their production is generally in small-batch sizes and the firms target niche segments in the market. The dominant form of knowledge here is tacit.

'Automotive components, systems design and manufacturing' includes three enterprises. Of these, two are manufacturing establishments belonging to a medium-sized enterprise and Osram GmbH. The third, the Carl Zeiss

Group, cooperates with automotive original equipment manufacturers and suppliers on design and development projects, as it did recently with the BMW Group for the development of an adaptive headlight system for automobiles.

*Table 11.2   Industrial data for metal working and treatment, machine building and automotive industries in EW and BW, 2004[a]*

|  | Enterprises | Total employment | Turnover[b] |
|---|---|---|---|
| East Württemberg | 184 | 32,180 | 5,451,401 |
| Baden Württemberg | 3,525 | 654,016 | 140,155,211 |

*Notes:*
a.   The same data are not available for the optics industry, as it is bundled with data on IT industry.   Despite efforts, it was not possible to receive separate statistics.
b.   The turnover amount is expressed in millions of euros, 2004.

*Source:* Statisches Landesamt Baden Württemberg.

The second prominent optics subfield is the 'life sciences, medical technology and laboratory equipment' group. Here, Carl Zeiss is the prime mover; it owns six of the 14 firms, and the rest of the group is linked to it in various forms, such as prior employment or commercial links through equipment, and service sales agreements.

The activities in the 'IT and consumer electronics' subfield are also dominated by Carl Zeiss. Of the five firms identified, two are SMEs, one of them offering higher-end digital cameras, mainly for professional users, and the other mainly involved in the supply of optical components. As for Carl Zeiss, the headquarters of its SMT AG division develops and manufactures a range of highly sophisticated products for the global chip industry, such as lithography production and process control systems, and wafer and mask inspection devices. This relatively recent investment in Oberkochen (in 2001) operates in coordination with premises in Wetzlar and Jena in Germany and Cambridge in the UK.

The 'optical communication and entertainment' subfield includes two medium-sized firms that develop comprehensive, upper-end laser show systems and the planetarium manufacture operations of Carl Zeiss.

'Space, geography and security' is another field where Carl Zeiss is present. It designs optronic systems for military forces and security organizations. Additionally, a start-up firm founded by a former Carl Zeiss top manager develops innovative aerial surveying mapping and digital photography systems for surveillance applications. Domestic and civil security systems incorporating optics technology are also developed and manufactured through two medium-sized firms.

The last subfield, 'environmental technology and renewable energy' contains relatively little activity, with optics systems for the inspection of wastewater and a solar panel manufactured by a single firm.

A considerable number of firms in the EW optics industry, except Carl Zeiss, are heavily dependent on the co-located sectors – such as manufacturing and surface treatment, and life sciences – as markets, which raises questions of longer-term sustainability, when one considers the concerns about the questionable future of manufacturing in western economies.

Carl Zeiss is clearly a crucial resource of knowledge for the optics industry in the region. The flow of products and expert individuals from Carl Zeiss into EW are the main tacit and explicit knowledge inputs that provide the industry with its competitiveness. This sort of dependence can be contrasted to other regions where the knowledge production is distributed and knowledge transfer is a two-way process between large enterprises and SMEs. An example for comparison is to be seen in the neighboring Stuttgart region. The Stuttgart automotive cluster is a well-known case discussed in the innovation systems literature and displays a very different industrial structure and distribution of activities compared to optics in EW (Morgan, 1999; Fuchs and Wasserman, 2005). DaimlerChrysler, Porsche and Bosch are pillar firms that are global leaders in their segments and carry out a significantly high proportion of added-value creation and R&D in the regional automotive industry, and they depend increasingly on the inputs of their suppliers (Grammel and Seibold, 2004; Caspar et al., 2005; Altvater-Mackensen et al., 2005). These often specialized automotive suppliers, consisting of SMEs and larger enterprises, are highly innovative and participate in reciprocal knowledge exchanges with heavyweights from the Stuttgart region. This is very different from the situation in EW where a disproportionate dependency on Carl Zeiss is apparent in the optics industry.

## LEARNING STREAMS IN EAST WÜRTTEMBERG

### Internal Resources

R&D has been a crucial activity for Carl Zeiss since the days of company founder and scientist Ernst Abbe. Even during the divided years of the cold war, both Carl Zeiss and Carl Zeiss Jena invested heavily in research in their respective strategic alignments (Kogut and Zander, 2000). Today, Carl Zeiss continues in the same vein, as Table 11.3 and Figure 11.3 exemplify. The firm actually spends a larger amount on R&D than its net income and the percentage value of R&D in terms of revenue has been on the increase for the last five business terms. The competitive nature of high-technology markets and a long-term business perspective, partly due to the institutional ownership of Carl Zeiss, are the main reasons for this outstanding focus on R&D.

*Table 11.3   Carl Zeiss Group: revenue, net annual income and R&D spending*

|  | 1999/00 | 2000/01 | 2001/02 | 2002/03 | 2003/04 |
|---|---|---|---|---|---|
| Revenue[*] | 1,998.0 | 2,056.0 | 2,257.0 | 2,029.0 | 2,135.0 |
| Yearly change (%) |  | 2.9 | 9.8 | -10.1 | 5.2 |
| Net annual income[*] | 53.0 | 110.0 | 106.0 | 16.0 | 77.0 |
| Yearly change (%) |  | 107.5 | −3.6 | −84.9 | 381.3 |
| R&D spending* | 139.0 | 146.0 | 186.0 | 190.0 | 209.0 |
| R&D / revenue (%) | 7.0 | 7.1 | 8.2 | 9.4 | 9.8 |

*Note:*   [*]Turnover expressed in millions of euros.

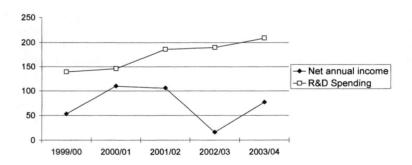

*Note:*   [*]Turnover expressed in millions of euros.

*Figure 11.3    Carl Zeiss Group: net annual income and R&D spending*

The 1,553 R&D staff employed by Carl Zeiss globally in 2004 have produced an increasing number of patents. The R&D effort is also apparent in the high ratio of revenue that is created by products up to three years in the market (Table 11.4).

*Table 11.4   Patent applications and revenue (%) of Carl Zeiss created through products up to 3 years in the market*

|  | 1999/00 | 2000/01 | 2001/02 | 2002/03 | 2003/04 |
|---|---|---|---|---|---|
| New patent applications | 150 | 240 | 260 | 344 | 371 |
| % of revenue from products less than 3 years old | 45 | 41 | 43 | 41 | 43 |

As optics becomes an enabler in different product and market segments, the demand for Carl Zeiss expertise increases. The increasing participation of Carl Zeiss in cooperative projects with other firms corresponds to the omnipresent rise of 'interactive' innovation approaches (based on cooperation and interaction between firms and between firms and institutions) co-existing with those of a linear kind (intra-company, research based and sequential). Carl Zeiss still practices both approaches for different business units and products.

SMEs are mostly founded by individuals with engineering degrees in optics or in related fields, and they employ a highly qualified workforce. For optics, basic research requires significant financial resources and SMEs often do not possess the means to bankroll such campaigns, therefore for them the focus is more on development than on research. Yet, due to the skills of their employees and open relations with customers, they manage to learn through practice and interaction. Development activity is undertaken predominantly in the region, although several SMEs have subsidiaries or contact offices outside EW and Germany. Trade fairs and sector-specific publications are also given as sources of information. Smaller firms seek to combine commercially available technologies to develop niche products that would satisfy the needs of their customers at the least possible development cost, for example, by incorporating off-the-shelf electronics components in systems instead of developing them in-house.

**Universities and Research Institutions**

Two of the more important functions that academic institutions serve for business enterprises are providing qualified employees and production of knowledge through research; firms' relations with these institutions permit firms to acquire knowledge and to pre-select future employees (Hendry et al., 2000; Wolfe, 2002). Aalen University of Technology and Economics (Fachhochschule Aalen – FH Aalen) serves both of these functions in EW for that optics industry. It is an applied science institution and like other German polytechnics, its curriculum is practice oriented. The faculty offers an undergraduate degree with different specialization streams in German, and a Master of Science degree in English, a first in Germany. Following the Bologna process, FH Aalen switched to a Bachelor of Science format for the undergraduate optics programs from the 2005/06 winter semester.

*Table 11.5     Distribution of theses by industry, 1994-2004*

| Industry | No. |
|---|---|
| Automotive | 93 |
| Medicine | 35 |
| Optics | 30 |
| Laser | 27 |
| Measurement and sensor technology | 26 |
| Communication | 11 |
| Automation | 10 |
| Aerospace | 9 |
| FH Aalen | 59 |
| Total | 300 |

The significance of FH Aalen for the region is multifold. First, numerous optics entrepreneurs in the region were trained there and it is still a leading resource for qualified employees for the region's firms. Second, there is a regular contact mechanism between the firms and FH Aalen through internships and degree projects. The latter allows the firms access to the laboratories at the university and the expertise of academic members. These diploma theses, where practice-oriented projects are carried out by students at the firms under the tutelage of faculty members, are a tool for know-how exchange and employee pre-selection. The duration of a project is relatively short, lasting only three to four months, which prevents complex research problems from being tackled. Nevertheless, student theses foster a multitude of knowledge flows between optics SMEs, their clients and FH Aalen. By allowing small and medium-sized optics firms to utilize the infrastructure and expertise at FH Aalen, thesis projects increase the real and perceived sophistication of the solutions offered to customers. FH Aalen faculty members admit to benefiting from this channel to refresh themselves, thereby compensating somewhat for their limited research time due to their heavy teaching load. Customers benefit from the expertise of both the firm and FH Aalen and contribute in their turn with specific field know-how.

As Table 11.5 shows, the number of theses conducted on automotive industry projects and medicine are leading the way. A closer look at the thesis topics reveals that those dealing with laser, measurement and sensor technology are also closely related to the metal processing and surface technology applications, which confirms the significance of co-located activities for the optics industry in EW.

*Table 11.6    Thesis distribution according to host firms, 1994–2004\**

| Host Firms | No. |
|---|---|
| FH Aalen | 59 |
| Carl Zeiss Group | 40 |
| DaimlerChrysler | 29 |
| Bosch Group | 18 |
| Institute of Laser Technologies in Medical Science and Measurement Technology at University of Ulm | 9 |
| Audi AG | 7 |
| Siemens Group | 5 |
| HB Laserkomponenten GmbH | 5 |
| Rest (<5) | 128 |
| Total | 300 |

*Note:* *The assistance of Prof. Dr. Thomas Hellmuth of FH Aalen in obtaining these statistical data is gratefully acknowledged.

The large enterprises constitute the majority of the thesis-hosting firms, with Carl Zeiss, DaimlerChrysler and the Bosch Group leading the field as shown in Table 11.6. Furthermore, the list of firms with less than five thesis projects is also heavily represented by bigger enterprises, with a relatively small percentage of SMEs. Significant two-way learning streams run between FH Aalen and bigger enterprises, of which some are from the vicinity. These student projects are also a pre-selection mechanism for firms.

On a different note, nodes of research-based learning relations in optics are found at Steinbeis Institutes and the Research Institute for Precious Metals and Metals Chemistry (FEM). The know-how pool of the two

Steinbeis Centers[6] is FH Aalen, and both of them are managed by academic members of the Optics Faculty. The first unit offering solutions on optometry is the low-key operation of the two, whereas the other, AWFE, covers almost all the other topics. The faculty members are the acting experts of AWFE, whose primary task is to endow the SMEs from different industries with the optics expertise in FH Aalen. FEM, a non-profit institution, makes heavy use of optoelectronics in its research on surface technology for testing and analysis purposes. As mentioned before, machinery and production technology is an important market for optics firms, which seek collaboration with FEM on application-oriented projects.

EW does not possess upstream, basic research resources, thus the depth of optics research is limited and the region's exposure to new knowledge often occurs during the publication or commercialization phase. Although EW firms can still develop sophisticated solutions in niche markets Carl Zeiss, the region's chances of technological leadership appear slimmer than otherwise, as it has to play catch-up each time.

**Interaction**

As discussed in previous sections, interaction is a strong motor of innovativeness; it not only encourages the improvement and upgrading of existing products and services, but also leads to the conception of new ones (Asheim, 1996; von Hippel, 2005). Especially for customized products in industrial markets, product development necessitates a dense interaction process where exchanged knowledge is to a large degree tacit. The specialized supplier understands the needs of the client in explicit detail and delivers customized solutions. Therefore, one can even go as far as to claim that tacitness here is the anchor of the process, due to the often uncodifiable knowledge related to future products. The relations between EW optics firms that specialize in manufacturing-related applications and their customers exemplify the case. These firms provide for SMEs, medium to large sized (TRUMPF GmbH +Co. KG) and large (Robert Bosch GmbH) enterprises. Many optics firms foster a mutual understanding of demands and competencies with their clients, which has been built up during a long period of cooperation. An interviewee remarked: 'customers know what is and what is not possible and what they need'. This is clearly a functioning learning mechanism for optics firms, where tacit knowledge forms the basis of exchanges. One potentially problematic consequence of these relations is the apparent low interest and investment in new geographical markets. The comfort of relatively secure markets increases the perception of opportunity costs and lowers the incentives to develop competencies to win new customers in new territories, thereby reducing further learning opportunities.

One curious point concerns the weak connections and interaction with the neighboring, economically vibrant Bavarian state. The differences in dialects and regional cultures between Swabian and Bavarian cultural spheres is the apparent cause, and underlines the importance of a shared cultural background.

The relationship between the optics SMEs and Carl Zeiss is both curious and crucial at the same time. Many SMEs in the region use Carl Zeiss products as the main input for their operations, yet Carl Zeiss has limited purchasing and cooperation activity in EW and, with the exception of several select applications and products, it does not have a comprehensive purchasing policy in optics components and services in EW. Carl Zeiss representatives explain the latter as the result of organizational differences, adding that they choose to engage in cooperative activities with larger enterprises. An ex-Carl Zeiss employee, who had held a managerial post in the firm, maintains that the corporate tradition and the very high quality and reliability levels it delivers oblige Carl Zeiss to be a strictly 'managed' company.[7] In his opinion, the structure and corporate culture render risk-taking with suppliers or providing support to entrepreneurial activity outside the group an uphill task for its employees. For the record, the metaphors he chose were 'army' and 'employees like soldiers'. However, Carl Zeiss does have some interaction with local suppliers. For instance, a medium-sized firm from EW took over part of the Carl Zeiss electronics prototyping activities in 2005 to operate onsite at Carl Zeiss premises. Therefore, it may follow that the difficulty is not merely an organizational mismatch, but rather a question of skill and organizational deficits of local SMEs. Compounded by the risk-aversion culture of Carl Zeiss, these deficits not only limit SMEs' business chances, but also remove any opportunity for learning by doing. It will be interesting to see, whether recent restructuring of Carl Zeiss operations into smaller companies will open up future supply possibilities for more SMEs.

Aversion to interaction with industry rivals and focusing on internal resources for innovation are not uncommon in spatial agglomerations (Tödtling and Kaufmann, 1999). In EW, interaction among the regional optics firms is very limited, lack of trust being seen as the primary culprit. The aggravated (negative) experiences of the past render incentives for interaction and/or cooperation with peers insufficient. This complies with the literature which maintains that trust is the basic building block of interaction, and confirms that it is not automatically produced with proximity. This state of collective retreat blocks a potential channel of learning. The deficiency of motivation is prevalent in the reluctance of firms to participate in the networking initiatives of the regional economic development office WiRO.[8] Therefore, at the time of writing in 2005, these initiatives have had a limited impact in the region.

As mentioned before, FH Aalen also hosts a Steinbeis Institute in its building and the faculty members function as experts in Steinbeis's customer projects. In addition, some faculty members offer technology-consulting services. Inevitably, in some cases the customers and the academics overlap with those of the optics SMEs. The resultant rivalry between FH Aalen and optics firms leads to strained relations, manifesting as friction even in the exchange of knowledge during student projects, which points at a rift that goes beyond a reluctance due to concerns over intellectual property (Bowie, 1994). In contrast, FH Aalen enjoys close relations with Carl Zeiss. The firm's employees undertake part-time teaching assignments; several faculty members have had a former career at Carl Zeiss; consequently, these contacts trigger apparent spillover effects. These relations have taken on a new dimension with the recent development of the manufacturing research lab for a-spherical lenses.[9] This important project, which is carried out on the premises of FH Aalen, is co-financed by public resources and Carl Zeiss. For the first five years, construction, equipment and additional starting costs will be covered by public funds, and the compensation of faculty members who carry the managerial responsibilities by Carl Zeiss. Apart from the significance of the research activity, the lab will contain a rapid-prototyping facility that will be commercially invaluable for the SMEs in product development and limited-series production. It will also function as an interactive learning experience for them. The production line in the lab has been modeled on that of Carl Zeiss, therefore it will directly benefit from research related to new manufacturing methods. After the period of financial support expires, the lab will function as an independent research establishment and will generate its revenue from client projects. Obviously, the effectiveness of this cooperation is to be judged by its results, but it clearly promises a significant learning potential for different regional actors.

In Germany, certain types of public research funding, such as, the initiatives of the Federal Ministry of Education and Research (BMBF), are fundamentally aimed at practical research and public–private partnerships, where universities, research institutions and enterprises cooperate. At the region-state level, the research funding activities by Landes-Stiftung Baden-Württemberg[10] also allocate grants to joint research initiatives of firms and academic institutions for similar ends. Although, the interaction during these projects creates a two-way exchange of know-how and production of knowledge, it is often the larger enterprises rather than the smaller ones that participate, due to the fact that SMEs often find it very difficult to allocate the time and capacity to deal with the necessary bureaucratic procedures and project activities.

## Assiduous Firms

In the absence of an upstream local research institution on optics technology, firms need a partner that can bring – in the words of an interviewee – 'new ideas', consequently, some firms seek supra-regional partners. According to the firms, academic and research institutions with a deeper breadth of research capability from neighboring Stuttgart, Ulm and Freiburg play a prominent role in this activity.[11] A recent and interesting example of these projects is the HDRC camera system for surface inspection for metals, which was jointly developed and commercialized by Stuttgart's Institute for Microelectronics (Institut für Mikroelektronik Stuttgart – IMS) and an EW-based optoelectronics firm. The firm differentiates itself by combining state-of-the-art electronics with optics in different applications, especially in industrial image processing and camera systems. IMS is a leader in image sensors and brings in its expertise on HDRC® (High-Dynamic-Range CMOS) sensor technology. Joining their respective competences, they developed an intelligent camera system suitable for environments with changing light behavior. This real-time system can be used in automotive, industrial image processing and security applications. At the time of investigation, the product was at the market launch phase. This is a prominent example of a firm, in its search for capabilities unavailable in its locality, engaging in a cooperative innovation project with a supra-regional party that is located in a neighboring metropolitan area.

To overcome the weak horizontal interaction with peers in the region, some EW firms choose to participate in the PhotonicsBW network, which functions at the BW level. It is a public-initiated, non-profit, multidimensional networking and knowledge dissemination organization for the optics industry[12] and its membership base consists of academic and research institutions and private enterprises. The last include not only optics firms, but users of optics technology as well: DaimlerChrysler AG (automotive), Heidelberger Druckmaschinen AG (printing machines), Trumpf Group (production technology), Robert Bosch GmbH (automotive, industrial technology, and household appliances), among others. The network hosts different activities for different ends: training programs for blue-collar employees, engineers and scientists, meetings for experts and most importantly six field-specific working groups composed of experts who discuss common issues, define the content of the training activities and provide feedback to policy makers on the direction of research funding. PhotonicsBW stimulates regular, institutionalized interaction and in this context it creates a platform for the sharing and production of knowledge and strong knowledge spillover effects. PhotonicsBW is a good example of public initiatives functioning as an interaction and learning platform and filling a gap in economic structures.

The support of larger enterprises is a critical factor for PhotonicsBW. For example, Carl Zeiss supports the initiative strongly, inasmuch as it provides the facilities for the coordination office for PhotonicsBW and lends its staff as instructors. The presence of Carl Zeiss, in addition to other important firms such as DaimlerChrysler and Trumpf, boosts the attractiveness of the initiative for smaller enterprises: the contacts are means not only to knowledge, but also to building commercial relationships, as well. From EW, apart from Carl Zeiss Group enterprises, only two firms are members PhotonicsBW. The annual membership fee, which varies between €1,000-€10,000, depending on the size of the enterprise or institution,[13] is a possible reason for the low participation; only certain firms choose to sustain the costs required to extend their competencies. Not coincidentally, one of these two enterprises is arguably the leading SME of the region and the other is a highly reputed one.

Even when the firms have functioning internal knowledge production processes and learning relationships with their customers, some enterprises with the necessary creative aggression seek further channels of learning to expand their competencies. The increasing sophistication of technology industries and the limited internal resources necessitate the expansion of in-house capacities and require these firms to look for complementary kinds of expertise in others. As some cases exemplify, supra-regional contacts are chosen when the expertise needed is not available in the vicinity of enterprises. Somewhat predictably, not all enterprises opt for this route, and most choose to maintain the status quo, if the current state of affairs is considered sufficiently satisfactory. The select minority of firms that decide to expand their knowledge and skills are the assiduous enterprises. Three such firms have already been identified in this research, but as the investigation did not cover all firms in EW, it is likely that there are more.

As for the partner research outside the region's borders, technological expertise is not the sole determinant, but geographical and cultural proximities also play a crucial role in that they reduce the actual and perceived costs of interaction and partnership. The relative proximity increases the instances of F2F contact; and a common language – even a common dialect – and similar cultural backgrounds facilitate the process of interaction and exchanges. Firms seem to seek out the path of least resistance when establishing a new partnership – and not only in terms of monetary cost. Metropolitan regions such as, Stuttgart, with their multifarious knowledge resources, can function as learning networks for smaller, nearby locations. Even when these resources are not globally the most sophisticated, the compromise they offer can be the next best thing. In this context, it appears to be a beneficial process for both sides: the resources of metropolitan regions are utilized to a greater capacity and the development of smaller locations is supported at less total cost. Coming back to the supra-regional contacts realm, as opposed to larger enterprises, which can finance global networks of contacts, for smaller enterprises the capacity and cost issues are more restrictive. Therefore, they reach out to other national and quasi-local contacts for partnerships for the optimal use of their resources.

## CONCLUSIONS

This chapter has tried to introduce the EW region as a low-key, yet interesting example of learning at the regional level. Considering the increasing importance of optics in manufacturing-related industries and the growing economic significance of health-related services, it can be said that the demand conditions for optics SMEs is positive rather than otherwise. Within EW, SMEs operate in a similar environment of opportunities and resources with no discernible barriers to access. From the 'learning' angle, the EW region boasts some very active and effective channels of knowledge creation and sharing, and some profoundly weak ones. That is, some, fruitful R&D activity is conducted by the region's firms internally and they derive significant strategy and know-how input from the close and lasting relations with their customers. FH Aalen offers application-based research on a broad spectrum and FEM Institute supports the most prominent fields of specialization of optics firms' machinery and surface technology. The know-how of Carl Zeiss is transferred to the region through commercial relations, FH Aalen and knowledge spillovers due to social interaction. However, a few important channels are barren: there is a lack of accessible up-stream research facilities, and horizontal interaction among the optics firms is profoundly weak. Because of the former, the main exposure of optics SMEs to latest developments often occurs only after the publication or commercialization phases, reducing any realistic chance of technology leadership. The limited horizontal contact among firms, a case of 'proximity without intimacy or interaction', limits peer to peer learning and synergy effects, although clusters are far from uncommon (Hendry et al., 2000).

With this background, most of the optics enterprises remain in the regional realm, avoiding taking steps into new, costly and potentially risky ventures. Yet some others choose to invest in supra-regional partnerships to develop new technological and business opportunities. These assiduous firms, which possess a creative aggression, go beyond the regional context they operate in. To borrow a metaphor from Bathelt et al. (2004), the firms that wish to learn further lay 'quasi-local global pipelines' to knowledge reservoirs in the vicinity. This national, supra-regional level of interaction provides an optimum solution to enterprises in terms of interaction costs. Common cultural backgrounds play decisive roles in location choices; *ceteris paribus*, firms would seek partnerships within their cultural sphere, for social proximity would ease cognitive relations over distance (Boschma, 2005).

The contrast between the relational distance between the optics firms and cultural proximity suggested by the shared Swabian culture, demands further research to test the effects of shared cultural space on commercial interaction. The intrinsic functioning of the conceivable knowledge spillovers from Carl Zeiss operations in EW and PhotonicsBW activities is also another topic for the future.

## ACKNOWLEDGEMENT

The support of the Regional Economic Development Corporation of East Württemberg (WiRO) is gratefully acknowledged.

## NOTES

1.  E-mail message to the Free Software Business mailing list from Brian Behlendorf, a prominent name in the Open Source software movement, 17 February 2004, <http://www.crynwr.com/fsb>, viewed on 17 February 2004.
2.  Hendry et al. (2000) indicates the presence of spin-off firms by ex-Carl Zeiss employees in Jena, and East Württemberg also has several enterprises founded by former Carl Zeiss employees.
3.  For this study, rather than internal mechanisms, the spatiality of the links to other parties will be discussed.
4.  Carl Zeiss AG is part of the Carl Zeiss Stiftung, which also owns Schott AG. Schott AG is a global glass manufacturer, headquartered in Mainz, Germany. It has no activity in the EW region and in this chapter, 'Carl Zeiss' will refer solely to Carl Zeiss AG.
5.  The European Union defines a medium-sized enterprise as having less than or equal to 250 employees and a €50 million yearly turnover, and a small enterprise as having less than or equal to 50 employees and a €10 million yearly turnover.
6.  Steinbeis Centers are an independently functioning, decentralized global network of technology transfer units. Inaugurated in Baden Württemberg, they are typically located close to a university and each carries out field-specific commissioned work for clients. They are an important element of the perceived regional innovation system in BW (Heidenreich and Krauss, 1998).
7.  This person swapped careers on his own initiative and still maintains close relations with Carl Zeiss and its employees.
8.  The regional economic development office WiRO (Wirschaftsförderungsgesellschaft mbH Region Ostwürttemberg) is financed by regional banks, and it runs networking and promotion initiatives for the promotion of surface technology and optics industries.
9.  Aspherical lenses achieve a higher performance than traditional designs with smaller dimensions, less weight and fewer components. As an example, they can reduce the number of lenses in adigital photo camera by half, while delivering higher imaging quality.

The importance of this new technology for EW is its potential for improved optical components and systems for quality assurance solutions.

10. Landesstiftung Baden-Württemberg is a foundation that promotes projects particularly in the fields of education, science and research. It is owned by Baden-Württemberg state.

11. Examples are the Institute of Applied Optics at the University of Stuttgart (surface technology), the Institute of Laser Technologies in Medical Science and Measurement Technology at the University of Ulm (medical and manufacturing fields), the Institute of Laser Tools (Institut für Strahlwerkzeuge – IFSW) in Stuttgart and the Materials Testing Institute at the University of Stuttgart.

12. PhotonicsBW was founded in 2000 by BMBF and is part of the OptecNet Deutschland initiative, a network of optics industry competence networks.

13. The start-up firms are granted a year's free membership.

# REFERENCES

Altvater-Mackensen, N., Balicki, G., Bestakowa, L., Bocatius, B. and Braun, J. (2005), 'Science and Technology in the Region', *Scientometrics*, **63** (3), 463–529.

Asheim, B.T. (1996), 'Industrial Districts as "Learning Regions". A Condition for Prosperity', *European Planning Studies*, **4** (4), 379–401.

Asheim, B. T. (2006), 'Learning Firms in Learning Regions: Innovation, Cooperation, and Social Capital', in Taylor, M. and Oinas, P. (eds), *Understanding the Firm: Spatial and Organizational Dimensions*, Oxford: Oxford University Press, pp. 214–34.

Bathelt, H., Malmberg, A. and Maskell, P. (2004), 'Clusters and knowledge: local buzz, global pipelines and the process of knowledge creation', *Progress in Human Geography*, **28** (1), 31–56.

Boschma, R.A. (2005), 'Proximity and Innovation: A Critical Assessment', *Regional Studies*, **39** (1), 61–74.

Bowie, N.E. (1994), *University–Business Partnerships: An Assessment*, Maryland: Rowman & Littlefield Publishers.

Carl Zeiss (2005), www.zeiss.de, 26 April 2005.

Caspar, S., Dispan, J., Krumm, R. and Seibold, B. (2005), *Strukturbericht Region Stuttgart 2005*, Stuttgart/Tübingen: IHK Region Stuttgart.

Cooke, P. (1998), 'Global Clustering and Regional Innovation', in Braczyk, H., Cooke, P., Heidenreich, M. and Krauss, G. (eds), *Regional Innovation Systems: The Role of Governances in a Globalized World*, London: UCL Press, pp. 245–62.

East Württemberg, www.ostwürttemberg.info, 5 April 2005.

Feldman, M. and Audretsch, D. (1999), 'Innovation in Cities: Science-Based Diversity, Specialisation and Localised Competition', *European Economic Review*, **43**, 409–29.

Florida, R. (1995), 'Toward the Learning Region', *Futures*, **27** (5), 527–36.

Fuchs, G. and Wasserman, S. (2005), 'The Regional Innovation System of Baden-Württemberg: Lock-in or Breakthrough?', in Fuchs, G. and Shapira, P. (eds), *Rethinking Regional Innovation and Change: Path Dependency or Regional Breakthrough?*, New York: Springer Science+Business Media, pp. 223–48.

Gertler M.S. (2003), 'Tacit Knowledge and the Economic Geography of Context, or the Undefinable Tacitness of Being (There)', *Journal of Economic Geography*, **3**, 75–99.

Grammel, R. and Seibold, B. (2004), *Automobil-Clusterreport 2003*, Stuttgart: Wirtschaftsförderung Region Stuttgart.

Granovetter, M. (1985), 'Economic Action and Social Structure: the Problem of Embeddedness', *American Journal of Sociology*, **91** (3), 481–510.

Heidenreich, M. and Krauss, G. (1998), 'The Baden-Württemberg Production and Innovation Regime', in Braczyk, H., Cooke, P., Heidenreich, M. and Krauss, G. (eds), *Regional Innovation Systems – The Role of Governances in a Globalized World*, London: UCL Press, pp. 214–44.

Hendry, C., Brown, J. and Defillippi, R. (2000), 'Understanding Relationships between Universities and SMEs in Emerging High Technology Industries: The Case of Opto-electronics', *International Journal of Innovation Management*, **4** (1), 51–75.

Herrigel, G. (1996), *Industrial Constructions: The Sources of German Industrial Power*, Cambridge: Cambridge University Press.

Kogut, B. and Zander, U. (2000), 'Did Socialism Fail to Innovate? A Natural Experiment of the Two Zeiss Companies', *American Sociological Review*, **65** (2), 169–90.

Krugman, P. (1991), *Geography and trade*, Leuven: Leuven University Press.

Lundvall, B. (1998), 'Why Study National Systems and National Styles of Innovation?', *Technology Analysis and Strategic Management*, **10** (4), 407–21.

Lundvall, B.Å. and Maskell, P. (2000), 'Nation States and Economic Development – From National Systems of Production to National Systems of Knowledge Creation and Learning', in Clark, G.L., Feldman, M.P. and Gertler, M.S. (eds), *The Oxford Handbook of Economic Geography*, Oxford: Oxford University Press, pp. 353–371.

Malmberg, A. (1997), 'Industrial Geography: Location and Learning', *Progress in Human Geography*, **21** (4), 573–82.

Malmberg, A. and Maskell, P. (2002), 'The Elusive Concept of Localization Economies: Towards a Knowledge-Based Theory of Spatial Clustering', *Environment and Planning A*, **34**, 429–49.

Marshall, A. (1925), *Principles of Economics, An Introductory Volume*, 8th edn, London: Macmillan.

Marx, K. (1976), *Capital, Volume 1*, Harmondsworth, UK: Penguin Books.

Maskell, P. (1998), 'Learning in the Village Economy of Denmark', in Braczyk, H., Cooke, P., Heidenreich, M., and Krauss, G. (eds), *Regional Innovation Systems: The Role of Governances in a Globalized World*, London: UCL Press, pp. 190–213.

Maskell, P. and Malmberg, A. (1999), 'Localised Learning and Industrial Competitiveness', *Cambridge Journal of Economics*, **23**, 167–185.

Morgan, K. (1999), 'Reversing Attrition?', in Barnes, T.J. and Gertler, M.S. (eds), *The New Industrial Geography: Regions, Regulation and Institutions*, London: Routledge, pp. 74–97.

Myrdal, G. (1957), *Rich Lands and Poor*, New York: Harper & Bros.

Nonaka, I. and Takeuchi, H. (1995), *The Knowledge–Creating Company: How Japanese Companies Create the Dynamics of Innovation*, New York: Oxford University Press.

Organization for Economic Cooperation and Development (OECD) (1999), *Boosting Innovation: The Cluster Approach*, Paris: OECD.

Organization for Economic Cooperation and Development (OECD) (2002), *Redefining Territories: The Functional Regions*, Paris: OECD.

Polanyi, M. (1983 [orig. 1966]), *The Tacit Dimension*, Magnolia, MA: Peter Smith.

Porter, M. (1998), *Competitive Advantage of Nations*, Basingstoke and New York: Palgrave.

Saxenian, A.L., Motoyama, Y. and Quan, X. (2002), *Local and Global Networks of Immigrant Professionals in Silicon Valley*, San Francisco, CA: Public Policy Institute of California.

Schumpeter, J.A. (1942), *Capitalism, Socialism and Democracy*, New York: Harper & Bros.

Scott, A.J. (1988), *Metropolis: From the Division of Labor to Urban Form,* Berkeley, CA and London: University of California Press.

Storper, M. (1997), *The Regional World*, New York and London: Guilford Press.

Storper, M. and Venables, A.J. (2004), 'Buzz: Face-To-Face Contact and the Urban Economy', *Journal of Economic Geography,* **4,** 351-70.

Storper, M. and Walker, R. (1989), *The Capitalist Imperative: Territory, Technology, and Industrial Growth*, Oxford: Basil Blackwell.

Tödtling, F. and Kaufmann, A. (1999), 'Innovation Systems in Regions in Europe – a Comparative Perspective', *European Planning Studies,* 7 (6), 699–717.

von Hippel, Eric (2005), *Democratizing Innovation*, Cambridge, MA: MIT Press.

Wolfe, D.A. (2002), 'Social Capital and Cluster Development in Learning Regions', in Holbrook, J.A. and Wolfe, D.A. (eds), *Knowledge, Clusters and Learning Regions*, Kingston: McGill-Queen's University Press, pp. 11–38.

# 12. Cluster Dynamics: Insights from Broadcasting in Three UK City-Regions

## Gary A.S. Cook and Naresh R. Pandit

## INTRODUCTION

Geographical clustering is a major characteristic of industrial growth and has recently become the subject of intense interest. The bulk of both theoretical and applied research to date has focused on manufacturing and, indeed, high-technology manufacturing. This chapter explores how benefits of clustering arise in the broadcasting industry, a service industry. As Hall (2000) and Scott (2000) argue, the cultural industries are highly concentrated in urban locations, with London dominant in the UK. Developing an understanding of variable performance among cultural industries in different city-regions is also important, given the prominence now given to culture-led development strategies (Bayliss, 2004) and in particular to basing such strategies around 'clusters' of creative industries (Department of Culture, Media and Sport, 2001). The broadcasting industry is still quite young, with large-scale broadcasting, and certainly commercial broadcasting, being essentially a post-war phenomenon in Britain. What is more, the broadcasting industry has been subject to a major shock in the form of extensive deregulation in the 1990s. This has led to rapid entry and a sea of change in the commercial possibilities within the industry. These industry dynamics make the broadcasting industry an interesting case study of clustering effects.

This chapter provides insights from two major studies of the broadcasting industry. The first was a two-year comparative case study of three important city-regions in the broadcasting industry in the UK, based on the cities of London, Bristol, and Glasgow. This investigation built on previous econometric work (Cook et al., 2001) which indicated that higher regional concentration of activity promoted positive spillovers in broadcasting. This is most apparent in London given its massive scale relative to other cities in the UK, yet controlling for cluster mass (measured by scale of industry employment), the South West region centred on Bristol emerged as being pound for pound even more dynamic than London in terms of firm growth rates and surviving new firm entry. South Scotland, centred on Glasgow, by contrast, emerged as being relatively less dynamic than the South West. The comparative case study was therefore aimed at trying to understand the reasons for these differences in dynamism. The second study was an in-depth questionnaire survey of broadcasting and related media activities in London, drawing some 204 usable responses. This study provided detailed evidence on cluster processes within one of the world's major media clusters, including the principal advantages and disadvantages perceived by incumbent firms. It thus provides a yardstick against which to judge the interview evidence from the comparative case studies. Throughout the chapter the geographic concentrations of activity in each city-region will be referred to by the shorthand term 'cluster', despite the valid criticism this term has received based on its very loose usage in policy debates (Martin and Sunley, 2003).

## ALTERNATIVE EXPLANATIONS OF RELATIVE CLUSTER SUCCESS

This literature review examines the features and processes which have been identified as being conducive to the formation of dynamic clusters. This will provide a conceptual framework for examining the essential features of dynamic broadcasting clusters. A central argument of this chapter is that the relative dynamism of the three city-regions considered is explained by the extent to which these features and processes have become established.

Scott and Storper (2003) suggest that the superior economic dynamism of cities rests on the coexistence of four key factors, each of which is important: economies of scale in capital-intensive infrastructure; dynamic forward and backward linkages among firms; dense local labour markets; and localised relational assets promoting learning and innovation. These relational assets have been dubbed 'untraded interdependencies' by Storper (1997) which he defines (p. 5) as 'conventions, informal rules and habits that coordinate economic actors under conditions of uncertainty'. A central assumption in the literature is that these untraded interdependencies, which are essential for realising cluster benefits, operate more effectively at more compact spatial scales. This list, while summarising important findings in both theoretical and empirical literatures, is somewhat incomplete for present purposes.

Malmberg and Maskell (2002) have recently argued that the emphasis on vertical linkages in clusters has led to a neglect of the importance of horizontal relationships, emphasising the benefits in terms of the pursuit of multiple R&D avenues, a source of important spillovers to rivals, and the competitive benefits of benchmarking and rivalry (Porter, 1990, 1998). The volume and sophistication of demand within the city may also be critical (Porter, 1990; Kitson et al., 2004). In Porter's conception, sophisticated, demanding customers will drive quality standards and innovation (von Hippel, 1988). The existence of concentrated demand for specialised services also provides an incentive for workers to invest in specialised skills and competencies (Scott and Storper, 2003), which is another dynamic of cumulative causation. Another important city-specific factor is 'quality of life', which is a very important consideration in terms of the ability of a city to attract the highest quality and most creative labour (Florida, 2002; Office of the Deputy Prime Minister, 2004). This has a variety of dimensions such as quality of schools, cultural amenities (Turok, 2004), tolerant social milieu, and availability of good housing at an affordable price. Entrepreneurship is also important to regional prosperity (Camagni, 2002). Coe and Townsend (1998) argue that the greater 'entrepreneurial culture' of the South East in the UK has been an important factor in the dynamism and growth of the region.

The importance of external connectivity for remaining at the forefront of innovation has been widely acknowledged in the literature (Boggs and Rantisi, 2003). Amin and Thrift (1992) argue persuasively that the emphasis on local production complexes is overdone for several reasons. Models which are locally based do not recognise the importance of emerging global corporate networks and interconnected global city-regions (Scott et al., 2001). They argue that centres are needed within which to generate and disseminate discourses, collective beliefs, and stories about what world production filieres are like and to develop, track and test innovations. Jacobs (1972, 1985), in her influential analysis of the sources of city dynamism, clearly lays considerable importance on the nature of external linkages a city has, such linkages providing a flow of new ideas and technology which provide a basis for local innovation and dynamism. A similar point is also emphasised by Hall (2000) as a powerful contributor to periods of creative flourishing in cities. This view has been articulated even more strongly in Pred's (1977) theory of city-systems. Much emphasis is placed in Pred's analysis on the importance of multilocational organisations (which may or may not be multinationals) as they will tend to be particularly wide conduits through which goods, services, capital and information may flow (Bathelt et al., 2004; Cumbers and McKinnon, 2004).

The relative importance of these various factors in the specific case of broadcasting is essentially an empirical question, nevertheless they provide likely sources of differences in cluster dynamism among the three cities investigated.

**Cluster Type**

The literature abounds with different typologies of geographic concentrations of economic activity (McCann and Sheppard, 2003). Markusen (1996) identifies a range of different types of cluster, each of which manifests a certain type of economic logic (see Coe, 2001 for an application to the Vancouver film industry). Markusen argues that these types have different implications for the success, variously defined, of the cluster and for its sustainability. One might go further and argue that what matter in addition are: the 'mass' of the cluster; the extent to which the processes indicative of the cluster type are formed; and the 'fit' between cluster type and line of activity. These ideal types thus provide an integrative framework within which to analyse the nature of the broadcasting clusters in each of the cities studied and also to seek for differences in their dynamism and sustainability:

1.  The Marshallian (Marshall, 1920, 1927) New Industrial District (NID), of which the third Italy is identified as an important variety. Markusen reports that in the Marshallian conception such districts are populated by small, locally owned firms. Major external economies exist in the form of labour market pooling, knowledge sharing and specialisation, including specialised supply of inputs.
2.  The hub-and-spoke district where regional structure revolves around one or several major corporations in one or a few industries. Among the examples Markusen gives are Toyota City in Japan and Boeing in Seattle. Suppliers tend to be subordinate to the hub firm(s), although they may enjoy externalities emanating from large firms without being particularly dependent on them. In addition, micro clusters may form within the more atomised supplier industries. Cooperation within the district tends to be on the terms of the hub firm(s).
3.  The satellite industrial platform is composed chiefly of branch plants of multinational corporations. Such districts may exist in any country and are typified by a lack of interaction among the firms located there. Firms are above all dependent on corporate parents.
4.  The state-anchored district where a major government tenant anchors the regional economy. The classic instance is where state defence establishments lead to clusters of defence-related firms, but a wide range of different types of government establishment may be the centre of such a district.

As Markusen suggests, many clusters manifest elements of more than one of these ideal types of industrial district. She suggests that Silicon Valley has an industrial district in electronics but also has a number of important hub firms, such as Lockheed, Hewlett Packard and Stanford University, hosts a number of branch plants as in the satellite platform model, such as IBM, OKI, NTK Ceramics, Hyundai and Samsung as well as benefiting from the defence industry as in the state-anchored district model. What is more, districts may metamorphose from one type to another.

## Summary

Drawing the threads of the literature review together, what has become the mainstream view in the literature is that clusters will be more sustainable when firms are embedded in the cluster through intricate relationships based on mutual dependency through a division of labour among firms. This division of labour works particularly well when underpinned by rich untraded interdependencies and social capital, referred to in the rest of the chapter as 'relational assets'. Powerful hub firms can be an asset to the cluster, but in the case of both hub-and-spoke and state-anchored districts the sustainability of the cluster may be threatened either by the fact that hub firms may falter or that they may be capable of shifting activity elsewhere through lack of embeddedness, responding to either commercial or political imperatives. Cluster type may also matter in so far as there may be a fit between basic economic characteristics of the industry and which of Markusen's types is best suited to it. Cluster scale matters as it influences the extent of the division of labour, the richness of networks that can be established and also the depth of the labour pool. Vertical linkages in local networks have received much emphasis as a source of dynamic capability both in production and innovation. More recently the literature has acknowledged the overlooked importance of both horizontal relationships among firms and also the external connectivity of the cluster and its constituent firms as a source of new learning and innovation.

## METHODOLOGY

The findings reported below are based on two sources. The first is a comparative case study of London, Bristol and Glasgow. This study was principally built around an interview survey consisting of 72 interviews conducted mainly with firms in the three cities between 2001 and 2002, and which also drew on secondary sources. The aim of the comparative case study was to compare the three broadcasting clusters in London, Bristol and Glasgow in order to understand the detailed processes that give rise to differential performance in these three cities. The majority of interviews were conducted with firms in the broadcasting, programme production and post-production sectors, which earlier econometric work had indicated were the most important in terms of cluster dynamics. This econometric work examined the influence of cluster size as measured by scale of employment on both firm growth rates and the rate of surviving new firm entry, finding a positive influence on both measures of cluster dynamism. The logic of the comparative case study design was to compare the largest cluster, London, with a dynamic region which performed more strongly than the growth and entry models predicted, Bristol, and one which performed less strongly, Glasgow. Table 12.1 provides a summary of the interviews conducted in each city-region. Fewer firms were interviewed in Glasgow as it has a smaller independent production and post-production sector. Interviews were semi-structured and the interview schedule was developed based on a prior literature review to explore themes identified as important. Notes were taken at interview and written up as soon as possible afterwards. Tape recording was not used in order to facilitate a more open discussion.

The second main body of evidence is a questionnaire survey of broadcasting and related media firms in London conducted in 2004. The questionnaire, available on request from the authors, was mailed to a stratified random sample of 1,500 companies drawn from a bespoke database built up from the FAME financial database and the Broadcast Production Guide, the leading industry trade directory. The largest 300 firms in the database were 100 per cent sampled, subject to the proviso that the sample was split *pro rata* to the numbers of advertising and broadcasting firms. The questionnaire was piloted with a small number of broadcasting firms before being sent. The importance of the questionnaire evidence is that it looks for evidence of dense interaction and cooperation in the place where it is most likely to arise, one of the world's most important media clusters. Combined with the interview evidence it provides a perspective on the extent to which smaller regional concentrations appear to manifest similar processes, albeit in the cases of Bristol and Glasgow on a much smaller scale. In all, 204 usable questionnaires were returned, an apparent response rate of 13.6 percent. Around 50 nil-responses were received which shed some light on the genuine response rate. The majority of these nil-responses related to either firms that had gone out of business, an important feature of the industry which has a high churn of firms, or firms that had been incorrectly classified as belonging to the broadcasting industry in the FAME database. These latter firms remained in the sample despite a lengthy effort to clean up the database. Taking these factors into account, the response rate among live firms in broadcasting and advertising was closer to 16 percent. The broad split of responses was broadcast television production 39 firms, film production 36 firms, post production 48 firms, advertising 18 firms, and miscellaneous broadcasting-related firms 63.

*Table 12.1  Respondents to the interview survey by sector*

|                          | London | Bristol | Glasgow |
|--------------------------|--------|---------|---------|
| Programme production     | 9      | 10      | 6       |
| Post production          | 6      | 5       | 1       |
| Broadcaster              | 3      | 3       | 4       |
| Equipment supply         | 3      | 2       | 2       |
| Industry expert/policy maker | 6  | 7       | 5       |

## LONDON, BRISTOL AND GLASGOW COMPARED

Before turning to a consideration of the broadcasting industry *per se*, attention will be given to the general context provided by each city and its governance. Sweeting et al. (2004) identify that each city has a different mode of governance. London is characterised as having *designed and focused* leadership centred on the mayor and the Greater London Authority. Clearly this regime is of very recent origin (Haywood, 1998) and essentially the shape to the broadcasting sector in London was established before such a degree of coordination came into being. Bristol is characterised as having *implicit and fragmented leadership*, which echoes other studies which have concluded that Bristol has had unhelpful governance in at least two respects. First, Bristol has suffered from fragmented and uncoordinated policy control across the functional city-region. Second, Bristol has essentially seen a *laissez-faire* policy approach, lacking a coherent policy, especially as concerns the cultural industries. The advent of the South West Regional Development Agency has done little, if anything, to correct this deficiency. Glasgow is characterised as having *emergent and formative leadership* which is typified by reasonable cooperation among agencies and a practical approach to getting the job done.

Glasgow has been identified by Turok et al. (2004) as possessing a number of general advantages, some of which weigh more heavily than others in terms of supporting the creative industries. Glasgow has effected an impressive transformation from an image of heavy industry and decline through initiatives such as 'Glasgow's Miles Better' and the European City of Culture, helping provide a focus for a culture-led regeneration strategy (Garcia, 2005). It is now an important retail, leisure and cultural centre and particularly in creative circles is seen as a favourable milieu. Glasgow also boasts both cheap labour and readily available graduate labour. In addition to its many cultural and leisure amenities, Glasgow offers attractive housing in its fashionable West End to tempt highly skilled and educated labour. Boddy et al. (2004) identify three particular advantages which Bristol enjoys as a business location. First, it has excellent transport connections to London and Heathrow airport, therefore is well connected nationally and internationally. Second, it has access via the M4 to a wide labour catchment area, including a wealth of technical and professional staff. Third, the cultural and physical attractions of the city and its environs support inward migration and retention of high calibre labour. London exerts a strong attraction based not only on its status as a major cultural metropolis but also by offering the best career opportunities in most of the broadcasting industry. Against this, London suffers from expensive housing, congested transport infrastructure and a reputation for poor schools.

Table 12.2 illustrates how the cities compare across a range of factors considered in the report across its six 'critical' characteristics of urban competitiveness.

*Table 12.2     Ranking within top 61 cities in Europe*

|  | London | Bristol | Glasgow | Edinburgh |
| --- | --- | --- | --- | --- |
| GDP per capita (2001) | 23 | 34[b] | 29 | 25 |
| European Innovation Index[a] | 8 | 14[b] | 38 | 38 |
| Airport passenger numbers | 1 | 75 | 38 | 44 |
| Internet hub | 1 | Not ranked | Not ranked | Not ranked |
| Healey & Baker index of best city to locate a business 1990 | 1 | Not ranked | 10 | Not ranked |
| Healey & Baker index of best city to locate a business 2002 | 1 | Not ranked | 22 | Not ranked |

*Notes:*
a.    This is based on a ranking of the region in which the city is based, e.g. South East in the case of London, South West in the case of Bristol and Scotland in the cases of both Glasgow and Edinburgh.
b.    Indicates that Bristol is the highest ranked of the English core cities, i.e. not including London.

*Source:*  ODPM (2004).

In addition to the above, Bristol emerges as also having a relatively strong performance in terms of the percentage of population with higher education, the percentage of employees working in high-tech services and to a somewhat lesser extent knowledge-intensive services. London also has a considerable advantage in terms of early-stage and expansion venture capital, per million of population and also business start-ups per 10,000 of population, however in both respects the South West comfortably outperforms Scotland. In sum, in almost every respect London eclipses the other two cities under consideration, understandable given its position at the apex of the hierarchy of world cities (Beaverstock et al., 1999, Taylor et al., 2002). What is more, Bristol is seen to have some important advantages over Glasgow in terms of connectivity to London, innovation and entrepreneurship. While Bristol is close to London geographically, several interview respondents in both Bristol and London expressed the clear view that they were regarded as being distinct broadcasting centres. Direct contrast was made with Birmingham, which it was felt had suffered from being too much within the sphere of influence of London.

## CLUSTER COSTS AND BENEFITS IN BROADCASTING

An obvious point about broadcasting is that in every country it is subject to heavy government regulation, which has generally had an influence on the location of broadcasting activity. First, the BBC was set up in the capital which remains an important strategic centre in the industry. Second, when independent television was set up in the UK, a deliberate policy was pursued of ensuring that network production (i.e., the production of television programmes that would be screened nationally) took place in the regions. Attempting to spread broadcasting activity around the regions, once a highly concentrated industry had been established in the capital, has proved difficult. The UK has imposed quotas for regional production, which have been circumvented to a substantial degree by independent companies from London setting up branch offices outside the capital to win business under the quota, but still essentially orchestrating operations from London. At the same time, many independent production companies in the regions have felt it necessary to set up offices in London in order to help secure commissions from the major broadcasters.

   The characteristics of some of the key regions in the broadcasting industry are shown in Tables 12.3 and 12.4. Table 12.3 illustrates two important facts. First, London dwarfs all other regions in terms of employment. This dominance is reinforced by similar dominance in allied industries such as publishing, music and entertainment (Turok, 2003). Second, there is a highly skewed pattern of employment. Table 12.4 provides a set of standard location quotients, focusing more narrowly on broadcast and broadcast-related activity. These location quotients compare the ratio of the proportion of regional employment in a given line of activity to the proportion of national employment in a given line of activity. A quotient above 1 indicates that a region has a disproportionate amount of employment in a particular line of activity relative to the country as a whole. Again this underscores

Table 12.3  Numbers employed in the audio-visual industries by sector and region

| | Wales | Scotland | Central London | West London | London ALL | South East | South West | West Midlands | North West |
|---|---|---|---|---|---|---|---|---|---|
| Broadcast TV | 1,300 | 1,400 | 5,400 | 6,900 | 12,300 | 1,300 | 1,100 | 1,100 | 1,900 |
| Cable and satellite television | 0 | 0 | 1,500 | 1,100 | 5,300 | 400 | 0 | 0 | 0 |
| Independent production (television) | 1200 | 500 | 5,400 | 700 | 8,200 | 1,500 | 800 | 200 | 1,100 |
| Broadcast radio | 700 | 1,500 | 4,600 | 5200 | 10,000 | 3,300 | 1,100 | 1,100 | 1,300 |
| Animation | 200 | 100 | 900 | 200 | 1,400 | 200 | 400 | 200 | 400 |
| Post production | 100 | 100 | 3,700 | 300 | 4,500 | 500 | 100 | 100 | 200 |
| Digital special effects | 0 | 0 | 600 | 0 | 600 | 100 | 0 | 0 | 0 |
| Facilities (studio/equipment Hire) | 100 | 300 | 300 | 1,200 | 2,100 | 800 | 300 | 100 | 200 |
| Web and internet | 1,100 | 600 | 12,100 | 2,200 | 20,100 | 6,100 | 1,000 | 400 | 400 |
| Electronic games | 0 | 800 | 600 | 500 | 1,400 | 3,400 | 200 | 1,000 | 900 |
| Offline multimedia | 1,300 | 300 | 1,000 | 400 | 2,400 | 3,200 | 300 | 200 | 200 |
| Commercials production | 0 | 0 | 2,100 | 0 | 2,500 | 100 | 0 | 0 | 200 |
| Corporate production | 200 | 100 | 600 | 200 | 1,100 | 900 | 200 | 0 | 100 |
| Film distribution | 0 | 0 | 400 | 100 | 500 | 0 | 0 | 0 | 0 |
| Processing laboratories | 0 | 0 | 400 | 0 | 400 | 200 | 0 | 0 | 0 |
| Other | 0 | 0 | 300 | 600 | 1,000 | 200 | 100 | 100 | 100 |

Source:  Skillset.

the dominance of London, which is especially marked in film distribution, cable and satellite broadcasting, post production and special effects and commercials production. The South West stands out in particular for its relative strength in animation.

*Table 12.4     Location quotients in selected regions in broadcasting-related industries*

|  | Wales | Scotland | London ALL | South East | South West | West Midlands | North West |
|---|---|---|---|---|---|---|---|
| Broadcast TV | 1.3 | 0.7 | 3.4 | 0.4 | 0.6 | 0.5 | 0.7 |
| Cable and satellite television | 0.0 | 0.0 | 6.0 | 0.5 | 0.0 | 0.0 | 0.0 |
| Independent production (television) | 1.9 | 0.4 | 3.6 | 0.7 | 0.6 | 0.2 | 0.7 |
| Broadcast radio | 0.7 | 0.8 | 2.9 | 1.0 | 0.6 | 0.6 | 0.5 |
| Animation | 1.5 | 0.4 | 3.0 | 0.5 | 1.5 | 0.7 | 1.2 |
| Post production | 0.4 | 0.2 | 5.1 | 0.6 | 0.2 | 0.2 | 0.3 |
| Digital special effects | 0.0 | 0.0 | 5.6 | 1.0 | 0.0 | 0.0 | 0.0 |
| Facilities (studio/equipment hire) | 0.5 | 0.8 | 3.0 | 1.2 | 0.8 | 0.2 | 0.4 |
| Commercials production | 0.0 | 0.0 | 5.6 | 0.2 | 0.0 | 0.0 | 0.6 |
| Corporate production | 1.8 | 0.4 | 2.7 | 2.3 | 0.9 | 0.0 | 0.3 |
| Film distribution | 0.0 | 0.0 | 6.5 | 0.0 | 0.0 | 0.0 | 0.0 |
| Processing laboratories | 0.0 | 0.0 | 4.4 | 2.3 | 0.0 | 0.0 | 0.0 |
| Other | 0.0 | 0.0 | 3.4 | 0.7 | 0.6 | 0.6 | 0.5 |

*Sources:* Skillset; ONS.

**Relational Assets**

Figure 12.1 indicates the top 10 benefits of locating in London according to the questionnaire. Scores were based on a simple summation of the Lickert scale responses ranging from 0 (not applicable) to 5 (very important). This leads to a maximum potential score of 1,020 (204 x 5). The mean score was

562 and the range across all 67 factors asked about in the questionnaire was from a maximum of 777, for face-to-face contact being an important benefit of co-location, to a minimum of 256, for support from local government being an important benefit of current location.

An important section of the questionnaire asked about why it was important to have close proximity to other firms in London. Collectively these factors achieved the highest ratings, with prime importance being placed on face-to-face contact and interpersonal relationships, providing three of the top 10 benefits of a London location.    Face-to-face contact is significantly more highly rated than maintaining personal contacts and emerges as the pre-eminent factor.  Maintaining personal contacts in turn is significantly more highly rated than building relationships of trust.   Why should these two things be so important? Here the interview evidence across all three cities was strong and consistent.  In large part it is due to the fact that what is being created is most importantly an image and sound which will convey meaning.  These are cultural artefacts whose most important qualities are the extent to which they convey meaning, emotion and information.  This makes it of paramount importance that those who are engaged in their production understand the meaning which is to be conveyed.   In order to come to that understanding, communication with the maximum 'bandwidth' is required, that is, face-to-face contact.

*Figure 12.1  Top 10 benefits of a London location*

A network of personal contacts smoothes the process of creative production in a variety of ways. It allows teams to be assembled quickly in order to carry out what by most industry standards is a short-term project, with the assurance that those engaged will be able to understand and produce what is required. Physical proximity in London promotes rich circuits of information about particular individuals which can be (and are) tapped into when assembling a team. Producers and editors in broadcast, film and advertising media often work hand in glove as the final product is fashioned during post production. Here there can be long, intense days where, by a process of verbal and nonverbal communication, the end result that is desired is fashioned. It is also important for allowing a frank exchange of views to take place without lasting offence or a breakdown in relations occurring. The path of production is sometimes smoothed by personal favours such as loans of staff and equipment and occasionally undercharging for work done on the implicit understanding that the favour would be returned should the occasion arise.

It is commonplace for those working in the industry in London to talk about the importance of 'the buzz' (Storper and Venables, 2004). This refers to the constant flow of ideas, gossip and rumour which inform people about the latest thinking on what are considered to be commercially viable ideas. This element of buzz in cities is seen as being especially important in respect of information-rich industries like the cultural industries (Turok, 2003). Soho is renowned for its clubs, bars and restaurants which provide important social spaces where those in the industry can meet and talk. The questionnaire evidence reveals that firms located in W1 (Soho) are significantly more likely to meet in such informal venues and to rate interpersonal interaction highly as a benefit of their location. One aspect of this is that the 'buzz' of London creates a constant flow of ideas which can contribute to the alchemy of a novel idea. As one respondent put it 'It's like sitting under a waterfall'. Much of the cross-fertilisation of ideas takes place at specific venues such as the bars and clubs of Soho. Bristol and Glasgow do not benefit to the same extent since their broadcasting and wider cultural industries clusters are so much smaller and less connected to international flows of people and ideas.

The advantage of physical proximity in promoting trust and cooperation with other companies was highly rated, 11th out of 67 factors in the questionnaire survey. Trust is very important within the production system in broadcasting, film and advertising due the tight time and money constraints which attend most projects. What adds to the importance of trust is the inherent uncertainty surrounding the quality of the ultimate output. The importance of trust and reputation permeates the production system in broadcasting. An independent production company may get a commission on the basis of the reputation of a key producer. The producer may then bring in a trusted director.  The director will bring in a trusted cameraman.  The cameraman will bring in trusted assistants.  Each is being brought in on the basis of an established reputation which they put on the line with each project and which they must at all times defend.  The dread prospect of being associated with a failure hangs over all and is the broadcasting equivalent of receiving the black spot.  Trust looms particularly large in the relationship between production and post production and provides an important part of the reason why they are almost always co-located.  Handing over the rushes (raw film footage) for post production is to entrust another with a valuable asset in which you have invested heart and soul.  To reduce this uncertainty, people like to work with those whom they can trust to 'get it right', both in terms of doing what they say they will do and doing it when they are expected to.  The extent to which this potential advantage is seen to be important in practice is associated with location, rather than with line of business, with the strongest association being location in W1 and to a lesser extent a wider definition of central London.

An important word used repeatedly in the London interviews was 'community'.  The same word was used somewhat less frequently in the Bristol interviews and far less frequently in Glasgow.  There are several important facets of the existence of this community.  First, there are overlapping communities, a wider broadcasting community and a more specific community relating to a particular craft or profession to which an individual will belong.  Second, access to the community is granted by certain rites of passage.  This ensures appropriate socialisation, imbuing the individual with attitudes, norms of behaviour and linguistic competence. A strong theme in the important literature of *innovative milieux* is that one of the keys to superior innovation in regional innovation systems is the ability for firms who may do quite different things, to share ideas through the ability to talk a common, or at least common enough, language.  What goes for innovation also goes for production.  Membership of the appropriate community is an important foundation of trust.  Another important aspect of community is accessibility, two important dimensions of which are knowing you can call on people without appointment and also knowing where people are likely to be available, for example, at meal times in local bars and restaurants.  It is important to acknowledge that communities also exist within large firms and are, therefore, not entirely a property of a vertically and horizontally disintegrated production system.

Glasgow differs from Bristol in some important respects.  The degree of cooperation and informal interaction among its independent companies is palpably lower, the lack of 'untraded interdependencies' being remarked upon by Turok (2003).  One possible reason for this is the much lesser degree of physical propinquity in Glasgow compared to Bristol.  In Bristol also there are more established meeting points such as the Tapas Bar and the BBC canteen. Several respondents in Bristol indicated how they meet socially with peers at ostensibly rival companies, indeed in one case going on holiday with them. No such evidence was forthcoming in Glasgow.

In sum, this evidence is consistent with the importance accorded in the literature to untraded interdependencies as being an important underpinning of dynamic and successful clusters. They also help anchor activity to a particular location. These untraded interdependencies are particularly important in a creative, project-based industry such as broadcasting. The less-developed relational assets in Glasgow are one reason for its lower dynamism.

## The Labour Market

The labour market is of undoubted importance in broadcasting clusters. A pool of talented labour with relevant skills stands as the pre-eminent *local* factor helping firms innovate according to the questionnaire survey. This is the third-highest ranked factor across the whole questionnaire and is significantly more important to large firms. From the employer's point of view, London is an attractive location, despite the obvious congestion, because it offers such an exceptional pool of creative talent relative to other areas of Britain. There is clearly a dynamic at work where the reputation of particular regional centres, above all London, attracts talent which makes the centre a more desirable place to do business. The strong pull of London on highly skilled labour is indicative of a much wider trend (HM Treasury, 2001; Dorling and Thomas, 2004). Most recruitment is done from the local labour market, although specialist skills may be sourced from much wider afield. An important counter-example is Bristol, which is the premier location for natural history producers, based around the Natural History Unit of the BBC (Bassett et al., 2002). Here anyone who aspires to work at the highest level in this genre has to operate in this location.

Labour market flexibility was generally viewed as being a source of advantage in a variety of ways, both in the questionnaire survey and the interviews. The most important advantage was seen as the ability to recruit good people at short notice, which stood apart from the other advantages of a flexible labour market. This is clearly important in media businesses which have a predominantly project-based mode of operation. For example, on securing a commission, an independent broadcast company may need to secure additional staff either on an employed or a freelance basis to undertake the work, but will have no guarantee of being able to offer continuity of employment to such staff. This fact is reflected in the high rating given to the ability to tailor the level of staff quickly to current requirements. Many independent production and post-production companies have a precarious existence, being generally squeezed by pressure on budgets and the problem of trying to ensure continuity of work. In this situation 'labour hoarding' is an expensive luxury most companies cannot afford.

The fine-grained division of labour which has been achieved in London has several benefits. First, it multiplies the range of possibilities for production in London. Related to this it is a source of advantage to the London cluster as it can provide specialised services which are not available elsewhere in the UK and possibly at very few locations globally. Third, it contributes to innovation as has already been explained. Finally, it is likely to lead to higher levels of skills within particular occupations or crafts within the industry. The last two points are partly related to the fact that there are denser 'craft communities' within London where ideas can be exchanged to mutual benefit.

Glasgow was generally described as having a 'maturing' labour market. As the independent sector has grown, so this has encouraged a process of labour market formation, one aided by a fair degree of mobility between film and television. Nevertheless, those with experience of production in both London and Glasgow acknowledged that there was a major difference between the depths of the two labour pools. Both Glasgow and Bristol suffer from the drain of talent to London, although this appears to be somewhat more troublesome for Glasgow. The reason is that Bristol is higher up the pecking order in its three main genres of natural history, factual and animation than Glasgow is in any of its main genres, lessening the relative attractiveness of London. Both also suffer from not having the critical mass to ensure year-round working for many staff. Again in this regard Bristol benefits from its focus on a small number of genres as skills, for example, as producer or director, are typically genre specific. Moreover, people like to belong to a professional community which Bristol is better able to offer in natural history or factual than Glasgow is in comedy (one of its successful areas in terms of winning network commissions).

Again the evidence is consistent with the received wisdom in the literature that labour market pooling is an important source of cluster strength. This factor is above all related to the scale of the cluster, which is an important and very obvious factor differentiating London from Bristol and Glasgow. Bristol fares better than Glasgow because its labour market resources are concentrated in a smaller number of genres, thus allowing stronger labour market pooling advantages pound for pound.

Figure 12.2 presents some evidence on the importance of co-location next to other firms. Three main things stand out. First, it appears that vertical relationships are more important than horizontal. Local customers and suppliers emerge as being important sources of help with innovation by

Porter (1990) and many other writers (e.g., von Hippel, 1988). Customers may demand innovation, a spur for both broadcast production and post-production companies competing for business against strong rivals. Moreover, customers may themselves be important innovators who are able to guide their suppliers to innovative solutions. Cook and Pandit (2005) document how post-production companies in Soho have produced a stream of innovations in hardware and software over recent years, sometimes alone and sometimes in collaboration with equipment and software suppliers. Another commonplace about innovation is that typically it requires many strands to be drawn together and the ability to find suppliers of necessary, and sometimes novel, inputs is an advantage of leading clusters. Evidence elsewhere in the questionnaire did indicate that benchmarking and competitive rivalry have positive influences in terms of providing a competitive spur, however, these horizontal relationships were much less important. The competitive spur of rivalry and the ability to benchmark against rivals are given somewhat lesser importance among this group and fall well below the mean score for all factors. These two factors are ranked 54th and 57th out of the 67 factors respectively. Second, there is some evidence that vertical relationships promote productive efficiency as well as innovation. Third, the importance of local demand is indicated.

## Dynamic Vertical and Horizontal Linkages

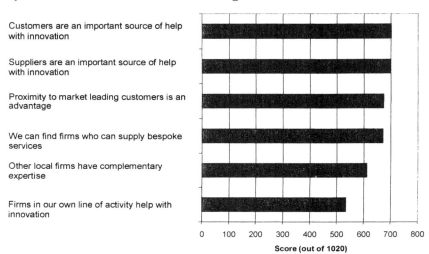

*Figure 12.2 Importance of co-location with other firms*

This evidence underscores the importance of linkages between firms. It agrees with the traditional emphasis in the literature on vertical linkages. It also points to the importance of cluster scale, as the size of the London cluster has led to a far richer specialised and disaggregated supply structure, contributing to dynamic efficiency and innovation.

## Demand

Demand is a fundamental consideration in location decisions.  In the UK system much depends on the personal judgement of the commissioning editor about what will work and what won't.  This places a premium on proximity for two main reasons.  First it economises on transaction costs as it is important to meet regularly with commissioning editors and others in the industry to keep up to date with the latest thinking on what types of programme are being sought.    Second, personal relationships with commissioning editors can be important in getting a hearing in which the opportunity may arise to convince them that the company has a viable idea. Understanding the personality of the commissioner is important in making a successful sales pitch.  Most network commissions, the most highly sought, are taken in London, providing a very strong rationale for setting up operations there.

The broad features of why proximity matters from the demand side are common to all three cities.  Several things differentiate them, however.  First the concentration of demand, both domestic and international, in London is massive compared to Bristol and Glasgow.  Bristol is, however, a focus of demand for natural history programmes and to a lesser extent animation. Demand for natural history in particular lends itself to export sales as it is less culture specific than other genres such as comedy.   Glasgow has the advantage of being the HQ of Channel 4's nations and regions whose head, Stuart Cosgrove, is wooed in a fashion similar to London-based commissioners.  By the same token there was a small flurry of London-based companies establishing a foothold in Bristol in the belief that Bristol was being viewed as a favoured region for commissions from Channel 4.

## Hub Firms

The strength of the broadcasters at the hub of the cluster is critical.  They will determine the extent and stability of demand for programming which in turn drives the derived demand for labour.  As has been argued above, the formation of the labour pool is a vital process in forming a dynamic regional concentration. The importance of hub broadcasters is demonstrated in the obverse by Edinburgh where the gravitation towards Glasgow of operations of the BBC and Scottish Television which had formerly been in Edinburgh was followed by a similar migration of independent production and post-production firms. The hub broadcasters have been responsible for many successful spin-outs which have reinforced the geographic concentration of activity, as almost all firms are set up close to where people currently live.

Bristol and Glasgow are on a roughly comparable scale as broadcasting centres and both are dwarfed by London. London is the headquarters of the BBC, Independent Television News, Channel 4, Channel 5 and now ITV (the main independent broadcaster). The presence of these major commissioners of programmes in London, above all the BBC, creates a strong attraction for new entry. It also hosts the headquarters of all the significant satellite and cable broadcasters. It is home to all of the larger UK independents such as Endemol, Celador, Tiger Aspect, Zenith, Lion TV and all of the major post-production companies such as the Moving Picture Company, the Mill and Liberty Media. London is also home to some powerful multinationals such as AOL-Time Warner, Paramount, Disney, Liberty Media and also in equipment supply such as Phillips and Sony. These multinationals are not only sources of demand, but also sources of new innovations and new ideas, as the next section illustrates.

# INNOVATION IN THE LONDON CLUSTER: A VIGNETTE

This brief vignette illustrates how the innovation systems in post production and equipment manufacture are focused on London and intertwine with each other. It gives an insight into how the various sources of advantage in London come together to create its pre-eminent status as a node in the global broadcasting industry. It also indicates the futility of trying to create a comparable cluster in the regions through some form of 'cluster strategy'.

Competition in both sectors is driven by innovation. Being first to be able to offer a new innovation allows a post-production company, and indeed in turn the manufacturer, the ability to earn what is typically a short-lived innovation rent. Imitation inevitably follows quickly and what was once fresh and striking very quickly becomes passé and clichéd. Innovation depends on having both the right equipment and the personnel who can operate it. Very often staff moves are linked with the acquisition of new equipment and software, and flurries of staff moves often accompany waves of adoption of new technologies. London is able to attract top talent from around the world, which means that there is a very well-developed labour pool of talented and energetic creative people who are willing to experiment and drive innovation forward. These people are attracted by the ability to do the most demanding and creative work using the latest technology. What is more, there is competition among these creative people for reputations, which provides a further competitive impulse to innovation. Labour mobility via spin-outs, often to exploit a new innovation, is also a distinctive feature of the industry (Cook and Pandit, 2005). The density of the London cluster and the greater entrepreneurialism of the South East both support this spin-out process.

Engineers form a highly important network. Particularly among engineers there are examples of knowledge trading which exemplify the processes analysed by von Hippel (1988). Engineers within post-production play a pivotal role. They understand the technical side, but also have great insight into the creative side of the business, therefore they can articulate what the customer is really after in a way it would be much more difficult to accomplish if engineers from the manufacturing companies were to attempt to talk to creative people directly. Post-production engineers are sometimes involved in client meetings with, for example, advertisers, where their role is to advise on how far it is possible technically to realise the advertiser's vision, and at what cost.

The ability to solve problems face to face is a more general advantage of proximity. First, the fact that people know each other personally means that they can discuss problems more candidly, rather than having to go through the niceties of normal communication channels. They are discussing problems engineer to engineer, rather than haggling company to company. The key advantage is that problems can be sorted out more quickly. This advantage is writ large where there are interface problems between different bits of equipment. These problems are easier to resolve if it is possible to get all the relevant engineers together in the same room to thrash it out. Proximity also helps in another way in sorting out gremlins with new products. All these trouble-shooting activities smooth the path of innovation.

The major equipment manufacturers make considerable efforts to keep abreast of what is happening in the market. They often maintain an engineering presence in Soho, part of which is to provide rapid trouble-shooting, but also to keep abreast of market trends. There is interaction with the engineers in the post-production houses in a number of ways. Engineers from the post-production houses are able to visit the R&D labs of the manufacturing companies which is beneficial to both sides. First, the post-production engineers are able to see what developments are in progress before products are formally unveiled at trade exhibitions. Second, the manufacturing engineers are able to get feedback on their developments, without waiting for a potentially costly flop in the marketplace. Third, such visits provide a forum for candid discussion which can involve discussing problems which the manufacturing engineers are working on but cannot, at present, solve. Occasionally this may lead to the post-production engineers going to help out the research and development (R&D) team in the manufacturing firm. This they are willing to do because they end up getting a product which is more closely suited to their needs. Again, the manufacturing engineers gain insight into what the end user actually requires.

Both Soho post production and the Thames Valley manufacturing clusters have the common distinction of being important nodes in a global industry. The way in which the local node interacts with the global network can be illustrated by a sketch of an actual innovation which is discussed in very general terms for reasons of confidentiality. An R&D facility in the UK was pursuing a particular line of R&D effort. In the process it was interacting with post production in London to get feedback on whether the developments in progress were meeting the requirements of the market. In this dialogue a need was established for which the UK facility had no ready solution. This fact was fed back to the corporate HQ which then relayed the problem to all its other R&D facilities around the world. These facilities then contributed something to the solution which was ultimately pooled by the UK R&D lab which worked up the prototype which was then referred back to the engineering department at corporate HQ to translate the design into production which was done in the multinational's home company. This provides a simple and sketchy example of how intensive knowledge flows within the node interacted with extensive knowledge flows within a global network to produce an innovation.

## CONCLUSIONS

Table 12.5 summarises the key findings regarding the factors which might bear on differences in cluster dynamism in the three cities identified in the literature review. Broadcasting in all three cities appears to be a blend of three of Markusen's types. Clearly the importance, almost since the inception of the industry in Britain, of the BBC, marks it as falling partly into the state-anchored model. The original geographic organisation of the industry was laid down by administrative fiat according to administrative and technical criteria. The existence of dominant firms surrounded by fringe suppliers indicates elements of a hub-and-spoke type cluster. Hub firms in London are larger, more numerous and have greater strategic decision-making capacity. Crucially, London is the centre for network commissioning and it is that which draws the highest quality labour.

344     *Entrepreneurship and Innovations in Functional Regions*

*Table 12.5  Summary of results*

| Factor | London | Bristol | Glasgow |
|---|---|---|---|
| Cluster type | Mix of state anchored and hub and spoke with well-developed 'industrial district' of networked small firms | Mix of state anchored and hub and spoke with small but partially well-developed 'industrial district' of networked small firms | Mix of state anchored and hub and spoke with more weakly developed 'industrial district' of small firms |
| Cluster scale | Very large | Small | Small |
| Cluster 'fit' | Good | Good | Fair |
| Relational assets | Excellent | Good | Fair |
| Labour pool | Excellent, deep and highly specialised | Fair | Fair |
| Inter-firm linkages | Excellent and benefits from a highly specialised division of labour among firms due to cluster scale | Fair, some benefits from a vibrant independent post-production, animation and effects sector | Fair to weak, has a less well-developed independent supply infrastructure |
| Demand | Very strong and international in scope | Fair and has demand for network and international commissions | Fair, but has more emphasis on national programmes and little international demand |
| External connectivity | Excellent | Good | Weak |
| Entrepreneurship | Very strong | Strong | Relatively weak |
| Local governance | Historically weak | Weak | Effective |
| Quality of life | Mixed | Good | Good |

London stands apart from Bristol and Glasgow in the extent to which it has developed a vibrant independent production and facilities sector in the 25 years since the formation of Channel 4. There is no doubt that this sector no longer stands in such a dependent relationship to the major UK broadcasters and several major independents are international competitors in their own right. Bristol also stands apart from Glasgow in that it too developed a relatively mature, if small-scale, independent programme production and post-production sector. Several natural history programme makers have conquered international markets, as has Aardman Animations. Bristol is also distinct from Glasgow in that there is evidence of a higher degree of collective identity and interaction among the firms there. Therefore in terms of developing from a hub-and-spoke cluster to a hub and spoke with functioning industrial district, London is in a class apart, but the relative success of Bristol explains why, at least until very recently, it has outperformed other regional clusters in the UK.

Contrary to the conclusions of a multi-city study which also included London, Bristol and Glasgow (Boddy and Parkinson, 2004a), this study did find evidence of cluster benefits of trust, cooperation and non-market relations, above all in London, but to a significant extent also in Bristol. Both studies clearly indicate that the sources of advantage firms in London gain are typical of those found in Saxenian's (1994) account of Silicon Valley. Above all, personal relationships are easier to build and maintain in a compact space and help both knowledge flows and also the close cooperation of many specialised suppliers, underpinned by trust, to deliver complex products and services to demanding customers. London strongly benefits from a large, specialised and highly talented labour pool. Not only does this give firms enormous flexibility and access to highly skilled and able individuals but it also acts as a magnet to the best new talent. Once there, individuals have strong incentives to invest in highly specific human capital by the density of demand which might call for their highly specialised services. This illustrates the self-sustaining nature of cluster success. Innovation in broadcasting clusters is a beguiling mix of high technology and artistic creativity and is driven not only by the stock of knowledge in the labour pool but also by rivalry, demanding customers, specialised suppliers and the ready flow of knowledge within a tightly bounded geographical space. As has become increasingly understood in the literature more generally, it is vertical relationships linking firms with customers and suppliers which are a highly important contributor to innovation. While broadly similar in type to London, both Bristol and Glasgow lack the scale, strength of demand and global connectivity to come close to creating a node with the strength and sophistication of London. The last two, in common with other regional centres in the UK, struggle to grow although their survival is not seriously in question, particularly given the political will to sustain broadcasting activity in the regions.

Regarding cluster dynamism generally and innovation more specifically, there was limited perceived importance of local government, academic institutions and professional bodies. This is a challenge to some of the received wisdom in the literature regarding the importance of such organisations, particularly in the context of innovation. Nevertheless it would be wrong to draw too hasty a conclusion that these organisations are of peripheral importance or that policies which entail action on their part are doomed to be impotent. As evidenced by the case of Glasgow, a sustained policy of support for business development within the cluster underpinned by joined-up thinking between the Scottish Executive and local agencies has yielded long-term benefits. The relative success of Bristol and London despite weaknesses in governance is consistent with Boddy and Parkinson's (2004b) view that policy has typically had a marginal influence on the relative success of particular urban centres, albeit a marginal influence which can tip the balance. There is little evidence that regional governance plays as strong a role in this industry as Cooke and Morgan (1998) suggest. National policy in terms of enforcing the requirement on broadcasters to commission at least 25 per cent of new production and quotas for regional commissioning has been far more influential.

## ACKNOWLEDGEMENTS

The authors acknowledge the support of the ESRC, award number R000223258, the British Academy, award number SG-36816 and Skillset who provided employment census data.

## REFERENCES

Amin, A. and Thrift, N. (1992), 'Neo-Marshallian Nodes in Global Networks', *International Journal of Urban and Regional Research*, **16**, 571–87.
Bassett, K., Griffiths, R. and Smith, I. (2002), 'Cultural Industries, Cultural Clusters and the City: the Example of Natural History Film-Making in Bristol', *Geoforum*, **33**, 165–77.
Bathelt, H., Malmberg, A. and Maskell, P. (2004), 'Clusters and Knowledge: Local Buzz, Global Pipelines and the Process of Knowledge Creation', *Progress in Human Geography*, **28**, 31–56.
Bayliss, D. (2004), 'Ireland's Creative Development: Local Authority Strategies for Culture-Led Development', *Regional Studies*, **38**, 817–31.
Beaverstock, J.V., Taylor, P.J. and Smith, R.G. (1999), 'A Roster of World Cities', *Cities*, **16**, 445–58.

Boddy, M., Bassett, K., French, S., Griffiths, R., Lambert, C., Leyshon, A., Smith, I., Stewart, M. and Thrift, N. (2004), 'Competitiveness and Cohesion in a Prosperous City-Region: the Case of Bristol', in Boddy and Parkinson (eds) (2004a), pp. 51–70.

Boddy, M. and Parkinson, M. (eds) (2004a), *City Matters. Competitiveness, Cohesion and Urban Governance*, Bristol: Policy Press.

Boddy, M. and Parkinson, M. (2004b), 'Introduction', in Boddy and Parkinson (eds) (2004a), pp. 1–11.

Boggs, J.S. and Rantisi, N.M. (2003), 'The "Relational Turn" in Economic Geography', *Journal of Economic Geography*, 3, 109–16.

Camagni, R. (2002), 'On the Concept of Territorial Competitiveness: Sound or Misleading?', *Urban Studies*, 39, 2395–411.

Coe, N.M. (2001), 'A Hybrid Agglomeration? The Development of a Satellite-Marshallian Industrial District in Vancouver's Film Industry', *Urban Studies*, 38, 1753–75.

Coe, N.M. and Townsend, A.R. (1998), 'Debunking the Myth of Localised Agglomerations: the Development of a Regionalised Service Economy in South-East England', *Transactions of the Institute of British Geographers*, 23, 385–404.

Cook, G.A.S. and Pandit, N.R. (2005), 'Clustered High Technology Small Firms and Innovation Networks: The Case of Post Production in London', in During, W., Oakey, R. and Kauser, S. (eds), *New Technology-Based Firms in the New Millennium*, Volume IV, London: Elsevier, pp. 165-84.

Cook, G.A.S., Pandit, N.R. and Swann, G.M.P. (2001), 'The Dynamics of Industrial Clustering in British Broadcasting', *Information Economics and Policy*, 13, 351–75.

Cooke, P. and Morgan, K. (1998), *The Associational Economy. Firms, Regions and Innovation*, Oxford: Oxford University Press.

Cumbers, A. and MacKinnon, D. (2004), 'Introduction: Clusters in Urban and Regional Development', *Urban Studies*, 41, 959–69.

Department of Culture, Media and Sport (2001), *Creative Industries Mapping Document 2000*, London: DCMS.

Dorling, D. and Thomas, B. (2004), *People and Places. A 2001 Census Atlas of the UK*, Bristol: Policy Press.

Florida, R. (2002), *The Rise of the Creative Class*, New York: Basic Books.

Garcia, B. (2005), 'Deconstructing the City of Culture: The Long-term Cultural Legacies of Glasgow 1990', *Urban Studies*, 42, 841–68.

Hall, P. (2000), 'Creative Cities and Economic Development', *Urban Studies*, 37, 639–49.

Haywood, I. (1998), 'London', *Cities*, 15, 381–92.

HM Treasury (2001), *Productivity in the UK: 3 – The Regional* Dimension, London: HM Treasury.

Jacobs, J. (1972), *The Economy of Cities*, Harmondsworth: Penguin.

Jacobs, J. (1985), *Cities and the Wealth of Nations: Principles of Economic Life*, Harmondsworth: Penguin.

Kitson, M., Martin, R. and Tyler, P. (2004), 'Regional Competitiveness: An Elusive Yet Key Concept?', *Regional Studies*, 38, 991–9.

Malmberg, A. and Maskell, P. (2002), 'The Elusive Concept of Localisation Economies: Towards a Knowledge-based Theory of Spatial Clustering', *Environment and Planning A*, 34, 429–49.

Markusen, A. (1996), 'Sticky Places in Slippery Space: A Typology of Industrial Districts', *Economic Geography*, 72, 293–313.

Marshall, A. (1920), *Principles of Economics*, London: Macmillan.

Marshall, A. (1927), *Industry and Trade*, London: Macmillan.

Martin, R. and Sunley, P. (2003), 'Deconstructing Clusters: Chaotic Concept or Policy Panacea?', *Journal of Economic Geography*, **3**, 5–35.

McCann, P. and Sheppard, S. (2003), 'The Rise, Fall and Rise Again of Industrial Location Theory', *Regional Studies*, **37**, 649–63.

Office of the Deputy Prime Minister (2004), *Competitive European Cities: Where Do The Core Cities Stand?*, London: ODPM.

Porter, M.E. (1990), *The Competitive Advantage of Nations*, Basingstoke: Macmillan.

Porter, M.E. (1998), 'Clusters and the New Economics of Competition', *Harvard Business Review*, November–December, 77–90.

Pred, A. (1977), *City-Systems in Advanced Economies.  Past Growth, Present Processes and Future Development Option,*, London: Hutchinson.

Saxenian, A. (1994), *Regional Advantage: Culture and Competition in Silicon Valley and Route 12*, Cambridge, MA: Harvard University Press.

Scott, A.J. (2000) *The Cultural Economy of Cities. Essays in the Geography of Image-Producing Industries*, London: Sage.

Scott, A.J., Agnew, J., Soja, E.W. and Storper, M. (2001), 'Global City-Regions', in Scott, A.J. (ed.), *Global City Regions*, Oxford: Oxford University Press, pp. 11–30.

Scott, A.J. and Storper, M. (2003), 'Regions, Globalization, Development', *Regional Studies*, **37**, 379–393.

Storper, M. (1997), *The Regional World: Territorial Development in a Global Economy*, New York: Guilford.

Storper, M. and Venables, A.J. (2004), 'Buzz: Face-to-Face Contact and the Urban Economy', *Journal of Economic Geography*, **4**, 351–70.

Sweeting, D., Hambleton, R., Huxham, C., Stewart, M. and Vangen, S. (2004), 'Leadership and Partnership in Urban Governance: Evidence from London, Bristol and Glasgow', in Boddy and Parkinson (eds) (2004a), pp. 349-66.

Taylor, P.J., Walker, D.R.F., Catalano, G. and Hoyler, M. (2002), 'Diversity and Power in the World City Network', *Cities*, **19**, 231–41.

Turok, I. (2003), 'Cities, Clusters and Creative Industries: the Case of Film and Television in Scotland', *European Planning Studies*, **11**, 549–65.

Turok, I. (2004), 'Cities, Regions and Competitiveness', *Regional Studies*, **38**, 1069–83.

Turok, I., Bailey, N., Atkinson, R., Bramley, G., Docherty, I., Gibb, K., Goodlad, R., Hastings, A., Kintrea, K., Kirk, K., Leibovitz, J., Lever, B., Morgan, J. and Paddison, R. (2004), 'Sources of City Prosperity and Cohesion: the case of Glasgow and Edinburgh', in Boddy and Parkinson (eds) (2004a), pp. 13-32.

von Hippel, E. (1988), *The Sources of Innovation*, Oxford: Oxford University Press.

# 13. Technology, Innovation and Latecomer Strategies: The Case of the Mobile Handset Manufacturing Sector in China

## Lei Ding and Kingsley E. Haynes

## BACKGROUND

Without going over the history of the literature in regional dynamics (Haynes et al., 1997), we know that there has been a recent growth in studies of international and interregional convergence using aggregate economic indices. This literature often examines the relationship between new technology and economic growth (Solow, 1956; Porter, 1990; Enos, 1992; Hobday, 1995; Anderson, 1996; Rigby, 2000). Much of that analysis indicates that chronological 'lateness' in the industrialization process does not relegate lagging regions permanently to their disadvantaged position. Positive changes due to increases in efficiency, rapid technological change, technological diffusion and spillovers, access to new markets and differential costs of factor inputs may all play a role in the reduction or elimination of gaps in competitive capacity, creating the possibilities for economic catch-up. Sharif (1989) recognized these 'late-industrializers' as latecomers in the context of technological innovation and diffusion. He noted that beneficial learning investments on the part of newcomers and the encumbrances of earlier investments on the part of mature industrializers might play compensating roles leading to different forms of convergence. Others have noted that late adoption generates advantage in the incorporation of new technology and may result in accelerated diffusion among lagging regions, creating newer opportunities for latecomers (Gerschenkron, 1962; Abramovitz, 1986; Perkins and Neumayer, 2005).

Other explanatory factors of empirically successful latecomer strategies include the degree of openness to international trade and investment and the level of integration into the globalization process (Storper, 1997; OECD,

1998; Rigby, 2000; Lall, 2002).  Perkins and Neumayer (2005) argue the importance of the neoclassical school's emphasis on the role of market liberalization among developing countries, including the removal of institutional barriers, the positive environment for foreign investment and the internationalization of trade, which both stimulate and accelerate technological diffusion and internal innovation.

Some of the literature on the emergence of the Asian economies – the so-called 'little tigers' – embodies this catch-up process of latecomer economies, particularly in manufacturing where many of them have reduced or eliminated the gap in production-related capabilities and in other cases have surpassed their advanced economy counterparts (Kim, 1980 and 1997; Ernst and O'Connor, 1992; Hobday, 1995, 2001; Lall, 2000; Mathews and Cho, 2000; Mathews, 2002; Liu, 2005).  In many cases, technological innovation has played a central role in this catch-up process in these latecomer regions (Ernst, 2004).  Specifically, innovation in electronics manufacturing is often cited in that literature and is based on advantageous production capacity, efficiency from low-cost production, rapid model changes to fit changing customer needs and tastes, available investment for technological change and refitting, and skilled engineering adaptation in production processes and in final product design (Bennett, 2002; UNIDO, 2002; Ernst, 2004). Latecomers have the advantage of being the 'first-second'. According to the literature this was for some products in particular industries, the most profitable strategy in regard to new products, in which the firm concentrates on analysis and 'reverse engineering' of competitors' developments and abandons its original research and development (R&D) (Baldwin and Childs, 1969). Of course, the assumptions here are that products of the industry can be analyzed fairly easily, and imitation processes do not require lengthy and costly retooling, improvement over original innovations will not involve patent infringement suits, demands are quite inelastic of prices, and so on.

The central idea is that international knowledge diffusion from leading regions to lagging regions can be expressed as a latecomer innovation strategy with respect to new innovations in process technologies, critical component development or in rapid changes in final product design.  This is the basis of Solow's (1956) neoclassical growth school where free technological spillovers produce long-run economic convergence.  Theories in the regional economic development literature, such as growth pole theory or trickle-down effects, can also be seen as expressions of these spillovers (Darwent, 1969; Higgins and Savoie, 1995; Stimson et al., 2006).  When intermediate development steps are shortened or eliminated these policies are often referred to as 'leapfrog' strategies – typical of some successful Asian economies (Singh, 1999).

Freeman (1987) and Nelson (1993) analyze the role of technological diffusion from a different perspective and conclude that rather than a simple flow of knowledge across country borders, technological advance and innovation rely on specific firms, networks, and economic institutions. They note the successful economic stories of the US in the nineteenth century, Japan in the 1960s, Korea and Singapore and other Asian economies in the 1980s, and more recently China, who all benefited from the exploitation of opportunities for technology catch-up (Liu, 2005). To some extent this view integrates the role of government into the technological innovation process, although most studies of Asian countries isolate the two processes of government and free market decision making (World Bank, 1993).

Product cycle theory also provides a different perspective of the technical catch-up for firms in a developing country (Vernon, 1966; Tan, 2002). When a multinational corporation starts to manufacture and sell a new product, the new product is made in developed countries and it is sold first in its domestic market and other developed markets and then in developing markets. But if the large-scale entry into a developing market becomes attractive and lucrative or if the lower costs in developing countries enable multinational companies to reduce their product costs, multinational firms start to engage in foreign direct investment (FDI) activities in developing countries. At the early stage, affiliates in developing countries are often assembly production lines. Over time, if there is a facilitating government policy and an appropriate cooperation from the foreign investors, these assembly and marketing facilities often localize the once-imported intermediate goods and even export the finished products to the global market. And eventually, large-scale local production by multinational firms foster the diffusion of technology know-how in the developing country. Domestic firms thus may grasp the opportunity to develop competitive local products.

Another perspective based on technological learning and the role of national innovation systems is also discussed (Kim, 1997; Lee and Lim, 2001). Lee and Lim observe that different technological regimes have different patterns of innovation and diffusion across industries and regions or even countries. However, it is important to remember that latecomer firms or sectors are not assured of catch-up performance with advanced economies even when following similar strategies, because the contextual economic environment is always changing. So what worked in one environmental situation may not be effective in another.

This chapter explores the closing of the gap in competitive capacity by decomposing the aggregate process and looking at one sector – telecommunications – in one developing economy – China.

## INTRODUCTION

China has the world's largest population. More than 60 percent live in the countryside. In 2003 approximately 20 percent of the population had fixed-line telephone access; approximately 21 percent had cell phones. Less than 10 percent of the mobile phone subscribers live in the countryside (Chinese Ministry of Information Industry (MII), 2006).

Telecommunications development in China was highly rigid and a low priority for 30 years (1949–79). A series of reforms followed during the next 12 years and mobile phone communications were introduced into China in 1987. The mid to late 1990s saw rapid development, competition and explosive growth (Figure 13.1). Mobile phone communications grew at an astounding rate, reaching 10 million users by 1997. The number of mobile subscribers exceeded fixed-line users seven years later. Since 2000 there has been full competition in value-added services and new technologies have been introduced (Network Weekly, 2004).

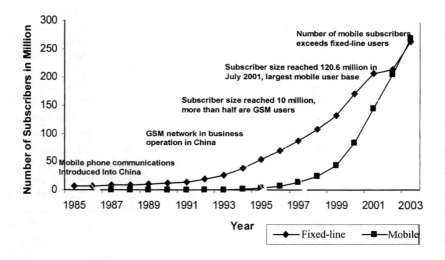

*Figure 13.1    Telecommunication events in China*

With a population of over 1.3 billion, China has the largest handset market in the world and this market continues to grow at a rapid rate. At the end of 2003 there were an estimated 268 million mobile subscribers, and more than 5 million people signed up for cellular phones each month (MII, 2004). Before 1999, China's mobile handset market had been completely dominated by foreign brand products, such as Motorola, Nokia, and Ericsson. As China applied its 'attracting and absorbing FDI' policies towards foreign mobile communications equipment providers, almost all major handset manufacturers were encouraged to establish joint ventures in China. As a result, all mobile phones sold were produced by foreign-owned enterprises or imported directly from abroad before 1998. Lacking scientific knowledge in local settings, with poorly developed or nonexistent support industries, with a history of heavily regulated telephony, and with a poorly developed hard-wire telephony infrastructure, China constrained indigenous firms from moving first in the domestic market.

However, since the entry of Chinese domestic mobile handset manufacturers in 1998, foreign brand products gradually lost their dominance in the handset market. In 2002, Chinese brands captured about 30 percent of the market, growing to approximately 55 percent in 2003. Chinese domestic suppliers have successfully established their position to surpass the market share of joint ventures, while direct imports have largely been phased out. Chinese brands are becoming the mainstream products in the domestic mobile phone market.

How did China's domestic firms catch up with the early movers, overcome inherent disadvantages and succeed in dominating the world's largest handset market in less than five years? By examining the mobile communications sector as a whole and taking the manufacturing of mobile handsets as a special case, this chapter examines how China's domestic firms have surmounted their inherent disadvantages and have taken a leadership position in limited product areas. This chapter concludes with a summary of factors that contributed to the success of China's domestic handset manufacturers.

## DEVELOPMENT OF CHINA'S MOBILE HANDSET MANUFACTURING SECTOR

The mobile communications market relied totally on direct imports in the late 1980s. During China's transition from a planned to a more market-oriented economy, telecommunications became a leading sector with an exponential growth rate in a dualistic economy (Jin and Haynes, 1997). Realizing the attractiveness of its potential market demand for mobile communications equipment and the bargaining power generated from its market size, China actively approached foreign suppliers with joint venture negotiations and technology transfer opportunities. With the establishment of Shanghai Bell in 1984, joint ventures in selected areas were strongly encouraged. Table 13.1 shows the digital cellular sector listed in the 'encouraged' category in the 'Government Guidelines for Foreign Investment in Telecommunications' issued by the State Council in 1995. In contrast, the analogue wireless system is listed as 'restricted' while the telecommunications service sector is completely prohibited from foreign investment.[1] Overall, foreign investment in the mobile communications equipment manufacturing sector was greatly encouraged by the Chinese government in the mid-1990s.

*Table 13.1     Regulatory categories of FDI in the telecom sector, 1995*

| Category | Details |
| --- | --- |
| Encouraged | Digital cellular, SDH, ATM switching system, satellite communications system, digital microwave system |
| Restricted | Analogue wireless system, PABX, non-ATM central office switches, TV and Radio Broadcasting systems, fax machines, low speed digital microwave system |
| Forbidden | Telecommunications basic service |

*Source:* Tan (2002).

When the 'attracting and absorbing FDI' policy was applied to the mobile communications equipment manufacturing sector it led to the emergence of FDI in mobile handset production in the early 1990s. In 1992, Motorola built its first manufacturing plant in the port of Tianjin. Now nearly all the world-famous mobile communications equipment providers, including Motorola, Ericsson, Nokia, Siemens, and Samsung, have established joint venture companies in China (see Table 13.2). Motorola, Nokia and Ericsson are the three largest. The total foreign investment in this sector was $1.9 billion in 1998 and over $4 billion in 2001 (Wang, 2003).

These foreign companies enjoyed a long period of success due to strong demand in China. Four primary joint-venture firms, Motorola, Ericsson, Nokia, and Siemens, dominated China's mobile handset market before 2002. The aggregate market share of these four companies was over 85 percent in 1999. China is also the single largest market for many large multinational companies. It accounts for 30 percent of Motorola's handset sales, making Motorola increasingly dependent on China for growth. Ericsson has established a primary base for production for worldwide sales in China and transferred R&D and production research to China, making it a regional presence. Nokia's largest market is China, with revenue of over $2.5 million and exports valued at $2.1 billion for 2003. Siemens's early, but smaller, commitment continued to pay dividends while Samsung, although late, was investing heavily (ChinaNex, 2004).

*Table 13.2  Primary foreign handset producers in China*

| | Motorola | Nokia | Ericsson | Siemens | Samsung |
|---|---|---|---|---|---|
| Date of entry | 1987 | 1985 | 1985 | 1982 | 1992 |
| First handset manufactured | 1992 | Mid-1990s | 1992 | 1993 | – |
| Subsidiaries in China | WO = 1<br>JV = 8<br>Controlled = 1<br>Local offices = 26<br>R&D facilities = 18<br>Employees = 13,000 | JV = 8<br>Local offices ~ 50<br>global R&D centers = 2<br>Employees = 4,700 | WO = 4<br>JV = 10<br>Local offices = 26<br>Employees= 4,500 | JV > 40<br>Local offices = 28<br>Employees= 21,000 | Manufacturing facilities = 11<br>Investment company = 1<br>Local offices = 3<br>R&D center = 1<br>after-sales service center = 1<br>Employees = 11,000 |
| Total investment | $3.4 billion (till 2002); R&D = $0.3 billion | More than $2.9 billion | More than 600 million | More than $660 million | More than $2.6 billion |
| Revenue (2003) | $6 billion | $2.5 billion | $1.8 billion | $1 billion | $6.4 million (sales in 2002) |
| Mobile phone production | – | – | – | 12.5 million (2003) | – |
| Mobile phones sold (2003) | about 12 million | about 10 million | – | 2–3 million | – |
| Market share (1999) (%) | 39.40 | 32.30 | 6.44 | 5.95 | – |
| Market share (2002) (%) | 25.76 | 18.17 | 2.09 | 4.66 | – |

*Note:* WO = 'wholly owned'; JV = 'joint venture'; – = 'not available'.

*Source:* The official websites of companies presented.

Local producers have captured more than 50 percent of China's domestic market, but joint ventures in China are still their primary production bases to supply the global market. In 2001, the total number of mobile handsets exported from China was 39.63 million, increasing to 63.15 million in 2002 and 95.23 million in 2003 (Chinese Ministry of Commerce, 2007). More than 98 percent of these exported handsets were manufactured by those joint ventures (MII, 2004). Although these foreign companies have lost their dominating role in China's domestic market, they are producing more handsets than the domestic firms (about 70 percent of total production in 2003) increasingly for export. However, as of 2004, foreign companies through joint ventures still dominated the domestic high-end handset market (with a price higher than 3,000 RMB/$400 per handset).

Local firms started supplying China's domestic handset market in 1998 when Kejian manufactured the first GSM handset with a domestic brand.

However, the development of the local manufacturers had been very slow prior to 2002 (see Figure 13.2).   A few large international companies dominated the internal market, especially in the urban areas.   The market share of domestic brands in China's domestic market was only 5 percent in 1999 and 10.7 percent in 2000.

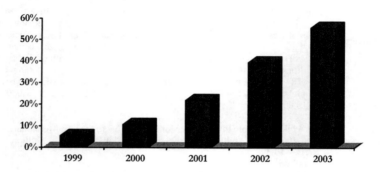

*Source*: Chinese Ministry of Information Technology, various years.

*Figure 13.2     Local Chinese brands – market share growth, 1999–2003*

Domestic companies lagged in all technological areas of handset manufacturing and design.   The government began to support domestic producers officially after 1999.   In January 1999, 'Several Issues on Speeding up the Development of Chinese Mobile Communications Industry' was issued by the State Council (Tan, 2002).   This document stipulated a list of measures to support local mobile communications equipment providers, including assignment of research grants for R&D, preferred interest rates, discounted tax rates, restriction of further foreign investment in the handset manufacturing sector, and other indirect measures, such as local governments' provision of free land in high-tech industrial parks for handset producers.

Encouraged by the government's support and lured by the rapidly growing handset market in China, many domestic firms entered this market after 1999. There are more than 20 domestic GSM or CDMA handset manufacturers now, which grew out of existing manufacturers in the four categories as listed in Table 13.3: consumer electronics producers, specialized mobile phone producers, telecommunications equipment manufacturers, and PC manufactures.   Mastering manufacturing skills and occupying the domestic market was a first priority for these domestic producers.   In fact, most domestic firms chose a 'brand-pasting' (*Tie Pai*) strategy, that is, they imported mobile phones directly from South Korea or Taiwan and then pasted their own brands on the phones.[2]  In this sense, most of the first-generation handsets of these firms are not 'real' domestic brand products since they were not designed and manufactured domestically.  But at the same time, firms invested heavily in manufacturing facilities and process technologies to achieve economies of scale and learning curve effects.  Later, most of these firms chose joint cooperation with foreign companies (not joint ventures) or developed R&D independently.  Some of the domestic manufacturers are still using the brand-pasting method for at least a portion of their products and enjoy the benefits of the government's preferential policies.  For example, as late as in 2003, a senior official of the MII condemned publicly the brand-pasting strategy and threatened to ban the import of mobile phones completely in 2004 (Wang, 2004).  Although there is some skepticism about the technical competency of China's domestic firms, clearly the capacity gap is closing.

*Table 13.3   Domestic handset manufacturers in China, 2003*

| Categories | Firms (date of first mobile phone manufactured) |
| --- | --- |
| Consumer electronics producers | TCL (2000), Haier (1999), Konka (2000), Xiaxin (1998), Hisense (2001) |
| Specialized mobile phone producers | Bird (1999), Kejian (1998), EastCom (1999), Capitel (2001), CECT (2001), Putian (2001) |
| Telecommunications equipment manufacturers | Datang (2001), Zhongxin (2000), Panda (1998), Panda Mobile (1998) |
| PC manufacturers | Legend (2002), Tide (2001) |

China's local producers gradually dominated the domestic mobile phone market.  Figure 13.3 shows that the domestic market share of local manufacturers increased gradually from 5.46 percent in 1999 to 10.7 percent in 2000, and 21.8 percent in 2001.  In 2002, the market share increased sharply to 39.4 percent.  In 2003, China's domestic firms produced 34.3 million and sold 34.1 million mobile handsets, taking a majority of China's mobile handset market with a share of 55.8 percent (ibid.).  In contrast, the share of the four leading foreign brands, Motorola, Nokia, Siemens, and Ericsson, declined from more than 85 percent in 1999 to 46 percent in 2002, and  24 percent in 2003 (MII, 2004).  Bird has been a leading producer with the largest market share of all domestic firms since 2000.  According to the MII, Bird held 15 percent of the handset market in 2003, and is a major contributor to lifting the share of Chinese brands to 55.8 percent in 2003. Overall, 10 domestic firms produced more than one million handsets in 2003.

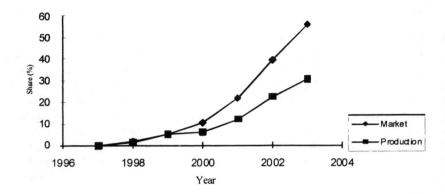

*Source:* Chinese Ministry of Information Technology, various years.

*Figure 13.3     Growth of market/production share of local-brand handsets, 1997–2003*

Chinese handset makers have successfully narrowed the technology gap with industry leaders by aggressive investment in manufacturing facilities. After 2002, handset manufacturers also significantly increased investment in R&D, focusing on upgrading their technological capabilities. Bird spent 6 percent of its revenue on R&D in 2003 (Network Weekly, 2004). But Chinese makers had not yet reached the stage of mastering the core technologies of handset products. In fact, by the close of 2004 no domestic firm had grasped the core technology of GSM and CDMA mobile phones. This is also true for many Japanese and South Korean companies (as of 2004) since core technologies of chip design were controlled by Texas Instruments (TI), Qualcomm and a few other companies.

Overall, there is a dynamic balance between Chinese domestic firms and foreign-owned enterprises in the handset market. China's policy has successfully empowered local firms to dominate the low-end and some medium-end Chinese markets with the help of foreign-owned and joint-venture enterprises. On the other hand, foreign-owned enterprises have continued to successfully dominate the high-end and some medium-end markets in China through joint ventures and intermediate goods export. China's domestic firms have occupied a large market share but have a long way to go to achieve technological leadership.

## BEHIND THE HYPERGROWTH

Chinese domestic mobile phone manufacturers are latecomers since they entered the handset market about 10 years later than the foreign producers. In this sense, the mobile phone manufacturing industry in China provides a good test case of the catch-up process by firms who are latecomers. The word 'latecomer' has been used extensively in previous economic and organizational studies. For example, the Korean semiconductor industry has been widely cited as an example of the successful latecomers (Cho et al., 1998; Mathews and Cho, 1999; Hobday, 1995; Choung et al., 2000). Cho et al. (1998) classified the sources of early-mover advantages, as well as latecomer advantages, into three areas: market, competition, and the characteristics of the early-moving firm (see Table 13.4).

*Table 13.4    Summary of early-movers/latecomers' advantages*

|  | Advantages of early movers | Opportunities for latecomers |
|---|---|---|
| Market | Brand loyalty; switching costs | Dynamic market; customer taste adjustments; new technological changes |
| Competition | Preemption | Incumbent inertia |
| Firm itself | Advantage through learning by doing | More-concrete information and less uncertainty; often resource-rich environment |

*Source*: Based on Cho et al. (1998).

Many factors contributed to the rapid development of China's mobile phone manufacturing. Following a similar framework as summarized by Cho et al., we classified success factors and examined the mobile communications sector as a whole. Here we combine those factors listed as 'competition' and 'firm' in Table 13.4 into a broad *competition* category while emphasizing another important factor – government policies.

### Market Structure

Local market conditions supported an immediate demand for mobile phones when local producers entered the market in late 1998. Before the late 1990s, owning a mobile phone was a rare luxury reserved only for leading bureaucrats or wealthy businessmen. But since 1998, ordinary persons have gradually accepted mobile phones because of the sharp decline in the mobile connection fees and mobile phone prices. In 1999, the total number of mobile phone users reached 43.3 million and nearly doubled in one year, reaching 84.5 million at the end of 2000. The number of mobile phone users increases by at least 50 million every year. New users need to buy handsets and existing subscribers also need to replace their old cell phones, which creates a large handset market in China (Figure 13.4). Since 2002, China has had the largest telecommunications network in terms of both fixed and mobile communications capacities (268 million cellular subscribers and 264 million fixed-line users in 2003). Even a small share of this large market would support the growth of a large producer.

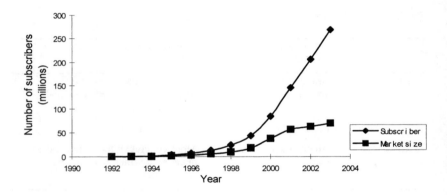

*Source:* Chinese Ministry of Information Technology, Chinese National Statistical Bureau, various years.

*Figure 13.4  Growth of the number of mobile phone subscribers and handset market size*

More important, the inherent nature of the mobile phone business was such that it created opportunities for latecomers to technologically leapfrog over early starters and assume industry leadership in certain fields. China's 2G (second-generation) mobile phone domestic producers could compete with foreign rivals at the chip-designing level because of technological patents. But many companies without chip technology, such as Samsung and LG, also established their position by succeeding in developing new application software and exterior designs. China's domestic producers also mastered design capability quickly, and now they provide more new GSM handset models than some of their foreign competitors.[3]  Domestic firms' knowledge of domestic markets also gives them advantages.  For example, since Chinese customers usually prefer folding handset over Nokia's traditional candy-bar handsets, domestic firms provided a variety of folding handset products to accord with customers' taste.  Although some foreign brands, such as Motorola, provide different folding models, Nokia's market share has declined steadily in China from 30 percent in 2000 to 13 percent in 2003, due partly to insipid flat design and lack of innovation (Sun, 2003).

Due to technological change, China's firms are at the same starting-point with foreign competitors for 3G mobile phone technologies.  It is not impossible for China's domestic firms to become involved and then control core technologies in some areas for 3G.  In fact, China had paid special attention to the TD-SCDMA standard and has jointly developed it with the China Academy of Telecommunications Technology (CATT) and Siemens.  TD-SCDMA is one of only three international standards recognized by the International Telecommunications Union (ITU) for 3G and is the first ITU standard proposed by China.  On 30 October 2002, the alliance of TD-SCDMA industry, consisting of eight domestic enterprises – Datang, Huawei, Soutec, Huali, Legend, ZTE, CEC and Putian – was established in Beijing.  Financially supported by the Chinese government, a meeting on TD-SCDMA prototype standards was set up by members of the Alliance in 2004 (RTX Telecom, 2003).  Although Motorola, Nokia, and Ericsson already have their own mature 3G products, these products cannot easily be introduced into China because of different standards.  China's domestic firms have the potential to build technological competency in this area.

**Competition**

In the intensely competitive handset market, domestic manufacturers compete directly with foreign-owned or joint-venture rivals.  China's diverse domestic mobile phone manufacturers have adopted a series of strategies to compete with their leading foreign competitors.  This competition has contributed to China's success.  As in many other Chinese industries, domestic competition among China's mobile handset manufacturers has been regarded as more important and threatening than competition overseas.

First, China's domestic firms focused on the low- or middle-end market and initiated severe price competition based on their advantages in low costs and local market characteristics.  The leading domestic firm, Bird, engages in competition by keeping prices lower than comparable products (ChinaNex, 2004).  Network Weekly (2004) estimates the average price of the mobile phones sold by Bird to be about RMB 919.21 (about $110) with an average profit of RMB 20.84 (less than $3) per handset, indicating that most mobile phones sold by Bird were low-end products. Joint ventures eventually lost the low-end market because of their relatively higher costs in labor and distribution. Even in the mid-range segments, joint ventures are facing strong competition – mainly from Chinese companies.

Second, local manufacturers usually have more extensive distribution channels which assist the capture and maintenance of their market throughout the country, especially in small cities and in the countryside. More than 20 handset manufacturers in China (including Bird, Kejian, TCL Mobile, and other small and medium-sized companies) primarily sell handsets through their own retail stores or dealers throughout the country. Especially for those domestic firms who are also consumer electronics producers or PC manufacturers, they have existing large distribution channels which can be used for handset sale. In recent years, some manufacturers also began to supply handsets to the mobile communications carriers. Figure 13.5 shows the distribution channels of a typical mobile handset manufacturer in China.

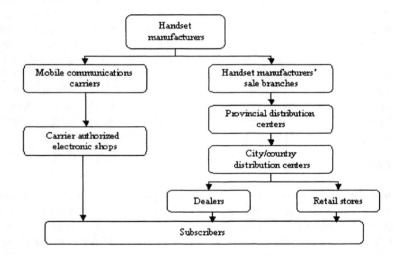

*Figure 13.5    Distribution channels of Chinese domestic firms*

Many specialized handset producers built their distribution channels on their own while electronic goods producers or PC manufacturers used their existing distribution networks. Manufacturers usually give the dealers a commission for each handset sold by the dealers. The commission rates vary in accordance with the number of handsets sold in a certain period. Some dealers offer incentives, reducing their commissions in an attempt to attract more customers and to obtain higher rates of commission later. Joint ventures usually do not have their own sales networks, but depend on a complicated three-level hierarchical agency system, which increases their distribution costs. As a result, domestic firms usually have more distribution channels than their foreign competitors. Nokia sells its handsets through a resale network with 900 outlets in China and has begun to work with regional distributors such as electronics store chains. In contrast, Bird sells its products through 40 distributors, 400 sales offices, 15,000 resale networks and 50,000 retail outlets (ChinaNex, 2004).[4]

Some Chinese producers also often provide better-quality after-sales services. Since many of these mobile phone manufacturers are also consumer-electric producers, they have experience and expertise in after-sales service. Bird built nearly 2,000 customers support centers, many in second- and third-tier cities.

## Government Intervention

Last and most important is the Chinese government's carefully planned intervention and support for the handset manufacturing sector. In the early stages, the government maintained policies promoting foreign investment in this industry. Diverse forms were adopted, including foreign wholly owned enterprises, joint-venture enterprises, joint cooperation enterprises and so on. The presence of many joint-venture handset manufacturers fostered the diffusion of technology expertise across the country. This was a broad-ranging knowledge diffusion and exchange which involved R&D, production, subcontracting, marketing, after-sales services, and local human resource training. China's domestic entrepreneurs, designers, workers, and engineers quickly grasped the opportunity to develop competitive local products. Since a local company, Kejian, produced the first GSM handset in 1998, local manufacturers' production of handsets gained rapid growth, built on the diffusion of technologies into China through various foreign investment and technology transfers and augmented them by local R&D efforts.

China's ultimate goal is to enable its local firms to compete with multinational companies, both in the Chinese and in the global market. The Chinese government shifted its role from *supporter* of joint ventures in the mobile communications manufacturing industry, including the handset sector, to one of *protector* when domestic firms began to compete with the foreign investment-controlled firms. The State Council adopted policies designed to allow Chinese firms to increase technological capacity and occupy the domestic market, to attract more investment and to collect special program funds to improve the technological competency of domestic mobile communications equipment producers (Network Weekly, 2004). The State Council financially supported R&D for mobile technologies by (i) transferring 5 percent of fixed-line telephone installation fees as a special grant from 1999 to 2003 and (ii) the MII invested 1.4 billion yuan ($169.7 million) from mobile connection fees. In addition, it stopped issuing licenses for joint ventures in mobile handset manufacturing after 1999.

Further, when GSM handset technology was becoming obsolete and CDMA technologies were maturing, the government established preferential policies toward domestic CDMA manufacturers. These policies limited domestic licenses for foreign competitors, restricted the sales of CDMA handsets produced by joint-venture firms and required domestic branding and R&D development. In 2001, licenses for CDMA mobile phone production were issued to 18 domestic firms and Motorola; Nokia received a license in 2003; no more licenses will be issued. The government restricts importation of CDMA handsets with quotas and charges an extra 2.5 to 5 percent of total sales volume if joint-venture firms sell CDMA handsets in China. The government required domestic CDMA mobile handset manufacturers to own their own brands, have independent R&D capability and/or possess appropriate patents.

In summary, tariff reduction, preferred interest rates, subsidies for R&D, regulations of market entry, and many other measures were implemented in China to support its mobile handset manufacturing sector. Telecommunications service providers are also encouraged by the government to purchase products of domestic venders. An extreme example is that the government organized supply–demand coordination conferences to promote the adoption of domestic products (Lu and Wong, 2003). In addition, numerical targets for export, production and R&D have been suggested by the government (MII, 2004). The government has been an important factor in the development of China's handset manufacturing sector and closing the technology capacity gap.

## CONCLUSIONS

China is the largest handset market in the world and this market continues to grow at an extremely rapid rate. Before 1999, China's mobile handset market was completely dominated by foreign brand products. However, since the entry of Chinese domestic mobile handset manufacturers in 1998, the domestic suppliers have gradually established their position to surpass the market share of joint ventures, while direct imports have been largely phased out. While products of joint ventures still control the high-end market, domestic brands are becoming the mainstream products in mobile handset market.

By examining China's mobile handset manufacturing sector as a whole and taking the manufacturing of mobile handsets as a special case, we found several factors that contributed to the success of the domestic handset manufacturers. Following a framework summarized by Cho et al. (1998), we classify these factors into three categories. First, China's large handset market supported an immediate demand for mobile phones. The inherent nature of the mobile phone business was such that it created opportunities for latecomers to technologically leapfrog. Second, in the intense competition with joint ventures, domestic producers occupied the domestic market with the advantages of low prices, extensive distribution channels, high performance–price ratios, better after-sales service, as well as a better understanding of the local market and tastes. Last, the growth of the industry has been carefully planned with intervention through government policies. By playing various roles in a timely manner, the government has provided crucial support for development of the mobile handset industry. The case of the mobile handset market suggests that China has localized the production of low-to-medium-end handset products, which gradually destroyed the direct import of these products and occupied the market which had been dominated by joint ventures. By actively investing in R&D and participating in the establishment of new technology standards, it is possible that local producers will build their technological competencies and become technological leaders in certain areas.

Taking the manufacturing of mobile handsets as a special case, this analysis suggests that China's policy and regulations have successfully helped local firms enhance the capacity of manufacturing and developing low-to-medium-end and some high-end products in the mobile handset manufacturing sector. Local firms have become dominant suppliers in the Chinese market. However, local firms have not become full-range competitive suppliers of high-end products either in domestic or in global markets. With China's accession to the World Trade Organization in November 2001, China's 'attract and absorb' strategy meets new challenges, since the way has been paved for foreign investment in all telecom sectors (see Lu and Wong, 2003). The selective industry and FDI policies as 'Government Guidelines for Foreign Investment in Telecommunications' will not be available in the future. Fiercer competition is expected and the survival of less-efficient domestic players will be threatened.

With further interaction between China and multinational companies, several scenarios could emerge to change or maintain the current market condition. The first scenario, maintaining the status quo, might be unacceptable either for multinational companies or for China. Even dominating the high-end products, multinational corporations still have sufficient incentive to occupy the medium-end and some low-end markets in

China. However, China's desire to develop into a capable global competitor would not be satisfied by this scenario. A second scenario could see the multinational companies develop a full range of products for low-to-medium-end as well as high-end markets and lower their prices. They would also extend and refine their distribution channels or cooperate with major service providers thus enabling them to reach the markets in small cities and in the countryside. This outcome is what foreign investors have been hoping for. Considering the fact that local manufacturers generally lack R&D capability and resource, this outcome is possible although China would try to block it. In the third scenario, there will be a close integration between Chinese local firms and foreign investors. Most local firms focus on providing low-to-medium-end products to domestic markets or supplying multinational companies with certain components in the short term. A few local manufacturers are gradually acquiring the capacity to develop a full range of handsets from low-end to high-end global markets and become technical leaders in certain areas. Foreign investors would keep their leadership in R&D and the high-end market in the short term. But in the long term, local firms will dominate the domestic market and occupy a significant portion of the global market. What has happened in China's television, personal computer, and central office switch markets suggests that this scenario could be a realistic and win–win solution both for China and for foreign investors.

## NOTES

1. China's general FDI policy for products in the 'encouraged' category is 'attracting and accepting whatever is possible'. Foreign investors usually can enjoy some preferential policies such as free land, tariff reduction, preferred interest rates, etc. Products in the 'Restricted' category are still in strong demand by the market but there are many joint ventures or domestic suppliers whose products can meet the demand in terms of quality, features, and prices. For products in this category, the Chinese government would usually use the strategy of 'picking up the best partners and limiting the number of joint ventures/other FDI ventures'. 'Forbidden' products are usually outdated technologies and foreign investment is prohibited in any form.
2. This is legal although it is not encouraged and is usually prohibited by the government. At the early stage, some firms just traded the devices in order to enjoy the government's preferential policies and incentives. But government policies prohibit domestic firms from doing so. More firms imported parts from Korea, Japan, or other countries for assembly. Now most manufacturers range from actual local production to imported parts.
3. For example, Bird launched 35 new models in 2003 and another 50 were scheduled for 2004. In contrast, Nokia launched only 14 GSM models in China in 2003.
4. The differences in sales systems among local firms and foreign players is primarily due to the firms' own choices because different players focus on different markets: foreign brands primarily focus on high-end customers in big cities while local firms focus on middle- or low-income users in middle or small cities and the countryside. Of course, since most local manufacturers are also consumer-electric or PC producers, they had extensive distribution channels even before they entered this market.

# REFERENCES

Abramovitz, M. (1986), 'Catching-up, forging ahead and falling behind', *Journal of Economic History,* **46** (2), 385–406.

Anderson, D. (1996), 'Energy and the environment: Technical and economic possibilities', *Finance and Development,* **33** (2), 10–13.

Baldwin, W.L. and Childs, G.L. (1969), 'The Fast Second and Rivalry in Research and Development', *Southern Economic Journal,* **36** (1), 18–24.

Bennett, D. (2002), *Innovative Technology Transfer Framework Linked to Trade for UNIDO Action,* Vienna: United Nations Industrial Development Organization.

ChinaNex (2004), 'China's telecommunications equipment providers: company profile', http://www.chinanex.com/company/index.htm, September 10, 2007.

Chinese Ministry of Commerce (2007), 'Statistical information' (in Chinese), http://cccme.mofcom.gov.cn/ztxx/ztxx.html, September 10, 2007.

Chinese Ministry of Information Industry (MII) (various years), 'Statistical information' (in Chinese), http://www.mii.gov.cn/col/col166/index.html, last September 10, 2007.

Chinese National Statistical Bureau (various years), *China Statistical Yearbook,* Beijing: China Statistics Press.

Cho, D.-S., Kim, D.J. and Rhee, D.K. (1998), 'Latecomer strategy: evidence from the semiconductor industry of Japan and Korean', *Organization Science,* **34** (2), 139–56.

Choung, J.Y., Hwang, H.R., Choi, J.H. and Rim, M.H. (2000), 'Transition of Latecomer Firms from Technology Users to Technology Generators: Korean Semiconductor Firms', *World Development,* **28** (5), 969–82.

Darwent, D.F. (1969), 'Growth Poles and Growth Centers in Regional Planning: A Review', *Environment and Planning,* **1** (1), 5–32.

Enos, J. (1992) *The Creation of Technological Capacity in Developing Countries,* London: Pinter.

Ernst, D. (2004), 'Late Innovation Strategies in Asian Electronics Industries: A Conceptual Framework and Illustrative Evidence', East-West Center Working Papers. Economic Series, No. 66, March.

Ernst, D. and O'Connor, D. (1992), *Competing in the Electronics Industry. The Experience of Newly Industrializing Economies,* Paris: Development Center Studies, OECD.

Freeman, C. (1987), *Technology Policy and Economic Performance,* London: Pinter.

Gerschenkron, A. (1962), *Economic Backwardness in Historical Perspective: A Book of Essays,* Cambridge, MA: Belknap Press of Harvard University Press.

Haynes, K.E., Button, K.J., Nijkamp, P. and Qiangsheng, L. (eds) (1997), *Regional Dynamics, Vols I and II,* Cheltenham, UK and Lyme, US: Edward Elgar.

Higgins, B. and Savoie, D.J. (1995), *Regional Development Theories and Their Application,* New Brunswick, NJ: Transaction Publishers.

Hobday, M. (1995), 'East Asian latecomer firms: Learning the technology of electronics', *World Development,* **23** (7), 1171–93.

Hobday, M. (2001), 'The Electronics Industries of the Asia-Pacific: Exploiting International Production Networks for Economic Development', *Asia-Pacific Economic Literature,* **15** (1), 13–29.

Jin, D. and Haynes, K.E. (1997), 'Economic Transition at the Edge of Order and Chaos: China's Dualist and Leading Sector Approach', *Journal of Economic Issues,* **31** (1), 79–101.

Kim, L. (1980), 'Stages of Development of Industrial Technology in a Developing Country: a Model', *Research Policy,* **9**, 254–77.

Kim, L. (1997), *Imitation to Innovation: The Dynamics of Korea's Technological Learning,* Boston, MA: Harvard Business School Press.

Lall, S. (2000), 'Technological Change and Industrialization in the Asian Newly Industrializing Economies: Achievements and Challenges', in Kim, L. and Nelson, R.R. (eds), *Technology, Learning and Innovation. Experiences of Newly Industrializing Economies*, Cambridge: Cambridge University Press, pp. 13–68.

Lall, S. (2002), 'Transnational Corporations and Technology Flows', in Nayyar, D. (ed.), *Governing Globalization: Issues and Institutions*, Oxford: Oxford University Press, pp. 78–107.

Lee, K. and Lim, C. (2001), 'Technological regimes, catching up and leapfrogging: finding from the Korean industries', *Research Policy,* **30**, 459–83.

Liu, X. (2005), 'China's Development Model: An Alternative Strategy for Technological Catch-Up Innovations', Working paper, Institute of Innovation Research, Hitotsubashi University, www.rieti.go.jp/en/events/bbl/05032202.pdf .(last accessed 10 September, 2007.

Lu, D. and Wong, C.K. (2003), *China's Telecommunications Market,* Cheltenham, UK and Northampton, MA, USA: Edward Elgar.

Mathews, J.A. (2002), 'Competitive Advantages of the Latecomer Firm: A Resource-Based Account of Industrial Catch-Up Strategies, *Asia Pacific Journal of Management,* **19**, 467–88.

Mathews, J.A. and Cho, D.S. (1999), 'Combinative capabilities and organizational learning in latecomer firms: the case of the Korean semiconductor industry', *Journal of World Business,* **34** (2), 139–56.

Mathews, J.A. and Cho, D.S. (2000), *Tiger Technology: The Creation of a Semiconductor Industry in East Asia*, Cambridge: Cambridge University Press.

Nelson, R.R. (ed.) (1993), *National Innovation System: A comparative analysis.* Oxford: Oxford University Press.

Network Weekly (2004), 'Implications of Bird's annual report: intention of a soft-landing',http://www.chinabird.com/birdnews/news-detail.asp?newsid=206, September 10, 2007.

OECD (1998), *Open Markets Matter: The Benefits of Trade and Investment Liberalization,* Paris: Organization for Economic Cooperation and Development.

Perkins, R. and Neumayer, E. (2005), 'The International Diffusion of New Technologies: A Multitechnology Analysis of Latecomer Advantage and Global Economic Integration', *Annals of the Association of American Geographers,* **95** (4), 2005, 789–908.

Porter, M.E. (1990), *The Competitive Advantage of Nations,* London: Macmillan.

Rigby, D.L. (2000), 'Geography and Technological Change', in Sheppard, E. and Barnes, T.J. (eds), *A Companion to Economic Geography*, Oxford: Blackwell, pp. 202–23.

RTX Telecom (2003), 'TD-SCDMA – China's chance', http://www.palowireless.com/3g/docs/TD-SCDMA-China.pdf, June 10 2005.

Sharif, M.N. (1989), 'Technological Leapfrogging: Implications for Developing Countries', *Technological Forecasting and Social Change,* **36**, 201–8.

Singh, J.P. (1999), *Leapfrogging Development? The Political Economy of Telecommunications Restructuring*, Albany, NY: State University of New York Press.

Solow, R.M. (1956), 'A Contribution to the Theory of Economic Growth', *Quarterly Journal of Economics,* **70**, 65–94.

Stimson, R.J., Stough, R.R. and Roberts, B.H. (eds) (2006), *Regional Economic Development*, second edition, Berlin: Springer.
Storper, M. (1997), *The Regional World: Territorial Development in a Global Economy,* New York: Guilford Press.
Sun, L. (2003), 'War of self-defense for foreign mobile handsets', *CEO&CIO*, **17**, 12–15.
Tan, Z. (2002), 'Product cycle theory and telecommunications industry-foreign direct investment, government policy, and indigenous manufacturing in China', *Telecommunications Policy,* **26**, 17–30.
UNIDO (2002), *Management of Technology: Selected Discussion Papers presented at the Vienna Global Forum,* Vienna: United Nations Industrial Development Organization.
Vernon, R. (1966), 'International investment and international trade in the product cycle', *Quarterly Journal of Economics*, **80** (2), 190–207.
Wang, B. (2003), 'Mobile phone sector is becoming the new economic growth pole for China', *China Electronic Daily*, January 17 (in Chinese).
Wang, Z. (2004), 'No. 5 Document will not be revoked and there will be no restrictions on the imports of mobile phones this year', *21st Century Report*, February 18 (in Chinese).
World Bank (1993), *The East Asian Miracle: Economic Growth and Public Policy*, Washington, DC: World Bank Group.

# 14.  Enterprise Development Policy: Modeling the Policy Context

## Roger R. Stough

---

## ENTERPRISE DEVELOPMENT TRENDS AND POLICY ISSUES: GENERAL

Many other parts of the world are experiencing a surge of interest in the formation of new businesses and this interest has become a central part of regional and national economic development strategy in many countries and regions. Strong emphasis on enterprise development as a platform for economic development is thus an important new dimension in development policy. It should not be surprising that much of enterprise development is located in cities and metropolitan areas and, moreover, is proximal to outlying centers such as edge cities or other planned peripheral developments such as special trade and/or technology development zones like those found in many developing countries (Stough and Kulkarni, 2001).

### The Role of Enterprise Development

In the US some 600,000 to 800,000 new jobs have been created annually over the past decade by new ventures (NCOE, 2004). The approximately 6 million small businesses in the US create the majority of these new jobs. Moreover, most of this majority of created jobs is produced by small businesses that experience rapid growth as they move from start-ups, to pre-growth to growth companies. The NCOE report also concludes that since the Second World War entrepreneurs have been responsible for 67 percent of the inventions and 95 percent of all radical innovations! Further, High (2004) provides an estimation model that shows that entrepreneurial enterprises contribute 45 percent of the total value added by all manufacturing between 1990 and 1999. In short, small businesses and the processes that create them contribute greatly both quantitatively and qualitatively to the national economy (Acs, 1999).

As these facts become more highly publicized, a surge of interest has arisen in how countries and regions can adopt policies that will support entrepreneurship and enterprise development, not just in the US but also in the European Union (EU) and Asia, and for that matter globally.  For example, China has adopted a large-scale technology business incubation program with tens of thousands of ventures already being developed in the metropolitan areas of that country (Stough, 2003b).  The large part of new company formation takes place in urban areas, not just in the US but also in other developed and developing countries as noted above in China and also the EU (European Commission, 2003).  There are a variety of factors responsible for variation in new firm formation rates (Armington and Acs, 2002), including exogenous and endogenous ones.

**Why is the Emphasis on Enterprise Development Increasing?**

Entrepreneurship is the way the economy and society take advantage of new wealth-creating opportunities that arise daily from constant change and idea creation.  However, when economic and social change accelerates, as during periods of rapid technological change like during the rise of the Industrial Revolution or during the rapid expansion of the ICT (information and communication technology) or knowledge age entrepreneurship and enterprise development also expand.  This is because technological change creates new pools of exploitable possibilities and opportunities.  Thus, it is not surprising that the recent period of rapid innovation in ICT has been one of increasing entrepreneurship.  Nor is it surprising that much of this activity is occurring in cities and more specifically often located in edge cites, that is, the outer parts of cities.  That this expansion has occurred primarily within an urban context is because that is where knowledge and human capital is concentrated and, thus, where innovation spillovers that drive new company formation are most concentrated (Acs, 2002).

Technological change is not the only reason for the surge of interest in new firm formation.  The break-up of the Soviet Union in 1989 signalled the end of a belief in the viability of centrally controlled economies (Fukuyama, 1995).  This, in turn, led to a widely held belief that at the very least, a more market-oriented economy was required.   The basis for this conclusion appeared earlier, during the 1980s, with increased reliance on liberalization and privatization policies in some of the more market-oriented economies of the world, for example, New Zealand, Great Britain, Canada and Australia – including many of the lagging economies in Asia, Africa and Latin America.  These political economy trends, amplified by intense technological change during the last two decades of the twentieth century, interacted to create a powerful context that begged for enterprise development supporting initiatives and policies. In this context, privatization also became a global policy phenomenon along with a belief in the need for increased enterprise and firm development (Kemp, 1991; Gomez-Ibanez and Meyer, 1993; and Savas, 2000). Thus, in addition to privatization, policies and programs to promote entrepreneurship and enterprise development also expanded. As evidence of this, it is interesting that US universities, during the 1980s and 1990s, formed 100 new entrepreneurship programs or 66 percent of all such entrepreneurship programs ever formed (Vesper and Gartner, 2002). Further, it is not surprising that since 1980, Fortune 500 companies have lost five million jobs while the US economy added 34 million new jobs through new ventures, start-ups and small businesses.

Globalization, partly driven by the ICT revolution that increased the availability of exploitable information, has also been a major contributor to the expansion of entrepreneurship. Audretsch (2001, p. 4) and others have observed, however, that globalization would not have become the pervasive force it has if only driven by the expansion and maturing of ICT. Political change in other parts of the world including Eastern and Central Europe, China, India and Vietnam resulted in new stability in formerly inaccessible markets. As this 'opening up' occurred, access to significantly lower cost but qualified labor increased in the world marketplace.

The reaction on the part of developed countries to this 'opening up' of access to lower-cost but qualified labor took two forms. One was to accelerate the substitution of capital for labor in general and more specifically the substitution of technology for labor in an effort to retain the higher end of the more traditional manufacturing activities. This of course resulted in some job loss due to productivity enhancement but not nearly as much as when operations moved offshore. Nevertheless, global wage differentials became so great that capital substitution was of limited effectiveness. This is the basic concern behind recent World Trade Organization demonstrations and the rapidly emerging immigration and 'off-shoring of jobs' issues in the US and at least the latter trend in other developed countries.

A second response of the developed countries to an inability to compete on the basis of wage cost and increasingly on the basis of capital substitution, involved shifting economic activity to high-wage and high-employment industries (Audretsch, 2001). In so doing, the competitive base shifted from factor cost inputs to technology and knowledge inputs. This, then, is a major reason for the global trend in the increasing adoption of firm formation and entrepreneurship-oriented development policy on the part of the developed countries. Namely, to enhance the ability to create more sustainable new companies and industries, and higher-wage/high-talent jobs. Thus, ICT and globalization are driving high-wage countries and regions to focus economic development policy on the creation of even higher-wage jobs and the maintenance of an environment that achieves competitiveness via innovation and high-end technology activities. How are they doing this? Such enterprises have the ability to *continuously innovate* their products which in turn delays or even denies the progression of the product development cycle, thus making it difficult, if not impossible, for low-wage-cost competitors to mimic or reengineer such products. Thus, continuous innovation products and companies form the foundation of competitiveness in developed countries. But this usually requires new companies that are not encumbered by the past and that are agile and capable of learning. This is another very important and basic reason for the expansion of enterprise development as an economic development strategy in developed countries.

However, this begs the question of why there is also a surge of interest in creating technology-intensive enterprise development programs in wage-competitive countries like China, as witnessed by the large-scale technology incubation programs that are in play in many cities there (Stough, 2003b). China's concern with learning how to compete on a continuous innovation basis stems in part from the fact that wages are rising in first-tier cities like Beijing, Shanghai and Shenzhen, making it increasingly difficult for firms there to compete with the more wage-competitive second-level cities often located more to the interior. There is also long-range concern on the part of national planners that as development occurs and wages rise, China will increasingly be forced to compete with developed countries, and to do this will require an ability to build and sustain continuous innovation enterprises. Thus, changed and changing competitive conditions globally are also driving the expansion of enterprise development initiatives in both developed and developing countries.

Faced with an environment driven by a new generic technology (ICT) and associated knowledge that enables a host of new innovations, globalization of information and access to information (partly as a result of the ICT revolution), opening up of new markets due to an acceptance of a more market-oriented philosophy and increased but transformed competitive conditions, it is not surprising that regions and nations have increasingly adopted stronger firm formation policies.

Theory (Schumpeter 1936 and 1942; and Kirzner, 1973) and experience (Birch, 1979) argue for and support a conclusion that the majority of new jobs are created in small companies and start-up ventures. While there is some debate on this (Harrison, 1994), it is difficult to argue against the evidence that the highest rates of entrepreneurship, that is, new ventures, and job growth, have occurred in the more technically advanced cities in the US over the past decade (Stough and Kulkarni, 2001). This provides another reason for the increasing attention that is being focused on venture formation policy.

## Enterprise Development Approaches and Policy Issues

A variety of arguments have been offered for why regions and nations are increasingly turning to enterprise development policies and programs as ways to increase jobs, wages and wealth. While it is clear that macro and micro economic policies and factors are important for achieving such goals, the reasons offered above provide a rationale for why the emphasis is disproportionately focused on enterprise development. The purpose here is to provide a framework for conceptualizing how cities are approaching the challenge of supporting enterprise development.

Given any region or nation for that matter, it can be assumed that there is a stock of individuals who are either contemplating formation of a company or are operating a small company. Figures 14.1 and 14.2 present or model this pool of entrepreneurs as a triangle called the 'entrepreneurial fountain'. The fountain mimics the entrepreneurial process, in that its base is composed of those who are thinking about starting a company and is subsequently partitioned into smaller and smaller parts as one moves up the triangle to existing businesses, pre-growth companies, growth companies and those that have spilled forward into a period of sustained growth.

Figure 14.3 shows the dynamic version of the fountain and recognizes that various forces ranging from macroeconomic effects and policy to endogenous efforts will result in its contraction or expansion. The economic development policy goals are to make the fountain as big as possible and to maximize the number of ventures that escape from the top of the fountain. These two policy objectives and related programs, *ceteris paribus*, have the potential to create a powerful engine for job creation and sustained economic development of regions as well as nations. This of course does not always happen because of the host of institutional barriers that face the developing country as it attempts to move up the development ladder (Rostow, 1960).

The fountain may also be viewed as a way to segment the enterprise development policy context. Policies and associated programs aimed at the base of the fountain are focused on company formation and include technical assistance for business start-ups. An example in the US is provided by its Small Business Administration's Small Business Development Center (SBDC) program. This is a national program with offices or centers located in major cities (metropolitan areas) in the US. SBDC centers provide free assistance to anyone who asks for help in starting a business. SBDCs also provide assistance to already existing small businesses requesting help, for example, to solve a business problem, improve or write a business plan,

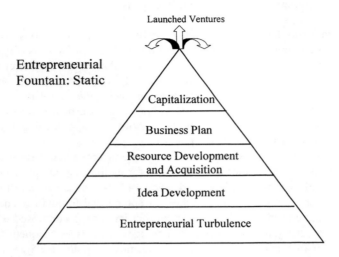

*Figure 14.1  Entrepreneurial fountain: the entrepreneurial process*

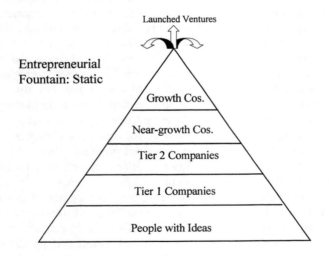

*Note:* Cos. = companies.

*Figure 14.2  Entrepreneurial fountain: static model*

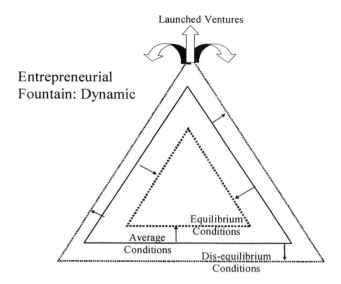

*Figure 14.3 Entrepreneurial fountain: dynamic model*

improve financials or to enter the export market and so on. The SBDC program provides basic assistance primarily at the first two levels or segments of the fountain (for Tier 1 companies) to help form a new business or to help develop an existing small business (Figure 14.2). The rationale for the subsidy to support this program is that information on company formation and growth and its availability is highly imperfect and not all individuals or small businesses have the resources to acquire, evaluate, access and use appropriate information. The policy and related programs of the SBDCs are justified first on equity or fairness grounds (asymmetric information market imperfection) on the one hand and on economic development grounds (job and wealth creation) on the other.

Programs like the SBDC provide a source of basic information and assistance but are unable to provide the in-depth and sustained business development assistance that is required and needed by companies that are beyond the Tier 1 level. Tier 2 companies can be loosely defined as having between $500,000 and $20 million in annual revenue, facing scalability issues, having basic operating capital and having a full-time professional management team in place or, if not, then readily available. Thus from most perspectives Tier 2 companies are viable businesses. Thus it is difficult to rationalize public assistance to these ventures on the basis of equity. But, it is

Tier 2 companies that move on to near-growth and then growth status, and where very large numbers of jobs are produced. Thus, from the perspective of job and wealth creation there is a rationale for focused assistance to increase the probability of such ventures reaching and going beyond the upper echelons of the entrepreneurial fountain. While it is presumed that private sector providers, for example, venture capital firms, provide the assistance that these firms need, such assistance is more often provided for near-growth and growth companies, not Tier 2 companies. With the exception of a few Tier 2 programs, there is thus a gap in the focused assistance that is needed to propel them into sustained growth. From the perspective of the pubic sector, this gap means that fewer Tier 2 companies reach growth status and thus less job and wealth creation occurs. All of this suggests a significant role for the public sector in assisting Tier 2 companies.

There are some public support programs for Tier 2 and more advanced companies but these are specialized in nature, for example, Small Business Investment Research (SBIR) grants to assist companies in the further development of pre-competitive technologies, or assistance programs that are highly dependent on and unique to local initiative, for example, local and state government support of business incubators (virtual or physical). But even with such support the availability of incubators in the US is limited and does not provide options for more than a small part of the potential Tier 2 market. In China, on the other hand, large technology incubation programs exist. For example, Qingdao, on the coast of China north of Shanghai with a population of about 4 million, supports a technology incubator with more than 600 ventures in residence. In Wuhan, with a population of more than 12 million, there are 26 technology incubation centers supporting several thousand Tier 2 type ventures, all attempting to excel to growth company status. Further, a federal government venture capital industry exists to support Tier 2 and other types of enterprise development, for example, the Innofund that supplies more than 20 percent of all the government venture capital made available to Tier 2 companies in China (Zhang and Sun, 2004; and Wang, 2006).

Finally, Tier 2 companies are often unable to obtain assistance from private sector providers of business development services because they are too under-resourced to afford to pay or not quite well enough developed to be attractive to the venture capital community. There appears to be a gap in support for Tier 2 ventures in many parts of the world. Regions and nations that opt to provide public support to these firms will potentially reap powerful competitiveness benefits in the form of sustained job and wealth creation, given the role of rapidly growing Tier 2-type companies in creating a large proportion of new jobs in the US economy (see Birch, 1979; High, 2004; and NCOE, 2004;). This, rather than equity and information imperfections, provides a rational basis for Tier 2 public subsidy policies and programs. However, steering public funding to support Tier 2 company development faces a value conflict problem in stronger market based economies like the US because it is seen as subsidizing viable businesses.

## Summary

There are a number of powerful technological, competitive, ideological, technical and political forces driving the interest in enterprise development. Further, most regions and nations have made investments in public policy initiatives to support enterprise development as a way of achieving job and wealth benefits. While public subsidy policies exist and have powerful rationales for supporting company formation, and provide assistance to fledgling businesses, policies to support ventures that are viable but facing a low probability of reaching sustained growth (Tier 2 companies) are minimally available in most market-dominated economies. But there is a development rationale for publicly subsidizing the development of these Tier 2 companies in that a region (or country) could reap significant additional job growth and wealth creation through their informed use. It is highly likely that there are strong benefit–cost-based reasons to pursue public support for Tier 2 companies, given the data on the high level of job and wealth creation that is produced by them when they grow rapidly. All of this of course assumes that appropriate procedures and skills exist not only to select Tier 2 companies with a higher probability of success than the market provides but also to guide a higher proportion of them to sustained growth. This knowledge remains in a relatively nascent stage of development. Despite this level of limited knowledge and information on how to capture the potential benefit of providing public support to Tier 2 companies, it is likely that more and more regions and countries will expand programs designed to help propel them to sustained growth.

Entrepreneurship and enterprise development are given special attention here because powerful forces support these activities and yet their evolution is in a relatively early stage. A major conclusion is that many regions are likely to make expanded public investments in policies and programs that will lead not only to the creation of more businesses but also to the creation and development of more growth ventures. This trend is likely to be stronger in the ascension and emerging regions (countries) and less strong in the more-established market-oriented economies because of the relatively taboo values associated with providing assistance to viable ventures, albeit ones with many of the cards stacked against them becoming a growth company.

# ENTERPRISE DEVELOPMENT AND POLICY/PROGRAM ISSUES: THE NATIONAL CAPITAL REGION

In this section two questions or topics are addressed. First, there are indications that there is considerable enterprise development activity in the National Capital Region and that it fluctuates in a countercyclical way with business cycles. Data are presented in support of this belief in an effort to begin to lay a quantitative base for future analysis. Second, the incubation infrastructure in the region is examined because of its infrastructural importance for Tier 2 company expansion.

Data on business start-ups and deaths should ideally be used as a measure of enterprise development. However, these data are not readily available, at least not at a cost that most organizations such as universities can afford in the US, for example, this author was quoted a price of $35,000 for a recent business birth and death database developed for US counties between 1994 and 1999. As a consequence of high cost, data on non-wage employment are used as a proxy for entrepreneurship activity. Clearly this is not a perfect measure because some non-wage employment is entrepreneurial in nature and some is routine. Nonetheless, that is what is available.

## Measuring Entrepreneurial Activity

Regarding the scale of entrepreneurship or enterprise development activity in the region it is instructive to note that 700,000 or 20 percent of the total labor force (3.5 million) in the Greater Washington region is non-payroll. This estimate is derived by subtracting the Bureau of Labor Statistics, estimate of employment (which only includes wage employment) from the Bureau of Economic Analysis estimates which also include non-wage employment (as illustrated in Figure 14.4). This estimate of 20 percent is about the same as the national average (21 percent). Yet, 25 percent of the labor force is employed either by the federal government or by federal contractors. If the total employment of 3.5 million is adjusted downward by 25 percent, then the percentage of non-wage employment in the region would be nearly 30 percent. This indicates that there is a relatively large concentration of entrepreneurial activity in the region, at least compared to the national average, and thus probably most other regions in the US.

Further, as presented in Figures 14.5 and 14.6 the amount of non-wage employment varies countercyclically. The amount of non-wage employment tends to expand during recessionary periods (early 1990s and the 2000–03 period). This is of interest given that the region had considerable entrepreneurial activity during the mid to late 1990s ICT boom. The data presented suggest that one way the region adjusts during recessionary periods

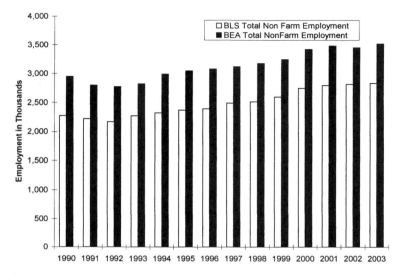

*Sources:* Bureau of Labor Statistics, Bureau of Economic Analysis.

*Figure 14.4   Total employment in the Washington DC area, 1990–2003*

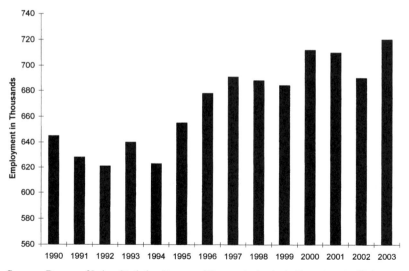

*Sources:* Bureau of Labor Statistics, Bureau of Economic Analysis, Department of Labor.

*Figure 14.5   Total Nonwage employment in the Washington DC area, 1990–2003*

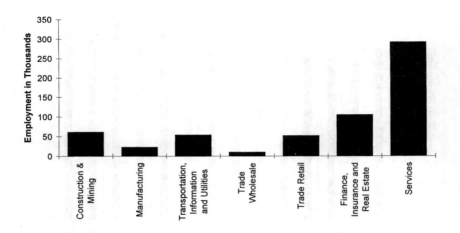

*Sources:* Bureau of Labor Statistics, Bureau of Economic Analysis, Department of Labor

*Figure 14.6  Sectoral Nonwage employment in Washington DC area, 2003*

is via an expansion of self-employment.  Much of this may take the form of private consultation in the areas of services in general and, more specifically, in the management and engineering services.  This is consistent with the structural composition of the region's economy with its considerable employment in computer software, systems integration and in the advanced services.

## Assistance for Tier 2 Ventures

The number and size of incubator (physical and virtual) facilities is one way to measure assistance for Tier 2 companies in a region or nation for that matter. Information on various attributes of incubators (number, type, goals, operational procedures and examples is presented in Stough, 1999, 85-107). Data were compiled (ibid., 82) on the incubation infrastructure of the National Capital Region in 1999 and it was found to be inadequate.  That year there were two incubators (one physical and one virtual) in Northern Virginia; one small business incubator in the District of Columbia; and three in Suburban Maryland (Stough, 2004).[1]  A conclusion was that the region needed to considerably expand the number of incubation facilities.

In January of 2004, based on membership of the National Business Incubator Association, information obtained from officials in various business support organizations in the region, and technology associations, 26 incubation programs (physical and virtual) were identified (Stough, 2004): 10 were located in Northern Virginia, four in the District of Columbia and twelve in Suburban Maryland part of the region. Judgment of which programs to include was liberal so the actual numbers may overstate the total by as much as three or four facilities. Yet, even with adjusting for this possibility there has been a huge expansion of incubation activity in the region over the last five years.

The increase of incubation facilities strongly suggests that infrastructure to support the development of what were called Tier 2 companies above has expanded. Yet, there is little information about success rates, that is, the rate at which incubated firms graduate to growth company status. Further, the combined facilities are probably not working with more than a pool of 200 to 250 companies, which leaves the remainder of Tier 2 companies in the region of some 140,000–170,00 (companies with 1–10 employees and $20 million or less in revenues). All incubation programs have intake requirements but they also need to meet revenue and performance goals. Together this sometimes (often in some cases) means that companies that are accepted into an incubator are not high-probability candidates for success but have the resources to pay the rent. Further, many incubators have minimal staff and program support to assist their companies: this means that the benefits may be limited to a minor rent reduction (over current market rates) and indirect benefits that may accrue from the un-organized and un-channelled spillover effects resulting from no more than being located with other businesses. Incubators that, at the minimum, provide events and settings for cross-tenant interaction at least contribute to the potential for knowledge and information spillovers to occur. In sum, the Greater Washington Metropolitan region has increased incubation infrastructure but it is not known in any meaningful way what contribution this is making to accelerating Tier 2 company development and to increases in the number of growth companies produced. This is critical information because that is where a large proportion of new jobs and thus regional wealth is created.

There appear to be two actions that are needed in the US National Capital Region regarding the development of Tier 2 companies. First, a careful and serious evaluation of the contribution that the expanded incubation infrastructure is making to company development (Tier 2 expansion) is needed. Without this it remains unclear what difference having this infrastructure means to sustained economic development and growth.

Second, it appears from the author's review and operating knowledge of the various incubation programs in the region that there is a need for a broadly conceived yet focused program to promote the transformation of Tier 2 companies into growth companies. Such a program would use existing business assistance programs including incubators to identify high-potential Tier 2 companies and channel them to a specific set of services designed to transform them into companies. These needs and services are well known and include such components as, for example, assistance with business plan development, management development or recruitment, market plan development, market research, technology vetting, intellectual property (IP) control, capital formation and competitive analysis. Many existing incubation and business assistance programs for companies beyond the Tier 1 level are trying to do just this. But they are under-resourced in many cases and/or lack the personnel or network to maintain the assistance that is needed over extended periods – which is often required to evolve a Tier 2 company.

## CONCLUSIONS

Enterprise development has become a central component of regional and national development strategy globally. There are multiple and powerful forces driving this trend and include the knowledge age or revolution and the expansion of the ICT industry, political change and the opening of new markets, increasing acceptance of market ideology, the need for institutional liberalization and changing or altered competitive conditions. All of these factors are pushing development policy in this direction in the emergent and ascension economies. However, in the developed countries this trend is driven heavily by competitive forces that make it almost impossible for them to compete on the basis of wage-cost differentials. These differentials are strong and in the wrong direction. This means that they can primarily compete by substituting capital and technology for labor or on the basis of continuous innovation. The former is only partly possible because the wage-cost differentials are very large, meaning that increased capital and technology in the production process can only compensate where products and services are highly sophisticated and have large amounts of knowledge creation, and also at the asymptote of this process where products and services are continuously innovated. Such a dynamic and continuous process is difficult to create and maintain in large organizations with process-slowing bureaucratic structures. Thus, new businesses need to be and are being increasingly created to enable the developed countries to compete.

The chapter also examined enterprise development policy approaches through the use of a model called the Entrepreneurial Fountain. The Fountain mimics the entrepreneurial process by segmenting the business development and growth context into parts that include people with ideas to start a company, small or Tier 1 businesses that are either quite small but with no intention to expand or whose existence is tenuous at best, Tier 2 or small but viable businesses, pre-growth and growth companies. The analysis concludes that the rationale for public support of business development services (start-up and very small and questionably viable ventures) is strong and based not just on economic development principles and benefits but also on equity and information access principles and considerations.

Support programs and policies for Tier 2 companies are minimal in comparison. This stems from the fact that Tier 2 businesses are for the most part viable in a business or profitability sense: they have predictable revenue flow, a professional management team, a definable product and an intelligible business model. Yet they are too small or still have significant imperfections in their business plans, management, IP, market concepts, and so on and thus are not so attractive to professional private sector business service providers, for example, PricewaterhouseCoopers, and thus not yet attractive to venture capitalists. But Tier 2 businesses that rise to pre-growth and growth company status are the source of a large portion of the jobs created by small businesses, and thus there is a job creation and economic development rationale that is strong for public sector support. The emergent and ascension economies are much better placed to create and implement public support programs for transforming Tier 2 companies into growth companies and thus reaping associated job and wealth-creation benefits. The developed countries that for certain have more institutional infrastructure and slack capital investment resources in place to support Tier 2 company transformation also have a longer market tradition and thus have and will face greater constraints and value conflicts in forming and implementing Tier 2 publicly supported programs.

This chapter also examined the question of how to measure enterprise development, and concluded that one of the more defensible ways to do this was by measuring business start-ups or births for a given period and subtracting from those business deaths in a region or country to obtain a net measure of enterprise creation (or a measure of the ratio of births to deaths called the 'churn' rate). In the US this is possible but the data are expensive to acquire. Consequently, an alternative approach was proposed using net non-wage employment as an indicator of propensity to entrepreneurship and enterprise development. The problem with this technique is that non-wage workers certainly include many entrepreneurs or those who have started and maintained their own small business, but they also include many others who are not entrepreneurs. Nonetheless, a case study application to the US National Capital Region enabled an estimate that suggests that there is much more than an average amount of entrepreneurial activity in the region.

Finally, a brief case study of enterprise development support activity in the US National Capital Region was provided. The analysis confirmed, as was expected given that the US is classified as a developed country, that public support was strong for firm formation and very small companies at the Tier 1 stage of development. It also confirmed that institutional infrastructure to support small ventures had increased during the last five years as measured by the change in virtual and physical incubation programs. The analysis concluded that the support for Tier 2 venture transformation was, while somewhat expanded in both the public and private sectors, not nearly as great as needed if the region wishes to reap the full potential of job and wealth benefits that appear to exist.

## NOTE

1. The Washington Metropolitan Region is composed of three state-level jurisdictions and includes Maryland, and Virginia counties, and the federal District of Columbia located at the geographic center of the region called Washington, DC.

## REFERENCES

Acs, Z. (ed.) (1999), *Are Small Firms Important?* Boston, MA: Kluwer.
Acs, Z. (2002), *Innovation and the Growth of Cities*, Cheltenham, UK and Northampton, MA, USA: Edward Elgar.
Armington, C. and Acs, Z. (2002), 'The Determinants of Regional Variation in New Firm Formation', *Regional Studies*, **36** (1), 33–46.
Audretsch, D. (2001), *Entrepreneurship Policy and the Strategic Management of Places*, Proceedings of Conference on Entrepreneurship Policy: What's Government got to do with it?, Cambridge: Kennedy School, Harvard University.
Birch, D.(1979), *The Job Creation Process*, Cambridge, MA: MIT Program on Neighborhood and Regional Change.
European Commission (2003), 'Entrepreneurship In Europe', Brussels: European Commission.
Florida, R. (2002), *The Rise of the Creative Class: And How It is Transforming Work, Leisure, Community and Everyday Lif,,* New York: Basic Books.
Fukuyama, F. (1995), *The Social Virtues and the Creation of Prosperity*, New York: Free Press.
Gomez-Ibanez, J.A. and J.R. Meyer (1993), *Going Private: The International Experience with Transportation Privatization*, Washington, DC: Brookings Institution.
Harrison, B. (1994), *Lean and Mean: The Changing Landscape of Corporate Power in the Age of Flexibility*, New York: Basic Books.
High, J. (2004), 'The Roles of Entrepreneurship in Economic Growth: Toward a Theory of Total Factor Productivity', in H.L.F. de Groot, P. Nijkamp and R.R. Stough (eds), *Entrepreneurship and Regional Economic Development: A Spatial Perspective*, Cheltenham, UK and Northampton, MA, USA: Edward Elgar.
Kemp, R. (1991), *Privatization: The Provision of Public Services by the Private Sector*, Jefferson: McFarland & Co.
Kirzner, I.M. (1973), *Competition and Entrepreneurship*, Chicago: University of Chicago Press.

National Commission On Entrepreneurship (NCOE) (2004), 'Fact Sheet', http://www.publicforuminstitute.org/nde/news/facts.htm.

Rostow, W.W. (1960), *The Process of Economic Growth*, 2nd edn, Oxford: Clarendon Press.

Savas, E.S. (2000), *Privatization and Public-Private Partnerships*, London: Chatham House.

Schumpeter, J.A. (1936), *The Theory of Economic Development: An Inquiry into Profits, Capital, Credit and the Business Cycle*, Cambridge, MA: Harvard University Press.

Schumpeter, J.A. (1942), *Capitalism, Socialism and Democracy*, New York: Harper & Row.

Stough, R.R. (1999), 'Building and Embedding an Innovation Culture in the Regional Economy', in Stough (ed.), *Proceedings of the Seventh Annual Conference on the Future of the Northern Virginia Economy*, Fairfax, VA: Mason Enterprise Center, School of Public Policy, George Mason University.

Stough, R.R. (2003a), 'Strategic Management of Places and Policy', *Annals of Regional Science* **37** (1), 179–201.

Stough, R.R. (2003b), 'The Rise of Global Enterprise Development: Patterns in China and India', *The Journal of Indian Management and Strategy*, **7**(6), April–June.

Stough, R.R. (2003c), 'Technology in the Washington Metropolitan Region in 2003', Paper presented at the 11th Annual George Mason University 'Forecasting the Greater Washington Area Economy', Fairfax, VA.

Stough, R.R. (2004), 'Technology in the Washington Metropolitan Region in 2004', Paper presented at the 12th Annual George Mason University 'Forecasting the Greater Washington Area Economy', Fairfax, VA.

Stough, R.R., Haynes, K.E. and Campbell, Jr., H.S. (1998), 'Small Business Entrepreneurship in the High Technology Services Sector: An Assessment for Edge Cities of the U.S. National Capital Region', *Small Business Economics*, **10**, 61–74.

Stough, R.R. and Kulkarni, R. (2001), 'Planning Issues and the New Generation Technology Economy: Comparative Regional Analysis and the Case of the U.S. National Capital Region', in J.F. Williams, and R.J. Stimson (eds), *International Urban Planning Settings: Lessons of Success*, Amsterdam: Elsevier Science.

Vesper, K.H. and Gartner, W.B. (2002), 'University Entrepreneurship Programs', Los Angeles: Lloyd Grief Center for Entrepreneurial Studies, Marshall School of Business, University of Southern California.

Wang, E. (2006), 'China's Public Venture Capital Programs and Innofund', PhD Dissertation, Fairfax, VA: George Mason University.

Zhang, Z. and Sun, H. (2004), 'The Enlightenment of Innofund's Success on Policy Venture Investment in Our Country', *Soft Science*, **18** (6), 21–23.

# 15. Entrepreneurial Business Support Networks: A Leader Institution Perspective

## Tõnu Roolaht

### INTRODUCTION

The internationalisation of start-up companies[1] is supported by their involvement in long-term relationships with other companies, public institutions, universities, private experts, and investors. These relationships should not be seen only as inevitable preconditions for expansion and commercialisation capabilities. In some respects, the network-embedded company trades some of its autonomy for shared resources and relational ties. These decisions about the start-up's relationships with other agents could be viewed as entrepreneurial choices.

Moreover, the formation of a business support network, which incorporates an innovative combination of public and private promotion efforts, could also be an entrepreneurial process. Although, some elements of the business support system can be established by learning from other countries' experience, absorptive capacity[2] concerning the adoption of pre-existing development scenarios is a necessary but often not a sufficient condition for successful promotion efforts. The environmental dynamism and characteristics of the local business environment are likely to call for new, flexible and innovative approaches that offer a mix of best practice with sufficient local responsiveness and leadership. Thus, entrepreneurial thinking and opportunity seeking are also the characteristics of business-supporting agents. The formation of well-functioning business support structures is often related to visionary ideas of lead entrepreneur(s) and leaders, who inspire entire communities or even societies (see Stimson et al., 2006).

The aim of this study is to examine the formation of the university-led entrepreneurial business support network for start-ups, where the focal role is played by technology transfer and incubation initiatives of the leader institution. This idea of entrepreneurship for supporting entrepreneurs stems from the fact that the market entry process is often very sensitive to the changes in business environment and cannot be effectively supported by rigid and formalised support procedures. The success of the relationships in this support network depends on shared vision and values. This means that in order to offer valuable support for entrepreneurial companies, private as well as public supporting agents should adopt an entrepreneurial mindset. Supporting leading-edge business activities, which are often based on recent scientific discoveries with uncertain market potential, is an inherently risky activity. The related risks cannot be avoided, but presumably they can be more successfully managed by sharing them within the support network.

This chapter is an interpretative description of business support networks and services based on desk research of the relevant literature and secondary data. However, it is not solely a theoretical conceptualisation. The described support framework is illustrated with empirical evidence from Estonia. The data sources used for the elaborated case of Estonian support networks include survey data, business plans, homepages and other documentation.

The chapter starts with a discussion of support measures for facilitating entrepreneurship via relational networks. This analysis of business support networks will undertake a synthesis of the experiences of several countries. The main focus is on a combination of domestic and international capabilities and resources within these networks via entrepreneurial activities. This analysis offers a preliminary framework for describing the role of entrepreneurship in support structures.

The empirical section thereafter is based on the exploratory case study of business support initiatives established in the Tartu region. Although the University of Tartu, as a leading research centre in the region, is an academic institution, the development of its industrial contacts could in many respects be described as an entrepreneurial process. The diversified role of the university in this network involves knowledge creation through research as well as the administrative tasks in supporting the commercialisation of its innovations. A successful combination of these two aspects requires the creation of lateral contacts between the faculties and departments beyond the capabilities of formal institutional structure. The University of Tartu as the leading agent in this support network can also attract international experts and lobby for governmental support. The chapter ends with a concluding discussion and suggestions for the continuation of research in the future.

# THE CONCEPTUAL ELEMENTS OF ENTREPRENEURIAL SUPPORT NETWORKS FOR START-UPS

## National Innovation Policy

The facilitation of entrepreneurship and abolition of barriers to entrepreneurship is often dependent on the formation of appropriate support networks. These support networks include public institutions offering programmes for the promotion of entrepreneurship, cooperation with other start-up companies, universities, private consultants and venture capitalists.

In her research on adjustment in Finnish universities, Häyrinen-Alestalo (1999) introduces interesting viewpoint on universities' support for innovations in the industrial sector. In this view, transformation of university teaching towards greater assistance to innovations by industrial companies can be seen as a reaction to national-level innovation policies. The adoption of new, more aggressive promotion policy has also reshaped the role expected of academic institutions. This offers an additional dimension to the government–university nexus. In addition to determining a large part of university financing, government policy explicitly or implicitly reshapes the position of academic institutions in a wider support network. However, the means by which universities react to change in this political setting can often vary considerably, depending on the intra-organisational and historical factors faced by a particular academic institution.

The suggestions for promoting linkages and interactions within the framework of national systems of innovation have also been derived from focused exploration of these linkages and their incorporation into an institutional linkage model (Mohannak, 1999). This model addresses all major policy issues that influence technological innovation and knowledge transfer between network participants. University–industry collaboration is also important for professional development, because industry needs to acquire, develop and retain a skilled and competent workforce, while academic life benefits from ideas, knowledge and practices outside the university setting (Slotte and Tynjälä, 2003).

Governments' broader role in supporting the creation of new innovative companies in different institutional structures and the strength of state institutions responsible for policy implementation has been investigated by Spencer et al. (2005). Shane (2004) suggests that entrepreneurship in universities can be substantially increased by suitable policy mechanisms and legislation, which offers initiatives for entrepreneurial behaviour such as patenting in order to transfer technology via licensing mechanisms.

**Regional Institutional 'Thickness'**

Looy et al. (2003) outline critical ingredients that help to make regional economic policies successful in promoting entrepreneurship and innovation. They stress the importance of a balanced mix based on the combination of research institutes and endogenous knowledge-intensive start-ups related to larger R&D-intensive incumbent companies. All this should be embedded in a professional environment that is able to provide sufficient advice and support services. Lahorgue and da Cunha (2003) found that in order to facilitate innovation among small and medium-sized enterprises (SMEs) in traditional industries, knowledge-sharing interlinks with high-technology-based enterprises were needed, thus enabling them to learn from this interaction.

The support network of start-up companies has also been described by the notion of regional institutional 'thickness'. This term refers to the interlocking and integrated web of support organisations and institutions, such as companies in the region, financial institutions, chambers of commerce, trading agencies and associations, government agencies, innovation centres and several other network partners. Thickness also means not just the incorporation of such institutions in a support network, but also synergies of interaction, joint representation and common purpose (Amin and Thrift, 1995). This co-location or spatial overlap of closely linked support agents is seen as a main determinant of economic development in a region.

Venkataraman (2004, p. 153) suggests that tangible infrastructural aspects are necessary, but not sufficient conditions for fostering regional technological entrepreneurship. Sufficient conditions offered by the intangibles of entrepreneurship to tangible infrastructure (hard and soft) such as risk capital may include access to novel ideas, role models, informal forums, region-specific opportunities, safety-nets, access to large markets, and executive leadership.

Keeble et al. (1999) studied the nature of collective learning processes by innovative technology-based SMEs in the Cambridge, UK region, and found that in addition to the University of Cambridge spin-offs and local inter-company networking, scientific and managerial recruitment development has been supported and accompanied by national-level influences and a 'thickening' institutional framework in the region. Thus, the synergies within support networks as well as alignment of purposes, set by different public or private agents, have an important influence on the effectiveness of support measures offered.

## Government Laboratories, Vocational Schools and the Wider Community

The Canadian experience shows that universities tend to be more catalytic for development activities than a driver of them because government laboratories and industry are primary factors that determine growth and success of knowledge clusters in Canada (Doutriaux, 2003). However, the laboratory–industry partnership is most efficient when parties have differentiated technological roles, but roles that are relatively closely related on the technology development spectrum so that coordination and integration of activities remains possible (Saavedra and Bozeman, 2004).

The analysis of the Massachusetts region in the United States, best known for the Massachusetts Institute of Technology (MIT) and other strong higher education institutions, showed that earlier university–industry linkage based on high-tech spin-offs has now been reorganised into a wider contextual cooperation on the level of vocational education, which has replaced, or more correctly amended, elite research linkages with diffusion-oriented models of academic outreach to lower educational levels and the wider community (Moussouris, 1998). A similar example of knowledge diffusion on a wider community-based level has been observed in the Ontario province of Canada (Hill, 2004).

## Triangular Cooperation

Public–private cooperation takes several forms. Some of these can support the emergence of private start-ups just by offering opportunities for collaboration. This aspect of public–private cross-boundary management has been investigated by Bergmann and Bliss (2004). However, the public–private partnership is in many respects too narrow a classification to provide sufficient elaboration on the nature of the support provided. Therefore, a triangular distribution of agents into government–university–industry partnerships is in many respects a more essential approach to describing the support structures. The governmental funding of universities is increasingly complemented by non-governmental funding links between university and industry. Such an industry–university partnership has gradually found more support in academic circles as an eligible way of funding research (Dagnino and Velho, 1998). According to Carayannis et al. (2000), these partnerships are facilitated by knowledge transfers across organisational boarders, which help to build trust and social capital for more advanced cooperation. They also support organisational learning and the emergence of trans-organisational knowledge interfaces, which constitute communities of innovation. This provides evidence of the paramount importance of applicable knowledge-sharing protocols in order to build well-functioning support networks.

## Leader Institution

Albino et al. (1999) suggest that the leader or anchor firm in an industrial district can considerably influence the nature of knowledge shared and build around itself new customer–supplier relationships in order to facilitate knowledge transfer. Although the knowledge transfer process can be shortened by using knowledge codification procedures, it might also weaken the relationship of the anchor firm with its supplier companies, because codification enables knowledge sharing with other competitors in the district. The notion of a leader firm can be justifiably generalised as a concept of leader institution within the setting of a complex support network. This generalisation helps to view academic research institutions – such as universities – as core contributors to knowledge–sharing networks, oriented towards facilitation of research-based spin-off companies. Taiwanese experience shows that with appropriate policy setting and legislative initiative, university research can become more oriented towards knowledge transfers between university and industry via an increased build-up of infrastructure, and patenting and licensing (Chang et al., 2005). R&D cooperation between companies can also increase information sharing and enhance knowledge spillovers, while helping to reduce research costs in sectors that rely predominantly upon own R&D for innovations (Lambertini et al., 2004).

## Entrepreneurial University

The commercialisation of knowledge created in universities is often viewed too narrowly as striving towards standardised intellectual property (IP) protection mechanisms, support for spin-off companies and establishment of venture capital funds for the transfer of technological knowledge. Although this challenge is very important, innovations and new solutions can also occur in new fields now denoted as 'creative industries', where new proprietary knowledge can also be successfully commercialised (Hearn et al., 2004).

Clark (1998) described the minimum required steps or elements to transform the traditional university into a more entrepreneurial one:

1.   strengthened steering at the core;
2.   expanded developmental periphery;
3.   diversified funding base;

4.   stimulating academic heartland; and
5.   integrated entrepreneurial culture.


This organisational transformation and change in academic disposition is a long-term process, which incorporates complex interaction between a university and its supporting environment. Schutte (1999) describes this process for the University of Twente in the Netherlands, which successfully used the creation of spin-off companies, an incubator in its business and science park and accumulation of venture capital to increase its economic and social impact in the surrounding region. In addition to these explicit means of increasing university–industry knowledge transfer, the change towards more applied academic research is part of the mental transformation or change in mindset.

Implementation of graduate degree programmes in entrepreneurship in Australia has proved to be a facilitator of start-up creation either as new companies or spin-offs from large ones. About 87 per cent of graduate survey respondents were engaged in such activity. It is also an important microeconomic effect in terms of new workplaces in start-up companies (McMullan and Gillin, 1998). Weinberg (2005) stresses the importance of student innovations and problem solving, student organisations and creation of social venture funds as ways to create an entrepreneurial campus culture. The more-theoretical view on teaching entrepreneurship stresses the importance of building teaching programmes around emerging theoretical concepts of entrepreneurship, especially contingency theories that support learning by doing (Fiet, 2000). Cope (2005) supports a similar idea on the dynamic learning perspective on entrepreneurship. He proposes three distinctive, interrelated elements of entrepreneurial learning:

1.   dynamic temporal phases, that demonstrate the complex relationship between learning prior to the start-up of the establishment and learning during the entrepreneurial process;
2.   interrelated processes that also stress the role of critical experiences, affective aspects of these and learning routines; and
3.   overarching characteristics between emotional and social aspects of entrepreneurial learning.


In the view of Politis (2005), entrepreneurial learning constitutes an experiential process, which has three main learning components: the entrepreneurs' career experience, the transformation process, and entrepreneurial knowledge, described as effectiveness in recognising and using entrepreneurial opportunities along with an ability to cope with the liabilities of newness. The review of teaching technology management, as academic discipline indicates, holds that the research focus of scientists from various countries differs substantially, thus creating further delays in developing technology management into a widely accepted academic discipline (Pilkington and Teichert, 2005).

## Business Incubators

Start-up promotion is often related to business incubators, which are often seen as infrastructural solutions for supporting the establishment and development of SMEs. Rice (2002) describes business incubators as 'producers' of business assistance programmes, which collaborate with the community where they operate and co-produce their services together with entrepreneurial ventures located in an incubator. This co-production process can have various forms, intensities and results. The time devoted by the incubator manager (or staff), intervention intensity, the number of co-production modes used and the readiness of the entrepreneur to participate actively in co-production are factors that affect the output dynamics related to joint inputs.

The four main types of traditional business incubators can be outlined as follows (Grimaldi and Grandi, 2005):

1. *Business Innovation Centres (BICs)*   The activities of BICs relate to offering a set of services to incubated companies, such as the provision of office space, basic infrastructure, communication possibilities, information about financing opportunities, visibility and other similar issues.
2. *University Business Incubators (UBIs)*  UBIs are established by universities for adoption of an entrepreneurial role in creating and diffusing scientific and/or technological knowledge; and for provision of assistance and supporting services to new knowledge-based ventures. They have features similar to traditional BICs but emphasise more the transfer of scientific and technological knowledge from universities to companies.
3. *Independent Private Incubators (IPIs)*  IPIs are incubators established by individuals or by groups of persons in order to assist talented entrepreneurs in establishing and expending their ventures. IPIs tend to take equity in new companies and rely on their own funds. They are often also called accelerators, because they engage in already launched projects in need of particular assistance.
4. *Corporate Private Incubators (CPIs)*  CPIs are owned and established by large companies for supporting the creation of new autonomous business units. These new corporate spin-offs are frequently established as

spillovers from intra-organisational research projects and result from diversification strategies used by large companies.

Grimaldi and Grandi differentiate between two models of business incubation. At one end of the continuum (model 1), they place public BICs and regional public incubators, which predominantly provide entrepreneurial ventures with tangible assets and market commodities. Thus, model 1 represents long- and medium-term support efforts based on government funding. At the other end (model 2) are private incubators (both CPIs and IPIs), whose assistance is oriented towards providing incubated companies with finance and more intangible high-value assets in a short-term perspective. UBIs have a unique mix of characteristics, with some representing features of model 1 and others those of model 2. Moreover, universities' incubating activities function as a gateway between public and private start-up support efforts.

**Technology Transfer Offices and Science Parks**

The intermediaries between university labs and spin-off-type start-up companies are also called university technology transfer offices (UTTOs). Markman et al. (2005) show that new venture establishment is positively related to the presence of profit-oriented UTTOs, while traditional university or non-profit UTTOs are more supportive of business incubation activities. New venture creation is also facilitated by licensing-for-equity, while the most common mode – licensing-for-cash – has the weakest connection to new venture formation. Researched UTTOs tended to overemphasise the importance of royalty income and to underemphasise the role of entrepreneurship (ibid.). According to the resource-based view of the company, the most important determinants of technology transfer performance, in terms of university spin-offs or licensing, are the amount of R&D revenue in industry, faculty quality in the university, age of the UTTO, and venture capital availability (Powers and McDougall, 2005).

One of the oldest examples of science/innovation park-type incubation centres in Central and Eastern European countries is INNOTECH in Budapest, co-owned by the university, local government and the Ministry of Education. The conception of the park was based on international experience but has been adapted to regional conditions and sees its main task as providing entrepreneurial incubation services to university professors (Pálmai, 2004). Bøllingtoft and Ulhøi (2005) discuss the emergence of so-called networked business incubators, which go far beyond the provision of necessary basic infrastructure. Reliance on accumulation of social capital and the use of social networks for the knowledge transfer process helps to improve the incubating effects of the support institutions. Social networks improve the know-how offered to start-up companies as well as the inter-company link between similar start-ups.

Neck et al. (2004) denote complex support frameworks for new venture creation 'entrepreneurial systems'. The results of their research showed that incubators, spin-offs, informal and formal networks, infrastructure and culture in certain regions tend to form unique interlinks, which support a high level of technically advanced entrepreneurship. Critical moments in the development cycle of incubators, such as, for example, the bankruptcies of older ventures and the subsequent layoffs, can also increase the rate of new venture creation, because incubators gain additional capabilities for providing suitable assistance.

## Spin-off Companies

The Italian experience is equally valuable in describing the role of academic spin-off companies in the exploitation and diffusion of public research results emanating from universities (Chiesa and Piccaluga, 2000). Knowledge-channelling through emergence of spin-offs can be seen as one of the core processes in promoting economic activities and entrepreneurship. It has shown itself as an efficient way to transfer research output to the marketplace. Spin-offs are the result of people and IP transfers from a parent institution (Davenport et al., 2002). Unlike in the case of a technology sale, licensing or development alliances spin-offs represent the exploitation of tacit knowledge embodied in human capital. That property of these specialised start-ups should offer further protection from involuntary diffusion of research results to competing companies, while preserving the effort to strive towards commercial application.

The extent to which spin-offs render large excess returns, in comparison to traditional companies, is a matter of dispute. Although *ex post* analysis suggests extra returns, the *ex ante* analysis of returns yields results that do not allow an unambiguous rejection of the efficient market hypothesis or the position that the returns from the post-spin-off phase might remain within the boundaries considered average for certain markets. Thus, the university-industry link achieved via spin-offs might, but should not be expected to, lead to extraordinary benefits (McConnell et al., 2001).

The capital structure of spin-offs is often determined by the parent institution, whereas the leverage ratio tends to be lower than that of the parent, but comparable to non-spin-off companies with similar characteristics. This leverage ratio is primarily determined by growth opportunities encountered by the spin-off, while profitability has no significant impact. The result explains in part the negative relationship between spin-offs' leverage and profitability, found earlier (Dittmar, 2004).

Pérez and Sánchez (2003) offer evidence about the role of university spin-offs, not in creating sales, innovative outputs and employment, but in facilitating university–industry network development and technology transfers. They found that the role of spin-offs from Spanish universities in establishing networks and transferring technology decreased over time, while relationships with customers increased. This indicates a clear spinning-off character with gradual mental detachment from the leader institution and growing ties with other businesses in the market.

Feldman and Klofsten (2000) offer a detailed investigation of growth barriers faced by spin-off companies that reach the status of a medium-sized company. Their analysis indicates that most problems occur because of planning, management and resource allocation failures concerning financing, competition by new entrants or organisational integration of available resources. Indeed, procedures initially set up for promotion of inter- and intra-company collaboration can, in the more advanced development stage that poses new challenges, solve adjustment problems. In essence the growth of a medium-sized spin-off might be slowed down by similar intra-organisational communication problems that usually characterise large corporations. Thus, a spin-off establishment is a necessary but not sufficient condition for achieving long-term survival and market development.

**International Manpower and Support**

Like the success of any institutional setting, the efficiency of support networks also depends on the availability of appropriate manpower. Experience from Singapore suggests that long-term resource allocations into the development of local research scientists and engineers, willing to pursue a career in R&D companies, should be supplemented by recruitment of international talent and various strategic measures. These include provision of R&D assistance, the reform of the education system, collaborations across business sectors and also the development of international R&D support networks (Liao and Chew, 2000). Thus, reliance on solely local manpower might leave the fast-growing networks short of qualified R&D personnel.

# THE NATURE AND MOTIVES OF ACADEMY–INDUSTRY COOPERATION

## The General Features of Collaboration between Research Institutions and Industries

The evidence from the US suggests that following the market for basic and applied academic research services in certain focus areas (for example, business marketing) can or may be a plausible way to establish strong university–industry collaboration (Lilien, 1990). Miyata (2000), however, argues that even US universities that have income from licence fees cannot rely solely on this income source and need additional contributions in most cases to maintain this function.

University–industry cooperation does not consist solely of commercialisation of innovative technologies, but should also incorporate a wider exchange of knowledge and personnel also for academic purposes. This indirect relationship can have equally important or even more widespread effects on a regional economy. Research results also indicate that taking equity in spin-off companies could be a more beneficial strategy in terms of non-governmental university income than using standard licensing contracts (Bray and Lee, 2000). This is because in the case of extraordinary market success, equity offers potentially better returns than licensing arrangements.

The study by Chang et al. (2005) reveals that knowledge transfers between university and industry tend to be dependent on short-term, personal and contract-based mechanisms and not on long-term, formal/organisational and cooperative capability development mechanisms. This result suggests future pathways and unused potential for reinforcing the short-term contacts with more permanent institutional frameworks for cooperation. The reason for universities and industrial companies to engage in cooperative R&D seems to lie in various resource interdependencies between these two agent groups (Geisler, 1995). Universities depend on private funding opportunities as well as on job opportunities offered by industrial companies to their graduates. Companies, however, need to gain access to technological innovations, to employ the results of academic research and access the universities' expertise for problem solving. Survivability of university–industry cooperation in R&D matters depends on the degree of institutionalisation of this interaction, whereas the intensity of interaction between the university and industrial companies seems to have an inverted U-type relationship with the long-term survival of these cooperative ties. This suggests that too intensive a relationship might lead to relationship dissolution much as too low intensity of the interaction between parties leads to the same result (ibid.).

A successful example of university–industry cooperation in diploma studies and curricula development, with strong linkages to business practice can also be found in Italy (Mengoni and Sami, 1998). This type of cooperation indicates that it is not solely the university that diffuses its research potential to private businesses in the region, but also industrial partners that contribute to the restructuring of academic life in a more entrepreneurial direction.

Brazilian universities also face growing pressure to adjust to the need for professional work in productive sectors. This growing orientation towards university–industry relationships makes universities actively seek partners in the productive sector. This indicates an important change in orientation towards more applicable and entrepreneurial knowledge and towards faster integration in the larger setting of support institutions (Meneghel et al., 2003).

## The Paths for Technology Transfer between Developers and Manufacturers

The support networks of start-up companies might adopt two main channels for transforming technological innovations into product innovations. The first is to have direct contact between technology developers, for example the research institute or university, and the manufacturer of consumer products, which are based on that new technology. The second option involves the intermediary company, which has expertise in helping to find suitable applications for new technologies. The research evidence provided by Tomes et al. (2000) suggests that this second type of development effort offers a more consistent success rate than the direct contact between developer and manufacturer of products. This shows that intermediary companies may have a very important role in efficiently relaying awareness of the needs posed by product innovations back to the developers of new technology. In a more detailed view, the university technology transfers to entrepreneurial companies can be differentiated into four main types (Shane, 2002):

1. *Industry-sponsored contract research*   Less likely to be used by entrepreneurial companies than by traditional companies, more geographically located and licence related and less used than customised agreements or government-funded research.
2. *Consulting*   Requires more intensive involvement by university faculty than consulting for large companies, a greater chance for conflict of interest than consulting for large companies, likely to be the result of personal ties and used as a channel for transferring technology out of the university.

3. *Technology licensing*    Licensing by entrepreneurial companies depends
   on complementary financing possibilities, lower royalty payments,
   possibility of capitalising patenting costs, availability of expertise, strong
   intellectual capital protection by licensees and access to technology
   families. Entrepreneurial companies license a different type of technology
   and from different innovators than large companies.
4. *Technology development and commercialisation*    Science and technology
   parks, subsidy programmes, and buffering institutions (for example,
   intermediary companies) influence university–industry interaction with
   entrepreneurial companies more than with large companies.

   This analysis shows that SMEs usually tend to rely on externally formed
support networks much more than large companies that can proactively build
their own R&D and commercialisation affiliates.

**National innovation policies and initiatives from regional governments**

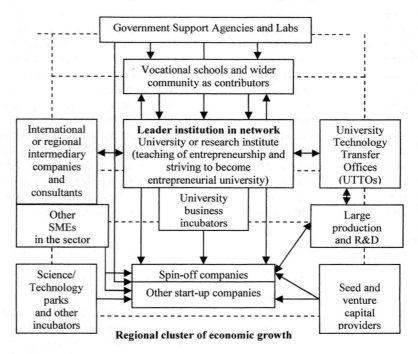

*Figure 15.1    Theoretical framework of university–industry entrepreneurial
support structure*

The university–industry support framework, which links national or regional policies with the emergence of growth clusters, is outlined in Figure 15.1. National innovation policies and regional initiatives that form the wider context for the particular network are shown. National policies are also implemented through government agencies and government-funded research labs. Along with vocational schools and the community they are important supportive contributors. The entrepreneurial university or research institute represents a leader institution in this model of the support network. Its role is to facilitate start-up establishment and technology transfers via UTTOs, international intermediation and business incubation services. Incumbent SMEs, technology parks, private incubators, R&D networks of large companies and venture capital providers reinforce and supplement these growth initiatives. The dashed represent loose network relationships and the arrows direct cooperative or other knowledge transfer contacts.

This model is the author's attempt to integrate the network elements and relational logic outlined above into a coherent depiction of the support network. Although one might argue that the differentiation between loose relationships and direct cooperation remains somewhat arbitrary, the model still represents a useful and heuristic tool for describing the formation of university–industry support networks. The following section introduces the research methodology to be used in the empirical analysis.

## METHODOLOGY

The empirical part of the chapter is build around the exploratory case study of business support initiatives established in the Tartu region. The case evidence was gathered predominantly in the form of desk research using several public sources. These sources of information include reports, surveys, homepages, development plans and strategies, the detailed citations of which are provided in the empirical part itself. However, the research is further facilitated by the author's personal involvement as assistant coordinator in international supporting activities. This experience offers the opportunity to use participant observation as one of the research methods. These observations refer to the personal experience and the body of information collected during the author's work as an employee of one network participant. This should also enable better access to the wider body of formal and informal information, which should in turn enrich the results.

The case study offers a more detailed picture of the efforts to develop an extended business support network and the role of entrepreneurship in facilitating local and international contacts. The roles of the lead institution and its main partners in this process, as well as the combined use of intrapreneurship and spin-offs, will also be addressed. On the basis of this exploratory case study, the initial theoretical framework of entrepreneurial support networks, depicted in Figure 15.1, will be revisited and elaborated. Thus, in the following this framework will be used for the investigation of the developing university–industry start-up support network in the Tartu region. The author adopts the perspective of the University of Tartu as the lead institution in this entrepreneurial initiative.

The purpose of the empirical analysis is to describe the network influences, participants and their relationships in order to outline the network formation process. Thus, the details about staffing and particular transfer efforts are outside the domain of this research effort, which focuses on the institutions as network participants.

## THE CASE OF ENTREPRENEURIAL START-UP SUPPORT NETWORK IN THE TARTU REGION

### The Features of Estonian Innovation Policy and Government Support Agencies

Until the new millennium, Estonia had predominantly relied upon imported technology from western economies and thus of its policy was based on cost competitiveness. The more-conscious development of national innovation policy began at the end of the 1990s, when it was accepted that in order to achieve and secure sustainable as well as socially and regionally balanced economic development, the role of R&D and innovation would have to be given greater importance.

In 2001, the Estonian parliament passed its national R&D strategy for the 2002–06 period in the document 'Knowledge-based Estonia', in which the Estonian government outlined the means for shifting from cost-based towards knowledge-based competitiveness. Thus, Estonian economic development was reoriented towards increasing the role of the knowledge-based sectors in its economy by stimulating private investment in R&D. This effort is supported and complemented by the participation of Estonian companies and research institutions in an intra-EU cooperation framework. The strategy stipulates that information society technologies, biotechnology and materials science are the fields with the greatest potential. The achievements of Estonian researchers in these target fields have received widespread international recognition.

The objectives of this strategy are to secure the reproduction of the knowledge and skills stock, which it is anticipated will enhance and increase competitiveness and increase the number of companies by initiating reform of traditional industries as well as through supporting the establishment of new technology-based companies. The quantitative purpose is to reach a total R&D expenditure level of 1.5 per cent of GDP (Estonian Ministry of Economic Affairs and Communications, 2005a).

In addition to this strategy, the characteristics of national innovation policies are outlined in the National Development Plan for 2004–06. The Estonian government has established several support programmes in order to promote the following (ibid.):

1. the strengthening of the knowledge-based economy – the consolidation, development and cooperative facilitation of R&D competence (Competence Centre Programme);
2. the financing of R&D and innovation activities – support to product development projects, market research and preparation of R&D projects (R&D Projects Support Programme, launching of technology programmes in key R&D areas);
3. the strengthening of innovation systems – the development of innovation support structures and the facilitation of strategic cooperation between scientists and entrepreneurs (SPINNO Programme, the Programme of Technology Development Centres, Business Incubation Programme, Research and Development Institutions' Infrastructure Development Programme, Research and Technology Park Infrastructural Investment Support Programme); and
4. the development of innovation competences and skills – the increase in societal awareness of innovations and the development of innovation competences and skills of companies (Innovation Awareness Programme).

The government has launched a risk capital fund (development fund) whose aim is to provide early-phase financing to innovative and high-technology business projects. The innovation policy and the new strategy for 2007–13 is concentrated around three keywords (competences, talents and technologies) and three projected objectives: an enriched set of competences and skills; the use of competences and skills for the creation of added value; and an efficient and innovation-supporting public sector. This new strategy also aims to increase the role of the private sector, and to promote international cooperation, coordination between Ministries and large local governments, and radical changes in R&D and innovation support (Estonian Ministry of Economic Affairs and Communications, 2005b).

The support measures foreseen in national innovation policies are implemented by the government agency Enterprise Estonia, which is financed from the central budget and has entrepreneurship development via support to technological and innovation projects as one of its primary objectives. Enterprise Estonia has a large network of regional development centres and it also facilitates the distribution of EU support funds (Enterprise Estonia, 2005). International cooperation networks of Enterprise Estonia are supported by ESTIRC (Estonian Innovation Relay Centre) programme, whose objective is to pursue the more effective utilisation of the potential innovation-supporting characteristics to Estonian companies and research institutions, in order to increase their competitiveness. ESTIRC is a unit of the pan-European system of Innovation Relay Centres, founded with the financial assistance of the European Commission as part of a sub-programme within the EU Sixth Framework Programme (ESTIRC, 2005).

In addition to establishing an R&D and innovation strategy, the government intends to reform its education system in order to increase the role of vocational education vis-à-vis that which supports the university education system. The need for these education policy readjustments comes from the feedback Estonian entrepreneurs, who see the lack of qualified professional labour as one of the major barriers to exporting (Survey of Estonian Exporters, 2004).

**The University of Tartu as Leader Institution in the Regional Network**

Tartu is a city of about 100,000 inhabitants located in Eastern Estonia. It has the largest and oldest university in the country, which has research and teaching programmes in the humanities, social sciences, natural sciences and medicine. The University of Tartu (UT) was established in 1632 by Swedish King Gustav II Adolf. It has gone through periods of being Swedish, Russian Imperial, Estonian, Soviet and now again an Estonian research and higher educational centre. At the end of 2004, the total number of students at UT was about 17,400 and the total number of graduates was 2,511 (UT, 2004b). The study programmes offered by UT closely follow the open university and web-based study formats. These differentiated cohorts of students help to improve the link between university teaching and practice. Research in Tartu University is conducted in various technological and scientific fields. It has six affiliated Estonian centres of excellence (UT, 2004b, p.10):

1. Centre for Basic and Applied Ecology;
2. Institute of Physics (also a Centre of Excellence of the European Commission);
3. Centre of Excellence for Gene and Environmental Technologies;
4. Centre of Excellence for Chemistry and Material Sciences;
5. Centre for Behavioural and Health Sciences; and

6. Centre for Molecular and Clinical Medicine (also a Centre of Excellence of the European Commission).

It can be seen from this list that many of the competence centres are established in research fields deemed as having the greatest potential according to the government policies outlined above. These centres show their relative strength in the fields of biotechnology, biomedicine and material sciences. This excellent match between university competence areas and political priorities as well as international market trends puts UT in a unique position as a lead institution not only in the Tartu region but within Estonia and in some specific fields at the European level.

While, these centres of excellence tend to have advanced competences in their particular field of expertise, they have somewhat insufficient entrepreneurship and technology management skills. In order to provide them with adequate support, the university enlists the services of social scientists from the Faculty of Economics and Business Administration (FEBA). In 2002, Tartu FEBA launched an additional pilot training programme in the field of entrepreneurship and technology management, which was targeted at scientists working on new technologies or people professionally involved in innovation support agencies.

By 2005 this pilot project had grown into an MBA programme in Entrepreneurship and Technology Management. The aim of this programme was to train specialists who could synthesise detailed knowledge about specific technologies with practical entrepreneurial skills. By offering knowledge about various technology management issues, further synergies are created, which in turn can be used for analysis and implementation of new business ideas (UT, 2005). This MBA programme consists of six modules: entrepreneurial environment, technology policy and management, marketing and sales management, financial planning and control, legal issues, and human resources and communications. Compulsory subjects account for 56 credit points, optional subjects for 4 credit points and an MBA thesis for 20 credit points, totalling 80 credit points per programme (ibid.). Several of the lecture courses and seminars are conducted by visiting foreign lecturers and experts, who have long experience in the field of entrepreneurship. The programme is offered in close cooperation with other UT faculties as well as with its foreign industrial partner, Zernike BV, to be introduced below.

The MBA programme is not the only support initiative offered by Tartu FEBA. In 2003, the Faculty established a Centre for Entrepreneurship as an interdisciplinary unit, which should provide other faculties, private companies and students with a wide range of support services and financing possibilities. The objectives of the Centre are (UT Centre for Entrepreneurship, 2006):

1. to raise entrepreneurship awareness at the UT and offer entrepreneurship training for students and the university staff, including the development of the MBA programme in Entrepreneurship and Technology Management;
2. to support commercialisation of the university's technological and scientific achievements, including analysis of business ideas for spin-out and spin-off companies, business consulting (undertaken jointly with the Institute of Technology couch entrepreneurs);
3. to cooperate in the development of Tartu, Southern Estonia and Estonia in general; and
4. to carry out research in entrepreneurship and innovation, and develop entrepreneurship teaching competence.

The centre is led by associate professor Tõnis Mets, who has developed well-established and accepted curricula in his role as a business consultant. This internal personal expertise is also used to provide various audiences with business planning courses. At present the centre is still very small, employing only four people – a general manager, two project managers and a consultant. The main activities of the centre have so far been related to participation in entrepreneurship facilitation partnerships (BEPART, SPINNO, ESUCO) and to the facilitation of student internships by companies. Tartu FEBA organises its support activities in close cooperation with the UT Institute of Technology, which is introduced in the next section.

**The UT Institute of Technology as UTTO and University Incubator**

The UT Institute of Technology (UTIT) is an R&D institution. Its purpose is to establish a new entrepreneurial culture in the scientific environment and thus support the generation of new technological solutions. The Institute was established in June 2001 (UTIT, 2005) and its stated mission is (UTIT, 2002, p. 2):

1. to create a basis for the high-technology economy in Estonia through R&D activities;
2. to increase the competitiveness of Estonian companies by facilitating and actively participating in the innovation process; and
3. to participate actively in the development of Estonian intellectual capital and cultivation of its future innovation leaders. The emphasis is on training scientists and current and future entrepreneurs with a technological profile.

The general objective of the Institute is the provision of new technological solutions by creating conditions in which innovative and well-equipped laboratories are established and pre-existing as well as new ideas can be developed (business incubation role). IP protection, enhanced cooperation with entrepreneurs, evaluation of the ideas and support for spin-off establishments, are guaranteed by the R&D support structure and will support the new entrepreneurial environment in the university for high-technology-driven innovation. In addition, the Institute will offer practical education based on success stories (UTIT, 2002).

In order to fulfil its mission, the UT Institute of Technology cooperates closely with its support units as well as with the R&D centres. The main structural units of the Institute are research and development centres (RDCs) (UTIT, 2005):

1. material and chemical technology;
2. biomedical technology;
3. environmental technology; and
4. information technology.

The central role in the commercialisation of the generated IP rests with the support units operating in close cooperation with RDCs, and having the following functions (UTIT, 2002, p. 3):

1. assessment and management of IP;
2. establishment and development of industrial liaison and project management;
3. supporting spin-off firms in the incubation and early development phases; and
4. providing research development and innovation (RDI) related educational programme to the RDCs and the University.

*Patenting and licensing* offers a full set of services for researchers in the university and in the region for high-technology discoveries and other innovative solutions. The *financial resources unit* ensures that the project has sufficient cash flow, especially in the first stage of development at the Institute, when spin-off companies are still too weak to raise enough income from their own activities. The *spin-offs support unit* offers assistance to already existing companies that had been spun off earlier, and need continuous support at all stages of development, and screens a number of newer ideas that could be converted into spin-offs in the near future. The quality of the support activities is expected to ensure the development of early-stage companies, professional leadership and the transformation of the new solutions into new companies. The *education unit* aims to increase the quality of human capital in the UT and to establish educational prógrammes that will prepare highly qualified personnel for the Institute's RDCs. This support structure has the longest experience in working with spin-offs and the related programme, and also significant competence for providing training in business plan development, spin-off establishments and management of technological projects (UTIT, 2002).

The UTIT continued to develop innovation support structures in 2004. In cooperation with several partners, it obtained support funds amounting to approximately €862,805 from Enterprise Estonia. This development project aims to achieve the sustainable cooperation of partners (Estonian Agricultural University and Tartu Science Park) in providing professional support services at the UT. The university's research groups and the UTIT also submitted 10 applications to Enterprise Estonia for preparatory grants and applied research grants for some €3 million in order to facilitate the increase of applied research at the university. Of these two preparatory projects and four applied research projects of the 10 proposed were funded. The UTIT also organised an international conference: 'Innovation Management in Estonia – the Needs of Enterprises' (May 2004). The conference provided for an exchange of ideas and offered solutions for problems raised by entrepreneurs, innovation policy makers and other representatives of innovation support structures (UT, 2004b, p. 12).

During the period from 1996 to 2005 the UT applied for patents concerning 12 different inventions. In May 2006, the university owned three patents and seven additional inventions for which international patent protection is being sought (UT, 2006). In 1999, UT's spin-off programme was launched and nine projects/companies were formed. Since then, two or three spin-off companies have been established each year but many of them are still very small (Puura, 2006).

## Support for Entrepreneurial Start-ups via Tartu–Zernike International Cooperation

The entrepreneurship facilitation partnership between UT (especially the FEBA) and the Zernike Group from Groningen, the Netherlands, began in 2002, when a Zernike expert participated in an entrepreneurship and technology management programme as a visiting lecturer.

The Dutch-based Zernike Group is an international company operating in the field of technology transfer, facility management, patenting and licensing, engineering, and consultancy (accounting, financing, marketing and sales). The development of Zernike was initiated in 1992 by the management of the Zernike Science Park. In 1983, the University of Groningen, regional authorities and the Dutch Ministry of Economic Affairs had created a commercial/academic organisation in the form of a science park in order to synergise science and business cooperation and development. Zernike offers seed capital as well as a methodology for protecting and selling developments, commercial marketing and sales of high-technology products, accounting and tax support, and business accommodation. Since 1996, the Zernike Group has also managed the Amsterdam Science Park and seed capital funds in Amsterdam (TIFAN BV), Alkmaar (ROF) and IJmond (IMKBIJ) as well as the three funds mentioned above. The Group is also active in consultancies for the EU and the United Nations (e.g., Hungary, Poland, the Czech Republic, and Slovakia) in technology transfer, training and business development. The organisation has over 180 staff and a growing number of joint ventures around the world – currently in Australia, Germany, Italy, and the UK. The Zernike Group operates in close cooperation with the University of Groningen that is in many respects a technological university. Together these two institutions have succeeded in creating a system that incorporates technological studies and entrepreneurship courses with the subsequent possibility of using the acquired skills by starting up spin-off companies (Zernike Group, 2001).

In 2004, the UT, represented by FEBA and the Zernike Group extended cooperation by successfully applying for an EU-FP6 Marie Curie industry–academy strategic partnership project on knowledge transfer. The general purpose of the proposed project was to facilitate the links between research at the UT and the commercial application of these research results by Estonian and/or EU companies. By increasing the economic and social returns, to research this project is seen to contribute to the economic growth and to the subsequent increase in welfare. The projected partnership between the UT (Estonia) and the Zernike Group (Netherlands) has the following objectives (UT, 2004a):

1. To develop UT post-graduate and other programmes in the fields of entrepreneurship and technology using the experts and scholars from Zernike.
2. To enhance the competence of experienced researchers from UT by training them in Zernike and its affiliates in following fields:
   a. the commercialisation of scientific results into marketable products;
   b. the protection of IP via licensing and patenting procedures; and
   c. the establishment of spin-off companies.
3. To facilitate the competence of market potential screening in the case of emerging innovative solutions and products.
4. To increase the possibilities for global marketing of the products and services developed by UT researchers, using the extensive corporate network of the Zernike Group.

These objectives are achieved by the secondment of Zernike's experts and affiliated researchers to UT as visiting lecturers and/or consultants as well as by the secondment of experienced researchers and non-scientific members at Zernike facilities as interns. The mutual exchange of experienced researchers has helped to merge the Dutch expertise in the commercial use of research results with new innovative solutions provided by Estonian researchers. The projected transfer of knowledge facilitates the establishment of stable and sustainable university–industry links of UT at the national and international levels. This project, however, is an integral part of a more extensive development effort led by the UTIT. Because the author of this contribution is involved as project manager in this joint effort, some aspects described below reflect the author's participative observations.

The visits to TU by Zernike's representatives and their contributions of lecture courses, seminars and meetings help to develop UT post-graduate programmes in the fields of entrepreneurship and technology management. For example, advanced schooling is an important aspect of projected enhancements in the protection of the intellectual property rights (IPR) of the UT researchers. Initially, general awareness about particular procedures and legal frameworks will have to be increased. Thus, the education and consulting services of Dutch participants will be appropriate with respect to the IPR-related objective of this project. The learning-by-doing knowledge transfer method employed during internships at Zernike is applicable as an important addition to the formal educational initiatives. It provides experienced Estonian research staff as well as project managers with first hand experiences of the commercialisation of scientific discoveries. The issues investigated and analysed at Zernike include: feasibility studies of new product market potential, the inclusion of a commercial perspective in the relatively early stages of applied research, sources for seed-funding, and the creation of investor contacts for producing and marketing the technological product globally.

Because Zernike has more than a decade of experience in these matters, the mobility of experienced researchers and non-research staff to Zernike facilities in the Netherlands and elsewhere provides a unique opportunity to acquire expertise in university–industry transfer, while providing Zernike with field-specific knowledge of scientific issues. The internship method is also appropriate in facilitating the establishment of spin-off companies. In this respect there are two interest groups. First, there are researchers who are interested in pursuing an entrepreneurial career by establishing their own start-up, and second, these are researchers who would like to offer consulting services for the first type of researcher in the future. This second category of personnel mobility is more within the focus of this transfer of knowledge project, which aims to develop local support structures.

The ongoing Tartu–Zernike project has clearly facilitated the commercialisation of research results achieved by UT researchers. The secondments to Zernike have had different purposes, related to the transfer of technological knowledge from UT to European markets. Some of them have been directly aimed at facilitating marketing contacts, while others in the form of internships set out to improve initial attempts to draft business plans. This extensive transfer of knowledge project continued until the end of 2006, and it is now being followed up with new cooperative projects between the UT and the Zernike Group.

## Tartu Science Park as a Business Incubation Partner and Company to Company Networking

The UT has close links with the Tartu Science Park (TSP) through its Institute of Technology. TSP was established in 1992, and was the first organisation in Estonia to support innovation. Because TSP is linked to Estonia's largest university (UT, which produces more than half of Estonian R&D) the main goal of the Science Park is to provide a variety of services needed in the support of the process of R&D commercialisation (TSP, 2005).

There are 26 companies located in approx 3,000 m$^2$ of office, laboratory and production space. The TSP's technology incubator offers a wide array of services to start-ups, ranging from fully developed infrastructure and office services to business and management consultancy. Currently, there are eight companies located in the incubator on TSP's premises. These companies are technically focused in the key areas of material, biotechnology and information–communication technology (ICT). In 2005, an additional 3,000 m$^2$ of incubator space was added and made available for use in 2006. TSP's ICT Centre provides seminars, courses and business competition events for students. The Centre also mediates several national and international ICT activities. The consultants at the Centre have assisted both starting and relocating ICT companies with personnel management problems by using their networks in the region (ibid.).

Services offered by the TSP include (ibid.):

1. *Rent and infrastructure*
   a. office and laboratory space 4–6 €/m$^2$;
   b. internet (fibre-optical connection) starting from 8 €/month (256 kbit); and
   c. phone, fax, copying, printing and computer desk facilities.
2. *Consultancy for start-up companies.* It also offers incubation services which include business consultation to realise a business plan. The status

of an incubation company may be applied for by innovative or knowledge-intensive start-ups. Activities include the following:

a. applied research and product development projects analysis and document preparation for Enterprise Estonia;

b. start-up consultancy: business plan, partnership search, project preparation for start-up aid application;

c. export plan analysis and preparation for Enterprise Estonia;

d. applied research and product development projects;

e. enterprise Estonia finances private technology-intensive and innovative projects with loans and grants. Consultants from TSP help the company to analyse its project and prepare the documents for submission to Enterprise Estonia according to requirements. Business consultancy grants of up to 12,780 are available from Enterprise Estonia. In relation to grants offered by Enterprise Estonia TSP offers the following types of consultancy for preparing applications (TSP, 2005):
   - consultancy for start-ups;
   - export plan consultancy; and
   - cooperation with local R&D institutions.

f. TSP also encourages young people to be active as entrepreneurs and offers support for company collaboration with research institutions. Short courses and business plan competitions for university students have led to the establishment of two new companies.

3. *International technology transfer*   Through an international network, TSP has helped to find partners in about 30 countries. TSP is also a participant in the Innovation Relay Centre (IRC) network covering 33 European countries (see ESTIRC above).

In terms of company-to-company network support, there are positive examples in the biotechnology sector where companies interact on the level of entrepreneurial employees who belong to the same research community or are studying as MBA students in the Tartu FEBA entrepreneurship and technology management programmes. These research and study contacts have helped to facilitate joint research on biotechnology industry development and management issues.

**National innovation policy towards knowledge-based competitiveness**
**(information technology, biotechnology and material technologies as key fields)**

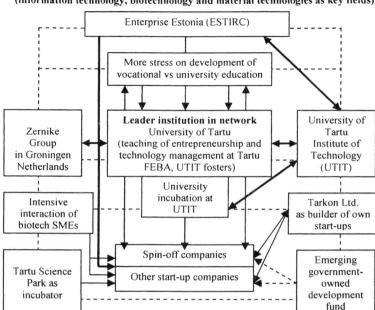

*Figure 15.2*    *Framework of university–industry entrepreneurial support in the Tartu region*

There is also one medium-sized fine-mechanics production company in the Tartu region (Tarkon), which extends its value chain by establishing new start-ups and attracting them to its own technology park centred around its core production activities. There is also personal-level linkage between Tarkon and TSP, because until recently the latter was led by an ex-CEO of Tarkon. Figure 15.2 recaptures the framework of the university–industry entrepreneurial support structure, based on the Estonian experience in the Tartu region. This should help to facilitate the understanding of relationships described in this empirical section. The arrows on the figure follow the same logic as with Figure 15.1. However, bolder arrows outline the most prominent network connections.

It can be seen from the figure that the support network in the region is characterised by the strong position of the UTIT that acts as a permanent facilitator of innovation. This network can also be characterised by strong involvement of the government promotion agency, Enterprise Estonia. International knowledge and technology transfers are well facilitated by long-term partnerships such as that with the Dutch Zernike Group, which has more than a decade's long experience in technology commercialisation and management. Another important partner is the local science park that also functions as a successful incubator, and offers extensive consulting, assistance and technology transfer services. Local input of venture capital is still sporadic, but a decision to establish state-owned risk capital has been made.

## CONCLUSIONS

The extensive investigation of the literature concerning the facilitation of entrepreneurship and technology transfer in academically led support networks of start-up companies has helped to outline the main elements of an entrepreneurial university–industry knowledge transfer support network. The orientation of universities towards more intensive support for applied research, innovation, and intra-campus entrepreneurship is often influenced by national-level innovation policies and regional support initiatives. In a wider network of technology diffusion, university-level support is likely to be extended towards vocational education and other educational levels. The use of intermediary companies or a university's technology transfer offices helps to increase the likelihood of stable and sustainable university–industry technology and knowledge sharing, although university technology transfer offices tend sometimes to favour licensing deals over facilitation of entrepreneurship. These intermediaries could and should be combined with well-structured incubation services and, preferably, networked incubation solutions.

The spin-off companies have proved themselves to be efficient means for transferring knowledge from an academic institution to the market. Unlike licensing deals and technology sales, spin-offs enable tacit intangible knowledge transfer. The extra returns from inefficient and superior market conditions of new business ideas have found support in *ex post* analysis, but not full support from an *ex ante* approach.

In the case of knowledge transfer, the demands of industry also pose new challenges for universities, which are adopting more market-driven or entrepreneurial attitudes. Similar to universities, large companies are likely to establish their own R&D commercialisation extensions. In support networks, dominant direct influences are often reinforced by more indirect network contacts, through which the entire structure is integrated.

The start-up support network in the Tartu region can be characterised by a strong leader position of the UT, although in terms of entrepreneurship and innovations this role is predominantly intermediated by its subunits – the Institute of Technology and the Faculty of Economics and Business Administration. These organisational units have taken a very proactive attitude towards facilitating entrepreneurship outside and intrapreneurship inside the university structures. This regional network has received considerable support from Enterprise Estonia, as well as from having advanced research capabilities in the technology-intensive fields denoted as most promising in the Estonian national R&D strategy for 2002–06.

These subunits have also initiated contacts with foreign industrial partners and consulting companies such as the Zernike Group as well as with the TSP, which is the most experienced innovation incubator in Estonia. The Tartu region even has one medium-sized production company which has an intrinsic interest in developing as a technology park rather than as a company with a highly internalised value-adding operation. Personal-level network contacts also establish a clear link between this company and the TSP. The same person has been, at different times, responsible for their institutional development, initially at the company level in Tarkon Ltd, and then as a director TSP.

This research has several limitations. Due to organisational reasons and time constraints, the study is predominantly based on desk research of publicly available research materials and documentation. Heavy reliance on official sources might offer a somewhat biased picture about the detailed nature of contacts in the support network, because the more problematic aspects of cooperation tend to remain in private hands and are not accessible via public information sources. The technology transfer and entrepreneurial contacts between university and industry can be very dynamic and complex, so much so that different viewpoints about these 'boiling structures' can render radically and irreconcilably different results. Even the triadic view of government–university–industry cooperative transfers might in certain situations remain too narrow to capture the most important catalysts and drivers of the system.

The theoretical implications of this study relate to the need to focus more research attention on the synergetic interconnections between the different levels, means and types of support agents, as well as the regional 'thickness' of various facilitating institutions and infrastructural solutions. Although, this more holistic view of the entire complex of different interactions might result in a loss of information about some important influential factors, at the same time, it helps to clarify not only the channels of direct impact, but also the indirect ones. In certain long-term cases, these indirect influences may come to dominate short-term direct impacts.

Managerial implications of this investigation point to the important role of intermediary companies or institutions in filling network gaps between the academic and industrial usage of technological knowledge. This idea of technological research intermediation needs to be brought to the frontline of R&D management solutions. This would help to utilise the most-experienced and cost-effective channels for knowledge diffusion into markets.

Future research in the field should rely more on in-depth interviews and group discussions in order to refine the proposed framework and the understanding of related phenomena. Also company-to-company interaction in addition to or side by side with the university–industry cooperation should be researched more. This potentially 'co-opetitive' relationship, which incorporates elements of competition and cooperation, can offer several interesting combinations. It could be the case that because of a virtual lack of domestic market for certain high-technology products, company-to-company relationships between peer start-ups tend to be solely supportive rather than fraught with competitive battles. Similarly, more attention should be paid to explaining the rationale behind the indirect and tacit network connections that were indicated in Figures 15.1 and 15.2 with leaders. Although these make sense in terms of defining the 'thickness' and boundaries of the regional support network, their exact functions are insufficiently transparent.

## ACKNOWLEDGEMENTS

The study was financially supported by the Estonian Science Foundation, Grants No. 6493 and 5840 and by the Ministry of Education and Research (Target Financing T0107).

## NOTES

1.  In general, start-up companies (in short, 'start-ups') are recently formed companies, particular definitions of which are often context specific. The Estonian promotion organisation Enterprise Estonia offers start-up grants to companies   whose estimated average annual revenue for the next three years is less than EEK 500,000 (about €32,000 in 2004) (Enterprise Estonia, 2005).
2.  Absorptive capacity is the ability to recognise new external knowledge, assimilate it and apply it to commercial ends (Cohen and Levinthal, 1990).

# REFERENCES

Albino, V., Garavelli, A.C. and Schiuma, G. (1999), 'Knowledge Transfer and Inter-Firm Relationships in Industrial Districts: The Role of the Leader Firm', *Technovation*, **19** (1), 53–63.

Amin, A. and Thrift, N. (1995), 'Globalisation, Institutional "Thickness" and the Local Economy', in Healey, P., Cameron, S., Davoudi, S., Graham, S. and Madani-Pour, A. (eds), *Managing Cities: The New Urban Context*, Chichester: John Wiley, pp. 92–108.

Bergmann, S.A. and Bliss, J.C. (2004), 'Foundations of Cross-Boundary Cooperation: Resource Management at the Public--Private Interface', *Society and Natural Resources*, **17** (5), 377–93.

Bøllingtoft, A. and Ulhøi, J.P. (2005), 'The Networked Business Incubator – Leveraging Entrepreneurial Agency?', *Journal of Business Venturing*, **20** (2), 265–90.

Bray, M.J. and Lee, J.N. (2000), 'University Revenues from Technology Transfer: Licensing Fees vs. Equity Positions', *Journal of Business Venturing*, **15** (5–6), 385–92.

Carayannis, E.G., Alexander, J. and Ioannidis, A. (2000), 'Leveraging Knowledge, Learning, and Innovation in Forming Strategic Government–University–Industry (GUI) R&D Partnerships in the US, Germany, and France', *Technovation*, **20** (9), 477–88.

Chang, Y.C., Chen, M.H., Hua, M. and Yang, P.Y. (2005), 'Industrializing Academic Knowledge in Taiwan', *Research Technology Management*, **48** (4), 45–50.

Chiesa, V. and Piccaluga, A. (2000), 'Exploitation and Diffusion of Public Research: The Case of Academic Spin-off Companies in Italy', *R&D Management*, **30** (4), 329–39.

Clark, B.R. (1998), *Creating Entrepreneurial Universities: Organisational Pathways of Transformation*, London and New York: International Association of Universities Press and Pergamon–Elsevier Science.

Cohen, W. and Levinthal, D. (1990), 'Absorptive Capacity: A New Perspective on Learning and Innovation', *Administrative Science Quarterly*, **35** (1), 128–52.

Cope, J. (2005), 'Toward a Dynamic Learning Perspective of Entrepreneurship', *Entrepreneurship: Theory and Practice*, **29** (4), 373–97.

Dagnino, R. and Velho, L. (1998), 'University–Industry–Government Relations on the Periphery: The University of Campinas, Brazil Minerva: A Review of Science', *Learning and Policy*, **36** (3), 229–51.

Davenport, S., Carr, A. and Bibby, D. (2002), 'Leveraging talent: Spin-off Strategy at Industrial Research', *R&D Management*, **32** (3), 241–54.

Dittmar, A. (2004), 'Capital Structure in Corporate Spin-Offs', *Journal of Business*, **77** (1), 9–43.

Doutriaux, J. (2003), 'University–industry Linkages and the Development of Knowledge Clusters in Canada', *Local Economy*, **18** (1), 63–79.

Enterprise Estonia (2005), http://www.eas.ee/?lang=eng, 7 August 2005.

Estonian Innovation Relay Centre (ESTIRC) (2005), http://www.eas.ee/?id=1169, 7 August 2005.

Estonian Ministry of Economic Affairs and Communications (2005a), 'National Development Plan for 2004–2006', http://www.mkm.ee/index.php?id=7172, 7 August 2005 (In Estonian).

Estonian Ministry of Economic Affairs and Communications (2005b), 'The Preliminary Vision and Objectives of Estonian R&D Strategy for a period 2007–2013,Available at http://www.mkm.ee/failid/Visioon_jaeesm_rgid_t__versioon.doc , 7 August 2005 (In Estonian).

Feldman, J.M. and Klofsten, M. (2000), 'Medium-Sized Firms and the Limits to Growth: A Case Study in the Evolution of a Spin-Off Firm', *European Planning Studies*, **8** (5), 631–50.

Fiet, J.O. (2000), 'The Theoretical Side of Teaching Entrepreneurship', *Journal of Business Venturing*, **16** (1), 1–24.

Geisler, E. (1995), 'Industry–University Technology Cooperation: A Theory of Inter-Organizational Relationships', *Technology Analysis and Strategic Management*, **7** (2), 217–29.

Grimaldi, R. and Grandi, A. (2005), 'Business Incubators and New Venture Creation: An Assessment of Incubating Models', *Technovation*, **25** (2), 111–21.

Häyrinen-Alestalo, M. (1999), 'The University under the Pressure of Innovation Policy – Reflecting on European and Finnish Experiences', *Science Studies*, **12** (1), 44–69.

Hearn, G., Cunningham, S. and Ordoñez, D. (2004), 'Commercialism of Knowledge in Universities: The Case of the Creative Industries', *Prometheus*, **22** (2), 189–200.

Hill, A.M. (2004), 'Secondary School, University, and Business/Industry Cooperation Yields Benefits to Technological Education Students', *Journal of Technology Studies*, **30** (3), 19–27.

Keeble, D., Lawson, C., Moore, B. and Wilkinson, F. (1999), 'Collective Learning Processes, Networking and "Institutional Thickness" in the Cambridge Region', *Regional Studies*, **33** (4), 319–32.

Lahorgue, M.A. and Cunha da, N. (2003), 'Introduction of Innovations in the Industrial Structure of A Developing Region', *International Journal of Technology Management and Sustainable Development*, **2** (3), 191–204.

Lambertini, L., Lotti, F. and Santarelli, E. (2004), 'Infra–industry Spillovers and R&D Cooperation: Theory and Evidence', *Economics of Innovation and New Technology*, **13** (4), 311–28.

Liao, Z., and Chew, I.K.H. (2000), 'The Development of Innovation Manpower for a Knowledge-Based Economy: The Singapore Approach', *International Journal of Innovation Management*, **4** (1), 123–35.

Lilien, G.L. (1990), 'Industry-University Cooperation at Penn State's Institute for the Study of Business', *Markets Interfaces*, **20** (6), 94–8.

Looy, B.V., Debackere, K. and Andries, P. (2003), 'Policies to Stimulate Regional Innovation Capabilities via University–Industry Collaboration: An Analysis and an Assessment', *R&D Management*, **33** (2), 209–29.

Markman, G.D., Phan, P.H., Balkin, D.B. and Gianiodis, P.T. (2005), 'Entrepreneurship and University-based Technology Transfer', *Journal of Business Venturing*, **20** (2), 241–63.

McConnell, J.J., Ozbilgin, M. and Wahal, S. (2001), 'Spin-offs, Ex Ante', *Journal of Business*, **74** (2), 245–80.

McMullan, W.E., and Gillin, L.M. (1998), 'Industrial Viewpoint – Entrepreneurship Education: Developing Technological Start-up Entrepreneurs: a Case Study of a Graduate Entrepreneurship Programme at Swinburne University', *Technovation,* **18** (4), 275–86.

Meneghel, S., Mello, D., Gomes, E. and Brisolla, S. (2003), 'The University–industry Relationship in Brazil: Trends and Implications for University Management',

*International Journal of Technology Management and Sustainable Development*, **2** (3), 173–90.

Mengoni, L. and Sami, M. (1998), 'Cooperation between University and Industries in Organizing a "Diploma Universitario" Curriculum: The Politecnico di Milano-Assolombarda Experience', *European Journal of Engineering Education*, **23** (4), 423–29.

Miyata, Y. (2000), 'An Empirical Analysis of Innovative Activity of Universities in the United States', *Technovation*, **20** (8), 413–25.

Mohannak, K. (1999), 'A National Linkage Programmes for Technological Innovation', *Prometheus*, **17** (3), 323–36.

Moussouris, L. (1998), 'The Higher Education–Economic Development "Connection" in Massachusetts: Forging A Critical Linkage?', *Higher Education*, **35** (1), 91–112.

Neck, H.M., Meyer, G.D., Cohen, B. and Corbett, A.C. (2004), 'An Entrepreneurial System View of New Venture Creation', *Journal of Small Business Management*, **42** (2), 190–208.

Pálmai, Z. (2004), 'An Innovation Park in Hungary: INNOTECH of the Budapest University of Technology and Economics', *Technovation*, **24** (5), 421–32.

Pérez, M.P. and Sánchez, A.M. (2003), 'The Development of University Spin-offs: Early Dynamics of Technology Transfer and Networking', *Technovation*, **23** (10), 823–31.

Pilkington, A. and Teichert, T. (2005), 'Management of Technology: Themes, Concepts and Relationships', *Technovation*, **26**, 288–99.

Politis, D. (2005), 'The Process of Entrepreneurial Learning: A Conceptual Framework', *Entrepreneurship: Theory and Practice*, **29** (4), 399–424.

Powers, J.B. and McDougall, P.P. (2005), 'University Start-up Formation and Technology Licensing with Firms that go Public: A Resource-based View of Academic Entrepreneurship', *Journal of Business Venturing*, **20** (3), 291–311.

Puura, E. (2006), 'Seven Years of Experience of Spin-Off Programmes in Tartu: Successes and Failures', http://www.tuit.ut.ee/orb.aw/class=file/action=preview/id=152427/7+years+of+experience+of+spin-off+programme+in+Tartu+-+successes+and+failures.pdf, 29 September 2006.

Rice, M.P. (2002), 'Co-production of Business Assistance in Business Incubators: An Exploratory Study', *Journal of Business Venturing*, **17** (2), 163–87.

Saavedra, P. and Bozeman, B. (2004), 'The "Gradient Effect" in Federal Laboratory-Industry Technology Transfer Partnerships', *Policy Studies Journal*, **32** (2), 235–52.

Schutte, F. (1999), 'The University-Industry Relations of an Entrepreneurial University: the Case of the University of Twente', *Higher Education in Europe*, **24**(1), 47–65.

Shane, S. (2002), 'Executive Forum: University Technology Transfer to Entrepreneurial Companies', *Journal of Business Venturing*, **17** (6), 537–52.

Shane, S. (2004), 'Encouraging university entrepreneurship? The Effect of the Bayh–Dole Act on University Patenting in the United States', *Journal of Business Venturing*, **19** (1), 127–51.

Slotte, V. and Tynjälä, P. (2003), 'Industry-University Collaboration for Continuing Professional Development', *Journal of Education and Work*, **16** (4), 445–64.

Spencer, J.W., Murtha, T.P. and Lenway, S.A. (2005), 'How Governments Matter To New Industry Creation', *Academy of Management Review*, **30** (2), 321–37.

Stimson, R.J., Stough, R.R. and Roberts, B.H. (2006) *Regional Economic Development: Analysis and Planning Strategy*, Berlin: Springer.

Survey of Estonian Exporters (2004), Online Report by Arico Marketing http://www.eas.ee/vfs/1901/Eksport%F6%F6ride%20uuring%202004%20kokkuv% F5te.pdf, 7 August 2005 (In Estonian).

Tartu Science Park (2005), http://park.tartu.ee/eng/, 7 August 2005.

Tomes, A., Erol, R. and Armstrong, P. (2000), 'Technological Entrepreneurship: Integrating Technological and Product Innovation', *Technovation*, **20** (3), 115–27.

University of Tartu (TU) (2006), 'The Indicators of Scientific Work in the University of Tartu 1996–2005', documentation from the University of Tartu intra-web (In Estonian).

University of Tartu (2005), 'The curricula outline of MBA program in entrepreneurship and technology management', http://www.mtk.ut.ee/doc/ETJIK.doc, 7 August 2005.

University of Tartu (UT) (2004a), Description of Work in the Marie Curie project 'Technological Knowledge Transfer Partnership between the University of Tartu and Zernike Group' Annex I to contract.

University of Tartu (UT) (2004b), 'University of Tartu Yearbook, 2004', http://www.ut.ee/orb.aw/class=file/action=preview/id=69552/aastaraamat2004veeb. pdf, 7 August 2005.

University of Tartu Centre for Entrepreneurship (2006), http://www.evk.ut.ee/99785 29 September 2006.

University of Tartu Institute of Technology (UTIT) (2005), http://www.tuit.ut.ee/index.php?lang=2andPHPSESSID=f26c9d50804a7653888e88 8a4f03beca, 7 August 2005.

University of Tartu Institute of Technology (UTIT), (2002), 'The Business Plan Summary of the Institute http://www.tuit.ut.ee/files/papers/Business%20Plan%20Summary.pdf?PHPSESSID =ae0e12b91883f50292dee4514af61b03, 7 August 2005.

Venkataraman, S. (2004), 'Regional Transformation through Technological Entrepreneurship', *Journal of Business Venturing*, 19(1), 153–67.

Weinberg, A. (2005), 'Creating an Entrepreneurial Campus Culture', *Peer Review*, **7** (3), 24–26.

Zernike Group (2001), 'Introductory Memo', Zernike (UK) Limited.

# Index